Readings in Social Welfare: Theory and Policy

BLACKWELL READINGS FOR CONTEMPORARY ECONOMICS

This series presents collections of writings by some of the world's foremost economists on core issues in the discipline. Each volume dovetails with a variety of existing economics courses at the advanced undergraduate, graduate, and MBA levels. The readings, gleaned from a wide variety of classic and contemporary sources, are placed in context by a comprehensive introduction from the editor. In addition, a through index facilitates research.

Readings in Social Welfare

Theory and Policy

Edited by

Robert E. Kuenne
Princeton University

BLACKWELL
Publishers

Copyright © Blackwell Publishers Ltd 2000
Editorial matter and organization copyright © Robert E. Kuenne 2000

First published 2000

2 4 6 8 10 9 7 5 3 1

Blackwell Publishers Inc.
350 Main Street
Malden, Massachusetts 02148
USA

Blackwell Publishers Ltd
108 Cowley Road
Oxford OX4 1JF
UK

Library of Congress Cataloging-in-Publication Data

Readings in social welfare: theory and policy/edited by Robert E. Kuenne.
     p. cm.—(Blackwell readings for contemporary economics)
   Includes bibliographical references and index.
   ISBN 0–631–22071–2 (hb: alk. paper)—ISBN 0–631–22072–0 (pb: alk. paper)
   1. Social policy—Economic aspects. 2. Public welfare. I. Kuenne, Robert E.   II. Series

  HB846 . R43 2000
  330.12′6—dc21

                    99–086003

British Library Cataloguing in Publication Data
A CIP catalogue record for this book is available from the British Library.

Typeset in 10/11.5 pt Ehrhardt
by Kolam Information Services Pvt. Ltd, Pondicherry, India
Printed in Great Britain by MPG Books, Bodmin, Cornwall

This book is printed on acid-free paper.

Dedicated to my grandchildren

Peter Andrew Kuenne

William Robert Kuenne

Charlotte Leigh Jeppsen

Isabelle Roxanne Jeppsen

Mia Anita Jeppsen

and to the Memory of the Princess

Olivia Michelle Kuenne

Contents

Authors

George A. Akerlof is professor of economics, the University of California at Berkeley, and a former senior staff economist for the Council of Economic Advisors.

Kenneth J. Arrow is Nobel laureate in economics, 1972, and professor of economics, emeritus, Stanford University. He is a fellow of the American Economic Association, American Association for the Advancement of Science, American Statistical Association, Econometric Society, and the Institute of Mathematical Statistics. He served as past president of the American Economic Association, the Econometric Society, the Institute of Management Sciences, the International Economic Association, and the Western Economic Association.

Harvey Averch is professor of public administration, Florida International University.

James M. Buchanan is Nobel laureate in economics, 1986, Holbert L. Harris University Professor, professor of economics and advisory general director of the Center for the Study of Public Choice, George Mason University. He is a fellow of the American Academy of Arts and Sciences, and the American Economic Association.

Keith Cowling is professor of economics and chair of the faculty board of social studies, University of Warwick.

Martin Feldstein is the George F. Baker Professor of Economics, Harvard University, and president of the National Bureau of Economic Research. He is the John Bates Clark Medallist, 1977, and a fellow of the American Academy of Arts and Sciences, and the Econometric Society.

Garrett Hardin is professor of biology, emeritus, the University of California at Santa Barbara.

Leland L. Johnson is a private consultant in the government regulation of business.

Alfred E. Kahn is R. J. Thorne Professor of Political Economy, emeritus, at Cornell University.

Kelvin Lancaster, deceased, was John Bates Clark Professor of Economics, Columbia University, and a fellow of the American Academy of Arts and Sciences, the American Economic Association, and the Econometric Society.

Robert C. Lind is professor of economics, management and public policy, Johnson Graduate School of Management, Cornell University.

Richard G. Lipsey is professor of economics, emeritus, Simon Fraser University.

R. Preston McAfee is the Rex G. Baker, Jr. Professor of Political Economy, University of Texas at Austin.

John McMillan is professor of economics, Graduate School of International Relations and Pacific Studies, University of California at San Diego.

Jeffrey A. Miron is professor of economics, Boston University.

Dennis C. Mueller is university professor, Institut für Wirtschaftswissenschaft, University of Vienna.

Richard A. Posner is Chief Judge of the U.S. Seventh Circuit Court of Appeals, and senior lecturer at the University of Chicago Law School.

Paul A. Samuelson, Nobel laureate in economics, 1970, is Institute Professor, emeritus, at the Massachusetts Institute of Technology. He is a National Medal of Science Recipient, 1996, past president of the American Economic Association, the Econometric Society, and the International Economic Association, and a fellow of the American Philosophical Society, and the British Academy.

Amartya Sen, Nobel laureate in economics, 1998, is Master at Trinity College, Cambridge University, and visiting professor of economics, Harvard University.

W. Kip Viscusi is the John Cogan Professor of Law and Economics, Harvard University.

Robert D. Willig is professor of economics and public affairs, Princeton University. He is a fellow of the Econometric Society and was deputy assistant attorney general for economics, Antitrust Division, U.S. Department of Justice.

Edward N. Wolff is professor of economics, New York University. He is a research associate of the Jerome Levy Economics Institute, and a council member of the International Input-Output Association.

Jeffrey Zwiebel is associate professor of finance, Graduate School of Business, Stanford University.

Preface

Few areas in microeconomics are in such active transition as that of social welfare and government policy pertaining to it. It is a field in which the positive and the normative have always interacted, leading to the enriching participation of social psychologists, philosophers, and political scientists; and it encompasses a body of policy discussion in which the political constrains the economically efficient more tightly than in most other fields of microeconomics.

Readings in Social Welfare: Theory and Policy seeks to give undergraduate students in advanced microeconomic theory courses and first-year graduate students in advanced economic theory an introduction into the richness of the debates that have characterized the subject and to focus on the important transformations of theory and policy in government regulation that have occurred over the last twenty-five years. This period has seen the deregulation of the airline industry, the reorientation of antitrust theory to the protection of the consumer, a revolution in the telecommunications industry and its regulation whose outcome is still but dimly known, the beginnings of deregulation in the electrical utility industry, a shift in utility regulation away from fair-return-on-a-fair-value basis to maximum price enforcement, a concern for the introduction of risk management in important custodial areas, and many more innovatory actions aimed largely at correcting economic inefficiencies.

In a persistent area of social concern, the vigor of recent economic performance and its impact on, or implications for, the distribution of wealth and income in both static and dynamic contexts have moved these issues once more to the fore. Paradoxically, although historically these debates have raged most vehemently in periods of economic depression, the lush economic progress of the 1990s has brought them to the fore in the guise of concern for the cross-sectional distribution of the fruits of progress as well as future ability of government programs to care for the aged.

The obvious richness of theory and policy that address such issues leads to painful decisions of inclusion and exclusion imposed by constraints of size and price. It was desired to include some of the most important classics of the postwar period that laid the foundations for research and government action. At the same time, we wanted to introduce debates over the future approaches to current problems, such as the most efficient methods of selling government property, the introduction of private investment accounts into Social Security, and the future of drug prohibition. We hope that a fruitful balance has been attained in the choice of selections that will introduce the student to the theoretical guidance given by seminal articles to the field, as well as to the many-sided arguments over current or prospective policy issues.

Although this book is, in every sense, a stand-alone volume coping with areas of the most important economic and social interest, it is also a complementary volume to *Readings in Applied Microeconomic Theory: Market Forces and Solutions*, edited by me and published concurrently by Blackwell. Both books were compiled simultaneously and permitted some salving of the pain of exclusion of an important selection from one book by inclusion in the other.

R. E. Kuenne
Genequil
Charlotte, Vermont

Acknowledgments

The editor and publisher wish to thank the following that have kindly given permission for the use of copyright material.

The American Association for the Advancement of Science for article:

Garrett Hardin, "The Tragedy of the Commons," *Science*, 162, (1968), 1243–8.

The American Economic Association and the authors for articles:

Kenneth J. Arrow and Robert C. Lind, "Uncertainty and the Evaluation of Public Investment Decisions," *American Economic Review*, 60, (1970), 364–78; Harvey Averch and Leland L. Johnson, "Behavior of the Firm Under Regulatory Constraint," *American Economic Review*, 52, (1962), 1052–69; Martin Feldstein, "The Missing Piece in Policy Analysis: Social Security Reform," *American Economic Review, Papers and Proceedings*, 86, (1996), 1–14; Alfred E. Kahn, "Surprises of Airline Deregulation," *American Economic Review, Papers and Proceedings*, 78, (1988), 316–22; R. Preston McAfee and John McMillan "Analyzing the Airwaves Auction," *Journal of Economic Perspectives*, 10(1), (1996), 159–75; John McMillan, "Selling Spectrum Rights," *Journal of Economic Perspectives*, 8(3), (1994), 145–62; Jeffrey A. Miron and Jeffrey Zwiebel, "The Economic Case Against Drug Prohibition," *Journal of Economic Perspectives*, 9(4), (1995), 175–92; Amartya Sen, "Rationality and Social Choice," *American Economic Review*, 85, (1995), 1–24; W. Kip Viscusi, "Economic Foundations of the Current Regulatory Reform Efforts," *Journal of Economic Perspectives*, 10(3), (1996), 119–34; Robert D. Willig, "Consumer's Surplus Without Apology," *American Economic Review*, 66, (1976), 589–97; Edward N. Wolff, "Recent Trends in the Size Distribution of Household Wealth," *Journal of Economic Perspectives*, 12(3) (1998), 131–50.

The London School of Economics & Political Science for article:

James M. Buchanan, "An Economic Theory of Clubs," *Economica*, 32, (1965), 1–14.

The MIT Press for articles:

George A. Akerlof, "The Market for 'Lemons': Qualitative Uncertainty and the Market Mechanism," *Quarterly Journal of Economics*, 84, (1970), 488–500; Paul A. Samuelson, "The Pure Theory of Public Expenditure," *Review of Economics and Statistics*, 36, (1954), 387–9.

The RAND Journal for article:

Richard A. Posner, "Theories of Economic Regulation," *Bell Journal of Economics*, 5, (1974), 335–58.

The Review of Economic Studies, Ltd. for article:

R. G. Lipsey and Kelvin Lancaster, "The General Theory of Second Best," *Review of Economic Studies*, 24, (1956), 11–32.

The Royal Economic Society for article:

Keith Cowling and Dennis C. Mueller, "The Social Costs of Monopoly Power," *Economic Journal*, 88, (1978), 727–48.

Every attempt has been made to trace copyright holders. The editor and publisher would like to apologize in advance for any inadvertent use of copyright material, and thank the individuals and organizations acknowledged above who have kindly given their permission to reproduce the selections noted.

PART I

The Distribution of Wealth: Static and Life Cycle Views

Introduction

The market economy distributes income extremely unequally, and wealth, as a cumulative stock magnitude, is even more subject to inequality. In Chapter 1 the data reveal that the variances of both measures of material reward are becoming wider among recipients. Wolff finds that, in the 1970s and 1980s, the USA moved from wealth inequality comparable with that of similarly developed nations to the most unequal of such societies in these regards. By 1995, for example, the highest 20 percent of households owned 85 percent of household wealth, and 93 percent of financial wealth, the latter being household wealth less equity in homes. The breakdown of wealth statistics by race, age, and occupation reveal similar patterns for several definitions of wealth, all of them confirming the high and increasing inequality in these dimensions in the USA.

Interestingly, Wolff's statistics reveal that, between 1983 and 1995, pension accounts rose from 1.5 percent to 9 percent of total assets, and total savings deposits fell from 15.3 percent to 7.3 percent of assets. The public is substituting tax-free pension accounts for savings deposits. These data do not include Social Security benefits, whose inclusion would somewhat temper the degree of inequality. The problems faced by that program are confronted in chapter 2.

Inequality in wealth and income distributions – even in the extremes revealed in these data – do not necessarily imply inequity. Social injustice can only be defined in terms of a widely accepted, consistently constructed theory of economic justice. Societies obtain a consensus on such theories only implicitly and, therefore, always indistinctly. Generally, their outlines are distinguished only when public outcry occurs if imperfectly drawn boundaries are transgressed. In the USA, extreme inequalities in income and wealth distributions have been tolerated with rather modest safety nets in place. Absent a more distinctly defined theory of economic justice, therefore, US political measures to alter such inequalities will occur only incrementally and largely as the result of power struggles among interest groups.

In chapter 2, Feldstein provides a sophisticated economic analytical framework with which to aid policy makers in making the fundamental alterations in the Social Security system that are required to keep it solvent at acceptable levels of income support. He deals with the economic effects of remaining with an unfunded (pay-as-you-go) system rather than replacing it with a funded system that invests in private sector stocks and bonds. The disadvantages of the present unfunded system spring from three sources: the deadweight loss that occurs from its distortions of labor supply and form of compensation; the intertemporal welfare loss from its depressing effects on private capital formation via savings reduction; and the sacrifice of benefits to recipients from the growth in the nation's capital stock that a movement to private investment of Social Security funds would permit.

CHAPTER ONE

Recent Trends in the Size Distribution of Household Wealth

EDWARD N. WOLFF

Source: *Journal of Economic Perspectives*, 12 (3), (1998), 131–50. Reprinted with the permission of the author and the American Economic Association. © American Economic Association.

Why is wealth important, over and above income? Family wealth by itself is a source of well-being, independent of the direct financial income it provides. There are four reasons. First, wealth in the form of owner-occupied housing provides services directly to its owners. Second, wealth is a source of consumption, independent of the direct money income it provides, because assets can be converted directly into cash and thus provide for immediate consumption needs. Third, the availability of financial assets can provide liquidity to a family in times of economic stress, such as occasioned by unemployment, sickness, or family break-up. Fourth, in a representative democracy, the distribution of power is often related to the distribution of wealth.

It would be foolish, of course, to expect even the best- functioning market economy to produce near-equality of wealth. The population is at different points in the life cycle, and one would expect the middle-aged and elderly to have accumulated more wealth than the young. People will have different tastes for accumulating human capital, for working and earning wages, and for saving. Entrepreneurial spirits are not distributed evenly across the population, nor is entrepreneurial success. Luck will play a role in economic outcomes. Who bought stock in Intel or Microsoft 15 years ago? Who happened to own a family farm that became coveted suburban real estate?

But even if economists can readily find reasons to be comfortable with some degree of wealth inequality, it is nonetheless troubling when that level rises substantially. In the 1970s, the level of wealth inequality in the United States was comparable to that of other developed industrialized countries. By the 1980s, the United States had become the most unequal society in terms of wealth among the advanced industrial nations. In the 1990s, the run-up in stock prices has added to the disparities in wealth. By 1997, one man, Bill Gates, was worth about as much as the 40 million American households at the bottom of the wealth distribution!

My earlier work, based on the 1983, 1989, and 1992 Surveys of Consumer Finances (SCF), presented evidence of sharply increasing household wealth inequality between

1983 and 1989, followed by a modest attenuation in 1992, though the level of wealth concentration was still greater in the later year than in 1983 (Wolff, 1994, 1996a). With the release of the Federal Reserve Board's *1995 Survey of Consumer Finances* (in July 1997), it is now possible to update some of my earlier figures on the distribution of household wealth to 1995. A number of issues will be addressed: how average and median wealth holdings have changed; how the overall concentration of wealth is changing; how the components of household assets and debts are changing; how wealth inequality is shifting by race and by age; which income classes are gaining most in wealth, and which have most to fear; what the wealth-holdings of the top 1 percent of the wealth distribution look like; what are the sources of changing wealth inequality; and how U.S. wealth inequality compares to that of other countries. But before addressing these questions, I will begin with a discussion of the measurement of household wealth and describe why I focus on the Survey of Consumer Finances in this discussion, rather than using evidence from some other possible data sources.

Data Sources and Methods

The sources used for this study are the 1983, 1989, 1992, and 1995 Survey of Consumer Finances (SCF) conducted by the Federal Reserve Board. The unit of observation is the "primary economic unit" of a household, which can be a family, a single individual, or two or more unrelated individuals who share expenses. Each survey consists of a core representative sample combined with a high-income supplement. The supplement is drawn from the Internal Revenue Service's Statistics of Income data file. For the 1983 SCF, for example, an income cut-off $100,000 of adjusted gross income is used as the criterion for inclusion in the supplemental sample. The advantage of the high-income supplement is that it provides a much "richer" sample of high income and therefore potentially very wealthy families. In 1989, for example, the supplement consisted of 866 out of 3,143 households. However, the presence of a high-income supplement creates some complications, because weights must be constructed to meld the high-income supplement with the core sample.[1] It should be stressed that this is a household survey, so that the quality of the information depends on the reliability of the respondents' answers. However, in the later surveys, at least, respondents were asked to check their actual financial records (such as stock and bond portfolios).

I will focus in the discussion that follows on two measures of wealth, which I will refer to as "net worth" and "financial wealth." Net worth (or marketable wealth) is defined as the current value of all marketable or fungible assets less the current value of debts. Net worth is thus the difference in value between total assets and total liabilities or debt. Total assets are defined as the sum of:

1 the gross value of owner-occupied housing;
2 other real estate owned by the household;
3 cash and demand deposits;
4 time and savings deposits, certificates of deposit, and money market accounts;
5 government bonds, corporate bonds, foreign bonds, and other financial securities;
6 the cash surrender value of life insurance plans;

   7 the cash surrender value of pension plans, including IRAs, Keogh, 401(k) plans, and other defined contribution plans;[2]
   8 corporate stock and mutual funds;
   9 net equity in unincorporated businesses; and
10 equity in trust funds.

Total liabilities are the sum of:

1 mortgage debt;
2 consumer debt, including auto loans; and
3 other debt.

   This measure of wealth is used because the primary interest here is in wealth as a store of value and therefore a source of potential consumption. Thus only assets that can be readily converted to cash (that is, "fungible" ones) are included. As a result, consumer durables (such as cars) and retirement wealth (for example, the present value of expected Social Security benefits), which are sometimes included in broader concepts of wealth, are excluded here.

   The second concept of wealth, which I call "financial wealth," is more restricted. It is defined as net worth minus net equity in owner-occupied housing. Financial wealth is a more "liquid" concept than marketable wealth, since it is somewhat difficult to liquidate one's housing wealth in the short term. (Remember, just taking out a home equity loan does not alter one's wealth, since in terms of personal wealth, the lower equity in the home and new cash available for spending offset each other.) Financial wealth thus reflects the resources that may be immediately available for consumption or various forms of investments.

   There are two other major surveys besides the SCF which provide time series data on household wealth inequality during the 1980s and 1990s: the U.S. Bureau of the Census's Survey of Income and Program Participation (SIPP) for 1984, 1988, 1991, and 1993; and the Panel Survey of Income Dynamics (PSID) for 1984, 1989, and 1994. Levels and trends in wealth and in the distribution of wealth differ substantially among the three sources. For example, the SCF data reveal somewhat greater inequality than the PSID, and substantially greater inequality than the SIPP. However, closer comparisons between the data sets quickly reveal the reason for such discrepancies. A comparison of mean wealth levels by income class between the SIPP and the SCF shows that they are quite close for the bottom four income quintiles, but over three times as great in the SCF as in the SIPP for the top income quintile. A comparison of mean wealth figures by asset type between the PSID and the SCF shows that the two sources are quite close for homes, vehicles, and liquid assets, but the mean value of stocks reported in the SCF is almost three times as great as that from the PSID and the mean value of unincorporated business equity is twice as great. These results indicate that the upper tail of the wealth distribution is missing from the SIPP and the PSID. These two datasets are probably useful for studying the wealth accumulation behavior of the middle class, but are not reliable for analyzing the behavior of the very rich.

   The Survey of Consumer Finances data series begins in 1983 because comparable data sources do not exist before this date. The SCF did exist prior to this date, but did not include a high income supplement and had only a limited number of questions on wealth. The closest cousin to the 1983 SCF is the 1962 Survey of Financial Characteristics of Consumers, also conducted by the Federal Reserve Board, but its sampling frame was notably different than the 1983 and subsequent Surveys of Consumer Finances. Even the PSID and the SIPP wealth series added special wealth "modules" only beginning in 1984. Prior to 1983, the best source for data on wealth concentration is the estate tax data compiled by the Internal Revenue Service. However, this source is limited to only about the top percent of wealth holders; Wolff (1996a) offers a further discussion of this source.

Wealth Has Fallen for the Median American Household

Median wealth for a U.S. household was about 10 percent lower in 1995 than in 1983, as shown in the first row of Table 1.[3] However, the decline was not continuous. After rising by 7 percent between 1983 and 1989, median wealth fell by 17 percent from 1989 to 1995. Mean wealth is much higher than the median – four to five times as great – implying that the vast bulk of household wealth is concentrated in the richest families. Mean wealth also showed a substantial increase from 1983 to 1989 followed by a rather precipitous decline, though overall it was 3 percent higher in 1995 than in 1983.[4] One reason for the decline in household wealth is evident from the third row of Table 1, which shows that the percentage of households reporting zero or negative net worth increased from 15.5 percent in 1983 to 18.5 percent in 1995.

When equity in owner-occupied housing is subtracted, median financial wealth was less than $10,000 in 1995, indicating that the average American household had very little savings available for its immediate needs. As shown in Table 1, the time trend for financial wealth is similar to that for household net worth. In particular, the fraction of households with zero or negative financial wealth rose over this period from 26 to 29 percent.

Table 1   Mean and median household wealth, 1983, 1989, 1992, and 1995 (1995 dollars)

	1983	1989	1992	1995	% change 1983–1995
Net worth					
Median	51,051	54,643	46,616	45,630	−10.6
Mean	198,770	227,718	221,384	204,529	2.9
Percent with zero or negative net worth	15.5	17.9	18.0	18.5	
Financial wealth					
Median	11,025	13,012	10,917	9,950	−9.8
Mean	144,245	169,977	168,770	156,935	8.8
Percent with zero or negative financial wealth	25.7	26.8	28.2	28.7	

Wealth Inequality is Still Much Higher in 1995 than in 1983

In 1995, the top 1 percent of families, as ranked by net worth, owned almost 39 percent of total household wealth; the top 20 percent of households held 84 percent. The richest 1 percent, as ranked by financial wealth, own 47 percent of total household financial wealth; the top 20 percent, 93 percent. A more detailed breakdown by various percentiles of the wealth distribution is presented in Table 2.

The figures also show that the wealth inequality, after rising steeply between 1983 and 1989, leveled off from 1989 to 1995.[5] For example, the share of wealth held by the top 1 percent rose by 3.6 percentage points from 1983 to 1989. Then, from 1989 and 1995, the share of the top percentile grew by a more modest 1.1 percentage points, while the share of the next 9 percentiles fell by 1.3 percentage points. However, the share of the bottom two quintiles also grew by 0.9 percentage points over this time.

The trend is similar for the inequality of financial wealth. The share of the top 1 percent climbed 4.0 percentage points between 1983 and 1989. In the ensuing six years, the share of the richest 1 percent grew by another 0.3 percentage points. At the same time, the share of the next 19 percentiles declined, as did the share of the second quintile, and that of the bottom two quintiles grew by 1.1 percentage points.[6]

Table 3 shows the striking changes in absolute wealth between 1983 and 1995. Over this period, the largest gains in both absolute and relative terms were made by the wealthiest households. The top 1 percent in 1995 saw their average wealth (in 1995 dollars) grow by $1.2 million or by 17 percent relative to their counterparts in 1983 (who may not necessarily be the same households). The only other group whose wealth increased was the next richest 4 percent of the wealth holders (0.5 percent). Average wealth fell for every other group, and the poorest 40 percent of households experienced the steepest decline in

Table 2   The size distribution of wealth, 1983, 1989, 1992, and 1995

| Year | Percentage share of net worth or financial wealth held by | | | | | | | |
	top 1.0%	next 4.0%	next 5.0%	next 10.0%	top 20.0%	2nd 20.0%	3rd 20.0%	bottom 40.0%
Net worth								
1983	33.8	22.3	12.1	13.1	81.3	12.6	5.2	0.9
1989	37.4	21.6	11.6	13.0	83.5	12.3	4.8	−0.7
1992	37.2	22.8	11.8	12.0	83.8	11.5	4.4	0.4
1995	38.5	21.8	11.5	12.1	83.9	11.4	4.5	0.2
Financial wealth								
1983	42.9	25.1	12.3	11.0	91.3	7.9	1.7	−0.9
1989	46.9	23.9	11.6	10.9	93.4	7.4	1.7	−2.4
1992	45.6	25.0	11.5	10.2	92.3	7.3	1.5	−1.1
1995	47.2	24.6	11.2	10.1	93.0	6.9	1.4	−1.3

For the computation of percentile shares of net worth, households are ranked according to their net worth; and for percentile shares of financial wealth, households are ranked according to their financial wealth.

Table 3   Mean wealth holdings by quantile, 1983, 1989, 1992, and 1995 (*in thousands, 1995 dollars*)

Year	Top 1%	Next 4%	Next 5%	Next 10%	Top 20%	2nd 20%	3rd 20%	Bottom 40%	All
Net worth									
1983	6,708	1,110	482.6	260.6	808.3	124.9	51.9	4.4	198.8
1995	7,875	1,115	471.7	246.8	858.1	116.8	45.9	0.9	204.5
% Change	17.4	0.5	−2.3	−5.3	6.2	−6.5	−11.5	−79.6	2.9
Financial wealth									
1983	6,187	906	354.0	158.7	658.3	57.0	12.3	−6.3	144.2
1995	7,400	963	352.2	158.5	730.0	54.0	11.3	−10.6	156.9
% Change	19.6	6.4	−0.5	−0.1	10.9	−5.3	−7.8	−68.3	8.8

their wealth holdings (a fall of 80 percent). The pattern is similar for financial wealth. The average financial wealth of the richest 1 percent grew by 20 percent and that of the next richest 4 percent by 6 percent. Financial wealth fell for all other groups, with the lower wealth groups suffering the greatest declines.

The Components of Household Wealth

Owner-occupied housing has been the single most important household asset accounting for about 30 percent of total assets, as shown in Table 4. The second biggest asset was business equity, at 18 percent of total assets; followed by corporate stock, including mutual funds (12 percent); real estate, other than owner-occupied housing (11 percent); pension accounts (9 percent); bank deposits and money market funds (7 percent); financial securities (4 percent); trust equity (3 percent); and the cash surrender value of life insurance (3 percent). Debt was 16 percent of gross assets.

The most striking change between 1983 and 1995 is that pension accounts grew from 1.5 percent to 9.0 percent of total assets. This increase almost exactly offset the decline in total deposits, from 15.3 percent to 7.3 percent of assets, so that it is reasonable to conclude that households have substituted tax- free pension accounts for taxable savings deposits.

Another interesting change is that while gross housing wealth remained almost constant as a share of total assets over this period, the amount of debt on principal residences rose substantially. As a result, net equity in owner-occupied housing as a share of total assets (substract the first row of debts from the first row of assets) fell from 23.8 percent to 19.5 percent. This reflected a rise in mortgage debt, which increased from 21 percent of the value of homeowner's property in 1983 to 36 percent in 1995. However, if mortgage debt on principal residence is excluded, then the ratio of other debt to total assets actually fell off slightly, from 6.8 percent in 1983 to 5.3 percent in 1995. The proportion of total assets in the form of other (non-home) real estate fell off sharply, from 15 percent in 1983 to 11 percent in 1995. Business equity fell slightly as a share of gross wealth over this period, as did financial securities. These declines were largely offset by a rise in the share of corporate stock in total assets, from 9.0 percent to 11.9 percent, reflecting the beginnings of the bull market.

Table 4   Composition of total household wealth, 1983, 1989, 1992, and 1995 (*percent of gross assets*)

	1983	1995
Principal residence (gross value)	30.1	30.4
Other real estate (gross value)	14.9	11.0
Business equity[a]	18.8	17.9
Total deposits[b]	15.3	7.3
Life insurance (cash surrender value)	2.2	2.7
Pension accounts[c]	1.5	9.0
Financial securities[d]	4.2	3.8
Corporate stock and mutual funds	9.0	11.9
Net equity in personal trusts	2.6	3.2
Other assets[e]	1.3	2.8
Total	100.0	100.0
Debt on principal residence	6.3	11.0
All other debt[f]	6.8	5.3
Total debt	13.1	16.3

[a] Net equity in unincorporated farm and non-farm businesses and closely-held corporations.
[b] Checking accounts, savings accounts, time deposits, money market funds and certificates of deposit.
[c] IRAs, Keogh plans, 401(k) plans, the accumulated value of defined contribution pension plans, and other retirement accounts.
[d] Corporate bonds, government bonds, open-market paper, and notes.
[e] Gold and other precious metals, royalties, jewelry, antiques, furs, loans to friends and relatives, future contracts, and miscellaneous assets.
[f] Mortgage debt on all real property except principal residence; and installment, consumer, and other debt.

There are marked differences in household portfolios by level of wealth. Table 5 provides a breakdown for the top 1 percent of households as ranked by wealth, who had a net worth exceeding $2.4 million (in 1995 dollars), the next 19 percent, with net worth between $177,000 and $2.4 million, and the bottom 80 percent, with net worth less than $177,000. The richest 1 percent of households invested about 80 percent of their savings in investment real estate, businesses, corporate stock, and financial securities in 1995. Housing accounted for only 6 percent of their wealth, liquid assets another 8 percent, and pension accounts 5 percent. Their debt-equity ratio (the ratio of debt to net worth) was 5 percent. Among the next richest 19 percent of U.S. households, 43 percent of their wealth took the form of investment assets – real estate, business equity, stocks, and bonds. Housing comprised 30 percent, liquid assets 11 percent, and pension assets 13 percent. Debt amounted to 13 percent of their net worth.

In contrast, almost two-thirds of the wealth of the bottom 80 percent of households was invested in their own home. Another 11 percent went into monetary savings of one form or another and 9 percent into pension accounts. The remaining 14 percent of their wealth was about evenly split among non-home real estate, business equity, and various financial securities and corporate stock. The ratio of debt to net worth was 73 percent, much higher than for the richest 20 percent.

Table 5   The composition of household wealth by wealth class in 1995 (*percent of gross assets*)

	All households	Top 1%	Next 19%	Bottom 80%
Principal residence	30.4	6.4	30.1	65.9
Other real estate	11.0	11.4	13.9	5.0
Liquid assets (bank deposits, money market funds, and cash surrender value of insurance).	10.0	7.7	11.3	11.1
Pension assets	9.0	4.7	12.6	8.5
Unincorporated business equity	17.9	36.8	11.0	3.1
Corporate stock, financial securities, mutual funds, and personal trusts	18.9	30.3	18.0	4.1
Miscellaneous assets	2.8	2.7	3.1	2.2
Total assets	100.0	100.0	100.0	100.0
Memo: Debt/net worth	19.4	4.8	12.9	73.0

Another way to portray differences between the middle class and the rich is to compute the share of total assets of different types held by each group, which is done in Table 6. In 1995, the richest 1 percent of households (again, this group has wealth exceeding $2.4 million) held half of all outstanding stock and trust equity, almost two-thirds of financial securities and over two-thirds of business equity, and 35 percent of investment real estate. The top 10 percent as a group, with household wealth of $352,000 and over, accounted for about 90 percent of stock shares, bonds, trusts, and business equity, and about three-quarters of non-home real estate. Moreover, despite the fact that 41 percent of households owned stock shares either directly or indirectly through mutual funds, trust accounts, or various pension accounts (up from 26 percent in 1983), a more detailed breakdown than is

Table 6   The percent of total assets held by wealth class, 1995

Asset type	Top 1.0%	Next 9.0%	Bottom 90.0%
Assets held primarily by the wealthy			
Stocks & Mutuals	51.4	37.0	11.6
Financial securities	65.9	23.9	10.2
Trusts	49.6	38.9	11.5
Business equity	69.5	22.2	8.3
Non-home real estate	35.1	43.6	21.3
Total for group	55.5	32.1	12.5
Assets and liabilities held primarily by the non-wealthy			
Principal residence	7.1	24.6	68.3
Deposits	29.4	32.9	37.7
Life insurance	16.4	28.5	55.1
Pension accounts	17.7	44.7	37.7
Total for group	12.8	29.7	57.5
Total debt	9.4	18.9	71.7

provided in the table shows that the richest 10 percent of households accounted for 82 percent of the total value of these stocks, only slightly less than their 88 percent share of directly owned stocks and mutual funds.

In contrast, owner-occupied housing, deposits, life insurance, and pension accounts were more evenly distributed among households. The bottom 90 percent of households, with wealth less than $352,000, accounted for over two-thirds of the value of owner-occupied housing, almost 40 percent of deposits, over half of life insurance cash value, and almost 40 percent of the value of pension accounts. Debt was the most evenly distributed component, with the bottom 90 percent of households responsible for 72 percent of total indebtedness.

There was relatively little change between 1983 and 1995 in the concentration of ownership of particular assets, with a few exceptions. The wealthiest 10 percent of households increased its share of total financial securities from 83 percent to 90 percent of the total amount of such securities over this period and its share of total deposits from 53 percent to 62 percent. The share of total pension accounts held by the top 10 percent fell from 68 percent in 1983 to 51 percent in 1989, reflecting the growing use of IRAs by middle income families, and then rebounded to 62 percent in 1992 and 1995 from the introduction of 401 (k) plans and their adoption by high-income earners. The share of total debt held by the top 10 percent also fell somewhat, from 32 to 28 percent.

The Racial Divide Widens

Households in the Survey of Current Finance are divided into four racial/ethnic groups: non-Hispanic whites; non-Hispanic blacks; Hispanics; and other races, including Asians, Native Americans, and others. The discussion here will focus on the striking differences in the wealth holdings of whites and blacks. Table 7 gives illustrative mean and median values for the wealth of black and white households, as well as ratios between them.

Table 7   Racial wealth differences, 1983–1995 (*in thousands of 1995 dollars, unless otherwise noted*)

Year	Mean values			Median values		
	Non-Hispanic whites	Non-Hispanic blacks	Ratio	Non-Hispanic whites	Non-Hispanic blacks	Ratio
Net worth						
1983	232.3	43.7	0.19	66.9	4.4	0.07
1989	274.8	46.1	0.17	79.4	2.0	0.03
1992	265.9	49.4	0.19	66.6	11.2	0.17
1995	242.4	40.8	0.17	61.0	7.4	0.12
Financial wealth						
1983	171.1	22.0	0.13	18.6	0.0	0.00
1989	207.7	22.5	0.11	25.1	0.0	0.00
1992	204.7	28.2	0.14	20.5	0.1	0.01
1995	188.4	21.2	0.11	18.1	0.2	0.01

In 1995, the ratio of black/white mean and median wealth holdings was 0.17 and 0.12, respectively, and that of financial wealth still lower, at 0.11 and 0.01, respectively. Underlying these trends, average real net worth rose for white households but fell for blacks from 1983 to 1995, so that the ratio fell from 0.19 to 0.17, whereas median wealth increased among black households while falling for whites, so that the ratio increased from 7 percent to 12 percent. Average financial wealth has remained relatively constant among black households while rising among whites, so that the ratio fell from 13 percent to 11 percent over this period. The median financial wealth of black households has also remained virtually constant over these years, at roughly zero.

If one searches the wealth data for positive notes, the homeownership rate of black households did grow from 44.3 percent in 1983 to 46.8 percent in 1995; while this is about two-thirds of the white level, it does represent a relative gain, since the homeownership rate among whites increased only from 68.1 percent to 69.4 percent over this time. Also, the percentage of black households reporting zero or negative net worth fell from 34.1 percent in 1983 to 31.3 percent in 1995; while this level is twice that of white households, the proportion of white households reporting zero or negative net worth rose from 11.3 percent in 1983 to 15.0 percent in 1995.[7]

Interestingly, it appears that the black/white wealth ratios held fairly steady from 1983 to 1992, or the relative position of blacks even improved somewhat, but then losses were sustained from 1992 to 1995. The most vivid example is that the median net worth of black households relative to white, which rose from 7 percent in 1983 to 17 percent in 1992, before slipping back to 12 percent in 1995.

One interesting issue is why the black/white wealth ratio is so much lower than the corresponding income ratio, which stood at 48 percent in 1995, particularly in light of the fact that black families appear to save more than white families at similar income levels (Blau and Graham, 1990). One important reason is differences in inheritances. According to the SCF data, 24 percent of white households had received an inheritance in 1995, compared to 11 percent of black households, and the average bequest among inheritors was $115,000 for whites and only $32,000 for blacks.

The Young are Getting Poorer

The life-cycle model predicts that wealth will follow a hump- shaped pattern over life, with accumulation in early and middle adulthood, followed by decumulation in old age (Modigliani and Brumberg, 1954). In general, the data on wealth does follow this pattern, as shown in Table 8. The table is scaled so that mean net worth of all households in any given year is normalized to 1.00; then, the levels for each age group is given relative to that level. Mean wealth increases with age up through age 65 or so and then falls off; however, the average wealth of elderly households (age 65 and over) still averages about 80 percent higher than the non-elderly.

Despite an apparent overall similarity in the age-wealth profiles for 1983, 1989, 1992, and 1995, some shifts in the relative holdings of wealth by age group are worth noting. From 1983 to 1995, the wealth of the youngest age group, under 35 years of age, fell in relative terms from 21 percent of the overall mean to 16 percent, and that of households between 35 and 44 of age dropped from 71 percent to 65 percent. In contrast, the wealth

Table 8 Age–wealth profiles, 1983–1995 (*ratio of mean net worth by age class to the overall mean*)

	1983	1989	1992	1995
All	1.00	1.00	1.00	1.00
Under 35	0.21	0.29	0.20	0.16
35–44	0.71	0.72	0.71	0.65
45–54	1.53	1.50	1.42	1.39
55–64	1.67	1.58	1.82	1.81
65–74	1.93	1.61	1.59	1.71
75 and over	1.05	1.26	1.20	1.32

of the oldest age group, age 75 and over, gained substantially, from 105 percent of the mean to 132 percent of it. The statistics point to a clear shifting of asset ownership away from younger towards older households.

The Mixed Relationship between Household Income and Wealth Gains

Another perspective is afforded by looking at average wealth holdings by income class. There has been some discussion, particularly in the *Wall Street Journal*, that the big winners over the 1980s in terms of wealth were middle-income families. I examine this by dividing households into those under age 65 and those 65 and over, because the elderly tend to have accumulated a large amount of wealth (as discussed in the previous section), but also tend to have lower incomes than younger families, especially after retirement. Lumping the two groups together might induce a spurious correlation between income and wealth gains due to age. The results are shown in Table 9.

Wealth and income are strongly correlated, with mean wealth rising monotonically with income for each age group and in each of the four years. It is also of note that among the non-elderly, only the top income class reported mean net worth exceeding the national average, while the top three income classes among the elderly did. Remember, of course, that these comparisons do not literally involve the same households in the different years, but rather those households that fall into a particular income group in a given year.

However, despite the strong correlation between income and wealth, there is no clear relation between income level and wealth gains. Among households under the age of 65, those in the two lower income classes and the upper middle income group ($50,000–$74,999) in 1983 experienced a very small growth in average wealth compared to their counterparts in 1995, while the middle income class in 1995 saw its net wealth drop sharply compared to those at that income level in 1983, and those in the top income class in 1995 also experienced a net decline compared to those at the top level in 1993, though a smaller one. Among the elderly, by far the greatest gain in net wealth is for the bottom income class, 34 percent. However, the net worth of the lower middle class elderly ($15,000–$24,999) in 1995 was 10 percent lower than that group had experienced in

Table 9 Mean household net worth by income class and age class, 1983–1995 (*in thousands, 1995 dollars*)

Income Class	Mean net worth				Percentage change 1983–95
	1983	*1989*	*1992*	*1995*	
All	198.8	227.7	221.4	204.5	2.9
Age Under 65	170.1	198.4	194.7	173.7	2.1
Under 15,000	31.5	20.8	25.9	31.9	1.2
15,000–24,999	49.7	71.4	44.0	50.2	1.0
25,000–49,999	87.0	103.6	79.3	77.3	−11.1
50,000–74,999	164.3	171.7	156.8	169.5	3.2
75,000 or over	825.9	826.8	930.9	774.3	−6.2
Age 65 or Over	319.2	333.5	316.4	314.5	−1.5
Under 15,000	54.7	55.8	58.9	73.4	34.2
15,000–24,999	151.3	165.1	149.5	135.8	−10.3
25,000–49,999	275.7	295.5	312.8	270.3	−2.0
50,000–74,999	558.2	706.8	618.0	594.6	6.5
75,000 or over	2,601.7	2,705.5	2,696.8	2,409.8	−7.4

1983, and that of the middle class fell by 2 percent. The wealth of the upper middle income group in 1995 was 7 percent higher than the comparable income group in 1983, but the wealth of the top income class diminished by 7 percent.

Another way of viewing the wealth holdings of each income class is in terms of the number of months its financial reserves can be used to sustain its normal consumption, which is done in Table 10. I use financial wealth as the basis of the calculation, since families still require a place to reside even if their income falls to zero, and focus on families where the householder is between 25 and 54 years of age, to reduce the potentially confounding effects of mixing in the elderly and retired. Annual consumption expenditures by income class are derived from the Bureau of Labor Statistics' Consumer Expenditure Surveys for 1989 and 1995. The first column shows the median financial wealth for the income group divided by the median monthly consumption expenditures for the group. The second column shows median financial wealth for the income group divided by 125 percent of the monthly poverty standard. As shown in Table 10, middle-income families between 25 and 54 years of age in 1989 had accumulated, on average, only enough financial wealth to sustain their normal consumption for a period of 3.6 months in case of income loss and to sustain consumption at 125 percent of the poverty standard for 9 months. Even the financial resources of the upper middle class, the fourth quintile, were only sufficient to maintain their normal consumption for 4.7 months and consumption at 125 percent of the poverty line for 14.6 months. The lower middle income class and the low income classes have virtually no financial reserves. In 1995, the bottom four income groups all had lower financial resources by this measure, while the top quintile is slightly better off by the first measure, but worse off by the second.

Table 10 Accumulated financial reserves of families aged 25–54, by income quintile, in terms of number of months reserves can sustain consumption, 1989 and 1995

Income quintile	Number of months current consumption can be sustained	Number of months consumption at 125% of poverty standard can be sustained
1989		
Top quintile	18.7	72.6
Fourth quintile	4.7	14.6
Middle quintile	3.6	9.0
Second quintile	0.7	1.0
Bottom quintile	0.0	0.0
1995		
Top quintile	19.0	61.3
Fourth quintile	3.5	7.9
Middle quintile	1.2	1.8
Second quintile	1.1	0.6
Bottom quintile	0.0	0.0

Who are the Rich? A View from the Top

Are the rich really different from the rest of us? Table 11 provides some information on the characteristics of the wealthiest 1 percent of households, defined as those with net worth of more than $1.5 million in 1983 or more than $2.4 million in 1995. In 1983, the rich were older than other people – about 12 years on average. While 43 percent of all householders were in age group 45–74, 84 percent of the rich were in this age group. Between 1983 and 1995, while the general population aged somewhat, the proportion of the top wealth holders under age 35 increased from 0.7 percent to 1.6 percent and the proportion in ages 35 to 44 from 9.2 percent to 21.1 percent. Correspondingly, the proportion of the very rich in age group 45–74 fell sharply, from 84 percent to 72 percent – a fall particularly striking relative to the overall demographic trends.

The rich are much better educated than the overall population. In 1983, 76 percent of the very rich were at least college graduates, compared to 21 percent of all householders. Between 1983 and 1995, overall educational attainment increased in the general population, with the proportion graduating from college climbing from 21 percent to 29 percent and median schooling rising by one year. Somewhat surprisingly, the proportion of the rich who had graduated college actually fell from 76 percent to 69 percent, though of this group the percentage who had gone to graduate school increased. There was a particularly large increase in the percentage of college drop-outs (one to three years of college) among the rich, from 11.6 percent in 1983 to 16.5 percent in 1995 – perhaps the Bill Gates phenomenon. As a result of these mixed trends, there is no clear evidence that more education paid off in terms of entry into the ranks of the top 1 percent of wealthholders over the period 1983 to 1992.

Table 11 Characteristics of the top one percent of wealthholders, 1983 and 1995 (*all figures are in percent*)

	1983		1995	
	Top 1%	*All*	*Top 1%*	*All*
Age				
Less than 35	0.7	30.6	1.6	24.8
35–44	9.2	19.5	21.1	23.0
45–74	84.1	42.8	72.3	42.4
75 and over	5.9	7.1	5.0	9.8
Education				
0–12 years	12.7	59.2	14.4	50.2
College 1–3	11.6	19.6	16.5	23.5
College graduate	40.0	10.6	29.1	15.0
Some graduate school	35.7	10.6	40.1	11.2
Race				
White (non-Hispanic)	97.9	80.9	95.3	77.7
Black (non-Hispanic)	0.5	12.7	0.7	12.8
Hispanic	0.0	3.5	0.0	5.7
Asian and others	1.6	2.8	3.9	3.9
Health				
Excellent	61.2	37.9	55.0	29.5
Good	32.1	39.6	33.0	46.1
Fair or Poor	6.7	22.5	12.0	24.4
Occupation of employment				
Self-Employed	37.5	15.4	71.1	15.0
Professionals, managers, & administrators	61.6	29.0	23.5	22.7
Sales, clerical, and all blue-collar workers	1.0	55.7	5.5	62.3
Industry of employment				
Trade	11.3	15.5	13.3	14.9
Finance & business services	47.8	31.8	58.3	39.3
Public administration	0.0	7.2	0.4	7.4
Other Industries	40.9	45.5	27.9	38.4

Figures are for household heads. All panels sum to 100.

The racial composition of the very rich differs significantly from that of the general population. Whereas 81 percent of households in 1983 were non-Hispanic whites, 98 percent of the rich fell into this category. Between 1983 and 1995, the proportion of white households among the top 1 percent fell somewhat, from 97.9 percent to 95.3 percent, but the population share of white households diminished even further. The largest growth was in the share of Asians and other races among the top 1 percent of wealthholders, from 1.6 percent to 3.9 percent.

The health statistics for the rich are a self-reported category, so a subjective element is involved. The results suggest that the rich are much healthier than the average population.

Between 1983 and 1995 there appears to be a slight deterioration in the health of both the overall population and the rich – trends which probably reflect the general aging of the population.

In terms of occupational composition, the self-employed (of any occupation) were substantially overrepresented in the ranks of the rich in 1983 – 38 percent versus 15 percent of all workers. The same was true for professionals, managers and administrators – 62 percent compared to 29 percent of all householders in the labor force. There were virtually no sales, clerical, craft, or other blue-collar workers found among the top 1 percent of wealthholders in 1983. Between 1983 and 1995, the most notable change was a huge gain in the share of the self- employed among the top 1 percent – almost doubling from 38 to 72 percent. This result tends to confirm our speculation about increased entrepreneurial activity in the ranks of the rich. Correspondingly, the proportion of salaried professionals, managers, and administrators in the ranks of the super-rich declined sharply over this time, from 62 percent to 24 percent.

Finally, the most common industry of employment for the very rich in 1983 was finance and business services, which includes finance, insurance, real estate, business, professional, or personal services. In 1983, 48 percent of the very rich who reported a job worked in this area, compared to 32 percent of all workers. The most notable change between 1983 and 1995 was a substantial gain in the share of finance and business services occupation in the ranks of the rich, from 48 to 58 percent (an increase relative to their overall employment share, which also increased). The proportion of workers employed in goods industries – which includes agriculture, mining, construction, manufacturing, transportation, communication, and utilities – in the ranks of the very rich fell steeply, from 41 percent in 1983 to 28 percent in 1995.

Sources of Changing Inequality

Why did wealth concentration increase so much over the 1980s and moderate in the 1990s? Though a full analysis of the factors involved is not possible here, two influences do stand out: the underlying trend in income inequality and the ratio of stock prices to median housing prices. The latter variable is used because stocks are highly concentrated among the rich while housing is the chief asset of the middle class.

Consider a simple regression. Let the dependent variable be wealth inequality, measured by the share of marketable wealth held by the top 1 percent of households. The independent variables are the share of income earned by the top 5 percent of households, the ratio of stock prices (measured by the Standard and Poor 500 index) to median housing prices, and a constant term.[8] Estimate the regression on 20 data points from 1922 and 1995, determined by the years in which either the estate tax data mentioned above or survey data are available, over that time. Both variables are statistically significant, the income variable at the 1 percent level and the stock price/housing price variable at the 5 percent level, and with the expected (positive) sign. Also, the fit is quite good for such a simple model, with an R^2 of .63.[9] The coefficients from such a regression imply that about two-thirds of the big run-up in wealth inequality between 1983 and 1989 can be accounted for by the substantial jump in income inequality over the same period, and about one-third by the increase in stock prices relative to housing prices (the residual is very small over this time frame – less than 3 percent). The more mitigated increase in wealth inequality between 1989 and 1995 is due to two offsetting effects: a huge gain in stock values relative to housing prices partially counterbalanced by a decline in underlying income concentration (with a residual of 20 percent).

U.S. Wealth Inequality in an International Context

In comparing wealth distributions across countries, it is important to derive such estimates from data sources collected in a relatively comparable way. Otherwise, different sampling frames and degrees of asset coverage can lead to wildly different estimates of household wealth inequality. Table 12 offers estimates of the distribution of household wealth for various OECD countries in the mid-1980s, based on a variety of sources.

Take the 1983 Survey of Consumer Finances as the baseline study for the United States. The first comparison is the 1984 Statistics Canada Survey of Consumer Finances. The original survey data from the two samples shows that wealth inequality is clearly greater in the United States, with a share of the top percentile almost double that of Canada's. However, the Canadian SCF does not include a high-income supplement, as does the American SCF. When Davies (1993) adjusted the Canadian data for this, he estimated a 22–27 percent share for the top 1 percent in Canada and a 41–46 percent share for the top 5 percent, figures still well below the corresponding figures for the United States.

Estimates for Japan are shown for Japan's 1984 National Survey of Family Income and Expenditures, suggesting that wealth inequality is considerably lower in Japan than in the United States. The low wealth concentration in Japan may be due to the extremely large share that owner-occupied housing has in the Japanese household portfolio; total real estate comprised 85 percent of Japan's household net worth in 1984.[10] Two sets of estimates are shown for Sweden in 1985/1986, one from a survey of Household Market and Non-Market Activities conducted at the University of Gothenburg, the other from a household survey conducted by Statistics Sweden. The concentration of wealth also

Table 12   The inequality of household wealth in selected countries, mid-1980s

	Percent of total wealth held by:	
	Top 1%	Top 5%
United States, 1983	35	56
Canada, 1984	17	38
France, 1986	26	43
Japan, 1984	25	
Sweden, 1985/86	16	31
Statistics Sweden, 1985/86	16.5	37
United Kingdom, 1983	25	
United Kingdom, 1986	22	

Source: Wolff (1996b). See the paper for details on sources and methods.

appears to be much greater in the United States than in Sweden. Estimates from the United Kingdom are based on marketable wealth for adult individuals derived from estate duty returns, taken from the Inland Revenue Statistics (the U.K. tax authority). Previous work of mine showed a remarkably close correspondence between the concentration shares of the top 1 percent of individuals computed from U.S. estate tax data and the top 1 percent of households derived from household survey data (Wolff, 1996b). If this relation also holds for the United Kingdom, then the results suggest that wealth inequality is considerably less in the United Kingdom than in the United States.

Evidence from a variety of other sources confirms that the inequality of the U.S. wealth distribution is markedly higher than in other countries. For example, the 1983 SCF was actually modified to match the asset coverage of a 1986 French survey done by the Institut National de les Statistique et des Etudes Economiques (INSEE). The comparable figures in this case are for gross assets. The study shows that the top 1 percent and 5 percent of U.S. households in the wealth distribution have 33 percent and 54 percent of gross assets, respectively, while the top 1 percent and 5 percent of French households have 26 percent and 43 percent of gross assets. A plausible comparison for the United States and Germany can be made based on another conformable database – the German Socio-Economic Panel (GSOEP) and the U.S. PSID-GSOEP Equivalent Data File for 1988 – which attempts to make the wealth concept used in the two databases consistent by including the same set of assets and liabilities. The results again show that the U.S. is the more unequal of the two countries.[11] For further discussions of these studies, their methods and limitations, see Wolff (1996b).

Concluding Comments

The distribution of wealth in the United States became much more unequal in the 1980s, and that trend seems to be continuing, albeit at a slower pace, in the 1990s. The only households that saw their mean net worth and financial wealth rise in absolute terms between 1983 and 1995 were those in the top 20 percent of their respective distributions and the gains were particularly strong for the top 1 percent. All other groups suffered real wealth or income losses, and the declines were particularly precipitous at the bottom. Slicing the numbers by black and white, or by young and old, only confirms the growth in inequality of wealth.

What has happened to the U.S. wealth distribution in the three years between 1995 and the publication of this article? It will take a few years before the evidence from the next SCF is available for analysis. However, some tentative comments can be offered. The very sharp rise in stock prices over the last three years (more than doubling) can only exacerbate further the divide between rich and poor. Though there has been talk about the "democratization" of stock ownership, stock shares are still heavily concentrated in the hands of the rich. Moreover, small business equity, which tends to move with stock prices, is also highly concentrated among the rich. If we conduct a simple simulation where we take asset holdings in 1995 as the baseline and run up asset values according to the actual change in asset prices over the last three years, the share of the top 1 percent would advance from 39 percent in 1995 to 41 percent in 1998.

Notes

1   Three studies conducted by the Federal Reserve Board – Kennickell and Woodburn (1992) for the 1989 SCF; Kennickell, McManus, and Woodburn (1996) for the 1992 SCF; and Kennickell and Woodburn (1997) for the 1995 SCF – discuss some of the issues involved in developing these weights.
2   This does not include pension reserves held by corporations or financial institutions.
3   The results for this section are based on the standard Consumer Price Index (CPI-U). Of course, if the increase in the CPI is overstated, as the Boskin Commission has recently argued, then the decline in wealth reported here may be likewise overstated.
4   The time trend is very similar when the value of vehicles is included in net worth. Similar results can also be derived from the revised estimates of Kennickell and Woodburn (1997) for 1989 and 1995.
5   On the basis of the estate tax data mentioned above, the steep rise in wealth inequality appears to begin in the mid-1970s. Moreover, similar trends are evident even when consumer durables and retirement wealth are included in household wealth. See Wolff (1996a) for more details.
6   These statements about inequality and financial wealth are borne out in more formal measures of inequality, like the Gini coefficient. The Gini coefficient for net worth rose from .80 in 1983 to .83 in 1989 – but remained at .83 in 1995, in part because of the rise in wealth in the bottom 40 percent of the distribution. For financial wealth, the Gini coefficient rose from .89 in 1983 to .93 in 1989, but fell back to .91 by 1995 – again because of improved (less negative) financial wealth in the lower part of the distribution.
7   There is a large amount of variation in the income and wealth figures for blacks on a year by year basis. This is probably a reflection of the small sample size for this group and the associated high sampling variability. The problem is even more severe for the Hispanic and the "other racial" group because of their smaller sample sizes.
8   The source for the income inequality series is the U.S. Bureau of the Census, Current Population Reports; the source for the Standard and Poor series is the 1997 *Economic Report of the President*; and the source for housing prices is various years of the *Statistical Abstract of the United States*. See Wolff (1996a) for more details.
9   Specifically, the regression is:

$$\text{WLTHTOP1} = 5.41 + 1.24 \text{ INCTOP5} + 0.28 \text{ } SP/HOUSE, R^2 = 0.63, N = 20$$
$$\quad\quad\quad\quad (0.6) \quad (3.3) \quad\quad\quad\quad\quad (2.6)$$

with t-ratios shown in parentheses.
10 Other reasonably comparable sources for wealth inequality in Japan include the 1981 Family Saving Survey and the 1981 Survey on Saving Behavior and Motivation. Summary measures of wealth inequality from these studies confirm that Japan's distribution of wealth is more equal; for example, the U.S. Gini coefficient from the 1983 SCF is .79, while Japan's Gini coefficient from these two sources is .58.
11 In particular, the U.S. wealth distribution had a Gini coefficient of .76, compared to .69 for Germany.

References and Further Reading

Blau, F. D. and Graham, J. W. (1990): "Black-White Differences in Wealth and Asset Composition," *Quarterly Journal of Economics*, May, 105 (2), 321–39.
Davies, J. B. (1993): "The Distribution of Wealth in Canada," in Edward N. Wolff (ed.), *Research in Economic Inequality*, 4. Greenwich, CT: JAI Press, 159–80.

Hurst, E., Luoh, M. C. and Stafford, F. P. (1996): *Wealth Dynamics of American Families, 1984–1994.* Institute for Social Research, University of Michigan, mimeo, August.

Kennickell, A. B. and Woodburn, R. L. (1992): *Estimation of Household Net Worth Using Model-Based and Design-Bases Weights: Evidence from the 1989 Survey of Consumer Finances*, mimeo, Federal Reserve Board of Washington, April.

——(1997): *Consistent Weight Design for the 1989, 1992, and 1995 SCFs, and the Distribution of Wealth*, mimeo, Federal Reserve Board of Washington, June.

Kennickell, A. B., McManus, D. A. and Woodburn, R. L. (1996): *Weighting Design for the 1992 Survey of Consumer Finance*, mimeo, Federal Reserve Board of Washington, March.

Modigliani, F., and Brumberg, R. (1954): "Utility Analysis and the Consumption Function: An Interpretation of Cross-Section Data," in K. Kurihara (ed.), *Post-Keynesian Economics*, New Brunswick, NJ: Rutgers University Press.

Wolff, E. N. (1994): "Trends in Household Wealth in the United States, 1962–1983 and 1983–1989," *Review of Income and Wealth*, June, 40, 143–74.

——(1996a) *TOP HEAVY: A Study of Increasing Inequality of Wealth in America.* Updated and expanded edition. New York: Free Press.

——(1996b) "International Comparisons of Wealth Inequality," *Review of Income and Wealth*, December, 42, 433–51.

CHAPTER TWO

The Missing Piece in Policy Analysis: Social Security Reform

MARTIN FELDSTEIN

Source: *American Economic Review, Papers and Proceedings*, 86 (1996), 1–14. Reprinted with the permission of the author and the American Economic Association. © American Economic Association.

Reforming the Social Security retirement program is an issue of enormous practical importance. Yet it remains the missing piece in American policy analysis. At a time when the Congress and the Administration are considering ways to reform welfare, Medicare, Medicaid, and the income tax, elected officials are still unwilling to confront the serious problems of our Social Security system. Eventually, however, its deteriorating financial condition will force major reforms. Whether those reforms are good or bad, whether they deal with the basic economic problems of the system or merely protect the solvency of existing institutional arrangements, will depend in part on whether we, as economists, provide the appropriate intellectual framework for analyzing reform alternatives.

Major policy changes that affect the public at large can only happen in our democracy when there is widespread public support for the new direction of policy. In the field of economics, the views of the media, of other private-sector opinion leaders, and of politicians and their advisers, depend very much on their perception of what economists believe is feasible and correct. Fundamental policy reforms in a complex area like social security also require the development of technical expertise, both in and out of government, about the options for change and their likely consequences.

Fortunately, an expanding group of economists is now thinking and writing about social security reform. I began to do research on the effects of Social Security and on Social Security reform nearly 25 years ago (Feldstein, 1974, 1975). A central concept in my analysis of Social Security has been the notion of 'Social Security wealth,' which I defined as the present actuarial value of the Social Security benefits to which the current adult population will be entitled at age 65 (or are already entitled to if they are older than 65) minus the present actuarial value of the Social Security taxes that they will pay before reaching that age. Social Security wealth has now grown to about $11 trillion or more than 1.5 times GDP.[1] Since this is equivalent to more than $50,000 for every adult in the country, the value of Social Security wealth substantially exceeds all other assets for the vast majority of American households. In the aggregate, Social Security wealth exceeds three-fourths of all private financial wealth, as conventionally measured.

Social Security wealth is of course not real wealth but only a claim on current and future taxpayers. Instead of labeling this key magnitude 'Social Security wealth,' I could have called it 'the nation's Social Security liability.' Like ordinary government debt, Social Security wealth has the power to crowd out private capital accumulation; and Social Security wealth will continue to grow as long as our current system remains unchanged, displacing an ever larger stock of capital.

The $11 trillion Social Security liability is three times as large as the official national debt. Although I certainly welcome the current political efforts to shrink future budget deficits, it is worth noting that, even if the traditional deficit is eliminated in the year 2002, so that the traditional national debt is then no longer increasing, the national debt in the form of the Social Security liability is likely to increase that year by about $300 billion.[2]

Looking further into the future, the aggregate Social Security liability will grow as the population expands, as it becomes relatively older, and as incomes rise. Government actuaries predict that, under existing law, the tax rate required to pay each year's Social Security benefit will rise over the next 50 years from the present level of slightly less than 12 percent to more than 18 percent, and perhaps to as much as 23 percent.[3]

The financial problems of the system are therefore very serious indeed. But my remarks today will not deal with the financial problems of Social Security but with the more fundamental economic effects of continuing with an unfunded system. I will begin with the deadweight loss that an unfunded system causes by distorting the supply of labor and the form of compensation. I will then discuss the intertemporal welfare loss that results from depressed capital accumulation and the potential gain from shifting to a funded system.

I take it as a given, in these remarks, that the nation is politically committed to a universal (or near universal) system of retirement benefits for the aged. An alternative would be to have a means-tested system that provides benefits only to those individuals who, through inadvertence, bad luck, or strategic behavior, reach old age with income and assets that are below some specified level. Although I believe that such an alternative deserves careful consideration, it lies beyond the scope of my remarks in this lecture.[4]

1. The Deadweight Loss of the Labor-Market Distortions[5]

The Social Security payroll tax distorts the supply of labor and the form of compensation. Moreover, although the link between the Social Security taxes that individuals pay and their subsequent benefits means that the statutory payroll tax rate overstates the effective individual marginal tax rates, the mandatory Social Security contributions are nevertheless real taxes with very substantial deadweight losses. These losses are inevitable because of the low return implied by the pay-as-you-go character of the unfunded Social Security system.

Let me explain. Unlike private pensions and individual retirement accounts, the Social Security system does not invest the money that it collects in stocks and bonds, but pays those funds out as benefits in the same year that they are collected.[6] The rate of return that individuals earn on their mandatory Social Security contributions is therefore far less than they could earn in a private pension or in a funded social-security system. As Paul Samuelson (1958) first taught us nearly 40 years ago, an unfunded social-security program with a constant tax rate provides a positive rate of return which, in equilibrium, is equal to the rate of growth of the social-security payroll tax base. The average annual rate of growth of real wages and salaries since 1960, 2.6 percent, is therefore a reasonable estimate of what an unfunded social-security program can yield over the long-term future.

I might just note that, in contrast to this 2.6-percent potential future yield, the rate of return on Social Security contributions since the inception of the program has been kept artificially high by the sharp increase in the Social Security tax rate.[7] The combined employer – employee rate rose from just 2 percent in 1940 to 3 percent in 1950, 6 percent in 1960, 10 percent in 1980, and 12 percent since 1988. Thus, those who got in on the ground floor of the Social Security program and are now retired paid taxes at relatively low rates but are receiving benefits that are financed by a much higher tax rate on current employees. The resulting double-digit return on Social Security contributions has sustained political support for the existing system. But such a sixfold increase in tax rates cannot happen again.[8]

In contrast to the 2.6-percent equilibrium return on Social Security contributions, the real pretax return on nonfinancial corporate capital averaged 9.3 percent over the same 35-year period since 1960.[9] That is the return that each individual's Social Security account could have earned in a fully funded government system or in a privatized system if the government credited the corporate tax receipts back to each account. The difference between the 2.6-percent Social Security return and that 9.3-percent real return implies that mandatory contributions to an unfunded social-security plan are real taxes with a very substantial deadweight loss.[10]

A simplified example will indicate the magnitude of the implied tax wedge. Consider an employee who contributes $1,000 to Social Security at age 50 to buy benefits that will be paid at age 75. With a 2.6-percent yield, the $1,000 grows to $1,900 after the 25 years. In contrast, a yield of 9.3 percent would allow the individual to buy the same $1,900 retirement income for only $206.[11] Thus, forcing individuals to use the unfunded system dramatically increases their cost of buying retirement income. In the current example, a funded plan would permit the individual to buy retirement income at just 21 percent of the price that he must pay in the unfunded program, allowing the 12-percent Social Security tax rate to be replaced by a 2.5-percent contribution. The remaining 9.5-percent excess mandatory contribution is a real tax for which the individual gets nothing in return.[12]

The deadweight loss caused by this 9.5-percent tax is much larger than one might imagine. It is not the 'small triangle' that typically comes to mind when one thinks of deadweight losses. Moreover, the size of the deadweight loss does not reflect the traditional low elasticity of labor supply that one associates with taxes on labor income. Let me explain both of these.

First, because the Social Security payroll tax is imposed on top of federal and state income taxes, the deadweight loss is not a small triangle but a much larger trapezoid. With a federal marginal tax rate of 28 percent (for single individuals with taxable incomes over $23,000 and married couples with combined incomes over $38,000) and a typical state income tax rate of 5 percent, the Social Security tax comes on top of an initial 33-percent marginal income tax rate.[13] A little arithmetic shows that the incremental deadweight loss that results from the additional 9.5-percent net Social Security tax is equal to 4.7 percent of the product of the payroll tax base and the compensated elasticity of that tax base with respect to the net-of-tax share.[14] This is about ten times as large as the deadweight loss that would result if the Social Security tax were the only tax.

That brings me to the second reason why the deadweight loss may be substantially larger than usually thought. The payroll tax distorts not only the number of hours that individuals work, but also other dimensions of labor supply like occupational choice, location, and effort. It also distorts the form in which compensation is taken, shifting taxable cash into untaxed fringe benefits, nice working conditions, and the like. These distortions to the form of compensation are in effect distortions to the individual's pattern of consumption. They are, dollar for dollar, as important as the distortions to labor supply. In a recent paper (Feldstein, 1995b), I showed that the deadweight loss caused by this full range of distortions – the number of working hours, the broader dimensions of labor supply, and the pattern of consumption implied by the form of compensation and by the use of tax deductions – can be evaluated quite simply in the traditional Harberger frame-work by using the compensated elasticity of taxable income (with respect to the net-of-tax share) in place of the usual compensated elasticity of labor supply. Because there are so many aspects of behavior that affect taxable income, this elasticity (and therefore the associated deadweight loss) is much larger than the traditional supply elasticity of working hours.

To estimate the elasticity of total taxable income with respect to the net of tax rate, I studied the tax returns of a panel of taxpayers before and after the 1986 Tax Reform Act (Feldstein, 1995c). These data imply a range of elasticity estimates between 1 and 1.5, all much larger than the traditional labor-supply elasticity.[15]

This elasticity of the income tax base is likely to exceed the elasticity of the Social Security payroll tax base because itemized deductions and changes in portfolio income do not influence the base of the payroll tax. To be very conservative, I will therefore assume for the current calculation that the relevant compensated elasticity of the payroll tax base with respect to the net-of-tax share is only 0.5.

Putting these pieces together implies that the deadweight loss due to the net Social Security tax is about 2.35 percent of the Social Security payroll tax base, a deadweight loss in 1995 of about $68 billion.[16] This deadweight loss is about 1 percent of GDP and nearly one-fifth of total Social Security payroll tax revenue. It increases the deadweight loss of the personal income tax by 50 percent.

In practice, the deadweight loss of the payroll tax is exacerbated by the haphazard relations between benefits and taxes that result from existing Social Security rules. For example, because benefits are based on the highest 35 years of earnings, most employees under age 25 receive no additional benefit for their payroll taxes. Because many married women and widows claim benefits based on their husbands' earnings, they also often receive no benefit in return for their payroll taxes. Because there is no extra reward for taxes paid at an early date, the effective tax rate on younger taxpayers can be a substantial multiple of the tax rate of older employees. Indeed, older men who are married can actually face a negative marginal Social Security tax rate, receiving more than a dollar in actuarially expected future benefits for every dollar that they now pay in payroll taxes (Feldstein and Andrew Samwick, 1992). The Social Security rules are so complex and so opaque that many individuals may simply disregard the benefits that they earn from additional working, therefore acting as if the entire payroll tax is a net tax no different in kind from the personal income tax.

The extra deadweight loss that results from these very unequal links between incremental taxes and incremental benefits would automatically be eliminated in a privatized funded system with individual retirement accounts. It can, however, also be eliminated within the existing unfunded system by creating individual Social Security accounts for each taxpayer (as James Buchanan [1968] suggested many years ago), crediting the account with the individual's tax payments and imputing the average pay-as-you-go return of 2.6 percent.[17] But the labor-market distortions and the resulting deadweight loss that result from the low rate of return in an unfunded system cannot be eliminated without shifting to either a funded public system or a privatized system of individual retirement accounts.[18]

2. The Welfare Loss of Reduced National Saving

The deadweight loss that results from labor-market distortions is not the only adverse effect of an unfunded social-security system or even the largest one. Even if there were no distortions to the labor supply or to the form of compensation (that is, even if the compensated elasticity of the tax base with respect to net of tax rate were zero), each generation after the initial one would lose by being forced to participate in a low-yielding unfunded program (i.e., by being forced to accept a pay-as-you-go implicit return of 2.6 percent when the real marginal product of capital is 9.3 percent). Even though capital income taxes now prevent each individual from receiving that 9.3 percent on his own savings, the public as a whole does receive that full return; what individuals do not receive directly, they receive in the form of reductions in other taxes or increases in government services.

The extent to which an unfunded social-security system causes a decline in national capital income and economic welfare depends on how individual saving responds to social-security taxes and benefits and on how the government acts to offset the reductions in private saving. Let's look at some facts.

An individual who has had average earnings during his entire working life and who retires at age 65 with a "dependent spouse" now receives benefits equal to 63 percent of his earnings during the full year before retirement. Since the Social Security benefits of such an individual are not taxed, those benefits replace more than 80 percent of peak preretirement net-of-tax income. Common sense and casual observation suggest that individuals who can expect such a high replacement rate will do little saving for their retirement. Such saving as they do during their preretirement years is more likely to be for precautionary balances to deal with unexpected changes in income or consumption. Not surprisingly, the median financial assets of households with heads aged 55–64 was only $8,300 in 1991, substantially less than six months' income. Even if one looks beyond financial wealth, the median net worth (including the value of the home) among all households under 65 years of age was only $28,000.

To get a sense of the order of magnitude of the annual loss, it is helpful to begin with the simplest case, in which each dollar of Social Security wealth reduces real private wealth by a dollar.[19] Since the forgone private wealth would have earned the marginal product of capital, while the unfunded Social Security system provides a return equal to the growth of aggregate wages, the population incurs a loss equal to the difference between those two returns. With a marginal product of capital of 9.3 percent and a Social Security return of 2.6 percent, the annual loss of real income is 6.7 percent of Social Security wealth. The Social Security wealth of $11 trillion in 1995 implies an annual loss in that year of $730 billion, or more than 10 percent of total GDP.

Of course, this loss is not directly comparable to the deadweight loss associated with the distortions to labor supply and to the form of compensation. Although this loss of investment income affects all generations that pay Social Security taxes, a full welfare evaluation requires comparing these losses to the gain of the initial generation of retirees who received benefits without making any contribution.

More generally, this massive potential loss must be qualified by addressing three questions. First, how much does the Social Security system actually depress real capital accumulation? The capital income loss occurs only to the extent that the capital stock would be higher with private saving or a funded program. Second, how should risk be taken into account in evaluating the loss of real income per dollar of forgone capital accumulation? And, third, how should the windfall gain to the initial generation that received Social Security benefits without making any contribution be balanced against these subsequent losses? I will deal briefly with each. Then I will turn to the potential benefit of shifting to a privatized funded social-security program.

3. The Induced Change in National Saving

To assess the effect of the existing Social Security system on national saving, one must recognize that Social Security affects public saving as well as private saving. Consider first the effect on public saving. The official surplus of the Social Security fund in fiscal year 1995 was $69 billion. To what extent does this Social Security surplus actually increase real national investment? The common criticism, that such a surplus does not raise real investment because it is invested exclusively in government bonds, is incorrect. If the Social Security trust fund buys government bonds that would otherwise have been sold to the public, it prevents an equal amount of crowding out and thereby does raise the level of real investment.

The critical issue is therefore how the existence of the Social Security surplus affects the size of the overall (unified) budget deficit. The current budget discussions about achieving a balanced budget in the year 2002 use the projected Social Security surplus of $111 billion in that year to offset projected deficits elsewhere in the budget. If the goal of a balanced budget in 2002 would have been set even if there were no projected Social Security surplus, then the existence of the surplus does not reduce the projected total budget deficit and therefore does not affect the projected future national savings available for investment. But if, as seems more likely, in the absence of a Social Security surplus, Congress and the President would have targeted a deficit in 2002 (with budget balance in some later year), then the projected Social Security surplus does increase projected national saving to some extent, although less than the full amount of the projected surplus.

Similarly, the actual deficit in 1995 would probably have been larger without the $69 billion Social Security surplus, but not $69 billion larger because Congress and the President would have enacted other legislation to reduce the budget deficit. Thus, some part, but only some part, of the $69 billion current Social Security surplus probably does help to offset the decline in private saving. But since the $69 billion annual surplus is only one-sixth of Social Security receipts and the entire Social Security trust fund is now less than 5 percent of Social Security wealth, the offsetting impact of public saving is not a major consideration.

The key issue is therefore the extent to which Social Security wealth reduces private saving. Economic theory alone cannot provide an unambiguous answer. Even if all individuals were rational life-cycle savers, each dollar of Social Security wealth would not necessarily replace exactly a dollar of real wealth. To the extent that the income-tested character of Social Security benefits induces earlier retirement, individuals will save more than they otherwise would. The relative importance of this induced retirement effect and of the more basic wealth replacement effect will vary from individual to individual (Feldstein, 1974). Social Security also affects private saving through an income effect and by providing a real annuity. My colleague Robert Barro argues that individuals who have operative utility-maximizing bequest motives offset fully the impact of Social Security wealth by increasing their saving in order to compensate future generations for the tax burdens implied by the Social Security liabilities (Barro, 1974). I doubt that this effect is empirically very important.[20] More important, I believe, is that an unknown number of individuals who are irrational or myopic may not respond at all to the provision of Social Security benefits.

Thus the extent to which Social Security wealth substitutes for private real wealth accumulation is an empirical issue. A substantial amount of research has been done on this question. Like every other important and complex issue in economics, different studies do not all point to the same conclusion. That is inevitable in empirical economics. As I have argued in a different context (Feldstein, 1982), all empirical specifications in economics are false models, oversimplifications that cannot be literally true. Statistical estimates must therefore be interpreted with a sensitivity to potential biases, simplifications, data quality problems, and the like. In the end, the researcher must make a judgment based on all of the evidence, rather than by applying traditional theories of statistical inference to each individual study.

What then does the evidence reveal about the effect of Social Security on private saving? At the most basic level is the fact, to which I have already referred, that most households accumulate little or no financial assets. This is consistent with a rational decision to substitute Social Security benefits for private wealth accumulation (Peter Diamond, 1977), but it could also be interpreted as evidence that individuals are completely myopic, providing nothing for their old age regardless of whether or not there are Social Security benefits. However, studies based on cross-sections of household data[21] support the substitution hypothesis. Although there remain serious problems of statistical identification and data quality and a wide range of parameter estimates, I interpret the cross-section evidence as implying that each extra dollar of Social Security wealth replaces about 50 cents of private wealth accumulation. Finally, there are the time-series studies linking Social Security wealth to aggregate private saving and consumption.[22] I recently reestimated the specification in my 1974 paper using time-series data through 1992 and tested some of the specifications that others had examined with earlier data (Feldstein, 1995a). The new parameter values are remarkably close to my original estimates and imply that the existing Social Security wealth reduces overall private saving by nearly 60 percent.

Although none of these is a definitive study that establishes a precise substitution of Social Security wealth for other household wealth, I believe that, taken together, these studies do imply that the Social Security program causes each generation to reduce its savings substantially and thereby to incur a substantial loss of real investment income.[23]

That the displacement of private saving by Social Security is less than complete reduces the loss that each generation incurs from the imposition of an unfunded program. But even if each dollar of Social Security wealth displaces only 50 cents of private wealth accumulation, the annual loss of national income would exceed 5 percent of GDP.[24]

However, in assessing the aggregate welfare impact of the Social Security program, the loss that results from the depressed level of real capital accumulation must be balanced against not only the windfall gain of the first generation of retirees, but also against the gain in protection to those myopic individuals who would otherwise have saved too little for their old age.[25] I shall not pursue that issue here but will ask instead what the loss is from using an unfunded program instead of a funded program to provide benefits. I will then examine what the gain would be in switching from our existing unfunded program to a funded one (in the form of a mandatory private program). In order to do so, it is necessary to consider first how the returns on real capital and on Social Security contributions should be adjusted for risk.

4. Adjusting Returns for Risks

Until this point in my remarks I have described the loss that results from substituting a pay-as-you-go program for real capital accumulation as the difference between the expected marginal product of capital and the expected growth of aggregate wages. Since both returns are uncertain, it would be appropriate to replace these expected yields with lower certainty-equivalence values.

The certainty-equivalent social rate of return on real capital depends on how the risk in that return is shared through the tax system between individual savers and the broader public.[26] Taxes paid by corporations have equaled about 42 percent of the 9.3-percent real pretax return over the past 35 years (Rippe, 1995), implying a net 5.4-percent average return to savers before personal taxes[27] and a 3.9-percent return collected by the government. Variations in this source of government revenue are reflected in the short run in the budget deficit and, in the longer run, in changes in taxes on all incomes (most of which are employment incomes) and in government spending.

I assume that most individuals do not invest in stocks and bonds because the costs of learning how to make such investments outweigh the small gains that would result relative to bank deposits on their very limited financial assets. The very small variations in net income imposed on them through their sharing in the tax on investment income can therefore be ignored, taking the mean value of that income as the certainty equivalent.[28] It is reasonable therefore to use the mean value (of 3.9 percent) as the relevant certainty equivalent for the part of the return to capital that is collected by the government.

What is the appropriate certainty equivalent for the 5.4-percent return that accrues to individual savers? A relatively conservative choice is the real yield on 10-year government bonds, a return of 2.5 percent between 1960 and 1994. Combining the 3.9-percent return collected in taxes and this 2.5-percent certainty-equivalent return received by individuals gives a total certainty-equivalent return of 6.4 percent, instead of the expected return of 9.3 percent.

It is less clear how the 2.6-percent return of the unfunded Social Security program should be adjusted for risk. The future return that an individual will receive on his or her Social Security taxes depends on the growth of aggregate real wages, on the changing age structure of the population, and on political decisions about taxes and benefits. During the period since 1960, the forward-looking increase in aggregate real wages for completed 20-year periods varied from a low of 1.5 percent to a high of 3.0 percent. Changes in demographic structure added to the fluctuations in available returns. And in recent years, the value of future Social Security benefits has been decreased by subjecting them to tax and by increasing the retirement age at which full benefits are paid.

One possibility would be to assume that the return on Social Security is as uncertain as the real return on investment in plant and equipment, suggesting that the appropriate difference between the two certainty equivalents may be the same as the difference between the two mean values, or 6.7 percent. An alternative extreme assumption would be to adjust the return on capital for risk but to make no adjustment in the return on the Social Security program, implying a risk-adjusted difference of only 3.8 percent (i.e., the difference between the 6.4-percent certainty-equivalent yield on real capital and the 2.6-percent expected return on Social Security wealth). Note that even this low 3.8-percent-age-point difference in returns implies that substituting the existing $11 trillion unfunded Social Security wealth for a funded program of equal size implies a risk-adjusted income loss of nearly 6 percent of GDP.[29]

In short, while risk adjustment might change the specific magnitude of the annual loss, even with a very conservative risk adjustment, the loss of having a funded rather than an unfunded program remains very substantial.

5. Initial Gains and Subsequent Losses

I turn now to the issue of how to balance the gain to the initial generation of beneficiaries in an unfunded system, who receive benefits without contributing, and the losses to all future generations who forgo the higher yield that would be earned on real capital.[30]

When a social-security program begins, the government collects an amount in taxes which it distributes to the then current retirees if the program is unfunded or which it invests in the national capital stock if the program is funded. The same thing happens again whenever the tax rate is increased to finance a relative increase in benefits or an expansion of coverage. To simplify my comments today, I will ignore the role of subsequent expansions and speak only of the windfall benefits to the initial generation.

If each dollar collected by an unfunded program reduces national saving by a dollar relative to a funded program of the same size,[31] each generation after the initial one incurs a loss that reflects the difference between the marginal product of capital and the growth of aggregate wages. The key question is whether the present value of the losses to all future generations exceeds the windfall benefit that the initial generation received without having paid any tax.

To compare these magnitudes, the future losses must be discounted at a rate that reflects the rate at which the marginal utility of consumption declines over time. The dollar loss to each subsequent generation grows at the same rate as aggregate wages. Discounting this growing stream of losses at a constant discount rate is therefore equivalent to applying a growth-adjusted discount rate (i.e., the difference between the discount rate and the growth rate) to a constant perpetual loss at the level incurred by the first generation of losers. Thus, the present value of the losses is equal to the taxes transferred to the initial beneficiaries multiplied by the ratio of the reduced rate of return (i.e., the difference between the risk-adjusted marginal product of capital and the risk-adjusted Social Security return) to the growth-adjusted discount rate.

Since the initial generation receives a benefit equal to the initial amount of the tax, the adoption of an unfunded plan rather than a funded plan causes a net-present-value loss if the return difference per dollar of forgone investment exceeds the growth-adjusted discount rate. This condition is satisfied for any plausible values of the parameters, implying that the present value of the future losses exceeds the value of the initial transfer.

Consider the following example. If one adopts the very conservative procedure of risk-adjusting the return to private capital but making no adjustment to the return on Social Security taxes, the lost rate of return is 3.8 percent. The present value of the future losses therefore exceeds the value of the initial generation's windfall if the growth-adjusted discount rate is less than 3.8 percent. Since the growth rate is 2.6 percent, this is satisfied if the discount rate itself is less than 6.4 percent, a condition that is certainly warranted.

With a more plausible but still very conservative high discount rate of 4 percent,[32] the risk-adjusted annual loss of 3.8 percent of displaced investment implies a present-value loss of an unfunded program that is nearly three times as large (when discounted back to the start of the program) as the windfall benefit to the initial retirees.[33,34]

6. The Potential Gain from Privatization

It is natural to ask, therefore, whether a large gain in economic welfare could be achieved by shifting now to a funded system. Several governments around the world are following Chile's example and making such a transition by privatizing their social-security programs.[35] Although the details differ, the essential feature of such privatizations is to require each employee to have a retirement account into which the employee or his employer must make regular periodic contributions that are then invested in stocks and bonds. At the time of privatization, the government recognizes its obligations to existing retirees and employees by depositing in these retirement accounts new government bonds equal to the present value of the benefits to which the individual is then entitled on the basis of past contributions to the unfunded system. Funds in these new retirement accounts can be used to purchase annuities, or withdrawn gradually when the individual reaches retirement age, or bequeathed to a spouse or other heirs.

A skeptic might ask whether this really accomplishes anything, since it merely converts the existing unfunded Social Security obligations into explicit government debt with the same present value. That skepticism would be warranted in a static economy but is not appropriate when economic growth is continually enlarging the size of the Social Security liability. Shifting from an unfunded program to a funded one is an application of the general principle that, when you discover you are in a hole, the first thing to do is to stop digging. Shifting to a funded system eliminates the future losses associated with future increases in the size of Social Security wealth.

In the first year after the privatization of a pay-as-you-go system, there is no increase in the capital stock, because the government would have to borrow all of the mandatory saving to pay benefits to existing retirees. But as time passes, the amount of net capital investment grows (because the mandatory saving rises with the number of employees and their average incomes) while the net Social Security debt that is explicitly recognized at privatization remains constant. As a result, the capital stock grows and with it the incremental income.

The net effect in each year consists of two parts: a gain equal to the real risk-adjusted return on the increase in the capital stock and a loss of the implicit Social Security return on the taxes paid. As the incremental capital stock grows, the net effect shifts from negative to positive and then increases without limit. If the capital stock grows by the amount of the mandated saving (in excess of the initial Social Security wealth), the present value of this gain at the time of privatization (using a 6.4-percent risk-adjusted return on capital, a 2.6-percent return on Social Security, and a 4-percent discount rate) is nearly twice the current value of the unfunded program. Approximating the current value of the unfunded program by the Social Security wealth implies a potential present-value gain of nearly $20 trillion. Even if the increase in the capital stock that results from shifting to a funded program is substantially less (because individuals reduce some private saving or because the mandated saving is less than the existing payroll tax), the potential present-value gain could easily exceed $10 trillion.

It is hard to put such a large sum in perspective. It may help to note that, with the assumed discount rate and GDP growth rate, that present-value gain from privatization is equivalent to about 2 percent of GDP in perpetuity. But when thinking about the political economy of reform, it is also worth bearing in mind that the potential gain from the one-time political act of shifting to a funded program has such an enormous positive present value.

This is just the gain from increasing real capital accumulation. In addition, as I noted earlier in my talk, the shift to a funded program would also reduce the deadweight losses that are now caused by a payroll tax that distorts labor supply and the form of compensation. Recall that this reduction in deadweight loss is the portion that cannot be obtained by redistributing the existing implicit return but depends on raising the rate of return on Social Security contributions from the rate of growth of wages to the real return on capital. This $68 billion deadweight loss for 1995 corresponds to an additional 1.0 percent of GDP.

Because privatization reduces the deadweight loss in perpetuity (by 1 percent of GDP) and provides individuals (after the first generation) with an opportunity to earn a higher rate of return on their mandatory retirement saving, it is possible to design a transition to a funded program that leaves each generation better off than it would be with the existing program. This can be done by using additional debt to smooth the cost of the transition over more than one generation. Although each of the transition generations would pay more in a combination of taxes and mandatory saving than under the existing laws, the improved return on their funded accounts and the resulting reduction in labor-market distortions would leave them better off.

During the transition, a system of payroll taxes that varies by age could increase the number of individuals who are net gainers by assigning more of the transition tax burden to those who, because they are younger, would gain more from the opportunity to invest their retirement savings at the higher rate of return.

Andrew Samwick and I are exploring yet an alternative approach to the transition problem that might make it possible to shift some or all employees from an unfunded system to a privatized funded system without raising taxes or reducing national saving. Our approach recognizes that some individuals, because of their age, financial circumstances, and preferences, would be willing to forgo their current claims on Social Security benefits without explicit compensation and to increase their total saving in exchange for not having to contribute to the pay-as-you-go program in the future. If we are successful in our research, we will have designed a Pareto-improving transition mechanism that improves the welfare of not only the current generation as a whole, but also of each participating individual. But that is work in progress and a subject for another day.

For now, my primary message has been that the reform of Social Security, and of other implicit life-cycle programs like Medicare and nursing-home care, is both urgent and enormously important. The payroll tax required by the current unfunded system distorts the supply of labor and the form of compensation, raising the deadweight loss of personal taxes by 50 percent. In addition, each generation now and in the future loses the difference between the return to real capital that would be obtained in a funded system and the much lower return in the existing unfunded program. Conservative assumptions imply a combined annual loss of more than 4 percent of GDP as long as the current system lasts. Although the transition to a funded system would involve economic as well as political costs, the net present value of the gain would be enormous.

The rapidly deteriorating financial position of Social Security will eventually force politicians to deal with the problem of Social Security reform. The very adverse impact of the current system on a wide variety of groups, including two-earner couples, the young, and the poor, may embolden some politicians to go beyond patching up the solvency of the current system to propose more fundamental reforms than have been considered in the past. When the politicians are ready to act, I hope that we in the economics profession will be ready to help them.

Notes

1   Note that this net Social Security wealth is the difference between Social Security benefits and Social Security taxes. The corresponding gross Social Security wealth that reflects only the present value of the benefits is about 60 percent higher. In Feldstein (1995a), I report an explicit calculation of net Social Security wealth in 1992 of $7.9 trillion in 1987 dollars. I have rescaled this to 1992 dollars by the rise in the consumer price index and extrapolated it to 1995 by the increase in nominal GDP from 1992 to 1995. Net Social Security wealth calculated in this way was $11.4 trillion in 1995.
2   These increases in Social Security wealth and its liability twin, together with the corresponding amounts for Medicare and Medicaid, are the core of the massive intergenerational transfers that Alan Auerbach, Jagdish Gokhale, and Laurence Kotlikoff have warned us about in their important studies of generational accounting (see Auerbach et al., 1991, 1994).

3 The 18-percent rate is based on what the Social Security actuaries call their intermediate Alternative-II assumptions, while the 23-percent rate is based on the somewhat more pessimistic Alternative-III assumptions. Experience suggests that even these alarming predictions may be too optimistic. In 1983, the Social Security actuaries calculated that a 12-percent rate would be enough to finance Social Security benefits until the year 2065. A dozen years later, these projections have been revised to show that the Social Security fund will be exhausted by 2035 if the tax rate is not increased or benefits reduced.

4 See Feldstein (1987) for an analysis of the conditions under which an unfunded means-tested system would provide a higher level of social welfare than an unfunded universal program. It would be desirable to extend this analysis to include the possibility of funding both alternatives.

5 I do not discuss the distortion to the retirement decision because that could be remedied by eliminating the retirement test and by other changes within the unfunded system.

6 Although the Social Security system has been accumulating a fund since 1983 to smooth the path of tax rates, more than 90 percent of payroll tax receipts are still paid out immediately as benefits, and the assets in the Social Security trust fund are less than 5 percent of the Social Security liabilities.

7 The Samuelson analysis shows that the rate of return is equal to the rate of growth of the tax base plus the rate of growth of the tax rate.

8 The tax rate increases that are projected for the next 50 years are needed just to offset the changing demographic structure and do not imply higher rates of return. Indeed, the rapid aging of the population and other recent changes imply that the return may be significantly lower than 2.6 percent for the current younger generation of employees.

9 This 9.3-percent return combines profits before all federal, state, and local taxes with the net interest paid. The method of calculation, described in Feldstein et al. (1983), has been applied to the more recent data in Richard Rippe (1995).

10 In practice, individual do not earn the full 9.3-percent pretax rate of return even on retirement saving. Individual retirement accounts and private pension plans earn that return net of federal, state, and local corporate taxes. Since those taxes averaged 42 percent of the pretax return (Rippe, 1995), the real net yield available to savers has been about 5.4 percent. In principle however a funded retirement system could deliver the full 9.3-percent pretax return to each individual saver. But even the lower 5.4-percent net return implies that the Social Security contributions are a substantial tax.

11 With a 5.4-percent net rate of return, the individual can buy that $1,900 retirement income for $510, about half of the cost with the unfunded Social Security program.

12 The extent of the effective tax depends on the taxpayers age (or, more generally, on the amount of time that will elapse between the payment of the tax and the receipt of the benefit). Replacing the 50-year-old man in the example with a 40-year-old man who has 35 years until retirement raises the net tax from 9.5 percent to 10.7 percent, while raising the age of the individual to 60 reduces the net tax to 7.3 percent.

13 The combination of the 33-percent rate and the 9.5-percent net Social Security tax implies a 42.5-percent rate. However, since half of the 9.5 percent is paid by employers, the marginal tax rate on the full pretax marginal product of labor is $42.5/1.0475 = 40.6$ percent.

14 Edgar Browning (1987) showed that, when the relevant behavioral elasticity is measured in the presence of the tax, the original Arnold Harberger (1974, pp. 25–68) formula for the deadweight loss of a tax with marginal tax rate t on a wage base of wL must be modified to:

$$DWL = 0.5\varepsilon t^2 wL/(1-t)$$

where ε is the compensated elasticity of the tax based (wL) with respect to the marginal net-of-tax share, $1-t$. The increase in the deadweight loss because the marginal tax rate is at t_2 rather than t_1 is therefore

$$\Delta \text{DWL} = 0.5\varepsilon(t_2^2 - t_1^2)wL/(1 - t_2)$$

Thus a pure payroll tax of 9.5 percent with no other tax present would induce a deadweight loss of $0.0045\varepsilon wL$. But in the presence of a preexisting income tax, the 9.5-percent payroll tax raises the deadweight loss by $\Delta \text{DWL} = 0.047\varepsilon wL$.

15   These estimates relate to the experience of taxpayers with 1985 incomes over $30,000 and may not be appropriate for the entire population. A similar study by Gerald Auten and Robert Carroll (1994), using a much larger set of panel data that is only available inside the Treasury Department, estimated the elasticity to be 1.33 with a standard error of 0.15. In a more recent study (Feldstein and Feenberg, 1995), Daniel Feenberg and I used the 1993 tax rate increases to estimate the elasticity implied by the experience after the 1993 tax rate increases. We found a short-run compensated elasticity of 0.74, although the interpretation of this is clouded by the lack of panel data and by transition issues.

16   Total wages taxable by the OASDI payroll tax in 1992 were $2.5 trillion. Scaling this up to the 1995 level by the increase in total wage and salary disbursements implies a 1995 tax base of $2.9 trillion. Since the payroll tax applied only to wages up to $61,200 per person in 1995, this $2.9 trillion should be reduced by the entire income of the individuals who earn $61,200 or more (for whom the payroll tax has no marginal tax consequence) and not just by the portion of their incomes over $61,200.

17   Tax payments or mandatory contributions of husbands and wives could be pooled and divided into two separate accounts, thereby providing protection in case of divorce. A fraction of the contributions could be automatically devoted to the purchase of life insurance. I will not explore these important issues further in the present talk.

18   Auerbach and Kotlikoff (1987) and Kotlikoff (1996) examine a special model in which the labor-market distortions can be eliminated in an unfunded system by having a higher *marginal* link, of benefits to taxes than the average benefit–tax ratio. They achieve this with a lump-sum tax on all employees. This creates no problem in their analysis, since all employees are assumed to have the same income. In practice, however, a lump-sum tax that is large enough to eliminate the marginal payroll-tax distortion would make the Social Security payroll tax very regressive.

19   I will discuss the evidence about the effect of Social Security on saving in the next section.

20   My own judgment on this "Ricardian equivalence" issue is that very few of the individuals who are affected by Social Security have operative bequest motives. Because future generations can be expected to have higher real incomes, even parents who include their children's consumption or utility in their own utility functions may prefer to receive gifts rather than to make bequests. If children do not wish to support their parents, the result is a corner solution in which loving parents do not compensate their children when the value of the Social Security liability increases. On the empirical irrelevance of Ricardian equivalence, see for example Joseph Altonji et al. (1992); see also Douglas Bernheim (1989).

21   These include studies by Feldstein and Anthony Pellechio (1979), Diamond and Jerry Hausman (1984), and Alan Blinder et al. (1990).

22   These studies include Feldstein (1974), Barro (1978), Louis Esposito (1978), and Dean Leimer and Selig Lesnoy (1982).

23   The decline in the size of the domestic capital stock depends also on the extent to which a lower rate of saving induces an increased net inflow of capital from abroad. If capital flowed internationally to maintain the same rate of return everywhere, a decline in the U.S. saving rate would induce an equal offsetting inflow from abroad. Although the net-of-tax return on this capital would go to the foreign suppliers of this capital, the U.S. government would collect taxes on the equity portion of this investment and the U.S. public would gain a corresponding amount. The evidence suggests, however, that the international capital market is sufficiently segmented that relatively little capital flows to replace the lost U.S. saving (see Feldstein and Charles Horioka, 1980; Michael Mussa and Morris Goldstein, 1993; Feldstein, 1994).

24   Increasing the capital stock by half of the 1995 net Social Security wealth of $11 trillion would raise capital income by $511 billion or about 7 percent of GDP if the rate of return remained unchanged at 9.3 percent. Such a large increase in the capital stock would of course reduce the marginal product of capital. If all of the increase in the capital stock went into the domestic capital stock (i.e., if there were no change in international capital flows), a Cobb-Douglas production function with a labor coefficient equal to the share of compensation in national income implies that the marginal product of capital would be depressed from 9.3 percent to 7.3 percent if the incremental capital went only into the business sector (i.e., excluding owner-occupied housing) and to 7.9 percent if the entire capital stock were increased. Of course, the lower return to capital would be matched by a higher return to labor. An increase in the capital stock equal to half of net Social Security wealth would raise the capital stock by one-fourth and would therefore raise national income by 5.7 percent.

25   If public policy is committed to an unfunded social-security program, setting the appropriate level of benefits requires balancing the protection of the myopic undersavers against the loss to others that results from replacing high-yield real capital accumulation with the low implicit Social Security yield. I have examined this optimization problem with the help of some simple models (Feldstein, 1985) and concluded that, with realistic estimates of the yield on capital and the return on the pay-as-you-go Social Security system, the replacement ratio of Social Security benefits to past earnings should be very much lower than it is in the current system. Indeed, even if all individuals substantially discount their utility during retirement when making their preretirement saving decisions, the optimal level of Social Security benefits may be zero (i.e., the loss in real income from reduced real saving may outweigh the benefit of the Social Security program in raising retirement income). This issue is of course closely related to the question of whether benefits should be means-tested (see Feldstein, 1987).

26   This issue is discussed in Feldstein (1995d). Kenneth Arrow and R. C. Lind (1970) explain that the fundamental principle for the evaluation of risky public expenditures is that the value of benefits should be reduced if a substantial risk is borne by the individual but that the expected value is an appropriate certainty equivalent for the part of the benefits and costs that the government spreads to all taxpayers through the tax system.

27   I assume that the alternative to the unfunded program would be a funded program in which the individual saver would get a return net of the corporate tax but not subject to any personal taxes. If additional personal taxes were levied, the certainty equivalent would get even closer to the expected value.

28   This implicitly assumes that the variation in portfolio income is uncorrelated with shocks to their income and consumption.

29   See note 24. An $11 trillion increase in the 1995 capital stock would raise the capital stock by 50 percent and, assuming a Cobb-Douglas technology, would raise national income by 11 percent. Labor would receive about three-fourths of this increase. This calculation ignores the risk adjustment and the offset for the implicit pay-as-you-go return on Social Security wealth. A 2.6-percent pay-as-you-go return on Social Security wealth would be about 4 percent of GDP.

30   For a formal analysis of this problem, see Feldstein (1995d).

31   This assumption of one-for-one substitution simplifies by abstracting from income effects. The funded program could be a funded public program or a private program with mandatory savings replacing the Social Security payroll tax.

32   The discount rate should reflect the decline in the marginal utility of per capita consumption that results from the growth of per capita real wages. With per capita real wage growth at about 1.6 percent per year, the appropriate discount rate is less than the critical value of 6.4 percent if the elasticity of the marginal utility function is less than the extremely high value of 4. An elasticity of 2, for example, which is high enough to imply that the marginal utility of consumption is halved about every 45 years, corresponds to a discount rate of 3.2 percent.

With aggregate wage growth of 2.6 percent, this implies a growth-adjusted discount rate of only 0.6 percent.

33   Recall that to simplify the discussion I have assumed that there was only one initial windfall. The actual loss reflects all subsequent program expansions as well.

34   A discount rate of 4 percent implies a growth-adjusted discount rate of 1.4 percent. The present value of the losses is thus $3.8/1.4 = 2.7$ times the initial transfer. With a more plausible discount rate of 3.2 percent, the corresponding loss would be 6.3 times the initial transfer. And if the return to Social Security is given the same risk adjustment as the return to real capital, the loss becomes $(9.3 - 2.6)/0.6 = 11.2$ times the initial transfer.

35   The use of the term "privatize" is ambiguous and raises political objections if it suggests a complete abrogation of government responsibility for the income of the aged. The benefits of a funded system that I discuss in this lecture refer to capital accumulation and to having separate accounts that link the mandatory contributions of each individual to subsequent benefits. I take the essence of privatizing to be whether individuals are also given control over their investments. In a funded but not privatized system, the government would have to invest in private stocks, bonds, and mortgages. There are obvious reasons for not wanting the government to acquire very large investments in individual private companies. Although the administrative costs may be higher when individuals have control over their investments, major U.S. mutual funds have reduced their expenses to less than one-quarter of 1 percent of assets on equity funds and to even less on fixed-income funds. Even in a private system, individuals might be constrained on the mix of assets in which they invest, and a general safety net might be provided to protect individuals whose investments did not produce adequate retirement income. Consideration of these issues lies beyond the scope of this lecture.

References

Altonji, J., Hayashi, F. and Kotlikoff, L. (1992): "Is the Extended Family Altruistically Linked? Direct Tests Using Micro Data," *American Economic Review*, December, 82 (5), 1177–98.

Arrow, K. and Lind, R. C. (1970): "Uncertainty and the Evaluation of Public Investment Decisions," *American Economic Review*, June, 60 (3), 364–78. [Reprinted as Ch. 16 in this volume.]

Auerbach, A. and Kotlikoff, L. J. (1987): *Dynamic fiscal policy*. Cambridge: Cambridge University Press.

Auerbach, A., Gokhale, J. and Kotlikoff, L. J. (1991): "Generational Accounts: A Meaningful Alternative to Deficit Accounting," in D. Bradford (ed.), *Tax Policy and the Economy*, vol. 5. Cambridge, MA: MIT Press, 55–110.

——(1994)"Generational Accounting: A Meaningful Way to Assess the Stance of Fiscal Policy," *Journal of Economic Perspectives*, 8 (1), Winter, 73–94.

Auten, G. and Carroll, R. (1994): "Taxpayer Behavior and the 1986 Tax Reform Act," working paper, Treasury Department Office of Tax Analysis, Washington, DC, July.

Barro, R. (1974): "Are Government Bonds Net Wealth?" *Journal of Political Economy*, 82 (6), November–December, 1095–117.

——(1978): *The Impact of Social Security on Private Saving*. Washington, DC: American Enterprise Institute.

Bernheim, D. (1989): "A Neoclassical Perspective on Budget Deficits," *Journal of Economic Perspectives*, 3 (2), Spring, 55–72.

Blinder, A., Gordon, R. and Wise, D. (1990): "Social Security, Bequests, and Life Cycle. Theory of Saving: Cross-Sectional Tests," in A. Blinder (ed.), *Inventory Theory and Consumer Behavior*, Ann Arbor: University of Michigan Press, 229–56. Previously published in 1983.

Browning, E. (1987): "On the Marginal Welfare Cost of Taxation," *American Economic Review*, 77 (1), March, 11–23.

Buchanan, J. (1968): "Social Insurance in a Growing Economy: A Proposal for Radical Reform," *National Tax Journal*, 21 (4), December, 386–95.

Diamond, P. (1977): "A Framework for Social Security Analysis," *Journal of Public Economics*, 8 (3), December, 275–98.

Diamond, P. A. and Hausman, J. A. (1984): "Individual Retirement and Savings Behavior," *Journal of Public Economics*, 23 (1–2), February–March, 81–114.

Esposito, L. (1978): "The Effect of Social Security on Saving: Review of Studies Using Time-Series Data," *Social Security Bulletin*, 41 (5), May, 9–17.

Feldstein, M. (1974): "Social Security, Induced Retirement, and Aggregate Capital Accumulation," *Journal of Political Economy*, 82 (5), September–October, 905–26.

——(1975): "Toward a Reform of Social Security," *Public Interest*, 40, Summer, 75–95.

——(1982): "Inflation, Tax Rules and Investment: Some Econometric Evidence," *Econometrica*, 50 (4), July, 825–62.

——(1985): "The Optimal Level of Social Security Benefits," *Quarterly Journal of Economics*, 10 (2), May, 303–20.

——(1987): "Should Social Security Be Means Tested?" *Journal of Political Economy*, 95 (3), June, 468–84.

——(1994): "Tax Policy and International Capital Flows," *Weltwirtschaftsliches Archiv*, 130 (4), 675–97.

——(1995a): "Social Security and Saving: New Time Series Evidence," National Bureau of Economic Research (Cambridge, MA) working paper 5054, March, *National Tax Journal*.

——(1995b): "Tax Avoidance and the Deadweight Loss or the Income Tax," National Bureau of Economic Research (Cambridge, MA) working paper 5055, March.

——(1995c): "Behavioral Responses to Tax Rates: Evidence from TRA86," *American Economic Review*, May (*Papers and Proceedings*), 85 (2), 170–4.

——(1995d): "Would Privatizing Social Security Raise Economic Welfare?" National Bureau of Economic Research (Cambridge, MA) working paper 5281, November.

Feldstein, M. and Feenberg, D. (1995): "The Effects of Increased Tax Rates on Taxable Income and Economic Efficiency: A Preliminary Analysis of the 1993 Tax Rate Increases," National Bureau of Economic Research (Cambridge, MA) working paper 5379, November, in J. Poterba (ed.), *Tax policy and the Economy*, Cambridge, MA: MIT Press.

Feldstein, M. and Horioka, C. (1980): "Domestic Savings and International Capital Flows," *Economic Journal*, 90 (358), June, 314–29.

Feldstein, M. and Pellechio, A. (1979): "Social Security and Household Wealth Accumulation: New Microeconometric Evidence," *Review of Economics and Statistics*, 61 (3), 361–8.

Feldstein, M. and Samwick, A. (1992): "Social Security Rules and Marginal Tax Rates," *National Tax Journal*, 45 (1), March, 1–22.

Feldstein, M., Dicks-Mireaux, L. and Poterba, J. (1983): "The Effective Tax Rate and the Pretax Rate of Return," *Journal of Public Economics*, 21 (2), July, 129–58.

Harberger, A. (1974): *Taxation and Welfare*. Chicago: University of Chicago Press.

Kotlikoff, L. (1996): "Privatization of Social Security: How It Works and Why It Matters," in J. Poterba (ed.), *Tax Policy and the Economy*, vol. 10. Cambridge, MA: MIT Press, 1–32.

Leimer, D. and Lesnoy, S. (1982): "Social Security and Private Saving: New Time Series Evidence," *Journal of Political Economy*, 90 (3), June, 606–29.

Mussa, M. and Goldstein, M. (1993): *The Integration of World Capital Markets, Changing Capital Markets: Implications for Monetary Policy*. Kansas City, MO: Federal Reserve Bank of Kansas City.

Rippe, R. (1995): "Further Gains in Corporate Profitability," *Economic Outlook Monthly* (Prudential Securities, Inc.), August, 95–3307.

Samuelson, P. (1958): "An Exact Consumption Loan Model of Interest With or Without the Social Contrivance of Money," *Journal of Political Economy*, 66 (4), December, 467–82.

PART II

Social Welfare
Judgments and
Measurement

Introduction

Chapter 3 by Lipsey and Lancaster codifies and illustrates a most important implication for searching for a welfare (or other) maximum under constraints that has far-reaching relevance for microeconomic methodology. Suppose one attains a Pareto optimum of some sort by maximizing some welfare function subject to well-recognized, non-policy derived constraints. For example, in an economy with given factor prices and factor availabilities (the constraints), one wishes to attain a Pareto optimum in the production of goods. Firms must then produce where goods' prices equal marginal costs within the factor availability constraints. This is a first-best solution to the problem. Now, however, let us suppose that, in two industries, monopoly conditions prevail and that prices are above marginal costs. Altering the environment to accommodate the new situation requires that two new constraints are added to the maximization problem, and new conditions must hold to attain a second-best welfare maximization.

In general, all of the conditions relating price to marginal cost for all firms in the economy in the new constrained maximum will change from the old price-equals-marginal cost conditions. Moreover, some industries will be required to raise prices above marginal cost, some to prices below marginal cost, and some to retain the equality. However, it is, in general, impossible to predict which industries will be required to move in which direction, if at all. That is, altering or adding constraints in a constrained maximization problem from a base case will alter all of the conditions of the base case in indeterminate directions and by indeterminate amounts. The second-best solution will differ fundamentally from the first-best, but in unknowable ways.

Consider the implications for policy. If the Antitrust Division of the Department of Justice could force both industries to price at marginal cost, clearly the first-best solution would be obtained; but, suppose the authorities can only follow a piecemeal policy, and it can force only one of the industries to price at marginal cost. Can it be assumed, or shown, that this action will increase social welfare? The analysis shows that it cannot be established, for the new situation will obtain a new constrained maximum welfare outcome that requires a completely new set of conditions among the industries. Failing these adjustments to be forthcoming, the antitrust authorities may have reduced social welfare by forcing a piecemeal adoption of first-best conditions. It follows: welfare economics, in essence, can be conducted only in a general equilibrium, not a partial equilibrium, framework.

Lipsey and Lancaster illustrate these principles for problems in international trade and taxation, in which the reader may not be interested. The core of their analysis may be found in sections 1, 2, 4, 7, and 8. In section 8, they show that even though a first-best problem can be shown to have a constrained maximum or minimum, it does not follow that a second-best variant will also have an extremum solution.

Along the spectrum of goods and services that runs from purely private goods which can be consumed by only one person (or family) to the pure public good that is nonrivalrous in the extreme, in that its consumption by any number of persons does not interfere with consumption by any number of additional consumers, there lie the types of goods whose utility to users is a function of the number of others who consume it simultaneously. In chapter 4, Buchanan christens such goods "club goods", or goods whose usage can be enjoyed by more than one agent, but are controlled by exclusion to a finite number of individuals. To a single user of such goods, the marginal benefit of increasing club size (i.e., number of persons consuming) may be expected to be positive over some domain of users, but then to become negative as congestion or other irritants arise. On the other hand, where costs are shared among users, the marginal cost of usage can be expected to be negative. For a *given size* (e.g., the number of members in a country club), the individual consumer will equate the marginal utility per dollar of the commodity (number of golf games per week) to the marginal cost of usage.

If all consumers have the same preferences and incomes, the number of users can be allowed to become variable. Then, the long-run equilibrium of the consumer occurs when the marginal utility per dollar of the services consumed equals the marginal cost of their provision equals the marginal cost of the number of consumers. Since all consumers have the same tastes for size, the optimal number of persons admitted is then determined.

Buchanan's contribution went beyond the designation of a new category of good to establish that the satisfaction derived from the consumption of few goods or services is independent of the number of persons enjoying them. Congestion is a problem with public goods, and is akin to Hardin's "tragedy of the commons" paradigm where consumers fail to value the commodity at its marginal social cost. The theory of clubs anticipated, or enlightened, these usage externalities.

In gauging the changes to a consumer's satisfaction with a price change, economists have resorted to using the area under the Marshallian demand curve between the base price and the new price. This change in consumer's surplus is calibrated in dollars and may be put into a ratio to base income to obtain a measure of the change in consumer satisfaction as a proportion of base income. However, such measures are accompanied by an apologetic addendum because the Marshallian demand curve incorporates changes in the marginal utility of money and, so, does not hold real income constant (a constant level of utility represented by movements along the initial indifference curve).

In chapter 5, Willig shows, most importantly, that, for realistic income elasticities of the demand function and base income levels, departures of consumer surplus, changes from the "true" changes in satisfaction, are small fractions of the ratio of consumer surplus changes to base income. These true measures are the compensating and equivalent variations, which measure changes in the consumer's welfare when real income (in the sense of positioning on the initial indifference curve) is held constant. Through the use of the income compensation function, Willig derives demand curves adjusted by the compensating variation and the equivalent variation, and juxtaposes them with the Marshallian function. This permits a graphic depiction of the differences in the sizes of the surplus changes in the three cases.

Then, since indifference curves are not observable, Willig moves to the derivation of bounds on these differences from knowledge of the demand parameters alone: income elasticities in the relevant region of the price change, base income, and the change in consumer surplus. His conclusion: for realistic values of these three sets of parameters, the economist need not apologize for use of the change in consumer surplus uncompensated for income effects.

What is the proper measure of the social costs of pricing power? Is it simply the sum of the deadweight losses associated with prices above marginal costs? Or is it the sum of the reductions in consumer surplus that occur thereby over the economy? Should we add advertising costs to social costs, on the assumption that most of such costs support non-informative purposes and are intended to protect monopoly rents? Are not the expenses of lobbying legislators also in this category? And what of investment costs in excess capacity intended to discourage potential entrants into industries? Should such global estimates follow the dictates of the theory of the second best (see chapter 3) and compare the sum of such costs against the welfare in a perfectly competitive economy? Is the sum of the social costs (whatever the measure adopted) derived by partial analyses industry by industry acceptable? Last, given the ambition of the goal and the inevitability of data paucity, what types of compromises does pragmatic need enforce on theory in the form of simplifying assumptions?

In a classic and seminal article, Harberger (1954) adopted the sum of consumer surplus reductions occurring from monopoly power as his measure, and estimated, in the period of the 1920s from which his data were derived, that social cost was about 0.1 percent of GNP. Chapter 6 presents a summary of the research results supporting and challenging the conclusion that such costs were trivial, and cataloging the criticisms of Harberger's methods. Cowling and Mueller then present four different measures of the social cost of pricing power in the USA and UK, with contrasting estimates that apply Harberger's methods to derive the same four measures. Broadly, their conclusions for both economies are that the social costs are far more important than Harberger and his supporters believe.

Chapter 6 is valuable as an introduction to the problems of definition and data manipulation that ambitious empirical projects enforce on skilled researchers, as well as the limits to which that sophisticated theory can be exploited in guiding such investigations, as it is for its empirical results.

Chapter 7 provides a rich, wide-ranging discussion of the important debate in social welfare theory between the "public choice-libertarian" school and the "social choice" school. Major proponents of the first school are Buchanan and Nozick, while Sen is a leading proponent of the second. To oversimplify in an effort to distinguish the major themes in Sen's treatment, the first school tends to assert three propositions:

1 There is no overarching concept of social welfare independent of the welfare of the individual members of the society.
2 The search for social justice is limited to the adoption of fair procedures for individuals to follow in their searches for satisfying their selfish preferences.

3 In their choice making, individuals, including public servants, are, and of right to be, driven by egoistic self interest.

On the other hand, social choice theorists believe

1 social welfare, in the form of a function ordering states enjoyed by individuals in the society, is a legitimate concept and its maximization a legitimate social goal;
2 social justice is a consequentialist-defined concept, not exclusively a proceduralist one; and
3 individuals and public servants are not wholly driven in their economic choices by self-interest but are capable of empathy for the plights of others.

Sen's discussion of the damage inflicted on social welfare theory by Arrow's "(Im) Possibility Theorem" and the means of escaping its narrow implications by enhancing wholly utility-relevant conditions with broader information revolves around the conflict in points (1) above. His view that social justice can never be wholly procedural or consequentialist concerns (2), and his view of the motivations of economic actors, illustrated by his seminal work on the origins of famines, as well as his view of the importance of discussion in liberal societies in altering motivations, is organized about points (3).

This outline is admittedly too simplistic as a summary of the richness of the menu in this chapter, but it may be valuable to the reader in providing a thread of continuity. The author's clarity in the introduction in stating the topics to be discussed, and his return to these aims in the conclusion, are models of presentation, and may eliminate the reader's need for the outline presented here.

References

Harberger, A. C. (1954): "Monopoly and Resource Allocation," *American Economic Review, Papers and Proceedings*, 44 (2), 77–87.

CHAPTER THREE

The General Theory of Second Best[1]

R. G. LIPSEY AND KELVIN LANCASTER

Source: Review of Economic Studies, 24 (1956), 11–32. Reprinted with the permission of The Review of Economic Studies, Ltd. © The Review of Economic Studies, Ltd.

There is an important basic similarity underlying a number of recent works in apparently widely separated fields of economic theory. Upon examination, it would appear that the authors have been rediscovering, in some of the many guises given it by various specific problems, a single general theorem. This theorem forms the core of what may be called *The General Theory of Second Best*. Although the main principles of the theory of second best have undoubtedly gained wide acceptance, no general statement of them seems to exist. Furthermore, the principles often seem to be forgotten in the context of specific problems and, when they are rediscovered and stated in the form pertinent to some problem, this seems to evoke expressions of surprise and doubt rather than of immediate agreement and satisfaction at the discovery of yet another application of the already accepted generalizations.

In this paper, an attempt is made to develop a *general* theory of second best. In Section 1 there is given, by way of introduction, a verbal statement of the theory's main general theorem, together with two important negative corollaries. Section 2 outlines the scope of the general theory of second best. Next, a brief survey is given of some of the recent literature on the subject. This survey brings together a number of cases in which the general theory has been applied to various problems in theoretical economics. The implications of the general theory of second best for piecemeal policy recommendations, especially in welfare economics, are considered in Section 4. This general discussion is followed by two sections giving examples of the application of the theory in specific models. These examples lead up to the general statement and rigorous proof of the central theorem given in Section 7. A brief consideration of the existence of second best solutions is followed by a classificatory discussion of the nature of these solutions. This taxonomy serves to illustrate some of the important negative corollaries of the theorem. The paper is concluded with a brief discussion of the difficult problem of multiple-layer second best optima.

1. A General Theorem in the Theory of Second Best[2]

It is well known that the attainment of a Paretian optimum requires the simultaneous fulfillment of all the optimum conditions. The general theorem for the second best optimum states that if there is introduced into a general equilibrium system a constraint which prevents the attainment of one of the Paretian conditions, the other Paretian conditions, although still attainable, are, in general, no longer desirable. In other words, given that one of the Paretian optimum conditions cannot be fulfilled, then an optimum situation can be achieved only by departing from all the other Paretian conditions. The optimum situation finally attained may be termed a second best optimum because it is achieved subject to a constraint which, by definition, prevents the attainment of a Paretian optimum.

From this theorem there follows the important negative corollary that there is no *a priori* way to judge as between various situations in which some of the Paretian optimum conditions are fulfilled while others are not. Specifically, it is *not* true that a situation in which more, but not all, of the optimum conditions are fulfilled is necessarily, or is even likely to be, superior to a situation in which fewer are fulfilled. It follows, therefore, that in a situation in which there exist many constraints which prevent the fulfillment of the Paretian optimum conditions, the removal of any one constraint may affect welfare or efficiency either by raising it, by lowering it, or by leaving it unchanged.

The general theorem of the second best states that if one of the Paretian optimum conditions cannot be fulfilled a second best optimum situation is achieved only by departing from all other optimum conditions. It is important to note that in general, nothing can be said about the direction or the magnitude of the secondary departures from optimum conditions made necessary by the original non-fulfillment of one condition. Consider, for example, a case in which the central authority levies a tax on the purchase of one commodity and returns the revenue to the purchasers in the form of a gift so that the sole effect of the tax is to distort relative prices. Then all that can be said in general is that given the existence and invariability of this tax, a second best optimum can be achieved by levying some system of taxes and subsidies on all other commodities. The required tax on some commodities may exceed the given tax, on other commodities it may be less than the given tax, while on still others a subsidy, rather than a tax, may be required.[3]

It follows from the above that there is no *a priori* way to judge as between various situations in which none of the Paretian optimum conditions are fulfilled. In particular, it is *not* true that a situation in which all departures from the optimum conditions are of the same direction and magnitude is necessarily superior to one in which the deviations vary in direction and magnitude. For example, there is no reason to believe that a situation in which there is the same degree of monopoly in all industries will necessarily be in any sense superior to a situation in which the degree of monopoly varies as between industries.

2. The Scope of the Theory of Second Best

Perhaps the best way to approach the problem of defining the scope of the theory of second best is to consider the role of constraints in economic theory. In the general economic problem of maximization a function is maximized subject to at least one constraint. For example, in the simplest welfare theory a welfare function is maximized subject to the constraint exercised by a transformation function. The theory of the Paretian optimum is concerned with the conditions that must be fulfilled in order to maximize some function subject to a set of constraints which are generally considered to be "in the nature of things". There are, of course, a whole host of possible constraints beyond those assumed to operate in the Paretian optimization problem. These further constraints vary from the "nature-dictated" ones, such as indivisibilities and boundaries to production functions, to the obviously "policy created" ones such as taxes and subsidies. In general, there would seem to be no logical division between those constraints which occur in the Paretian optimum theory and those which occur only in the theory of second best. All that can be said is that, in the theory of the Paretian optimum, certain constraints are assumed to be operative and the conditions necessary for the maximization of some function subject to these constraints are examined. In the theory of second best there is admitted at least one constraint additional to the ones existing in Paretian optimum theory and it is in the nature of this constraint that it prevents the satisfaction of at least one of the Paretian optimum conditions. Consideration is then given to the nature of the conditions that must be satisfied in order to maximize some function subject to this new set of constraints.[4]

It is important to note that even in a single general equilibrium system where there is only one Paretian optimum, there will be a multiplicity of second best optimum positions. This is so because there are many possible combinations of constraints with a second best solution for each combination.[5] For this reason one may speak of the existence of *the* Paretian optimum but should, strictly speaking, refer to *a* second best optimum.

It is possible to approach problems in the theory of second best from two quite different directions. On the one hand, the approach used in this paper is to assume the existence of one constraint additional to those in the Paretian optimum problem (e.g., one tax, one tariff, one subsidy, or one monopoly) and then to investigate the nature of the conditions that must be satisfied in order to achieve a second best optimum and, where possible, to compare these conditions with those necessary for the attainment of a Paretian optimum. On the other hand, the approach used by Professor Meade is to assume the existence of a large number of taxes, tariffs, monopolies, *et cetera*, and then to inquire into the effect of changing any one of them. Meade, therefore, deals with a system containing many constraints and investigates the optimum (second best) level for one of them, assuming the invariability of all the others (Meade, 1955b, p. 9). It would be futile to argue that one of these approaches was superior to the other. Meade's is probably the appropriate one when considering problems of actual policy in a world where many imperfections exist and only a few can be removed at any one time. On the other hand, the approach used in the present paper would seem to be the more appropriate one for a systematic study of the general principles of the theory of second best.

3. The Theory of Second Best in the Literature of Economics

The Theory of Second Best has been, in one form or another, a constantly recurring theme in the post-war literature on the discriminatory reduction of trade barriers. There can be no doubt that the theory of customs unions provides an important case study in the application of the general theory of second best. Until customs union theory was subjected to searching analysis, the "free trader"[6] often seemed ready to argue that any reduction in tariffs would necessarily lead to an improvement in world productive efficiency and welfare. In his path-breaking work on the theory of customs unions Professor Viner (1950) has shown that the removal of tariffs from some imports may cause a decrease in the efficiency of world production.

One important reason for the shifts in the location of production which would follow the creation of a customs union was described by Viner (1950, p. 43) as follows:

> There will be commodities which one of the members of the customs union will now newly import from the other, whereas before the customs union it imported them from a third country, because that was the cheapest possible source of supply even after payment of the duty. The shift in the locus of production is now not as between the two member countries but as between a low-cost third country and the other, high-cost, member country.

Viner used the term trade diversion to describe production shifts of this sort and he took it as self-evident that they would reduce the efficiency of world production. Since it is quite possible to conceive of a customs union having only trade diverting production effects, it follows, in Viner's analysis, that the discriminatory reduction of tariffs may reduce, rather than raise, the efficiency of world production.

Viner emphasized the production effects of customs unions,[7] directing his attention to changes in the location, and hence the cost, of world production. Recently Professor Meade (1955a) has shown that a customs union has exactly parallel effects on the location, and hence the "utility" of world consumption. Meade isolates the "consumption effects" of customs unions by considering an example in which world production is fixed. In this case Viner's problem of the effects of a union on the cost of world production cannot arise. Meade argues that, under these circumstances, a customs union will tend to raise welfare by encouraging trade between the member countries but that, at the same time, it will tend to lower welfare by discouraging the already hampered trade between the union area and the rest of the world. In the final analysis a customs union will raise welfare, lower it, or leave it unchanged, depending on the relative strength of these two opposing tendencies (Meade, 1955a, ch.III). The Viner-Meade conclusions provide an application of the general theorem's negative corollary that nothing can be said a priori about the welfare and efficiency effects of a change which permits the satisfaction of some but not all of the Paretian optimum conditions.

Another application of second best theory to the theory of tariffs has been provided by S. A. Ozga (1955, p. 489) who has shown that a non-preferential reduction of tariffs by a single country may lead "away from the free trade position". In other words, the adoption of a free trade policy by one country, in a multi-country tariff ridden world, may actually lower the real income of that country and of the world. Ozga demonstrates the existence of this possibility by assuming that all commodities are, in consumption, rigidly complementary, so that their production either increases or decreases simultaneously. He then shows that in a three country world with tariffs all around, one country may adopt a policy of free trade and, as a result, the world production of all commodities may decrease. This is one way of demonstrating a result which follows directly from the general theory of second best.

In the field of Public Finance, the problems of second best seem to have found a particularly perplexing guise in the long controversy on the relative merits of direct *versus* indirect taxation. It would be tedious to review all the literature on the subject at this time. In his 1951 article, I. M. D. Little has shown that because of the existence of the "commodity" leisure, the price of which cannot be directly taxed, both direct and indirect taxes must prevent the satisfaction of some of the conditions necessary for the attainment of a Paretian optimum. An indirect tax on one good disturbs rates of substitution between that good and all others while an income tax[8] disturbs rates of substitution between leisure and all other goods. Little then argues that there is no *a priori* way to judge as between these two positions where some Paretian optimum conditions are satisfied while others are not. This is undoubtedly correct. However, Little might have gone on to suggest that there is an *a priori* case in favour of raising a given amount of revenue by some system of *unequal indirect taxes* rather than by either an income tax or an indirect tax on only one commodity. This interesting conclusion was first stated by W. J. Corlett and D. C. Hague (1953–54). These authors have demonstrated that the optimum way to raise any given amount of revenue is by a system of unequal indirect taxes in which commodities "most complementary" to leisure have the highest tax rates while commodities "most competitive" with leisure have the lowest rates (Corlett and Hague, 1953–54, p. 24). The reason for this general arrangement of tax rates should be intuitively obvious. When an equal *ad valorem* rate of tax is placed on all goods the consumption of leisure will be too high while the consumption of all other goods will be too low.[9] The consumption of untaxed leisure may be discouraged by placing especially high rates of tax on commodities which are complementary in consumption to leisure and by placing especially low rates of tax on commodities which are competitive in consumption with leisure.

Professor Meade (1955c, ch. III) has recently given an alternate analysis of the same problem. His conclusions, however, support those of Corlett and Hague. In theory at least, the tables have been completely turned and the indirect tax is proved to be superior to the income tax, provided that the optimum system of indirect taxes is levied.[10] This conclusion is but another example of an application of the general theorem that if one of the Paretian optimum conditions cannot be fulfilled then a second best optimum situation can be obtained by departing from all the other optimum conditions.

What is perhaps not so obvious is that the problem of direct *versus* indirect taxes and that of the "consumption effects" of customs unions are analytically identical. The Little analysis deals with a problem in which some commodities can be taxed at various rates while others must be taxed at a fixed rate. (It is not necessary that the fixed rate of tax should be zero). In the theory of customs unions one is concerned with the welfare and efficiency effects of varying some tariff rates while leaving others unchanged. In Little's analysis there are three commodities, X, Y and Z; commodity Z being leisure. By renaming Z home goods and X and Y imports from two different countries one passes immediately to the theory of customs unions. An income tax in Little's analysis becomes a system of non-discriminatory import duties while a single indirect tax becomes the discriminatory tariff introduced after the formation of a customs union with the producers of the now untaxed import. A model of this sort is considered further in Section 5.

An application of the general theory of second best to yet another field of economic theory is provided by A. Smithies (1936) in his article, *The Boundaries of the Production and Utility Function*. Smithies considers the case of a multi-input firm seeking to maximize its profits. This will be done when for each factor the firm equates marginal cost with marginal revenue productivity. Smithies then suggests that there may exist boundaries to the production function. These boundaries would take the form of irreducible minimum amounts of certain inputs, it being possible to employ more but not less than these minimum amounts. It might happen, however, that profit maximization called for the employment of an amount of one factor less than the minimum technically possible amount. In this case production would take place "on the boundary" and the minimum possible amount of the input would be used. However, in the case of this input, marginal cost would no longer be equated with marginal productivity, the boundary conditions forcing its employment beyond the optimum level. Smithies then shows that given the constraint, marginal cost does not equal marginal productivity for this input, profits will be maximised only by departing from the condition marginal cost equals marginal productivity for all other inputs. Furthermore, there is no *a priori* reason for thinking that the nature of the inequality will be the same for all factors. Profit maximization may require that some factors be employed only to a point where marginal productivity exceeds marginal cost while other factors are used up to a point where marginal productivity falls below marginal cost.

Problems of the "mixed economy" provide an application of second best theory frequently encountered in popular discussion. Consider, for example, a case where one section of an economy is rigidly controlled by the central authority while another section is virtually uncontrolled. It is generally agreed that the economy is not functioning efficiently but there is disagreement as to the appropriate remedy. One faction argues that more control over the uncontrolled sector is needed, while another faction pleads for a relaxation of the degree of control exercised in the public sector. The principles of the general theory of second best suggest that *both sides* in the controversy may be advocating a policy appropriate to the desired ends. Given the high degree of control in one sector and the almost complete absence of control in another, it is unlikely that anything like a second best optimum position has been reached. If this is so, then it follows that efficiency would be increased either by increasing the degree of control exercised over the uncontrolled sector or by relaxing the control exercised over the controlled sector. Both of these policies will move the economy in the direction of some second best optimum position.

Finally mention may be made of the problem of "degrees of monopoly". It is not intended to review the voluminous literature on this controversy. It may be mentioned in passing that, in all but the simplest models, a Paretian optimum requires that marginal costs *equal* marginal revenues throughout the entire economy.[11] If this equality is not established in one firm, then the second best conditions require that the equality be departed from in all other firms. However, as is usual in second best cases there is no presumption in favour of the same degree of inequality in all firms. In general, the second best position may well be one in which marginal revenues greatly exceed marginal costs in some firms, only slightly exceed marginal costs in others, while, in still other firms, marginal revenues actually fall short of marginal costs.

A similar problem is considered by Lionel W. McKenzie (1951) in his article "Ideal Output and the Interdependence of Firms". He deals with the problem of increasing the money value of output in situations in which marginal costs do not equal prices in all firms. The analysis is not conducted in a general equilibrium setting and many simplifying assumptions are made such as the one that resources can be shifted between occupations as desired without affecting their supplies. McKenzie shows that even in this partial equilibrium setting if allowance is made for inter-firm sales of intermediate products, the condition that marginal costs should bear the same relation to prices in all firms does not provide a sufficient condition for an increase in the value of output. Given that the optimum condition, marginal costs equals price cannot be achieved, McKenzie shows that a second best optimum would require a complex set of relations in which the ratio of marginal cost to price would vary as between firms. Although the analysis is not of a full general equilibrium, the conclusions follow the now familiar pattern:

1 If a Paretian optimum cannot be achieved a second best optimum requires a general departure from all the Paretian optimum conditions and
2 there are unlikely to be any simple sufficient conditions for an *increase* when a *maximum* cannot be obtained.

4. The Theory of Second Best and "Piecemeal" Policy Recommendations

It should be obvious from the discussion in the preceding sections that the principles of the general theory of second best show the futility of "piecemeal welfare economics".[12] To apply to only a small part of an economy welfare rules which would lead to a Paretian optimum if they were applied everywhere, may move the economy away from, not toward, a second best optimum position. A nationalized industry conducting its price-output policy according to the Lerner–Lange "Rule" in an imperfectly competitive economy may well diminish both the general productive efficiency of the economy and the welfare of its members.

The problem of sufficient conditions for an increase in welfare, as compared to necessary conditions for a welfare maximum, is obviously important if policy recommendations are to be made in the real world. Piecemeal welfare economics is often based on the belief that a study of the *necessary* conditions for a Paretian welfare optimum may lead to the discovery of *sufficient* conditions for an increase in welfare.[13] In his *Critique of Welfare Economics*, I. M. D. Little (1950, p. 120) discusses the optimum conditions for exchange and production "…both as necessary conditions for a maximum, and as sufficient conditions for a desirable economic change". Later on in his discussion Little says "…necessary conditions are not very interesting. It is *sufficient* conditions for improvements that we really want…" (Little, 1950, p. 129). But the theory of second best leads to the conclusion that there are in general no such sufficient conditions for an increase in welfare. There are necessary conditions for a Paretian optimum. In a simple situation there may exist a condition that is necessary and sufficient. But in a general equilibrium situation there will be no conditions which in general are sufficient for an increase in welfare without also being sufficient for a welfare maximum.[14]

The preceding generalizations may be illustrated by considering the following optimum condition for exchange: "The marginal rate of substitution between any two 'goods' must be the same for every individual who consumes them both". (Little, 1950, p. 121). Little concludes (p. 122) that this condition gives a sufficient condition for an increase in welfare provided only that when it is put into effect, "…the distribution of welfare is not thereby made worse". However, the whole discussion of this optimum condition occurs only after Little (p. 121) has postulated "...a fixed stock of 'goods' to be distributed between a number of 'individuals'". The optimum condition that all consumers should be faced with the same set of prices becomes in this case a sufficient condition for an increase in welfare, because the problem at hand is merely how to distribute efficiently a fixed stock of goods. But in this case the condition is a necessary and sufficient condition for a Paretian optimum. As soon as variations in output are admitted, the condition is no longer sufficient for a welfare maximum and it is also no longer sufficient for increase in welfare.

The above conclusion may be illustrated by a simple example. Consider a community of two individuals having different taste patterns. The "government" of the community desires to raise a certain sum which it will give away to a foreign country. The community has made its value judgement about the distribution of income by deciding that each individual must contribute half of the required revenue. It has also been decided that the funds are to be raised by means of indirect taxes. It follows from the Corlett and Hague analysis that the best way to raise the revenue is by a system of *unequal* indirect taxes in which commodities "most complementary" to leisure are taxed at the highest rates while commodities "most substitutable" for leisure are taxed at the lowest rates. But the two individuals have different tastes so that commodity X is substitutable for leisure for individual I and complementary to leisure for individual II, while commodity Y and leisure are complements for individual I and substitutes for II. The optimum way to raise the revenue, therefore, is to tax commodity X at a low rate when it is sold to individual I and at a high rate when it is sold to individual II, while Y is taxed at a high rate when sold to I but a low rate when sold to II. A second best optimum thus requires that the two individuals be faced with different sets of relative prices.

Assume that the optimum tax rates are charged. The government then changes the tax system to make it non-discriminatory as between persons while adjusting the rates to keep revenue unchanged. Now the Paretian optimum exchange condition is fulfilled, but welfare has been decreased, for both individuals have been moved to lower indifference curves. Therefore, in the assumed circumstances, this Paretian optimum condition is a sufficient condition for a *decrease* in welfare.

5. A Problem in the Theory of Tariffs

In this section the simple type of model used in the analysis of direct *versus* indirect taxes is applied to a problem in the theory of tariffs. In the Little–Meade–Corlett & Hague analysis it is assumed that the government raises a fixed amount of revenue which it spends in some specified manner. The optimum way of raising this revenue is then investigated. A somewhat different problem is created by changing this assumption about the disposition of the tax revenue. In the present analysis it is assumed that the government returns the tax revenue to the consumers in the form of a gift so that the only effect of the tax is to change relative prices.[15]

A simple three commodity model is used, there being one domestic commodity and two imports. It is assumed that the domestic commodity is un-taxed and that a fixed rate of tariff is levied on one of the imports. The optimum level for the tariff on the other import is then investigated. This is an obvious problem in the theory of second best. Also it is interesting to note that the conclusions reached have immediate applications to the theory of customs unions. In the second part of this section the conclusions of Section 5.1 are applied to the problem of the welfare effects of a customs union which causes neither trade creation nor trade diversion, but only the expansion and contraction of the volumes of already existing trade.

5.1. Second best optimum tariff systems with fixed terms of trade

The conditions of the model are as follows: Country A is a small country specializing in the production of one commodity (Z). Some of Z is consumed at home and the remainder is exported in return for two imports, X from country B and Y from country C. The prices of X and Y in terms of Z are unaffected by any taxes or tariffs levied in country A. It is further assumed that none of the tariffs actually levied by A are high enough to protect domestic industries producing either X or Y,[16] that country B does not produce commodity Y and that country C does not produce commodity X.[17] The welfare of country A is defined by a community welfare function which is of the same form as the welfare functions of the identical individuals who inhabit A.

It is assumed that A levies some fixed tariff on imports of commodity Y and that commodity Z is not taxed. It is then asked. What tariff ($\leqq 0$) on imports of commodity X will maximize welfare in country A? This tariff will be termed the optimum X tariff.[18]

The model may be set out as follows: Let there be three commodities, X, Y and Z. Let p_x and p_y be the prices of X and Y in terms of Z. Let the rate of ad valorem tariff charged on X and Y be $t_x - 1$ and $t_y - 1$.[19]

$$u = u(x, y, z) \tag{5.1}$$

$$\frac{\partial u}{\partial x} = \frac{\partial u}{\partial z} p_x t_x \tag{5.2a}$$

$$\frac{\partial u}{\partial y} = \frac{\partial u}{\partial z} p_y t_y \tag{5.2b}$$

$$X p_x + Y p_y + Z = C \tag{5.3}$$

Equation (5.1) expresses country A's community welfare function. Equations (5.2a and b) are the demand equilibrium conditions. Equation (5.3) gives the condition that A's international payments be in balance.[20]

These equations will yield a solution in general for any t_x and t_y in X, Y and Z. Hence, for given p_x, p_y, C and whatever parameters enter into (5.1):

$$X = f(t_x, t_y) \tag{5.4a}$$
$$Y = g(t_x, t_y) \tag{5.4b}$$
$$Z = h(t_x, t_y) \tag{5.4c}$$

Attention is directed to the sign of the change in U when t_x changes with $t_y > 1$ kept constant. From equations (5.1) and (5.4):

$$\frac{\partial u}{\partial t_x} = \frac{\partial u}{\partial x} \cdot \frac{\partial x}{\partial t_x} + \frac{\partial u}{\partial y} \cdot \frac{\partial y}{\partial t_x} + \frac{\partial u}{\partial z} \cdot \frac{\partial z}{\partial t_x} \tag{5.5}$$

Substitute (5.2a and 5.2b) into (5.5):

$$\frac{\partial u}{\partial t_x} = p_x t_x \frac{\partial u}{\partial z} \cdot \frac{\partial x}{\partial t_x} + p_y t_y \frac{\partial u}{\partial z} \cdot \frac{\partial y}{\partial t_x} + \frac{\partial u}{\partial z} \cdot \frac{\partial z}{\partial t_x} \tag{5.6}$$

$$= \frac{\partial u}{\partial z} \left(p_x t_x \frac{\partial x}{\partial t_x} + p_y t_y \frac{\partial y}{\partial t_x} + \frac{\partial z}{\partial t_x} \right) \tag{5.6}$$

Next, take the partial derivative of (5.3) with respect to t_x.

$$p_x \frac{\partial x}{\partial t_x} + p_y \frac{\partial y}{\partial t_x} + \frac{\partial z}{\partial t_x} = 0$$

or:

$$p_x \frac{\partial x}{\partial t_x} + p_y \frac{\partial y}{\partial t_x} = -\frac{\partial z}{\partial t_x} \tag{5.7}$$

Substitute (5.7) into (5.6):

$$\frac{\partial u}{\partial t_x} = \frac{\partial u}{\partial z} \left(p_x t_x \frac{\partial x}{\partial t_x} + p_y t_y \frac{\partial y}{\partial t_x} - p_x \frac{\partial x}{\partial t_x} - p_y \frac{\partial y}{\partial t_x} \right)$$

$$= \frac{\partial u}{\partial z} \left[p_x \frac{\partial x}{\partial t_x} (t_x - 1) + p_y \frac{\partial y}{\partial t_x} (t_y - 1) \right] \tag{5.8}$$

It is assumed, first, that some tariff is levied on Y but that X is imported duty free. Therefore, $t_x = 1$ and $t_y > 1$. Equation (5.8) reduces to:

$$\frac{\partial u}{\partial t_x} = \frac{\partial u}{\partial z} \left[p_y \frac{\partial y}{\partial t_x} (t_y - 1) \right] \tag{5.9}$$

In (5.9) $\partial u / \partial t_x$ takes the same sign as $\partial y / \partial t_x$.[21] It follows that the introduction of a marginal tariff on X will raise welfare if it causes an increase in imports of commodity Y, will leave welfare unchanged if it causes no change in imports of Y and will lower welfare if it causes a decrease in imports of Y. Therefore, the optimum tariff on X is, in fact, a subsidy, if imports of Y fall when a tariff is placed on X, it is zero if the X tariff has no effect on imports of Y and it is positive if imports of Y rise when the tariff is placed on X.

It is now assumed that a uniform rate of tariff is charged on X and Y. Therefore, $t_x = t_y \equiv T$ and equation (5.8) becomes:

$$\frac{\partial u}{\partial t_x} = \frac{\partial u}{\partial z}(T - 1)\left(p_x \frac{\partial x}{\partial T} + p_y \frac{\partial y}{\partial T}\right)$$

Substituting from (5.7):

$$\frac{\partial u}{\partial t_x} = -\left[\frac{\partial u}{\partial z} \cdot \frac{\partial z}{\partial t_x}(T - 1)\right] \tag{5.10}$$

In (5.10) the sign of $\frac{\partial u}{\partial t_x}$ will be opposite to the sign of $\frac{\partial z}{\partial t_x}$. It follows that a marginal increase in the tariff on X will increase welfare if it causes a decrease in the consumption of Z, will leave welfare unchanged if it causes no change in the consumption of Z and will lower welfare if it causes an increase in the consumption of Z. It may be concluded, therefore, that the optimum tariff on X exceeds the given tariff on Y if an increase in the X tariff reduces the consumption of Z, that the optimum X tariff equals the given Y tariff if there is no relation between the X tariff and the consumption of Z and that the optimum X tariff is less than the given Y tariff if an increase in the X tariff causes an increase in consumption of Z.

In the case where an increase in the tariff on X causes an increase in the consumption of Y and of Z the optimum X tariff is greater than zero but less than the given tariff on Y.

5.2. Welfare effects of a customs union causing only trade expansion and trade contraction

It is assumed that country A initially charges a uniform *ad valorem* rate of tariff on imports of X and Y. A then forms a customs union with country B. Now X is imported duty free while the pre-union tariff still applies to Y. What is the effect on A's welfare of such a customs union? Some answers[22] follow immediately from the previous analysis:

Case 1: Any increase in the tariff on X causes a fall in the consumption of Y. The optimum tariff on X is, in fact, a subsidy. Therefore, the customs union must raise A's welfare.

Case 2: Variations in the tariff on X have no effect on consumption of Y. The optimum tariff on X is now zero. The customs union raises welfare in A. Furthermore, it raises it to a second best optimum level (assuming that only the X tariff can be varied).

Case 3: Variations in the tariff on X have no effect on the purchases of Z. The optimum tariff on X is equal to the Y tariff. The customs union lowers A's welfare. Furthermore, the union disturbs an already achieved second best optimum.

Case 4: An increase in the tariff on X causes a fall in the consumption of Z. In this case the optimum tariff on X exceeds the given Y tariff. Therefore, the customs union lowers A's welfare.

Case 5: An increase in the tariff on X causes an increase in the consumption of both Y and Z. The optimum X tariff is greater than zero but less than the given Y tariff. The effect of the customs union on welfare is not known. Assume, however, that the X tariff is removed by a series of stages. It follows that the initial stages of tariff reduction must raise welfare and that the final stages must lower it. Although nothing can be said about the welfare effect of a complete removal of the X tariff, another important conclusion is suggested. A small reduction in tariffs must raise welfare. A large reduction may raise or lower it. It follows, therefore, that a partial preferential reduction of tariffs is more likely to raise welfare than is a complete preferential elimination of tariffs. Of course, this conclusion depends upon the specific assumptions made in the present model but it does provide an interesting and suggestive hypothesis for further investigation.[23,24]

6. Nationalized Industry in an Economy with Monopoly: A Simple Model

An interesting, and not unlikely, situation in which a "second best" type of policy may have to be pursued is that of a mixed economy which includes both nationalized industries and industries which are subject to monopoly control.

The monopoly is assumed to be one of the data: for one reason or another this monopoly cannot be removed, and the task of the nationalized industry is to determine that pricing policy which is most in "the public interest".

When there is full employment of resources then, if the monopoly is exercising its power, it will be producing less of the monopolized product than is required to give an optimum (in the Paretian sense) allocation of resources. Since there is less than the optimum production of the monopolized good, there will be more than the optimum production of the non-monopolized goods as a group.

Suppose that one of the non-monopolized industries is now nationalized. What should be its price/output policy? If it behaves competitively then it will tend to produce more of its product, relative to the monopolized good, than the Paretian optimum would require. If, on the other hand, it behaves monopolistically itself, then it will cut down the excess of its own production relative to that of the monopoly but will increase the excess of the remaining goods relative to both its own product and that of the monopolized industry. This is a typical "second best" situation: any policy will make some things worse and some better.

It is clear that no policy on the part of the nationalized industry can restore the Paretian optimum, for the existence of the monopoly prevents this. The nationalized industry must aim at a second best policy, designed to achieve the best that still remains open to the economy. In purely general terms it is impossible to be more definite than this, as will be shown in Section 9. Intuitively, however, one might expect that, in some situations at least, the best policy for the nationalized industry would be to behave something like the monopoly, but to a lesser extent. In the case of the simple model to be presented in this section, one's intuitions would be correct.

There are assumed to be, in the present model, three industries producing goods x, y, z. Labour is the only input, costs are constant, and the total supply of labour is fixed. These assumptions define a unique linear transformation function relating the quantities of the three goods:

$$ax + by + cz = L \tag{6.1}$$

The production functions from which this is derived are:

$$x = \frac{1}{a} l_x$$

$$y = \frac{1}{b} l_y \tag{6.2}$$

$$z = \frac{1}{c} l_z$$

$$l_x + l_y + l_z = L$$

The marginal costs are constant and proportional to a, b, c.

The "public interest" is assumed to be defined by a community preference function, which is of the same form as the preference functions of the identical individuals who make up the society. For simplicity, this preference function is assumed to take the logarithmic form:

$$U = x^\alpha y^\beta z^\gamma \qquad \alpha, \beta, \gamma > 0 \tag{6.3}$$

The partial derivatives of this are:

$$\frac{\partial U}{\partial x} = \alpha \frac{U}{x}$$

$$\frac{\partial U}{\partial y} = \beta \frac{U}{y}$$

$$\frac{\partial U}{\partial z} = \gamma \frac{U}{z}$$

so that the marginal utilities of x, y, z are proportional, respectively, to α/x, β/y, γ/z. For a utility function of this type, all goods are substitutes in both the Edgeworth–Pareto and Hicksian senses.

If there were no constraints in the economy (other than the transformation function itself), the Paretian optimum would be that found by maximizing the expression $U - \lambda(ax + by + cz - L)$, where λ is the Lagrangian multiplier. This would lead to the three equations:

$$\frac{\partial U}{\partial x} - \lambda a = 0$$

$$\frac{\partial U}{\partial y} - \lambda b = 0 \tag{6.4}$$

$$\frac{\partial U}{\partial z} - \lambda c = 0$$

which can be expressed in the proportional form:

$$\frac{a}{\alpha} x = \frac{b}{\beta} y = \frac{c}{\gamma} z \tag{6.5}$$

These conditions are of the familiar Paretian type, namely that the marginal utilities (or prices which, assuming the ordinary consumer behaviour equations, are proportional to them) are proportional to the marginal costs. There being no monetary conditions, and the supply of labour being fixed, equality between prices and marginal costs is not necessarily implied.

Suppose now that the industry producing x is a monopoly. The monopoly will set the price of x higher (in terms of some numéraire, which will be taken to be z) in relation to marginal cost than in the conditions of the Paretian optimum. A numéraire is necessary since money, and money prices, are not being considered.

For the present purposes, the exact margin between marginal cost and price in the monopolized industry (relative to the numéraire) does not matter. It is necessary only for the problem that the monopolist set the prices of x higher, relative to the price of z, than the ratio of the marginal cost of producing x to the marginal cost of producing z.

In other words, the monopolist's behaviour can be expressed by:

$$\frac{p_x}{p_z} > \frac{mc_x}{mc_z}$$

Substituting for

$$\frac{p_x}{p_z} \left(= \frac{\partial U}{\partial x} \Big| \frac{\partial U}{\partial z} = \frac{\alpha z}{\gamma x} \right) \quad \text{and} \quad \frac{mc_x}{mc_z} \left(= \frac{a}{c} \right)$$

this gives:

$$\frac{\alpha z}{\gamma x} > \frac{a}{c}$$

$$c\alpha z > a\gamma x \tag{6.6}$$

$$= ka\gamma x \text{ where } k > 1$$

The actual value of k (provided it is > 1) does not matter for the analysis. It is not necessary for the argument that k is constant as the monopolist faces the changes brought about by the policies of the nationalized industries, but it simplifies the algebra to assume this.

The behaviour of the monopolist, assumed unalterable, becomes an additional constraint on the system. The best that can be done in the economy is to maximize U subject to two constraints, the transformation function (6.1) and the monopoly behaviour condition (6.6). The conditions for attaining the second best optimum (the Paretian optimum being no longer attainable) are found, therefore, as the conditions for the maximum of the function $U - \mu(c\alpha z - ka\gamma x) - \lambda'(ax + by + cz - L)$, where there are now two Lagrangian multipliers μ, λ'. Neither of these multipliers can be identified with the multiplier λ in the equations (6.4).

The conditions for attaining the second best are, therefore:

$$\alpha \frac{U}{x} - \mu ka\gamma - \lambda'a = 0 \tag{6.7}$$

$$\beta \frac{U}{y} - \lambda'b = 0 \tag{6.8}$$

$$\gamma \frac{U}{z} + \mu c\alpha - \lambda'c = 0 \tag{6.9}$$

To appreciate these conditions, it is necessary to compute the ratio p_y/p_z, compare it with the ratio mc_y/mc_z, and relate the result to both the Paretian optimum conditions and the mode of behaviour of the monopolist.

Although there are three equations (6.7), (6.8), (6.9) above, these involve the two Lagrangian multipliers, so that there is actually only one degree of freedom. Hence, the policy of the nationalized industry (that which produces y) is sufficient for attaining the second best. If the nationalized industry sets its price, relative to its marginal cost, so as to satisfy the above conditions, it will have done all that is within its power to further the public interest.

To complete the solution it is necessary to determine μ and λ'.

From (6.7)

$$\mu ka\gamma x = \alpha U - \lambda'ax \tag{6.10}$$

and from (6.9)

$$-\mu c\alpha z = \gamma U - \lambda'cz \tag{6.11}$$

Hence,

$$\mu(ka\gamma x - c\alpha z) = (\alpha + \gamma)U - \lambda'(ax + cz)$$

but, from (6.6), $ka\gamma x - c\alpha z = 0$ so that,

$$(a + \gamma)U - \lambda'(ax + cz) = 0$$

$$\lambda' = \frac{(a + \gamma)U}{ax + cz} \tag{6.12}$$

Substituting for λ' in (6.10)

$$\begin{aligned}
\mu ka\gamma x &= \alpha U - \frac{(\alpha + \gamma)U}{ax + cz} \cdot ax \\
&= \frac{c\alpha z - \gamma ax}{ax + cz} U \\
&= (k - 1)\frac{\gamma ax}{ax + cz} U \quad [c\alpha z = k\gamma ax, \text{ from } (6.6)] \\
\mu &= \frac{k - 1}{k} \cdot \frac{U}{ax + cz} \tag{6.13}
\end{aligned}$$

The correct pricing policy for the nationalized industry is given from the ratio p_y/p_z which is implicit in the equations (6.7), (6.8), (6.9).

$$
\begin{aligned}
\frac{p_y}{p_z} &= \frac{\frac{\partial U}{\partial y}}{\frac{\partial U}{\partial z}} \\[2mm]
&= \frac{\beta \frac{U}{y}}{\gamma \frac{U}{z}} \\[2mm]
&= \frac{\lambda' b}{-\mu c \alpha + \lambda' c} \qquad \text{[From (6.8), (6.9)]} \\[2mm]
&= \frac{b}{c - \frac{\mu}{\lambda'} c \alpha} \qquad \text{[From (6.12), (6.13)]} \\[2mm]
&= \frac{\frac{b}{c}}{1 - \frac{k-1}{k} \cdot \frac{\alpha}{\alpha + \gamma}}
\end{aligned}
$$

(6.14)

Now $b/c = MC_y/MC_z$, from (6.2), so that:

$$
\frac{p_y}{p_z} = \frac{MC_y}{MC_z} \cdot \left(\frac{1}{1 - \frac{k-1}{k} \cdot \frac{\alpha}{\alpha + \gamma}} \right)
$$

(6.15)

Consider the expression

$$
\left(\frac{k-1}{k} \cdot \frac{\alpha}{\alpha + \gamma} \right)
$$

Since $k > 1, 0 < (k-1)/k < 1$, and $\alpha/(\alpha + \gamma) < 1$ since $\gamma > 0$. Thus the bracketed expression on the right hand side of (6.15) is greater than unity.

In other words, $p_y/p_z > MC_y/MC_z$, so that, relative to the numéraire, the nationalized industry should set its price higher than its marginal cost and, to that extent, behave like the monopoly.

But now consider the relationship between the nationalized industry and the monopoly.

$$
\begin{aligned}
\frac{p_y}{p_x} &= \frac{\beta \frac{U}{y}}{\alpha \frac{U}{x}} \\[2mm]
&= \frac{\frac{b}{a}}{\frac{\mu}{\lambda'} k \gamma + 1} \\[2mm]
&= \frac{\frac{b}{a}}{\frac{k-1}{\alpha + \gamma} \cdot \gamma + 1} \\[2mm]
&= \frac{b}{a} \cdot \frac{\alpha + \gamma}{\alpha + k \gamma}
\end{aligned}
$$

(6.16)

In this case, since $k > 1, \alpha, \gamma > 0, (\alpha + \gamma)/(\alpha + k\gamma) < 1$. Since $b/a = MC_y/MC_x$, the nationalized industry should set its price less high, in relation to marginal cost, than the monopoly.

In short, in the particular model analysed, the correct policy for the nationalized industry, with monopoly entrenched in one of the other industries, would be to take an intermediate path. On the one hand, it should set its price higher than marginal cost (relative to the numéraire) but, on the other hand, it should not set its price so far above marginal cost as is the case in the monopolized industry.

These conclusions refer, it should be emphasized, to the particular model which has been analysed above. This model has many simplifying (and therefore special) features, including the existence of only one input, constant marginal costs and a special type of utility function. As is demonstrated later, in Section 9, there can be no *a priori* expectations about the nature of a second best solution in circumstances where a generalized utility function is all that can be specified.

7. A General Theorem of the Second Best

Let there be some function $F(x_1 \cdots x_n)$ of the n variables $x_1 \cdots x_n$, which is to be maximized (minimized) subject to a constraint on the variables $\Phi(x_1 \cdots x_n) = 0$. This is a formalization of the typical choice situation in economic analysis.

Let the solution of this problem – the Paretian optimum – be the $n - 1$ condition $\Omega^i(x_1 \cdots x_n) = 0, i = 1 \cdots n - 1$. Then the following theorem, the theorem of the second best, can be given:

If there is an additional constraint imposed of the type $\Omega^i \neq 0$ for $i = j$, then the maximum (minimum) of F subject to both the constraint Φ and the constraint $\Omega^i \neq 0$ will, in general, be such that none of the still attainable Paretian conditions $\Omega^i = 0, i \neq j$, will be satisfied.

PROOF   In the absence of the second constraint, the solution of the original maximum (minimum) problem is both simple and familiar. Using the Lagrange method, the Paretian conditions are given by the n equations:

$$F_i - \lambda\Phi_i = 0 \quad i = 1 \cdots n \tag{7.1}$$

Eliminating the multiplier, these reduce to the $n - 1$ proportionality conditions:

$$\frac{F_i}{F_n} = \frac{\Phi_i}{\Phi_n} \quad i = 1 \cdots n - 1 \tag{7.2}$$

where the nth commodity is chosen as numéraire.

The equations (7.2) are the first order conditions for the attainment of the Paretian optimum. Now let there be a constraint imposed which prevents the attainment of one of the conditions (7.2). Such a constraint will be of the form (the numbering of the commodities is, of course, arbitrary):

$$\frac{F_1}{F_n} = k\frac{\Phi_1}{\Phi_n} \quad k \neq 1 \tag{7.3}$$

It is not necessary that k be constant, but it is assumed to be so in the present analysis. There is now an additional constraint in the system so that, using the Lagrangian method, the function to be maximized (minimized) will be:

$$F - \lambda'\Phi - \mu\left(\frac{F_1}{F_n} - k\frac{\Phi_1}{\Phi_n}\right) \qquad (7.4)$$

The multipliers λ', μ will both be different, in general, from the multiplier λ in (7.1).

The conditions that the expression (7.4) shall be at a maximum (minimum) are as follows:

$$F_i - \lambda'\Phi_i - \mu\left\{\frac{F_nF_{1i} - F_1F_{ni}}{F_n^2} - k\frac{\Phi_n\Phi_{1i} - \Phi_1\Phi_{ni}}{\Phi_n^2}\right\} = 0 \qquad i = 1\cdots n \qquad (7.5)$$

If the expression $F_nF_{1i} - F_1F_{ni}/F_n^2$ is denoted by Q_i and the equivalent expression for the Φ's by R_i, then the conditions (7.5) can be re-written in the following form:

$$\frac{F_i}{F_n} = \frac{\Phi_i}{\Phi_n}\frac{\left[1 + \frac{\mu}{\lambda'}(Q_i - kR_i)\right]}{\left[1 + \frac{\mu}{\lambda'}(Q_n - kR_n)\right]} \qquad (7.6)$$

These are the conditions for the attainment of the second best position, given the constraint (7.3), expressed in a form comparable with the Paretian conditions as set out in (7.2).

Clearly, any one of the conditions for the second best will be the same as the equivalent Paretian condition only if the expression:

$$\frac{1 + \frac{\mu}{\lambda'}(Q_i - kR_i)}{1 + \frac{\mu}{\lambda'}(Q_n - kR_n)}$$

is unity. Now this will only be the case if:

(i) $\mu = 0$,
(ii) $\mu \neq 0$, but $Q_i - kR_i = Q_n - kR_n$.

The first of these cannot be true for, if it were, then, when $i = 1$, F_1/F_n would be equal to Φ_1/Φ_n, in contradiction with the constraint condition (7.3).

It is clear from the nature of the expressions Q_i, Q_n, R_i, R_n that nothing is known, in general, about their signs, let alone their magnitudes, and even the signs would not be sufficient to determine whether (ii) was satisfied or not.

Consider $Q_n = (F_nF_{1n} - F_1F_{nn})/F_n^2$. If F were a utility function then it would be known that F_1, F_n were positive and F_{nn} negative, but the sign of F_{1n} may be either positive or negative.[25] Even if the sign of F_{1n} were known to be negative, the sign of Q_n would still be indeterminate, since it would depend on whether the negative or the positive term in the expression was numerically the greater. In the case of Q_i, where $i \neq n$, the indeterminacy is even greater, since there are two expressions F_{i1} and F_{ni} for which the signs may be either positive or negative.

The same considerations as apply for the Q's also apply for the R's of course. In general, therefore, the conditions for the second best optimum, given the constraint (7.3), will all differ from the corresponding conditions for the attainment of the Paretian optimum. Conversely, given the constraint (7.3), the application of these rules of behaviour of the Paretian type which are still attainable will not lead, in general, to the best position in the circumstances.

The general conditions for the achievement of the second best optimum in the type of case with which this analysis is concerned will be of the type $F_i/F_n = k_i\Phi_i/\Phi_n$, where $k_i \neq k_j \neq 1$, so that $F_i/F_j = \Phi_i/\Phi_j$, $F_i/F_j \neq F_k/F_j$, $\Phi_i/\Phi_j \neq \Phi_k/\Phi_j$, and the usual Paretian rules will be broken all round.

8 The Existence of a Second Best Solution

The essential condition that a true second best solution to a given constrained situation should exist is that, if there is a Paretian optimum in which F has a maximum (minimum) when the constraint is removed, then the expression (7.4) must also have a true maximum (minimum). There is no reason why this should, in general, be the case.

For one thing, whereas well-behaved functions F and Φ will always have a solution which satisfies the comparatively simple first order conditions for a Paretian optimum, it is by no means certain that the much more complex first order conditions (7.5) for a second best solution will be satisfied, since these conditions involve second order derivatives whose behaviour (subject only to convexity-concavity conditions of the functions) is unknown.

If the first order conditions for the existence of second best solutions present difficulties, the difficulties are quite insurmountable in the case of the second order conditions. Let it be supposed, for concreteness, that the nature of the case is such that F is to be maximized. Then the existence of a second best solution requires that the first order conditions (7.5) shall give a maximum, not a minimum or a turning point. This requires that the second differential of the expression (7.4) shall be negative. But the second differential of (7.4) involves the *third* order derivatives of F and Φ. Absolutely nothing is known about these in the general case, and their properties cannot be derived from the second order condition that the Paretian optimum represents a true maximum for F.

9 The Nature of Second Best Solutions

The extraordinary difficulty of making *a priori* judgements about the types of policy likely to be required in situations where the Paretian optimum is unattainable, and the second best must be aimed at, is well illustrated by examining the conditions (7.6) in the light of possible knowledge about the signs of some of the expressions involved.

In order to simplify the problem, and to render it less abstract, the function F will be supposed to be a utility function and Φ, which will be supposed to be a transformation function, will be assumed to be linear. The second derivatives of Φ disappear, so that $R_i = 0$ for all i, and attention can be concentrated on the expressions Q.

With the problem in this form, the derivatives F_i are proportional to the prices p_i, and the derivatives Φ_i are proportional to the marginal costs MC_i. As an additional simplification which assists verbal discussion but which does not affect the essentials of the model, it will be supposed that price equals marginal cost for the nth commodity, which will be referred to as the numéraire.

From (7.6), with these additional assumptions, therefore:

$$\frac{\frac{F_i}{F_n}}{\frac{\Phi_i}{\Phi_n}} = \frac{\frac{p_i}{p_n}}{\frac{MC_i}{MC_n}} = \frac{p_i}{MC_i} = \frac{1 + \frac{\mu}{\lambda'}Q_i}{1 + \frac{\mu}{\lambda'}Q_n} = \frac{1 + \theta Q_i}{1 + \theta Q_n} \qquad \left(\theta = \frac{\mu}{\lambda'}\right) \tag{9.1}$$

Thus, for the ith commodity, price is above / equal to / below marginal cost, when the second best optimum is attained, according as:

$$P = \frac{1 + \theta Q_i}{1 + \theta Q_n} \gtreqless 1$$

The problem is reduced to that of discovering what can be said, *a priori*, about the magnitude of this expression.

Now $Q_i = (F_n F_{1i} - F_1 F_{ni})/F_n^2$. At most, it may be possible to deduce the *sign* of Q_i but the order of its magnitude will remain unknown unless a specific utility function is given.

With knowledge of signs, and no more, the most that can be said can be summarized very simply:

$$\begin{align}
(i) \quad &\text{If } \theta > 0, \ P > 1 \text{ if } Q_i > 0, Q_n < 0. \notag \\
&\qquad\qquad P < 1 \text{ if } Q_i < 0, \ Q_n > 0. \notag \\
(ii) \quad &\text{If } \theta < 0, \ P > 1 \text{ if } Q_i < 0, \ Q_n > 0. \notag \\
&\qquad\qquad P < 1 \text{ if } Q_i > 0, \ Q_n < 0. \notag
\end{align} \tag{9.2}$$

Nothing can be said about P if Q_i, Q_n are of the same signs.

Now consider Q_i. The denominator is always positive, and F_1, F_n are both positive, so that the determining factors are the signs of the mixed partial derivatives F_{1i} and F_{ni}. It is assumed that goods are known to be substitutes $(F_{ij} < 0)$ or complements $(F_{ij} > 0)$ in the Edgeworth–Pareto sense. There are four possible cases:

(a) If $F_{1i} > 0, F_{ni} > 0$, then $Q_i \gtreqless 0$.
(b) If $F_{1i} < 0, F_{ni} < 0$, then $Q_i \gtreqless 0$.
(c) If $F_{1i} > 0, F_{ni} < 0$, then $Q_i > 0$.
(d) If $F_{1i} < 0, F_{ni} > 0$, then $Q_i < 0$.

In cases (c) and (d), but not in cases (a) and (b), therefore, the sign of Q_i is determinate.

To complete the picture the sign of θ is also needed. Where the sign of this can be found at all, it is found by putting $i = 1$ and substituting in the constraint condition (7.3). For concreteness, let k be > 1 (the first good will be referred to as the monopolized good).

Then, since

$$\frac{1 + \theta Q_1}{1 + \theta Q_n} = k > 1$$

it can be deduced that, if $Q_1 < 0$, $Q_n > 0$, then $\theta < 0$, and if $Q_1 > 0$, $Q_n < 0$, then $\theta < 0$. In all other cases the sign of θ is indeterminate.

For Q_1, Q_n, it is known that F_{11}, $F_{nn} < 0$, and $F_{n1} = F_{1n}$ so that there are only two cases, $F_{n1} > 0$ and $F_{n1} < 0$. The information conveyed in each of the two cases is as follows:

I $F_{n1} > 0$: $Q_1 < 0, Q_n > 0$, so that $\theta < 0$.

II $F_{n1} < 0$: $Q_1 \gtreqless 0$, $Q_n \gtreqless 0$, so that $\theta \gtreqless 0$.

The combination of cases I and II with the independently determined cases (a), (b), (c), (d) gives a total of eight cases. Table 1 shows the information which can be derived about the signs of Q_i, Q_n and θ, and the consequent information about P using the conditions (9.2).

Of the eight cases tabulated, the signs of Q_i, Q_n and θ are simultaneously determinate in only two, I(c) and I(d), and in only one of these two, I(d), does this lead to a determinate relationship between price and marginal cost. This sole case leads to the only *a priori* statement that can be made about the nature of second best solutions on the basis of the signs of the mixed second order partial derivatives of the utility function:

Table 1

Case		Sign of			Relationship of price to marginal cost for x_i
		Q_i	Q_n	θ	
I $F_{n1} > 0$	(a) $F_{ij}, F_{ni} > 0$	?	+	−	?
	(b) $F_{ij}, F_{ni} < 0$	?	+	−	?
	(c) $F_{1i} > 0, F_{ni} < 0$	+	+	−	?
	(d) $F_{1i} < 0, F_{ni} > 0$	−	+	−	Price exceeds marginal cost
II $F_{ni} < 0$	(a) $F_{1i}, F_{ni} > 0$	?	?	?	?
	(b) $F_{1i}, F_{ni} < 0$	?	?	?	?
	(c) $F_{1i} > 0, F_{ni} < 0$	+	?	?	?
	(d) $F_{1i} < 0, F_{nt} > 0$	−	?	?	?

Table 2

Relationship between monopolized good and numéraire	Relationship of ith good to:		Signs of			Price of ith good relative to marginal cost
	monopolized good	Numéraire	Q_i	Q_n	θ	
Complements, or weak	Complements	Complements	?	+	−	?
	Substitutes	Substitutes	?	+	−	?
	Complements	Substitutes	+	+	−	?
	Substitutes	Complements	−	+	−	Higher
	Complements	Weak	+	+	−	?
	Substitutes	Weak	−	+	−	Higher
	Weak	Complements	−	+	−	Higher
	Weak	Substitutes	+	+	−	?
Substitutes	Any	Any	$\left.\begin{matrix} + \\ - \\ ? \end{matrix}\right\}$	?	?	?

If the monopolized commodity is complementary (in the Edgeworth–Pareto sense) to the numéraire, and the ith commodity is also complementary to the numéraire, but a substitute for the monopolized good, then, in order to attain a second best solution, the price of the ith commodity must be set higher than its marginal cost.

Since knowledge of the sign alone of the derivatives F_{ij} reveals only one determinate case, it would seem worthwhile to examine the situation if more heroic assumptions can be made about the knowledge of the utility function. The additional information which is assumed is that two commodities may be known to be "weakly related", that is, that the derivative F_{ij} is either zero or of the second order relative to other quantities.

In the expression $Q_i = (F_n F_{1i} - F_1 F_{ni})/F_n^2$, for example, if the ith commodity and the numéraire are weakly related in this sense, then the term $F_1 F_{ni}$ can be neglected relative to the term $F_n F_{1i}$ and the sign of Q_i is wholly determined by the sign of F_{1i}.

If the monopolized good and the numéraire are weakly related, then $Q_1 < 0$ and $Q_n > 0$. This is similar to the case I, in which the two goods were complements, leading to the same conclusions. There are now, however, four additional cases to add to $(a), (b), (c), (d)$, for various combinations of weak relatedness with substitution and complementarity as between the ith commodity and the monopolized good and the numéraire. All the cases which can be given in terms of the three relationships (weakly related, complements, substitutes) are tabulated in Table 2. There are now three determinate cases, which can be summarized as follows:

If the monopolized good and the numéraire are either complements or only weakly related, then the second best solution will certainly require the price of the ith good to be set above its marginal cost either if the good is a substitute for the monopolized good and either complementary or only weakly related to the numéraire, or if the good is weakly related to the monopolized good but complementary to the numéraire.

With any other combinations of relatedness among the goods, it cannot be determined, *a priori*, whether the second best solution will require the price of any particular good to be above or below its marginal cost. In particular, if there is no complementarity between any pairs of goods, and the relationship between the monopolized commodity and the numéraire is not weak, then there are no determinate cases.

As a matter of interest it is possible to work out conditions that may be likely to bring about any particular result. For example, a possible case in which the price of a good might be set below its marginal cost would be that in which the monopolized good, the numéraire, and the other good were all substitutes, but the rate at which marginal utility diminished was small in the case of the monopolized good (so that Q_1, Q_n would both be positive, with Q_1 large compared with Q_n, giving a positive value for θ), and the relationship of the good under discussion was much stronger with the monopolized good than with the numéraire (so that Q_i might be negative). There can be few real cases, however, where such guesses about the magnitudes of the quantities involved could be made.

10. The Problem of Multiple-layer Optima

In all the preceding analysis, the problems have been conceived in terms of a single-layer optimum. It has been assumed that the constraint which defined the Paretian optimum (the transformation function, for example) was a technically fixed datum, and was not, itself, the result of an optimization process at a lower level.

The characteristic of general economic systems is, however, that they usually involve several successive processes of optimisation, of increasing generality. The transformation function, for example, may have been derived as the result of competitive firms maximizing their profits. Firms are assumed to have minimized their costs before proceding to maximize their profits, and these costs are themselves derived from processes involving optimisation by the owners of the various factors of production.

It is of the nature of the economic process, therefore, that optimization takes place at successive levels, and that the maximization of a welfare function subject to a transformation function is only the topmost of these. It is also of the nature of Paretian optima (due to the simple proportionality of the conditions) that the optimization at the different levels can be considered as independent problems.

In the case of a second best solution, however, the neat proportionality of the Paretian conditions disappears: this immediately poses the question whether a second best solution in the circumstances of a multiple-layer economic system will require a breaking of the Paretian conditions at lower levels of the system, as well as at the level at which the problem was initiated.

The present paper does not propose to examine the problem, for it is a subject that would seem to merit full-scale treatment of its own. There seems reason to suppose, however, that there may well be cases in which a breaking of the Paretian rules at lower levels of the process (moving off the transformation function, for example) may enable a higher level of welfare to be obtained than if the scope of policy is confined to one level only.

A two-dimensional geometric illustration that is suggestive, although not conclusive, is set out in Figure 1. Ox, Oy represent the quantities of two goods x, y. The line AB represents a transformation function (to be considered as a boundary condition) and CD a constraint condition. In the absence of the constraint CD the optimum position will be some point, such as P, lying on the transformation line at the point of its tangency with one of the contours of the welfare function.

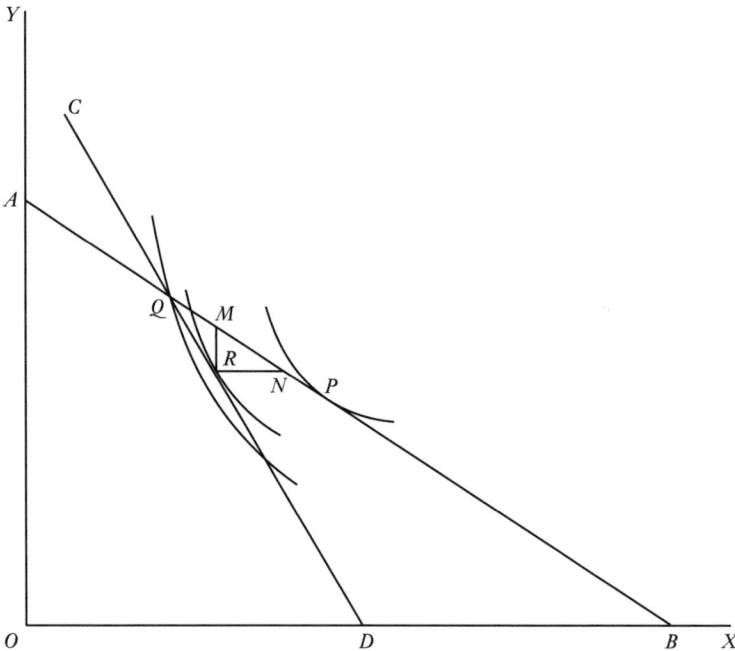

Figure 1

If the constraint condition must be satisfied, only point along *CD* can be chosen, and the optimum point *P* is no longer attainable. A point on the transformation line (*Q*) is still attainable. Will the second best solution be at the point *Q*, or should the economy move off the transformation line? If the welfare contours and the constraint line are as shown in the diagram, then the second best point will be at the point *R*, inside the transformation line.

It is obvious, of course, that the second best will never be at a point which is technically inefficient (has less of one commodity and no more of the other) relative to any *attainable* point. Although there are points (the segment *MN*) on the transformation line which are technically more efficient than *R*, these are not attainable. *R* is *not* technically inefficient relative to *Q*, even though *R* lies inside the transformation line.

If the line *CD* had a positive slope (as have the types of constraint which have been exemplified in the preceding analyses), the second best would always lie at its point of intersection with the transformation line, since all other points on *CD* would be technically inefficient relative to it.

Notes

1   The appelation, "Theory of Second Best," is derived from the writings of Professor Meade (1955b). Meade has given, in *Trade and Welfare*, what seems to be the only attempt to date to deal systematically with a number of problems in the theory of second best. His treatment,

however, is concerned with the detailed case study of several problems, rather than with the development of a general theory of second best.

2   See section 7 for formal proofs of the statements made in this section.

3   See section 5.

4   The general theory of second best is, thus, concerned with all maximization problems not just with welfare theory. See Section 3 for examples of non-welfare applications.

5   There may be more than one second best optimum for any given set of constraints. See Section 8.

6   i.e., one who believes that trade carried on in the absence of any restraints necessarily leads to an optimum situation. Of course, as soon as there exist restrictions preventing the satisfaction of at least one of the Paretian optimum conditions in the domestic market of any of the trading countries, there is no longer a case for perfectly free trade "... the general case for free trade rests on the contention that in a world of *utopian* domestic policies (i.e., where domestic economic policies ensure the satisfaction of all the Paretian optimum conditions) it sets internationally the proper *marginal* conditions for economic *efficiency*". Meade (1955b, p. 139).

7   His neglect of the demand side of the problem allowed him to reach the erroneous conclusion that trade diversion necessarily led to a decrease in welfare. It is quite possible for an increase in welfare to follow from the formation of a customs union whose sole effect is to divert trade from lower- to higher-cost sources of supply. Furthermore, this welfare gain may be enjoyed by the country whose import trade is diverted to the higher-cost source, by the customs union area considered as a unit and by the world as a whole.

8   In this analysis an income tax may be treated as a uniform *ad valorem* rate of tax on all commodities except leisure.

9   Too high and too low in the sense that a decrease in the consumption of leisure combined with an increase in the consumption of all other goods would raise the welfare of any consumer.

10 Of course two special cases are always possible. In the first the optimum rates of tax will be equal for all commodities (i.e., the income tax is the optimum tax). This will occur if the supply of effort (the demand for leisure) is perfectly inelastic. In the second case the optimum rates will be zero for all but one commodity (i.e., an indirect tax on one commodity is the optimum tax). This will occur if the demand for one commodity is perfectly inelastic.

11 For example, if the supply of effort is not perfectly inelastic an equal degree of monopoly throughout the entire economy has the same effect as an income tax on wage earners. Following Little's analysis it is obvious that this tax will prevent the attainment of a Paretian optimum.

12 For a description of this type of welfare economics see Little (1950, p. 89).

13 Indeed any economics that attempts piecemeal policy recommendations must be based on the belief that there can be discovered sufficient conditions for an increase in, as distinct from necessary conditions for a maximum of, whatever it is that is being considered.

14 This conclusion follows directly from the negative corollary stated in the second paragraph of Section 1.

15 If consumers have different utility functions then each consumer must receive from the government an amount equal to what he pays in taxes. However, if all consumers have identical homogeneous utility functions then all that is required is that the tax revenue be returned to some consumer or consumers.

16 Therefore, there can be no question of a reduction of A's tariffs causing trade creation.

17 Therefore, there can be no question of a preferential reduction of A's tariffs causing trade diversion.

18 Obviously, this is a problem in the theory of second best. The initial tariff on Y causes the consumption of Y to be too low relative to both X and Z. If the consumption of Y can be encouraged at the expense of X, welfare will be increased. However, if the consumption of Z is encouraged at the expense of X, welfare will be lowered. A tariff on X is likely to cause both sorts of consumption

shift and the optimum X tariff will be that one where, at the margin, the harmful effect of the shift from X to Z just balances the beneficial effect of the shift from X to Y.

19   We are greatly indebted to Dr. George Morton for suggesting the following mathematical demonstration. It now replaces a much more cumbersome demonstration.

20   i.e. The value of imports $(Xp_x + Yp_y)$ plus the value of domestic production *consumed at home* (Z) equals the total value of domestic production (C).

21   These relationships are not as simple as they might appear. If worked out $\partial y/\partial t_x$ and $\partial z/\partial t_x$ would be found to be of the same order of complexity as are the Q_i's in Section 9.

22   Only the most obvious applications of the conclusions reached in Section 5.1 are given in this section. This is not the place for a detailed report on original work in the theory of customs unions.

23   This conclusion is also reached by Professor Meade (1955a, p. 51).

24   Another conclusion suggested by the analysis is that the higher are the tariffs reduced by the union relative to all other tariffs, the more likely is it that the union will raise welfare, cf. Meade (1955a, pp. 108–9).

25   The Hicksian definitions of complementarity and substitution give no information about the signs of the individual F_{ij}'s, where F is a utility function. The Edgeworth–Pareto definitions do, and Section 9 considers the extent to which the knowledge of these signs enables *a priori* statements to be made about the nature of second best solutions.

References

Corlett, W. J. and Hague, D. C. (1953–54): "Complementarity and the Excess Burden of Taxation," *Review of Economic Studies*, 21 (54), 21–30.

Little, I. M. D. (1950): *A Critique of Welfare Economics*. Oxford: The Clarendon Press.

——(1951): "Direct *Versus* Indirect Taxes," *The Economic Journal*, 61 (243), September, 577–84

McKenzie, L. W. (1951): "Ideal Output and the Interdependence of Firms," *The Economic Journal*, 61 (244), 785–803.

Meade, J. E. (1955a): *The Theory of Customs Unions*. Amsterdam: The North-Holland Publishing Co.

——(1955b): *Trade and Welfare*. London: Oxford University Press.

——(1955c): *Trade and Welfare, Mathematical Supplement*. London: Oxford University Press.

Ozga, S. A. (1955): "An Essay in the Theory of Tariffs," *Journal of Political Economy*, 63 (6), December, 489–99.

Smithies, A. (1936): "The Boundaries of the Production and Utility Function," in *Exploration in Economics*, London: McGraw-Hill.

Viner, J. (1950): *The Customs Union Issue*. New York: Carnegie Endowment for International Peace.

CHAPTER FOUR

An Economic Theory of Clubs

JAMES M. BUCHANAN

Source: *Economica*, 32 (1965), pp. 1–14. Reprinted with the permission of The London School of Economics & Political Science. © The London School of Economics & Political Science.

The implied institutional setting for neo-classical economic theory, including theoretical welfare economics, is a régime of private property, in which all goods and services are privately (individually) utilized or consumed. Only within the last two decades have serious attempts been made to extend the formal theoretical structure to include communal or collective ownership–consumption arrangements.[1] The "pure theory of public goods" remains in its infancy, and the few models that have been most rigorously developed apply only to polar or extreme cases. For example, in the fundamental papers by Paul A. Samuelson (1954, 1955), a sharp conceptual distinction is made between those goods and services that are "purely private" and those that are "purely public". No general theory has been developed which covers the whole spectrum of ownership–consumption possibilities, ranging from the purely private or individualized activity on the one hand to purely public or collectivized activity on the other. One of the missing links here is "a theory of clubs", a theory of co-operative membership, a theory that will include as a variable to be determined the extension of ownership–consumption rights over differing numbers of persons.

Everyday experience reveals that there exists some most preferred or "optimal" membership for almost any activity in which we engage, and that this membership varies in some relation to economic factors. European hotels have more communally shared bathrooms than their American counterparts. Middle and low income communities organize swimming-bathing facilities; high income communities are observed to enjoy privately owned swimming pools.

In this paper I shall develop a general theory of clubs, or consumption ownership–membership arrangements. This construction allows us to move one step forward in closing the awesome Samuelson gap between the purely private and the purely public good. For the former, the optimal sharing arrangement, the preferred club membership, is clearly one person (or one family unit), whereas the optimal sharing group for the purely public good, as defined in the polar sense, includes an infinitely large number of members. That is to say, for any genuinely collective good defined in the Samuelson way, a club that has an infinitely large membership is preferred to all arrangements of finite size. While it is evident that some goods and services may be reasonably classified as purely private, even in the extreme sense, it is clear that few, if any, goods satisfy the conditions of extreme collectiveness. The interesting cases are those goods and services, the consumption of which involves some "publicness", where the optimal sharing group is more than one person or family but smaller than an infinitely large number. The range of "publicness" is finite. The central question in a theory of clubs is that of determining the membership margin, so to speak, the size of the most desirable cost and consumption sharing arrangement.[2]

1.

In traditional neo-classical models that assume the existence of purely private goods and services only, the utility function of an individual is written,

$$U^i = U^i\left(X_1^i, X_2^i, \ldots, X_n^i\right) \tag{1}$$

where each of the X's represents the amount of a purely private good available during a specified time period, to the reference individual designated by the superscript.

Samuelson extended this function to include purely collective or public goods, which he denoted by the subscripts, $n + 1, \ldots, n + m$, so that (1) is changed to read,

$$U_i = U^i\left(X_1^i, X_2^i, \ldots, X_n^i; X_{n+1}^i, X_{n+2}^i, \ldots X_{n+m}^i\right) \tag{2}$$

This approach requires that all goods be initially classified into the two sets, private and public. Private goods, defined to be wholly divisible among the persons, $i = 1, 2, \ldots, s$, satisfy the relation

$$X_j = \sum_{i=1}^{s} X_j^i$$

while public goods, defined to be wholly indivisible as among persons, satisfy the relation,

$$X_{n+j} = X_{n+j}^i$$

I propose to drop any attempt at an initial classification or differentiation of goods into fully divisible and fully indivisible sets, and to incorporate in the utility function goods falling between these two extremes. What the theory of clubs provides is, in one sense, a "theory of classification", but this emerges as an output of the analysis. The first step is that of modifying the utility function.

Note that, in neither (1) nor (2) is it necessary to make a distinction between "goods available to the ownership unit of which the reference individual is a member" and "goods finally available to the individual for consumption". With purely private goods, consumption by one individual automatically reduces potential consumption of other individuals by an equal amount. With purely public goods, consumption by any one individual implies equal consumption by all others. For goods falling between such extremes, such a distinction must be made. This is because for such goods there is no unique translation possible between the "goods available to the membership unit" and "goods finally consumed". In the construction which follows, therefore, the "goods" entering the individual's utility function, the X_js, should be interpreted as "goods available for consumption to the whole membership unit of which the reference individual is a member".

Arguments that represent the size of the sharing group must be included in the utility function along with arguments representing goods and services. For any good or service, regardless of its ultimate place along the conceptual public–private spectrum, the utility that an individual receives from its consumption depends upon *the number of other persons with whom he must share its benefits*. This is obvious, but its acceptance does require breaking out of the private property straitjacket within which most of economic theory has developed. As an extreme example, take a good normally considered to be purely private, say, a pair of shoes. Clearly your own utility from a single pair of shoes, per unit of time, depends on the number of other persons who share them with you. Simultaneous physical sharing may not, of course, be possible; only one person can wear the shoes at each particular moment. However, for any finite period of time, sharing is possible, even for such evidently private goods. For pure services that are consumed in the moment of acquisition the extension is somewhat more difficult, but it can be made none the less. Sharing here simply means that the individual receives a smaller quantity of the service. Sharing a "haircut per month" with a second person is the same as consuming "one-half haircut per month". Given any quantity of final good, as defined in terms of the physical units of some standard quality, the utility that the individual receives from this quantity will be related functionally to the number of others with whom he shares.[3]

Variables for club size are not normally included in the utility function of an individual since, in the private-goods world, the optimal club size is unity. However, for our purposes, these variables must be explicitly included, and, for completeness, a club-size variable should be included for each and every good. Alongside each X_j there must be placed an N_j, which we define as the number of persons who are to participate as "members" in the sharing of good, X_j, including the ith person whose utility function is examined. That is to say, the club-size variable, N_j, measures the number of persons who are to join in the consumption-utilization arrangements for good, X_j, over the relevant time period. The sharing arrangements may or may not call for equal consumption on the part of each member, and the peculiar manner of sharing will clearly affect the way in which the variable enters the utility function. For simplicity we may assume equal sharing, although this is not necessary for the analysis. The rewritten utility function now becomes,

$$U^i = U^i \left[\left(X_1^i, N_1^i \right), \left(X_2^i, N_2^i \right), \ldots, \left(X_{n+m}^i, N_{n+m}^i \right) \right]^4 \tag{3}$$

We may designate a numeraire good, X_r, which can simply be thought of as money, possessing value only as a medium of exchange. By employing the convention whereby the lower case u's represent the partial derivatives, we get u_j^i / u_r^i, defined as the marginal rate of substitution in consumption between X_j and X_r for the ith individual. Since, in our construction, the size of the group is also a variable, we must also examine, u^i_{Nj}/u^i_r, defined as the marginal rate of substitution "in consumption" between the size of the sharing group and the numeraire. That is to say, this ratio represents the rate (which may be negative) at which the individual is willing to give up (accept) money in exchange for additional members in the sharing group.

We now define a cost or production function as this confronts the individual, and this will include the same set of variables,

$$F = F^i\left[\left(X^i_1, N^i_1\right), \left(X^i_2, N^i_2\right), \ldots, \left(X^i_{n+m}, N^i_{n+m}\right)\right] \tag{4}$$

Why do the club-size variables, the N_j's, appear in this cost function? The addition of members to a sharing group may, and normally will, affect the cost of the good to any one member. The larger is the membership of the golf club the lower the dues to any single member, given a specific quantity of club facilities available per unit time.

It now becomes possible to derive, from the utility and cost functions, statements for the necessary marginal conditions for Pareto optimality in respect to consumption of each good. In the usual manner we get,

$$\frac{u^i_j}{u^i_r} = \frac{f^i_j}{f^i_r} \tag{5}$$

Condition (5) states that, for the ith individual, the marginal rate of substitution between goods X_j and X_r, in consumption, must be equal to the marginal rate of substitution between these same two goods in "production" or exchange. To this acknowledged necessary condition, we now add,

$$\frac{u^i_{Nj}}{u^i_r} = \frac{f^i_{Nj}}{f^i_r} \tag{6}$$

Condition (6) is not normally stated, since the variables relating to club size are not normally included in utility functions. Implicitly, the size for sharing arrangements is assumed to be determined exogenously to individual choices. Club size is presumed to be a part of the environment. Condition (6) states that the marginal rate of substitution "in consumption" between the size of the group sharing in the use of good X_j, and the numeraire good, X_r, must be equal to the marginal rate of substitution "in production". In other words, the individual attains full equilibrium in club size only when the marginal benefits that he secures from having an additional member (which may, and probably will normally be, negative) are just equal to the marginal costs that he incurs from adding a member (which will also normally be negative).

Combining (5) and (6) we get,

$$\frac{u^i_j}{f^i_j} = \frac{u^i_r}{f^i_r} = \frac{u^i_{Nj}}{f^i_{Nj}} \tag{7}$$

Only when (7) is satisfied will the necessary marginal conditions with respect to the consumption-utilization of X_j be met. The individual will have available to his membership unit an optimal quantity of X_j, measured in physical units and, also, he will be sharing this quantity "optimally" over a group of determined size.

The necessary condition for club size may not, of course, be met. Since for many goods there is a major change in utility between the one-person and the two-person club, and since discrete changes in membership may be all that is possible, we may get,

$$\frac{u^i_j}{f^i_j} = \frac{u^i_r}{f^i_r} > \frac{u^i_{Nj}}{f^i_{Nj}}\bigg|_{Nj=1} \qquad \frac{u^i_j}{f^i_j} = \frac{u^i_r}{f^r} < \frac{u^i_{Nj}}{f^i_{Nj}}\bigg|_{Nj=2} \qquad (7a)$$

which incorporates the recognition that, with a club size of unity, the right-hand term may be relatively too small, whereas, with a club size of two, it may be too large. If partial sharing arrangements can be worked out, this qualification need not, of course, be made.

If, on the other hand, the size of a co-operative or collective sharing group is exogenously determined, we may get,

$$\frac{u^i_j}{f^i_j} = \frac{u^i_r}{f^i_r} > \frac{u^i_{Nj}}{f^i_{Nj}}\bigg|_{Nj=k} \qquad (7b)$$

Note that (7b) actually characterizes the situation of an individual with respect to the consumption of any purely public good of the type defined in the Samuelson polar model. Any group of finite size, k, is smaller than optimal here, and the full set of necessary marginal conditions cannot possibly be met. Since additional persons can, by definition, be added to the group without in any way reducing the availability of the good to other members, and since additional members could they be found, would presumably place some positive value on the good and hence be willing to share in its costs, the group always remains below optimal size. The all-inclusive club remains too small.

Consider, now, the relation between the set of necessary marginal conditions defined in (7) and those presented by Samuelson in application to goods that were exogenously defined to be purely public. In the latter case, these conditions are,

$$\sum_{i=1}^{s}\left(\frac{u^i_{n+j}}{u^i_r}\right) = \frac{f_{n+j}}{f_r} \qquad (8)$$

where the marginal rates of substitution in consumption between the purely public good, X_{n+j}, and the numeraire good, X_r, summed over all individuals in the group of determined size, s, equals the marginal cost of X_{n+j} also defined in terms of units of X_r. Note that when (7) is satisfied, (8) is necessarily satisfied, provided only that the collectivity is making neither profit nor loss on providing the marginal unit of the public good. That is to say, provided that,

$$\frac{f_{n+j}}{f_r} = \sum_{i=1}^{s}\left(\frac{f^i_{n+j}}{f^i_r}\right) \qquad (9)$$

The reverse does not necessarily hold, however, since the satisfaction of (8) does not require that each and every individual in the group be in a position where his own marginal benefits are equal to his marginal costs (taxes).[5] And, of course, (8) says nothing at all about group size.

The necessary marginal conditions in (7) allow us to classify all goods only after the solution is attained. Whether or not a particular good is purely private, purely public, or somewhere between these extremes is determined only after the equilibrium values for the N_j's are known. A good for which the equilibrium value for N_j is large can be classified as containing much "publicness". By contrast, a good for which the equilibrium value of N_j is small can be classified as largely private.

2.

The formal statement of the theory of clubs presented in Section 1 can be supplemented and clarified by geometrical analysis, although the nature of the construction implies somewhat more restrictive models.

Consider a good that is known to contain, under some conditions, a degree of "public-ness". For simplicity, think of a swimming pool. We want to examine the choice calculus of a single person, and we shall assume that other persons about him, with whom he may or may not choose to join in some club-like arrangement, are identical in all respects with him. As a first step, take a facility of one-unit size, which we define in terms of physical output supplied.

On the ordinate of Fig. 1, we measure total cost and total benefit per person, the latter derived from the individual's own evaluation of the facility in terms of the numeraire, dollars. On the abscissa, we measure the number of persons in possible sharing arrangements. Define the full cost of the one-unit facility to be Y_1, and the reference individual's evaluation of this facility as a purely private consumption good to be E_1. As is clear from the construction as drawn, he will not choose to purchase the good. If the single person is required to meet the full cost, he will not be able to enjoy the benefits of the good. Any enjoyment of the facility requires the organization of some co-operative-collective sharing arrangement.[6]

Two functions may now be traced in Fig. 1, remaining within the one-unit restriction on the size of the facility. A total benefit function and a total cost function confronting the single individual may be derived. As more persons are allowed to share in the enjoyment of the facility, of given size, the benefit evaluation that the individual places on the good will, after some point, decline. There may, of course, be both an increasing and a constant range of the total benefit function, but at some point congestion will set in, and his evaluation of the good will fall. There seems little doubt that the total benefit curve, shown as B_1, will exhibit the concavity property as drawn for goods that involve some commonality in consumption.[7]

The bringing of additional members into the club also serves to reduce the cost that the single person will face. Since, by our initial simplifying assumption, all persons here are identical, symmetrical cost sharing is suggested. In any case, the total cost per person will fall as additional persons join the group, under any cost-sharing scheme. As drawn in Fig. 1, symmetrical sharing is assumed and the curve, C_1, traces the total cost function, given the one-unit restriction on the size of the facility.[8]

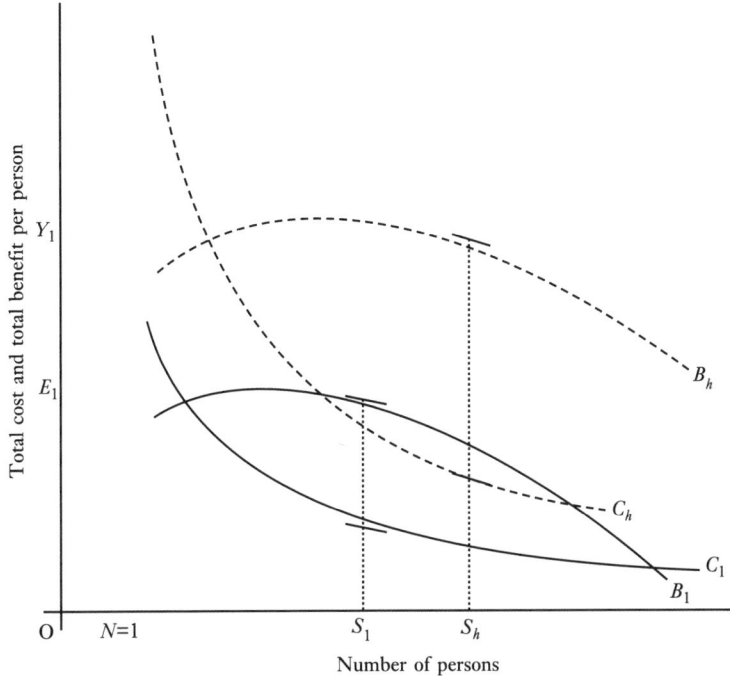

Figure 1

For the given size of the facility, there will exist some optimal size of club. This is determined at the point where the derivatives of the total cost and total benefit functions are equal, shown as S_1 in Fig. 1, for the one–unit facility. Consider now an increase in the size of the facility. As before, a total cost curve and a total benefit curve may be derived, and an optimal club size determined. One other such optimum is shown at S_h, for a quantity of goods upon which the curves C_h and B_h are based. Similar constructions can be carried out for every possible size of facility; that is, for each possible quantity of good.

A similar construction may be used to determine optimal goods quantity for each possible size of club; this is illustrated in Fig. 2. On the ordinate, we measure here total costs and total benefits confronting the individual, as in Fig. 1. On the abscissa, we measure physical size of the facility, quantity of good, and for each assumed size of club membership we may trace total cost and total benefit functions. If we first examine the single-member club, we may well find that the optimal goods quantity is zero; the total cost function may increase more rapidly than the total benefit function from the outset. However, as more persons are added, the total costs to the single person fall: under our symmetrical sharing assumption, they will fall proportionately. The total benefit functions here will slope upward to the right but after some initial range they will be concave downward and at some point will reach a maximum. As club size is increased, benefit

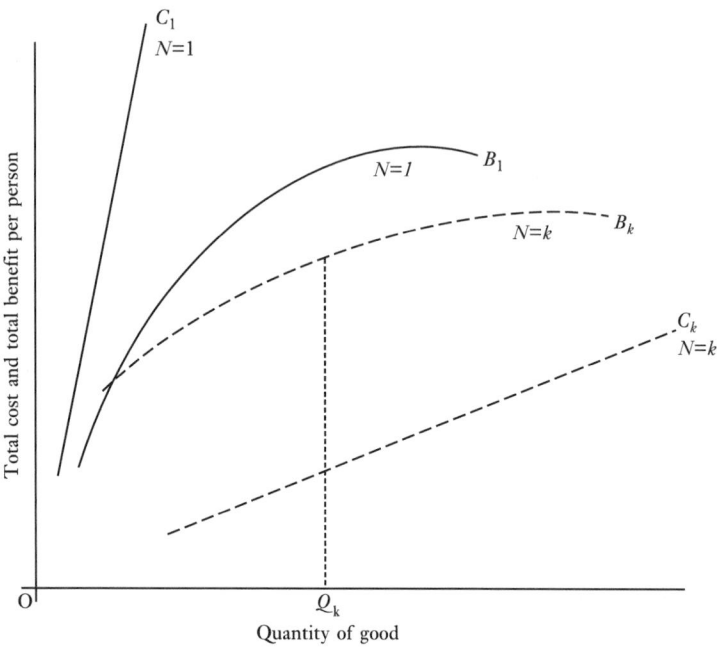

Figure 2

functions will shift generally downward beyond the initial non-congestion range, and the point of maximum benefit will move to the right. The construction of Fig. 2 allows us to derive an optimal goods quantity for each size of club; Q_k is one such quantity for club size $N = K$.

The results derived from Figs. 1 and 2 are combined in Fig. 3. Here the two variables to be chosen, goods quantity and club size, are measured on the ordinate and the abscissa respectively. The values for optimal club size for each goods quantity, derived from Fig. 1, allow us to plot the curve, N_{opt}, in Fig. 3. Similarly, the values for optimal goods quantity, for each club size, derived from Fig. 2, allow us to plot the curve, Q_{opt}.

The intersection of these two curves, N_{opt} and Q_{opt}, determines the position of full equilibrium, G. The individual is in equilibrium both with respect to goods quantity and to group size, for the good under consideration. Suppose, for example, that the sharing group is limited to size, N_k. The attainment of equilibrium with respect to goods quantity, shown by Q_k, would still leave the individual desirous of shifting the size of the membership so as to attain position L. However, once the group increases to this size, the individual prefers a larger quantity of the good, and so on, until G is attained.

Fig. 3 may be interpreted as a standard preference map depicting the tastes of the individual for the two components, goods quantity and club size for the sharing of that good. The curves, N_{opt} and Q_{opt}, are lines of optima, and G is the highest attainable level for the individual, the top of his ordinal utility mountain. Since these curves are lines of optima within an individual preference system, successive choices must converge in G.

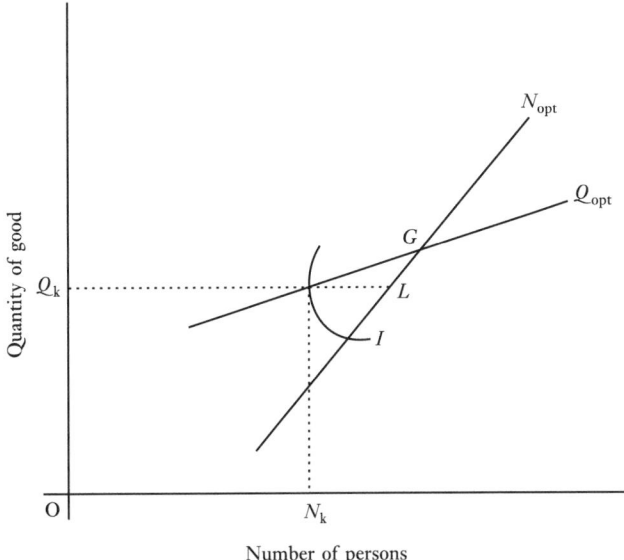

Figure 3

It should be noted that income–price constraints have already been incorporated in the preference map through the specific sharing assumptions that are made. The tastes of the individual depicted in Fig. 3 reflect the post-payment or net relative evaluations of the two components of consumption at all levels. Unless additional constraints are imposed on the model, he must move to the satiety point in this construction.

It seems clear that under normal conditions both of the curves in Fig. 3 will slope upward to the right, and that they will lie in approximately the relation to each other as therein depicted. This reflects the fact that, normally for the type of good considered in this example, there will exist a complementary rather than a substitute relationship between increasing the quantity of the good and increasing the size of the sharing group.

This geometrical model can be extended to cover goods falling at any point along the private–public spectrum. Take the purely public good as the first extreme case. Since, by definition, congestion does not occur, each total benefit curve, in Fig. 1, becomes horizontal. Thus, optimal club size, regardless of goods quantity is infinite. Hence, full equilibrium is impossible of attainment; equilibrium only with respect to goods quantity can be reached, defined with respect to the all-inclusive finite group. In the construction of Fig. 3, the N curve cannot be drawn. A more realistic model may be that in which, at goods quantity equilibrium, the limitations on group size impose an inequality. For example, in Fig. 3, suppose that the all-inclusive group is of size, N_k. Congestion is indicated as being possible over small sizes of facility, but, if an equilibrium quantity is provided, there is no congestion, and, in fact, there remain economies to scale in club size. The situation at the most favourable attainable position is, therefore, in all respects

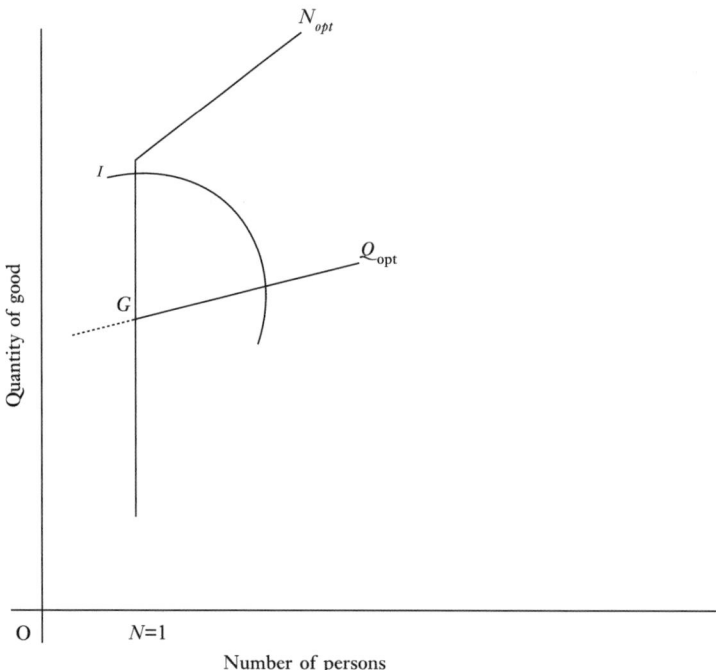

Figure 4

equivalent to that confronted in the case of the good that is purely public under the more restricted definition.

Consider now the purely private good. The appropriate curves here may be shown in Fig. 4. The individual, with his income–price constraints is able to attain the peak of his ordinal preference mountain without the necessity of calling upon his fellows to join him in sharing arrangements. Also, the benefits that he receives from the good may be so exclusively his own that these would largely disappear if others were brought in to share them. Hence, the full equilibrium position, G, lies along the vertical from the $N = 1$ member point. Any attempt to expand the club beyond this point will reduce the utility of the individual.[9]

3.

The geometrical construction implies that the necessary marginal conditions are satisfied at unique equilibrium values for both goods quantity and club size. This involves an oversimplification that is made possible only through the assumptions of specific cost-sharing schemes and identity among individuals. In order to generalize the results, these restrictions must be dropped. We know that, given any group of individuals who are able to evaluate both consumption shares and the costs of congestion, there exists some set of marginal prices, goods quantity, and club size that will satisfy (7) above. However, the quantity of the good, the size of the club sharing in its consumption, and the cost-sharing arrangements must be determined simultaneously. And, since there are always "gains from trade" to be realized in moving from non-optimal to optimal positions, distributional considerations must be introduced. Once these are allowed to be present, the final "solution" can be located at any one of a sub-infinity of points on the Pareto welfare surface. Only through some quite arbitrarily chosen conventions can standard geometrical constructions be made to apply.

The approach used above has been to impose at the outset a set of marginal prices (tax-prices, if the good is supplied publicly), translated here into shares or potential shares in the costs of providing separate quantities of a specific good for groups of varying sizes. Hence, the individual confronts a predictable set of marginal prices for each quantity of the good at every possible club size, independently of his own choices on these variables. With this convention, and the world-of-equals assumption, the geometrical solution becomes one that is relevant for any individual in the group. If we drop the world-of-equals assumption, the construction continues to hold without change for the choice calculus of any particular individual in the group. The results cannot, of course, be generalized for the group in this case, since different individuals will evaluate any given result differently. The model remains helpful even here, however, in that it suggests the process through which individual decisions may be made, and it tends to clarify some of the implicit content in the more formal statements of the necessary marginal conditions for optimality.[10]

4.

The theory of clubs developed in this paper applies in the strict sense only to the organization of membership or sharing arrangements where "exclusion" is possible. In so far as non-exclusion is a characteristic of public goods supply, as Musgrave (1959) has suggested, the theory of clubs is of limited relevance. Nevertheless, some implications of the theory for the whole excludability question may be indicated. If the structure of property rights is variable, there would seem to be few goods the services of which are non-excludable, solely due to some physical attributes. Hence, the theory of clubs is, in one sense, a theory of optimal exclusion, as well as one of inclusion. Consider the classic lighthouse case. Variations in property rights, broadly conceived, could prohibit boat operators without "light licenses" from approaching the channel guarded by the light. Physical exclusion is possible, given sufficient flexibility in property law, in almost all imaginable cases, including those in which the interdependence lies in the act of consuming itself. Take the single person who gets an inoculation, providing immunization against a communicable disease. In so far as this action exerts external benefits on his fellows, the person taking the action could be authorized to collect charges from all beneficiaries under sanction of the collectivity.

This is not, of course, to suggest that property rights will, in practice, always be adjusted to allow for optimal exclusion. If they are not, the "free rider" problem arises. This prospect suggests one issue of major importance that the analysis of this paper has neglected, the question of costs that may be involved in securing agreements among members of sharing groups. If individuals think that exclusion will not be fully possible, that they can expect to secure benefits as free riders without really becoming full-fledged contributing members of the club, they may be reluctant to enter voluntarily into cost-sharing arrangements. This suggests that one important means of reducing the costs of securing voluntary co-operative agreements is that of allowing for more flexible property arrangements and for introducing excluding devices. If the owner of a hunting preserve is allowed to prosecute poachers, then prospective poachers are much more likely to be willing to pay for the hunting permits in advance.

Notes

1   It is interesting that none of the theories of Socialist economic organization seems to be based on explicit co-operation among individuals. These theories have conceived the economy either in the Lange–Lerner sense as an analogue to a purely private, individually oriented social order or, alternatively, as one that is centrally directed.

2   Note that an economic theory of clubs can strictly apply only to the extent that the motivation for joining in sharing arrangements is itself economic; that is, only if choices are made on the basis of costs and benefits of particular goods and services as these are confronted by the individual. In so far as individuals join clubs for camaraderie, as such, the theory does not apply.

3   Physical attributes of a good or service may, of course, affect the structure of the sharing arrangements that are preferred. Although the analysis below assumes symmetrical sharing, this assumption is not necessary, and the analysis in its general form can be extended to cover all possible schemes.

4   Note that this construction of the individual's utility function differs from that introduced in an earlier paper, where "activities" rather than "goods" were included as the basic arguments Buchanan and Stubblebine (1962). In the alternative construction, the "activities" of other persons enter directly into the utility function of the reference individual with respect to the consumption of all other than purely private goods. The construction here incorporates the same interdependence through the inclusion of the N_j's although in a more general manner.

5   In Samuelson's diagrammatic presentation, these individual marginal conditions are satisfied, but the diagrammatic construction is more restricted than that contained in his earlier more general model.

6   The sharing arrangement need not be either co-operative or governmental in form. Since profit opportunities exist in all such situations, the emergence of profit-seeking firms can be predicted in those settings where legal structures permit, and where this organizational form possesses relative advantages (Coase, 1937). For purposes of this paper, such firms are one form of club organization, with co-operatives and public arrangements representing other forms. Generally speaking, of course, the choice among these forms should be largely determined by efficiency considerations.

7   The geometrical model here applies only to such goods. Essentially the same analysis may, however, be extended to apply to cases where "congestion", as such, does not appear. For example, goods that are produced at decreasing costs, even if their consumption is purely private, may be shown to require some sharing arrangements in an equilibrium or optimal organization.

8   For simplicity, we assume that an additional "membership" in the club involves the addition of one separate person. The model applies equally well, however, for those cases where cost shares are allocated proportionately with predicted usage. In this extension, an additional "membership"

would really amount to an additional consumption unit. Membership in the swimming club could, for example, be defined as the right to visit the pool one time each week. Hence, the person who plans to make two visits per week would, in this modification, hold two memberships. This qualification is not, of course, relevant under the strict world-of-equals assumption, but it indicates that the theory need not be so restrictive as it might appear.

9   The construction suggests clearly that the optimal club size, for any quantity of good, will tend to become smaller as the real income of an individual is increased. Goods that exhibit some "publicness" at low income levels will, therefore, tend to become "private" as income levels advance. This suggests that the number of activities that are organized optimally under co-operative collective sharing arrangements will tend to be somewhat larger in low-income communities than in high-income communities, other things equal. There is, of course, ample empirical support for this rather obvious conclusion drawn from the model. For example, in American agricultural communities thirty years ago heavy equipment was communally shared among many farms, normally on some single owner-lease-rental arrangment. Today, substantially the same equipment will be found on each farm, even though it remains idle for much of its potential working time.

The implication of the analysis for the size of governmental units is perhaps less evident. In so far as governments are organized to provide communal facilities, the size of such units measured by the number of citizens, should decline as income increases. Thus, in the affluent society, the local school district may, optimally, be smaller than in the poor society.

10 A note concerning one implicit assumption of the whole analysis is in order at this point. The possibility for the individual to choose among the various scales of consumption sharing arrangements has been incorporated into an orthodox model of individual behaviour. The procedure implies that the individual remains indifferent as to which of his neighbours or fellow citizens join him in such arrangements. In other words, no attempt has been made to allow for personal selectivity or discrimination in the models. To incorporate this element, which is no doubt important in many instances, would introduce a wholly new dimension into the analysis, and additional tools to those employed here would be required.

References

Buchanan, J. M. and Stubblebine, W. C. (1962): "Externality," *Economica*, 31, 371–84.
Coase, R. H. (1937): "The Nature of the Firm," *Economica*, 4, 386–405.
Musgrave, R. A. (1959): *The Theory of Public Finance*. New York: McGraw-Hill.
Samuelson, P. A. (1954): "The Pure Theory of Public Expenditure," *Review of Economics and Statistics*, 36, 387–9. [Reprinted in Ch. 15 of this volume.]
Samuelson, P. A. (1955): "Diagrammatic Exposition of a Theory of Public Expenditure," *Review of Economics and Statistics*, 37, 350–5.

CHAPTER FIVE

Consumer's Surplus Without Apology
ROBERT D. WILLIG

Source: *American Economic Review*, 66 (1976), pp. 589–97. Reprinted with the permission of the author and the American Economic Association. © American Economic Association.

The purpose of this paper is to settle the controversy surrounding consumer's surplus[1] and, by so doing, to validate its use as a tool of welfare economics. I will show that observed consumer's surplus can be rigorously utilized to estimate the unobservable compensating and equivalent variations – the correct theoretical measures of the welfare impact of changes in prices and income on an individual.

I derive precise upper and lower bounds on the percentage errors of approximating the compensating and equivalent variations with consumer's surplus. These bounds can be explicitly calculated from observable demand data, and it is clear that in most applications the error of approximation will be very small. In fact, the error will often be overshadowed by the errors involved in estimating the demand curve. The results in no way depend upon arguments about the constancy of the marginal utility of income.

Consequently, this paper supplies specific empirical criteria which can replace the apologetic caveats frequently employed by those who presently apply consumer's surplus. Moreover, the results imply that consumer's surplus is usually a very good approximation to the appropriate welfare measures.

To preview, below I establish the validity of these rules of thumb: For a single[2] price change, if $|\bar{\eta}A/2m^0| \leq .05, |\underline{\eta}A/2m^0| \leq .05,$ and if $|A/m^0| \leq .9$, then

$$\frac{\underline{\eta}|A|}{2m^0} \leq \frac{C-A}{|A|} \leq \frac{\bar{\eta}|A|}{2m^0} \tag{1}$$

and

$$\frac{\underline{\eta}|A|}{2m^0} \leq \frac{A-E}{|A|} \leq \frac{\bar{\eta}|A|}{2m^0} \tag{2}$$

Here, $A =$ consumer's surplus area under the demand curve and between the two prices (positive for a price increase and negative for a price decrease)

C = compensating variation corresponding to the price change
E = equivalent variation corresponding to the price change
m^0 = consumer's base income
$\bar{\eta}$ and $\underline{\eta}$ = respectively the largest and smallest values of the income elasticity of demand in the region under consideration.

The formulae place observable bounds on the percentage errors of approximating the C or E conceptual measures with observable A. For example, if the consumer's measured income elasticity of demand is 0.8 and if the surplus area under the demand curve between the old and new prices is 5 percent of income, then the compensating variation is within 2 percent of the measured consumer's surplus.

The ratio $|A|/m^0$ can be interpreted as a measure of the proportional change in real income due to the price change.[3] In most applications, the ratio will be very small. Measured income elasticities of demand tend to cluster closely about 1.0, with only rare outliers. Thus it can be expected that $\bar{\eta}|A|/2m^0$, the most important of the terms in (1) and (2), will usually be small enough to permit conscious and unapologetic substitution of A for C or E in studies of individual welfare.[4]

Should $\underline{\eta}|A|/2m^0$ be large, A would not be close to C and E. For such rare cases, formulae are provided below in Section 4 which enable the estimation of C and E from the observable $\bar{\eta}, \underline{\eta}, m^0$, and A.

1. The Compensating and Equivalent Variations

In this section, I present definitions of conceptual tools to measure the costs or benefits of price changes to an individual consumer. While these theoretical measures are not directly observable, the analysis that follows in succeeding sections will show that they can be empirically estimated with consumer's surplus.

Throughout I will be assuming that the consumer behaves as though he were choosing his consumption bundle $X = X^1, X^2, \ldots, X^n$ to maximize an increasing strictly quasi-concave ordinal utility function $U(X)$ subject to the budget constraint $\sum p_i X^i = m$. The resulting demand functions, denoted $X^i(p, m)$, are assumed to be differentiable. The indirect utility function, defined by

$$l(p, m) \equiv U\left[X^1(p, m), X^2(p, m), \ldots, X^n(p, m)\right]$$

relates the price and income parameters to the maximum level of utility the consumer can achieve under the resulting budget constraint. Clearly, by nonsatiation, $l(p, m)$ is monotone increasing in income m, and decreasing in prices p.

The indirect utility function can be used to make statements about individual welfare. Let the base, initial situation be characterized by prices p^0 and income m^0, while an alternative situation can be summarized by p', m'. The economic well-being of the consumer in the different situations can be compared by means of the ordinal ranking of the numbers $l(p^0, m^0)$ and $l(p', m')$.

Another way to effect this welfare test is to compare the income change $m' - m^0$ to the smallest income adjustment needed to make the consumer indifferent to the change in prices from p^0 to p'. If $m' - m^0$ is larger, then welfare is greater in the new situation, and inversely.

This test level of income adjustment is called the compensating income variation, denoted by C below. Symbolically,

$$l(p^0, m^0) = l(p', m^0 + C) \tag{3}$$

The welfare test above

$$l(p', m') \gtreqqless < l(p^0, m^0) \qquad \text{as } m' - m^0 \gtreqqless < C \tag{4}$$

follows immediately from (3) by nonsatiation. Thus the compensating variation is an individual's cost–benefit concept which makes price changes perfectly commensurable with changes in income.

Similarly, the equivalent variation in income (E) can be defined[5] by

$$l(p^0, m^0 - E) = l(p', m^0) \tag{5}$$

In words, $-E$ is the income change which has the same welfare impact on the consumer in the base situation as have the changes in prices from p^0 to p'. It reduces the impacts of different price changes down to the single dimension of income. As such, the equivalent variation concept can be used to rank the consumer's levels of well-being under various sets of prices. With the definitions $l(p^0, m^0 - E') = l(p', m^0)$ and $l(p^0, m^0 - E'') = l(p'', m^0)$, these welfare tests, too, follow from nonsatiation:

$$\begin{aligned}
l(p', m^0) &\gtreqqless l(p'', m^0) \text{ as } E'' \gtreqqless E' \\
l(p', m^0) &\gtreqqless l(p^0, m') \text{ as } m^0 - E \gtreqqless m'
\end{aligned} \tag{6}$$

The welfare tests (4) and (6) show that the compensating and equivalent variations are cost–benefit concepts which can be used to evaluate the impact of micro-economic policy on an individual.[6] These concepts derive practical importance from the fact that they can be estimated from observable consumer's surplus.

2 Consumer's Surplus

The compensating and equivalent variations can be most incisively studied and related to consumer's surplus by means of the income compensation function.[7] This is denoted by $\mu(p|p^0, m^0)$ and is defined to be the least income required by the consumer when he faces prices p to achieve the same utility level he could enjoy (by maximizing behavior) under the parameters p^0, m^0. Thus, by definition,

$$l[p, \mu(p|p^0, m^0)] = l(p^0, m^0) \tag{7}$$

Trivially, we have

$$\mu(p^0 | p^0, m^0) = m^0 \tag{8}$$

Now, we can see that the compensating and equivalent variations can be expressed or redefined in terms of the income compensation function. From (3), $m^0 + C = \mu(p' | p^0, m^0)$, or combining with (8),

$$C = \mu(p' | p^0, m^0) - \mu(p^0 | p^0, m^0) \tag{9}$$

Similarly, from (5), $m^0 - E = \mu(p^0 | p', m^0)$, or

$$E = \mu(p' | p', m^0) - \mu(p^0 | p', m^0) \tag{10}$$

These relationships serve as the bridge to consumer's surplus. It is well known[8] that

$$\frac{\partial \mu(p | p^0, m^0)}{\partial p_i} = X^i(p, \mu(p | p^0, m^0)) \tag{11}$$

This system of partial differential equations, together with the boundary condition (8), is the heart of analytical welfare economics.[9] The compensating and equivalent variations, or any measure of individual welfare that accepts the individual's own consumption preferences, can be calculated from the complete demand functions via (11) and (8).

Restricting attention to changes in a single price, p_1, let $p^0 = (p_1^0, p_2^0, \ldots, p_n^0)$ and $p' = (p_1', p_2^0, \ldots, p_n^0)$. Use the Fundamental Theorem of Calculus and (11) to rewrite (9) and (10) as

$$C = \int_{p_1^0}^{p_1'} X^1(p_1, p_2^0, \ldots, p_n^0, \mu(p_1, p_2^0, \ldots, p_n^0 | p_1^0, p_2^0, \ldots, p_n^0, m^0)) dp_1 \tag{12}$$

$$E = \int_{p_1^0}^{p_1'} X^1(p_1, p_2^0, \ldots, p_n^0, \mu(p_1, p_2^0, \ldots, p_n^0 | p_1', p_2^0, \ldots, p_n^0, m^0)) dp_1 \tag{13}$$

These formulae express the compensating and equivalent variations as areas under demand curves, between the old and new price horizontals. The demand curves are not Marshallian in that the income parameters are not constant. Instead, they are Hicksian compensated demand curves, because the income parameters include compensation which varies with the price to keep the consumer at a constant level of utility. The only distinction between C and E in (12) and (13) is the level of utility the compensation is designed to reach.

Referring to Figure 1, C is the area $p_1^0 p_1' be$ under the demand curve compensated to $l(p^0, m^0)$. This curve crosses the Marshallian curve $X^1(p, m^0)$ at p_1^0 since

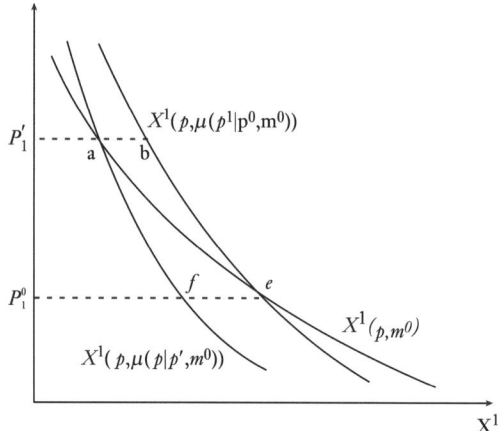

Figure 1

$\mu(p^0|p^0, m^0) = m^0$. With $p'_1 > p^0_1$, if X^1 is noninferior $(\partial X^1/\partial m \geq 0)$ this compensated curve lies above the Marshallian one for $p_1 > p^0_1$, since $\mu(p_1, p^0_2, \ldots, p^0_n|p^0, m^0) \geq m^0$ whenever $p_1 > p^0_1$. Similarly, E is the area $p^0_1 p'_1 af$ under the demand curve compensated to $I(p', m^0)$. This Hicksian curve crosses the Marshallian one at p'_1, and lies below it for $p_1 < p'_1$. The area usually called consumer's surplus is $p^0_1 p'_1 ae$, defined by the observable Marshallian demand curve. Denoting this area by A, we have, then, $C \geq A \geq E$, for noninferior X^1 (the inequalities reverse for X^1 inferior). Of course, it also follows immediately that if there is no income effect $(\partial X^1/\partial m \equiv 0)$, $C = A = E$.

These qualitative results may be useful for some cost–benefit analyses. For example, suppose a policy would raise both an individual's income and the price of a non-inferior good. If the observable consumer's surplus area A were greater than the income boost, it could be inferred from the inequality that C also would be greater. Then, from the welfare test (4), an analyst could conclude that the policy would be injurious to the consumer.

However, usually more information than this is needed about C and E. What is required is a methodology to estimate the welfare measures from observable data. In the next section I show how C and E can be explicitly calculated from observables when the income elasticity of demand is constant.

3. Constant Income Elasticity

Constant income elasticity of demand for X^1 means that

$$\frac{\partial X^1(p, m)}{\partial m} \frac{m}{X^1(p, m)} \equiv \eta$$

Then, we have the simple differential equation $dX^1/X^1 = \eta(dm/m)$ which can be integrated from $X^1(p, m^0)$ to yield

$$X^1(p, m) = X^1(p, m^0)\left[\frac{m}{m^0}\right]^{\eta}$$

The entire income compensation function can be derived by substituting this expression into (11) and solving the resulting differential equation with boundary condition (8). We have, suppressing unchanging arguments,

$$\frac{d\mu}{dp_1} = X^1(p_1, \mu) = X^1(p_1, m^0)\left[\frac{\mu}{m^0}\right]^{\eta}$$

or

$$\mu^{-\eta}d\mu = (m^0)^{-\eta}X^1(p_1, m^0)dp_1$$

Then, integration between p_1^0 and p_1', remembering that $\mu(p_1^0) = m^0$, yields

$$\frac{\left[\mu(p_1')\right]^{1-\eta} - \left[m^0\right]^{1-\eta}}{1-\eta} = (m^0)^{-\eta}\int_{p_1^0}^{p_1'} X^1(p_1, m^0)dp_1 \tag{14}$$

for $\eta \neq 1$, and for $\eta = 1$

$$\ln \mu(p_1') - \ln m^0 = \frac{1}{m^0}\int_{p_1^0}^{p_1'} X^1(p_1, m^0)dp_1$$

Hence, after rearranging we have these explicit expressions for the income compensation function:

$$\mu(p_1'|p_1^0, m^0) = m^0\left[1 + \left(\frac{1-\eta}{m^0}\right)\int_{p_1^0}^{p_1'} X^1(p_1, m^0)dp_1\right]^{\frac{1}{1-\eta}} \qquad \eta \neq 1 \tag{15}$$

$$\mu(p_1'|p_1^0, m^0) = (m^0)\exp\left[\frac{1}{m^0}\int_{p_1^0}^{p_1'} X^1(p_1, m^0)dp_1\right] \qquad \eta = 1 \tag{16}$$

These give the welfare measure μ in terms of the potentially observable constant income elasticity of demand and the consumer's surplus area under the Marshallian demand curve. Let us denote this area by

$$A \equiv \int_{p_1^0}^{p_1'} X^1(p_1, m^0)dp_1 \tag{17}$$

From (15), we see that if $\eta = 0$, $\mu(p'_1|p^0_1, m^0) = m^0 + A$. However, from (16) we see that if preferences are homothetic, the consequent unitary η does not imply any equalities among C, E, and A. Below, for expositional convenience, I ignore the case $\eta = 1$.

Recalling the definitions of C and E, (9) and (10), and loosely applying to (15) this Taylor approximation,

$$(1+t)^{1/1-\eta} \approx 1 + \frac{t}{1-\eta} + \frac{\eta t^2}{2(1-\eta)^2}$$

(where $\approx$ means "approximately equal to"), we get:

$$C \approx A + \frac{\eta A^2}{2m^0} \quad E \approx A - \frac{\eta A^2}{2m^0}$$
$$\frac{C-A}{A} \approx \frac{\eta A}{2m^0} \quad \text{and} \quad \frac{A-E}{A} \approx \frac{\eta A}{2m^0}$$

This was the striking result on the percentage error of approximating C with A which was previewed in the introduction. The next section will establish this formula rigorously for nonconstant income elasticity of demand.

4. Estimation Results

Assume that in the region of price–income space under consideration,[10] $\bar{\eta}$ and η are upper and lower bounds, respectively, on $(\partial X^1(p,m)/\partial m)(m/X^1(p,m))$, with neither equal to 1.[11] It follows from the Mean Value Theorem that

$$\left(\frac{m_2}{m_1}\right)^{\eta} \leq \frac{X^1(p,m_2)}{X^1(p,m_1)} \leq \left(\frac{m_2}{m_1}\right)^{\bar{\eta}} \qquad \text{for } m_2 \geq m_1 \tag{18}$$

Let us consider the welfare impact of a price increase from p^0_1 to p'_1. Since $\mu(p_1|p^0, m^0) \geq \mu(p^0_1|p^0, m^0)$ for $p_1 \geq p^0_1$, we can set $m_2 = \mu(p_1)$ and $m_1 = \mu(p^0_1) = m^0$ in (18):

$$\left[\frac{\mu(p_1)}{m^0}\right]^{\eta} \leq \frac{X^1(p_1, \mu(p_1))}{X^1(p_1, m^0)} \leq \left[\frac{\mu(p_1)}{m^0}\right]^{\bar{\eta}}$$

Rearranging, and substituting from (11) yields

$$0 \leq X^1(p, m^0)^{-\eta}$$
$$\leq \frac{\partial \mu(p)}{\partial p_1}[\mu(p)]^{-\eta} = \frac{\partial\left[\frac{\mu(p)^{1-\eta}}{1-\eta}\right]}{\partial p_1}$$

and

$$0 \leq \partial \frac{\left[\frac{\mu(p)^{1-\bar{\eta}}}{1-\bar{\eta}}\right]}{\partial p_1}$$

$$= \frac{\partial \mu(p)}{\partial p_1} \mu(p)^{-\bar{\eta}}$$

$$\leq X^1(p, m^0)(m^0)^{-\bar{\eta}}$$

Integrating these relationships with respect to p_1 between p_1^0 and p_1' (as in (14)) preserves the inequalities. Rearrangement of the resulting relationships yields these bounds:

$$m^0 \left[1 + (1 - \underline{\eta}) \frac{A}{m^0} \right]^{\frac{1}{1-\underline{\eta}}}$$

$$\leq \mu(p'|p^0, m^0) \qquad (19)$$

$$\leq m^0 \left[1 + (1 - \bar{\eta}) \frac{A}{m^0} \right]^{\frac{1}{1-\bar{\eta}}}$$

provided

$$\underline{\eta}, \bar{\eta} \neq 1, 1 + (1 - \underline{\eta}) \frac{A}{m^0} > 0$$

and

$$1 + (1 - \bar{\eta}) \frac{A}{m^0} > 0$$

For the case of a price decrease from p_1^0 to p_1', since $\mu(p_1|p_1^0, m^0) \leq m^0$ for $p_1 \leq p_1^0$, we can set $m_2 = m^0$ and $m_1 = \mu(p_1)$ in (18), and then follow the same sequence of steps. Once again, (19) emerges, but reference to (17) shows that here A is negative.

Invoking the definition (9), (19) can be rewritten as

$$\frac{\left[1 + (1-\underline{\eta})\frac{A}{m^0}\right]^{\frac{1}{1-\underline{\eta}}} - 1 - \frac{A}{m^0}}{\frac{|A|}{m^0}} \leq \frac{C-A}{|A|} \leq \frac{\left[1 + (1-\bar{\eta})\frac{A}{m^0}\right]^{\frac{1}{1-\bar{\eta}}} - 1 - \frac{A}{m^0}}{\frac{|A|}{m^0}} \qquad (20)$$

Also, using (10) and reversing the roles of p' and p^0 in (19) (but not in the definition of A) gives

$$\frac{\left[1 - (1-\underline{\eta})\frac{A}{m^0}\right]^{\frac{1}{1-\underline{\eta}}} - 1 + \frac{A}{m^0}}{|A|/m^0} \leq \frac{A-E}{|A|} \leq \frac{\left[1 - (1-\bar{\eta})\frac{A}{m^0}\right]^{\frac{1}{1-\bar{\eta}}} - 1 + \frac{A}{m^0}}{|A|/m^0} \qquad (21)$$

The measures of a consumer's welfare can be tightly estimated from observables via (19)–(21), regardless of the size of A/m^0, if $1 \pm (1 - \eta)A/m^0 > 0$, $1 \pm (1 - \bar{\eta})A/m^0 > 0$, and if η, and $\bar{\eta}$ are sufficiently close in value.[12] Of course, in the limit, as η approaches $\bar{\eta}$, (19) reduces to the constant elasticity formula (15). Moreover, we shall see that if the absolute values of $\underline{\eta}A/2m^0$ and $\bar{\eta}A/2m^0$ are small, then (20) and (21) reduce to elegant rules of thumb.

Table 1 displays the numerical values of the following coefficients for selected choices of η and a: $\eta a/2$,

$$\frac{[1 + (1 - \eta)a]^{1/1-\eta} - 1 - a}{a}$$

and

$$\frac{[1 - (1 - \eta)a]^{1/1-\eta} - 1 + a}{a}$$

The latter two expressions encompass the forms of the bounds in (20) and (21), when a is interpreted as $|A|/m^0$.[13] It can be readily seen from the table that for the ranges of parameter values studied,[14] when $|\eta a/2|$ is small (say less than .05), $\eta a/2$ is close enough (within .005) to the actual bounds for most practical purposes. This numerical observation corroborates the loose application to (15) of the Taylor Series expansion in Section 3. More importantly, it establishes the rules of thumb previewed in (1) and (2).[15]

Addition of (1) and (2) yields a check on the numerical proximity of C and E: when $|\underline{\eta}A/2m^0| \leq .05$, $|\bar{\eta}A/2m^0| \leq .05$, and $|A/m^0| \leq .9$,

$$\frac{\underline{\eta}|A|}{m^0} \leq \frac{C - E}{|A|} \leq \frac{\bar{\eta}|A|}{m^0} \tag{23}$$

So, the analysis hinges on the magnitudes of η and A/m^0. As discussed in the introduction, in most practical applications $|\eta A/2m^0|$ and $|A/m^0|$ are likely to be small enough for the rules of thumb to apply. If not, equations (19)–(21) and Table 1 will be useful. Even if the calculated error bounds are too large to be ignored, the compensating and equivalent variations may still be usefully estimated from the data via the formulae.

5. Individual Welfare and Consumer's Surplus

With the approximation results in hand, let us return to the question of how to make statements about individual welfare, based on observable data. Remember from (4) that $l(p', m') \gtreqless l(p^0, m^0)$ as $m' - m^0 \gtreqless C$. With the empirical information that $\underline{C} \leq C \leq \bar{C}$, where $\underline{C}$ and $\bar{C}$ can be calculated from (20) or (22), it can be concluded that

Table 1

$\eta\backslash\varepsilon$	.001	.005	.010	.020	.030	.040	.050	.075	.100	.150	.200	.250
	−.001	−.005	−.010	−.020	−.030	−.040	−.050	−.075	−.100	−.150	−.200	−.250
−2.00	−.001	−.005	−.010	−.019	−.029	−.038	−.046	−.067	−.086	−.121	−.152	−.180
	−.001	−.005	−.010	−.021	−.032	−.043	−.054	−.086	−.121	−.205	−.316	−.480
	−.001	−.003	−.005	−.010	−.015	−.020	−.025	−.038	−.051	−.076	−.101	−.126
−1.01	−.001	−.003	−.005	−.010	−.015	−.019	−.024	−.035	−.046	−.066	−.085	−.102
	−.001	−.003	−.005	−.010	−.016	−.021	−.027	−.041	−.056	−.090	−.129	−.174
	.000	.001	.002	.003	.005	.006	.008	.011	.015	.023	.030	.038
.30	.000	.001	.002	.003	.005	.006	.008	.011	.015	.023	.029	.036
	.000	.001	.002	.003	.005	.006	.008	.011	.015	.023	.031	.039
	.000	.001	.003	.005	.008	.010	.013	.019	.025	.038	.050	.063
.50	.000	.001	.003	.005	.008	.010	.013	.019	.025	.038	.050	.063
	.000	.001	.003	.005	.008	.010	.013	.019	.025	.038	.050	.063
	.000	.002	.004	.007	.011	.014	.018	.026	.035	.053	.070	.088
.70	.000	.002	.004	.007	.011	.014	.018	.027	.035	.054	.072	.090
	.000	.002	.004	.007	.010	.014	.017	.026	.035	.051	.068	.085
	.000	.002	.005	.009	.014	.018	.023	.034	.045	.068	.090	.113
.90	.000	.002	.005	.009	.014	.018	.023	.034	.046	.070	.095	.120
	.000	.002	.004	.009	.013	.018	.022	.033	.044	.065	.085	.105
	.001	.003	.005	.010	.015	.020	.025	.038	.051	.076	.101	.126
1.01	.001	.003	.005	.010	.015	.020	.026	.039	.052	.080	.108	.138
	.001	.003	.005	.010	.015	.020	.025	.037	.049	.072	.094	.116
	.001	.003	.006	.011	.017	.022	.028	.041	.055	.083	.110	.138
1.10	.001	.003	.006	.011	.017	.022	.028	.043	.057	.088	.119	.152
	.001	.003	.006	.011	.016	.022	.027	.040	.053	.078	.102	.125
	.001	.003	.006	.012	.018	.024	.030	.045	.060	.090	.120	.150
1.20	.001	.003	.006	.012	.018	.024	.031	.047	.063	.097	.132	.169
	.001	.003	.006	.012	.018	.024	.029	.043	.057	.084	.110	.134
	.001	.004	.008	.015	.023	.030	.038	.056	.075	.113	.150	.188
1.50	.001	.004	.008	.015	.023	.031	.039	.059	.080	.125	.173	.224
	.001	.004	.007	.015	.022	.029	.036	.054	.070	.102	.132	.160
	.001	.005	.010	.020	.030	.040	.050	.075	.100	.150	.200	.250
2.00	.001	.005	.010	.020	.031	.042	.053	.081	.111	.176	.250	.333
	.001	.005	.010	.020	.029	.038	.048	.070	.091	.130	.167	.200
	.002	.008	.015	.030	.045	.060	.075	.113	.150	.225	.300	.375
3.00	.002	.008	.015	.031	.047	.064	.082	.129	.180	.302	.455	.657
	.002	.008	.015	.029	.043	.056	.069	.100	.129	.180	.226	.266
	.003	.013	.025	.050	.075	.100	.125	.188	.250	.375	.500	.625
5.00	.003	.013	.026	.053	.082	.114	.147	.244	.362	.716	1.477	**
	.002	.012	.024	.047	.069	.089	.109	.154	.193	.261	.317	.364
	.005	.025	.050	.100	.150	.200	.250	.375	.500	.750	1.000	1.250
10.00	.005	.026	.053	.115	.186	.271	.374	.774	1.916	**	**	**
	.005	.024	.047	.089	.126	.160	.191	.257	.312	.396	.460	.509

* Each group of three numbers includes, from the top, $\eta\,a/2$, $[(1 + (1 − \eta)a)^{1/1-\eta}-1 - a]/a$, and $[(1 − (1 − \eta)a)^{1/1-\eta} − 1 + a]/a$. The entry ** indicates that $(1 + (1 − \eta)a) < 0$.

$$l(p', m') > l(p^0, m^0) \quad \text{if } m' - m^0 > \bar{C}$$
$$l(p', m') < l(p^0, m^0) \quad \text{if } m' - m^0 < \underline{C} \tag{24}$$

If $\underline{C}$ and $\bar{C}$ are close in value, (24) provides a welfare test of considerable power.[16] If $|\bar{\eta}A/2m^0|$ and $|\eta A/2m^0|$ are small enough, both $\underline{C}$ and $\bar{C}$ can be safely replaced in (24) by A. Otherwise, they can be calculated from η, $\bar{\eta}$, A, and m^0.

To conclude, at the level of the individual consumer, cost–benefit welfare analysis can be performed rigorously and unapologetically by means of consumer's surplus.

Notes

1 Throughout, the term consumer's surplus is used to refer to the area to the left of an individual's fixed-income (Marshallian) demand curve and between the relevant price horizontals. The concept of consumer's surplus originated in 1844 (see Jules Dupult) and has been controversial ever since. Alfred Marshall, who popularized the tool, stipulated that for it to be validly used the marginal utility of money must be constant (Marshall, 1961, p. 842 or David Katzner, 1970, p. 152). However, Harold Hotelling wrote that consumer's surpluses "give a meaningful measure of social value. This breaks down if the variations under consideration are too large a part of the total economy of the person..." (1969, p. 289). John Hicks (1956) too, stated only a gentle caution: "In order that the Marshallian measure of consumer's surplus should be a good measure, one thing alone is needful – that the income effect should be small" (p. 177). More recently, though, Paul Samuelson (1947, pp. 194–95) concluded that consumer's surplus is a worse than useless concept (because it confuses), and I.M.D. Little (1957, p. 180) agreed, calling it no more than a "theoretical toy." Nonetheless, theorists and cost–benefit analysts have persisted in their use of the tool. For justification they resort (see E. J. Mishan, 1971, pp. 337–38, for example), with no formal theoretical support, to statements similar to those quoted above from Hotelling and Hicks.
2 While I restrict attention to single price changes here, analogous, but more complex formulae are derived for multiple price changes in my papers (1973a, b).
3 Or the ratio can be interpreted using the words of Hotelling quoted in note 1 as the relative size of the variation.
4 Formulae (1) and (2) reflect the cautions (see note 1) of both Hotelling and Hicks.
5 The definitions (3) and (5) correspond to those of Hicks, 1956, p. 177, and Samuelson, 1947, p. 199.
6 They also can serve as building blocks for methodologies to make social welfare judgments. The Compensation Principle is a well-known example (see Tibor Scitovsky, 1969).
7 This theoretical tool was introduced by Lionel McKenzie (1957), and definitively studied by Leonid Hurwicz and Hirofumi Uzawa (1971).
8 See Hurwicz and Uzawa (1971) for a state-of-the-art derivation. Heuristically, (11) says that the first-order income change, $d\mu$, required to compensate for the price increase, dp_1 is just the augmentation needed to buy the old consumption bundle, $X(p, \mu, (p|p^0, m^0))$, at the new prices $p_1 + dp_1, p_2 \ldots, p_n$ rather than at the old prices p. The irrelevance to this calculation of the concomitant substitution effects is the result of the envelope theorem.
9 This point of view was taken by Herbert Mohring (1971).
10 This region is $\{(p, m) : p_1 = \alpha p_1^0 + (1 - \alpha)p_1', \ 0 \le \alpha \le 1; \ p_i = p_i^0, \ i \ne 1; \ m = \gamma m^0 + (1 - \gamma)\mu(p|p^0, m^0), 0 \le \gamma \le 1; \text{ and } X^1(p, m) > 0\}$.
11 Either $\bar{\eta}$ or η can be arbitrarily close to 1.
12 The most plausible cause of the negation of these conditions is $(\partial X^1/\partial m)(m/X^1) \to \infty$. However, regions in which X^1 is identically zero can be ignored, since there both μ and A

are unchanging. To handle the case in which $X^1 = 0$ and $\partial X^1/\partial m \neq 0$ near the boundary of the relevant region, bounds on μ can be derived from bounds on $\partial X^1/\partial m$. Because these are generally more gross than (19), the best approach is to take this tack only in the vicinity of the singularity, use (19) on the rest of the path of integration, and splice the sets of inequalities together. The formulae for such procedures can be found in my 1973a, b papers. An explicit solution for μ when $\partial X^1/\partial m$ is independent of m is also reported there.

13 For example, the value of the lower bound in (20) when $\eta = 2$ and $A/m^0 = -.05$ is .048. This can be found in Table 1 as the value of $\left[(1 - (1 - \eta)a)^{1/1-\overline{\eta}} - 1 + a\right]/|a|$ when $\eta = 2$ and $a = .05$.

14 These seem to include most values that would be found for these parameters in actual applications.

15 When $|\eta A/2m^0| \leq .05$ and $|\overline{\eta}A/2m^0| \leq .05$, it suffices for $1 \pm (1 - \eta)A/m^0 > 0$ and $1 \pm (1 - \overline{\eta})A/m^0 > 0$ that $|A/m^0| < .9$.

16 Another welfare comparison (which may be useful for an analysis of social welfare with a Bergsonian social welfare function) is made possible by the fact (see Hurwicz and Uzawa, 1971) that $\mu(p^0|p, m)$, viewed as a function of p and m, is a proper indirect utility function.

$$\mu(p^0|p, m) = E + m$$

where E is the equivalent variation associated with a change from p^0 to p. Hence this particular ordinal indirect utility function can be exactly expressed by areas under compensated demand curves, as in (13), or it can be estimated from consumer's surplus via (19), (21), or (2).

References

Arrow, K. J. and Scitovsky, T. (1969): *Readings in Welfare Economics*, vol. 12. Homewood, Ill.: Irwin.

Dupuit, J. (1969 [1844]): "On the Measurement of the Utility of Public Works," translated and reprinted in K. J. Arrow and T. Scitovsky, 255–83.

Hicks, J. R. (1956): *A Revision of Demand Theory*. Oxford: Clarendon Press.

Hotelling, H. (1969): "The General Welfare in Relation to Problems of Taxation and of Railway and Utility Rates," in Arrow and Scitovsky.

Hurwicz, L. and Uzawa, H. (1971): "On the Integrability of Demand Functions," in J. S. Chipman, L. Hurwicz, M. K. Richter and H. Sonnenschein (eds), *Preferences, Utility, and Demand*, New York, 114–48.

Katzner, D. (1970): *Static Demand Theory*. New York: Macmillan.

Little, I. M. D. (1957): *A Critique of Welfare Economics*. Oxford: Clarendon Press.

Marshall, A. (1961): *Principles of Economics*, 9th edn. New York: Macmillan.

McKenzie, L. W. (1957): "Demand Theory without a Utility Index," *Review of Economic Studies*, 24, June, 185–9.

Mishan, E. J. (1971): *Cost-Benefit Analysis: An Introduction*. New York: Praeger.

Mohring, H. (1971): "Alternative Welfare Gain and Loss Measures," *Western Economic Journal*, 9, December, 349–68.

Samuelson, P. A. (1947): *Foundations of Economic Analysis*. Cambridge, Mass.: Harvard University Press.

Scitovsky, T. (1969): "A Note on Welfare Propositions in Economics," reprinted in Arrow and Scitovsky.

Willig, R. (1973a): "*Consumer's Surplus: A Rigorous Cookbook*," technical report no. 98, Economics Series, Inst. for Mathemat. Stud. in the Soc. Sci., Stanford University 1973.

—— (1973b): "*Welfare Analysis of Policies Affecting Prices and Products*," memo. no. 153, Center for Research in Economic Growth, Stanford University 1973.

CHAPTER SIX

The Social Costs of Monopoly Power

KEITH COWLING AND DENNIS C. MUELLER

Source: *Economic Journal*, 88 (1978), pp. 727–48. Reprinted with the permission of The Royal Economic Society. © The Royal Economic Society.

In 1954, Arnold Harberger estimated the welfare losses from monopoly for the United States at 0.1 of 1% of GNP. Several studies have appeared since, reconfirming Harberger's early low estimates using different assumptions (e.g. Schwartzman, 1960; Scherer, 1970; Worcester, 1973). These papers have firmly established as part of the conventional wisdom the idea that welfare losses from monopoly are insignificant.

The Harberger position has been, almost from the start, subject to attack, however (e.g. Stigler, 1956); Kamerschen (1966) followed essentially the Harberger methodology, but assumed an elasticity of demand consistent with monopoly pricing behaviour at the industry level and obtained welfare loss estimates as high as 6%. Posner (1975) made some rough estimates of the social costs of acquiring monopoly power, but, using Harberger's calculations, concluded that the real problem was the social cost imposed by regulation rather than of private market power.

The most sophisticated critique of Harberger's approach has been offered by Abram Bergson (1973). Bergson criticises the partial equilibrium framework employed by Harberger and all previous studies, and puts forward a general equilibrium model as an alternative. He then produces a series of hypothetical estimates of the welfare losses from monopoly, some of them quite large, for various combinations of the two key parameters in this model, the elasticity of substitution in consumption and the difference between monopoly and competitive price. Not surprisingly Bergson's estimates, suggesting as they do that monopoly can be a matter of some consequence, have induced a sharp reaction (see Carson, 1975; Worcester, 1975).[1]

The present paper levels several objections against the Harberger-type approach. It then calculates estimates of the welfare loss from monopoly using procedures derived to meet these objections, and obtains estimates significantly greater than those of previous studies. Although several of the objections we make have been made by other writers, none has systematically adjusted the basic Harberger technique to take them into account. Thus all previous estimates of monopoly welfare losses suffer in varying degrees from the same biases incorporated in Harberger's original estimates.

We do, however, employ a partial equilibrium framework as followed by Harberger and all subsequent empirical studies. Although a general equilibrium framework would be preferable, such an approach requires simplifying assumptions which to our mind are just as restrictive as those needed to justify the partial equilibrium approach. For example, Bergson must assume that social welfare can be captured via a social indifference curve, and further that this indifference curve is the CES variety. The assumption that the elasticity of substitution (σ) is constant further implies, for a disaggregated analysis, that the elasticity of demand for each product (η_i) is the same, since $\eta_i \rightarrow \sigma$ as the share of the ith product in total output approaches zero. But the assumption that η_i is the same for all i is the same assumption made by Harberger and most other previous studies. It introduces a basic inconsistency between the observed variations in price – cost margins and the assumed constant elasticities in demand, which the present study seeks to avoid. Given such problems, we have adopted the partial equilibrium framework, with all the necessary assumptions it requires (see Bergson, 1973). We present estimates for both the United States and the United Kingdom based on data gathered at the firm level.

1. Theoretical Analysis

We have four substantive criticisms of the Harberger approach:

1 In the partial equilibrium formula for welfare loss $\frac{1}{2} dp\, dq$, where dp is the change in price from competition to monopoly and dq is the change in quantity, dp and dq were considered to be independent of each other. Generally low values of dp were *observed* and low values of dq were *assumed*. In Harberger's case he assumed that price elasticities of demand in all industries were unitary. This must inevitably lead to small estimates of welfare loss.

2 The competitive profit rate was identified with the mean profit rate and thus automatically incorporated an element of monopoly. In fact the underlying approach was a "constant degree of monopoly" – one in which distortions in output were associated with deviations of profit rate from the mean, rather than from the competitive return on capital.

3 The use of industry profit rates introduces an immediate aggregation bias into the calculation by allowing the high monopoly profits of those firms with the most market power to be offset by the losses of other firms in the same industry. Given assumption (1), a further aggregation bias is introduced, which can easily be shown to result in additional downward bias in the estimates.

4 The entire social loss due to monopoly was assumed to arise from the deviation of monopoly output from competitive levels. To this should be added the social cost of attempts to acquire monopoly positions, existing or potential.

We now seek to justify each of these four criticisms.

1.1. Interdependence of dp_i and dq_i

Assuming profit maximising behaviour we can define the implied price elasticity of demand for a specific firm by observing the mark-up of price on marginal cost:

$$\hat{\eta}_i = \frac{p_i}{(p_i - mc_i)} \tag{1}$$

For a pure monopolist or perfectly colluding oligopolist $\hat{\eta}_i$ is the industry elasticity of demand. In other cases $\hat{\eta}_i$ reflects both the industry demand elasticity and the degree of rivals' response to a change in price the ith firm perceives (Cubbin, 1975). Using (1) we shall obtain welfare loss estimates by individual firms from their price/cost margins. These estimates indicate the amount of welfare loss associated with a single firm's decision to set price above marginal cost, given the change in its output implied by $\hat{\eta}_i$.[2] To the extent other firms also charge higher prices, because firm i sets its price above marginal cost, the total welfare loss associated with firm i's market power exceeds the welfare loss we estimate. To the extent that a simultaneous reduction to zero of all price cost margins is contemplated, however, $\hat{\eta}_i$ overestimates the net effect of the reduction in p_i on the ith firm's output. What the latter effect on output and welfare would be is a matter for general equilibrium analysis and is not the focus here. Rather, we attempt an estimate of the relative importance of the distortions in individual firm outputs, on a firm by firm basis, on the assumption that each does possess some monopoly power, as implied by the price cost margin it chooses, and uses it.

This approach emphasising the interdependence of observed price distortions and changes in output contrasts with the methodology of Harberger (1954), Schwartzman (1960), Worcester (1973) and Bergson (1973), who observe (or, in Bergson's case, assume) $(p_i - mc_i)/p_i$ and then *assume* a value of η_i.[3] Harberger observed generally low values of dp_i and yet chose to assume that $\eta_i =$ one, and therefore that dq_i was also very small. But, it is inconsistent to observe low values of dp_i and infer low elasticities unless one has assumed that the firm or industry cannot price as a monopolist, i.e. unless one has already assumed the monopoly problem away.[4] Assuming interdependence we obtain the following definition of welfare loss:

$$dW_i = \frac{1}{2}\frac{dp_i}{p_i}\frac{dq_i}{q_i}p_iq_i, \tag{2}$$

where[5]

$$\frac{dp_i}{p_i} = \frac{1}{\hat{\eta}_i} \quad \text{and} \quad \frac{dq_i}{q_i} = \hat{\eta}_i\frac{dp_i}{p_i} = 1$$

therefore

$$dW_i = \frac{dp_i}{p_i}\frac{p_iq_i}{2} \tag{3}$$

Assuming constant costs we can rewrite (3) in terms of profits:

$$dW_i = \frac{\Pi_i}{p_iq_i}\frac{p_iq_i}{2} = \frac{\Pi_i}{2} \tag{4}$$

This formulation obviously contrasts sharply with Harberger's:

$$dW_i = \frac{1}{2} p_i q_i \eta_i t_i^2 \tag{5}$$

where

$$t_i = \frac{dp_i}{p_i} \qquad \eta_i = 1$$

It is obvious that if t_i is small the welfare loss is going to be insignificant. If t_i were a price increase due to tariff or tax then it might be assumed to be independent of η_i[6] and equation (5) would give a reasonable estimate of welfare loss. But where t_i is a firm decision variable, η_i and t_i must be interdependent, and formulae for calculating welfare losses should take this interdependence into account. Interesting here is the Worcester (1975) critique of Bergson for doing essentially this with his hypothetical general equilibrium calculations when Worcester himself followed the Harberger line without demur (Worcester, 1973).[7] In contrast to Harberger and Worcester, Bergson (1973) allowed himself to pick some combinations of t_i and η_i, which implied high values of welfare loss.

Harberger defended his choice of a demand elasticity of 1.0 across all products on the grounds that what was "envisage[d was] not the substitution of one industry's product against all other products, but rather the substitution of one great aggregate of products (those yielding high rates of return) for another aggregate (those yielding low rates of return)" (p. 79). Thus, the use of $\eta = 1.0$ was an attempt at compensating for the disadvantages of employing a partial equilibrium measure of welfare loss to examine a general equilibrium structural change. But certainly this is a very awkward way of handling the problem which neither answers the criticisms raised by Bergson (1973) against the partial equilibrium approach, nor those we have just presented. For this reason we have chosen to define the partial equilibrium methodology properly and obtain the best estimates we can with this approach, recognising that it leaves unanswered the issues raised by general equilibrium analysis and the theory of second best regarding the net effect of a simultaneous elimination of all monopoly power. We return to this point below in Subsection 1.5.

1.2. The measurement of monopoly profits

The obvious measure of monopoly profit is the excess of actual profits over long-run competitive returns. For an economy in equilibrium, the competitive profit rate is the minimum profit rate compatible with long-run survival, after making appropriate allowances for risk. Monopoly profit is thus the difference between actual profits and profits consistent with this minimum rate.

Harberger (1954) and all subsequent studies have based their monopoly profit estimates on the size of the deviation between actual profit rates and the mean rate. To the extent that observed profits contain elements of monopoly rent, the mean profit rate exceeds the minimum rate consistent with long-run survival. The deviations between profit rates above the mean and the mean rate underestimate the level of monopoly returns, and the estimate of monopoly welfare is biased downwards.[8] Indeed, if all firms and industries were in long-run equilibrium, all would earn profits equal to or greater than the minimum and the use of deviations from the mean would minimise the size of the measured monopoly profits.

It is unreasonable to assume that the time periods investigated in Harberger's study, the others which followed, or our own, are long enough or stable enough so that all firms and industries are in equilibrium. The presence of firms earning profits less than the competitive norm creates a methodological problem for a study of monopoly welfare losses. All studies to date have implicitly assumed that a monopolist's costs are the same as those of a firm in competitive equilibrium, and that all welfare loss is from the loss of consumers' surplus from a monopoly price above marginal cost. But, what is the appropriate assumption to make for a firm experiencing losses? It seems unrealistic to assume that its costs are at competitive levels and its prices below them. More reasonable seems the assumption that these firms are in disequilibrium, probably with costs currently above competitive levels. When calculating monopoly welfare losses, therefore, we simply drop all firms (or industries where relevant) with profits below the competitive return on capital, in effect assuming that they will eventually return to a position where they are earning normal profits or disappear. In either case, they represent no long-run loss to society. (It is possible that some of these losses represent expenditures by firms hoping to secure monopoly positions from other firms in the industry, as discussed below. These losses are then part of the social costs of monopoly. We attempt to account for them in one of our welfare loss formulae.)

Previous studies, to the extent we can ascertain, have followed Harberger and treated deviations in profits below and above the mean symmetrically. That is, an industry whose profit rate was 5% below the mean profit rate was considered to have created as large a welfare loss as an industry whose profits are 5% above the mean.[9] Thus, these studies have not actually estimated welfare loss under monopoly using perfect competition as the standard of comparison, but have effectively compared welfare loss under the present regime with that which would exist were the degree of monopoly equalised across all firms and industries. Under their procedures, a constant degree of monopoly power, however high, would result in no welfare loss. While such an approach has some theoretical support, it raises practical difficulties. How is this elusive concept of a constant degree of monopoly defined and measured? How is such a world created without an omniscient planner or regulator? In addition, monopoly in product markets could be expected to induce distortions in factor markets. Finally, as developed below, the existence of monopoly power in product markets attracts resources to its acquisition and protection, which are part of the social cost of monopoly apart from the distortions in output accompanying it. For these reasons, and because it appears to be most directly in the spirit of the analysis, we have compared monopoly profits to competitive returns, and considered only deviations above the competitive rate when estimating welfare losses.

Following Harberger and other previous studies we have attempted to minimise the transitory component in our estimates by using averages of firm profits over several years.[10] Nevertheless, some of the companies earning profits above competitive levels in our samples are in temporary disequilibrium, and the welfare losses associated with these firms can be expected to disappear over time. Thus, our estimates of monopoly profits are a combination of both long-run monopoly profits and short-run disequilibrium profits. To the extent the time periods we have chosen are representative of the U.K. and U.S. economies under "normal" conditions, our calculations are accurate estimates of the annual losses from monopoly, both permanent and transitory, that can be expected in these countries. A further effort to eliminate the transitory monopoly components from the data would require a specification of what is meant by "permanent" and "transitory" monopolies. Many economists would take it for granted that in the "long run" all monopolies are dead and thus monopoly like unemployment is a "short-run" phenomenon. As with unemployment, the question is how serious is the problem when it exists, and how long does it last. Our paper addresses the first of these questions. A full answer to the second question is clearly beyond the scope of our essentially cross-section analysis.

1.3. The aggregation biases from using industry data

Previous studies of monopoly welfare losses with the exception of Worcester (1973) used industry data at a fairly high level of aggregation. At any point in time some firms in an industry are likely to be earning profits below the competitive level. We have already discussed the methodological issues raised in a study of monopoly welfare losses by firms earning negative economic profits. If our interpretation of these firms as being in short-run disequilibrium is correct, then they should be dropped from an industry before calculating the industry's profit rate. Previous studies which have based their calculations solely on industry data have effectively combined the negative profits of some firms with the positive profits of others in estimating the welfare losses from monopoly. Thus they have implicitly assumed that the monopoly profits earned by the most profitable firms in the industry are somehow offset or mitigated by those experiencing transitory losses. But if there is a monopoly problem in an industry, it is represented by the positive rents earned by those firms with profits above the norm, and the losses of firms that are temporarily unable to compete successfully in no way alleviates the social costs arising from the monopoly positions of the other firms. The present study therefore measures monopoly welfare losses using firm level monopoly profit estimates.

A second aggregation bias is introduced into the estimates of all previous studies other than Kamerschen's (1966) through the assumption of a constant elasticity of demand across all industries. This results in the profit margin's appearance as a squared term in the welfare loss formula. The use of average firm profit margins (including firms with negative profits) implicit in the use of industry data, further biases the welfare loss estimates downwards. The extent of this bias is measured below.

1.4. Welfare loss in the acquisition of monopoly power

Tullock (1967) and Posner (1975) have argued that previous studies understate the social costs of monopoly by failing to recognise the costs involved in attempts to gain and retain monopoly power. These costs could take the form of investment in excess production capacity, excessive accumulation of advertising goodwill stocks, and excessive product differentiation through R and D.[11] Efforts to obtain tariff protection, patent protection and other types of preferential government treatment through campaign contributions, lobbying or bribery are parts of the social costs of the existence of monopoly as defined by Tullock and Posner. To the extent that these expenditures enter reported costs in the form of higher payments to factor owners and legitimate business expenses, firm costs in the presence of monopoly exceed costs under perfect competition. Estimates of welfare loss based on those profits remaining *net* of these expenditures *under*estimate the social cost of monopoly in two ways: first, by understanding monopoly rents they understate the distortions in output monopoly produces; secondly, by failing to include these additional expenditures as part of the costs of monopoly.

Three adjustments to the usual welfare triangle measure of monopoly welfare loss are made to account for the additional expenditures to redistribute monopoly rents, monopoly power induces. First, advertising is added to monopoly profit in calculating the welfare triangle loss to allow for the understatement of monopoly profit expenditures of this type produce. Second, all of advertising is added to the welfare loss. This takes the extreme view of advertising as merely an instrument for securing market power. To the extent advertising provides useful information to consumers, this measure overstates the cost of monopoly.[12] Third, all of measured, after-tax profits above the competitive cost of capital are used as the estimate of the expenditures incurred by others to obtain control of these monopoly rents. Obviously this estimate is but a first approximation. It is an under-estimate, if the firm has incurred expenditures in the acquisition and maintenance of its monopoly position, which are included in current costs. It is an overstatement if actual and potential competitors can successfully collude to avoid these wasteful outlays. This type of argument can always be rebutted, however, by carrying the Tullock/Posner analysis one stage back and positing expenditures of resources to enter the potential competitor's position, and so on. The arguments that after-tax profits underestimate the additional costs associated with monopoly seem at least as reasonable as those suggesting over-estimation.

1.5. An objection and alternative estimating technique

The assumption that demand elasticity equals the reciprocal of the price–cost margin, equation (1), can give rise, when price–cost margins are small, to firm level elasticity estimates much greater than existing industry level estimates, and imply large increases in output from the elimination of monopoly. This has led several observers to criticise the use of the Lerner formula, and the underlying assumption that firms set price as if they possess and utilise market power. Worcester (1969) has made the argument most forcefully.

> Serious error . . . arise[s] if the "monopolist" is only an oligopolist who fears entry, unfavour-able publicity, government regulation or a weaker position at the bargaining table should profits be too high, and for such reasons prices at P_0 (Fig. 1) and sells output Q_E in spite of the fact that the marginal revenue is far below zero at that point. [1969, p. 237, note that our Fig. 1 and Worcester's are drawn to scale.]

The elasticity of demand is lower at P_0 than at P_M, and the expansion in output following a reduction in price to competitive price P_c is obviously much smaller if we assume the "monopolist" sets price equal to P_0. Thus Worcester's depiction of the problem does meet the objections many have raised against the use of the Lerner formula to estimate demand elasticities. We observe only that if one assumes from the start that "monopolists" are so constrained in their behaviour that they must set price so low that marginal revenue is

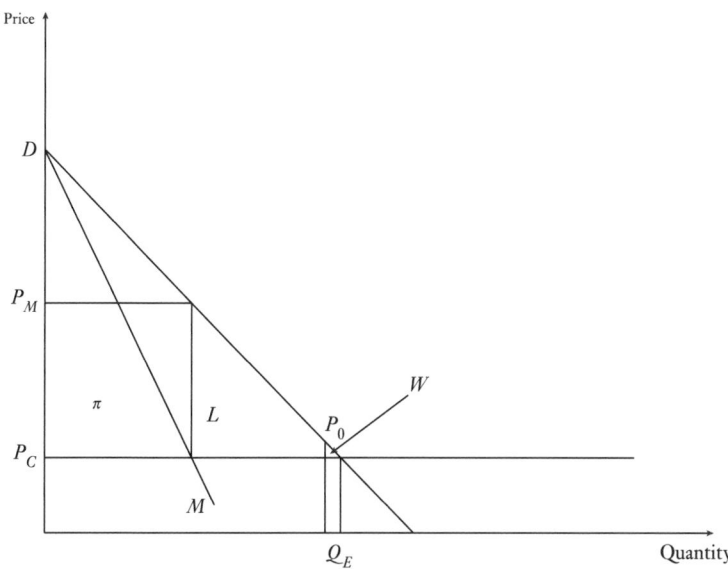

Figure 1 π, Monopoly profit rectangle. L, Deadweight loss assuming firm exercises monopoly power. W, Worcester's proposed deadweight loss.

negative, it can be no surprise that calculations incorporating this assumption indicate insignificant welfare losses. But any estimates of welfare losses within a partial equilibrium framework, which impose demand elasticities significantly below those implied via the Lerner formula, must implicitly be assuming that firms set price in such an environment, if the data on price–cost margins are accepted at face value.

The latter assumption may not be valid, however, and its abandonment allows a reconciliation of existing profit-margin data with lower demand elasticity figures without also introducing the assumption that monopolists are either irrational or impotent. The preceding section discusses several business outlays that are made to maintain or preserve monopoly positions. Conceptually these are best treated as *investments* out of current profits made to secure future monopoly rents than as current production costs as is done for accounting purposes, and is carried through into the economist's calculations based on accounting data. A rational monopolist will not take these into account in making his short-run pricing decision. We can thus reconcile the monopoly pricing assumption with small demand elasticity estimates by assuming that average costs contain much investment-type expenditure and that marginal production costs are below these.

In Fig. 2 let C_0 be observed costs, including investment-type outlays, and P_0 observed price. For such price and cost figures to be consistent with monopoly pricing behaviour the firm's demand schedule would have to be D_0. Price P_0 would be consistent with a much more inelastic demand schedule, D_a say, if actual production costs were at C_a. Note that both profits (π), and the welfare triangle losses (L) are much larger under the more inelastic demand schedule assumption.

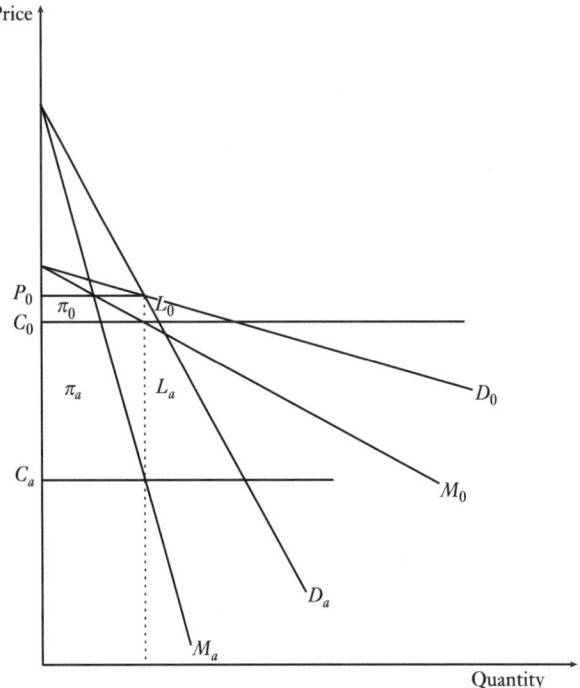

Figure 2

Thus, an alternative procedure for calculating the welfare losses from monopoly to the one described above would be to estimate price–cost margins from data on demand elasticities, where now we estimate demand elasticities from data on price–cost margins. We do not pursue these calculations here. First, because we do not have demand elasticity data applicable to firms, and the imposition of any constant η across all firms is obviously *ad hoc*. Second, the choice of any η in line with existing industry estimates would lead to welfare loss estimates far greater than those calculated here. The highest of the elasticities used in previous studies has been $\eta = 2 \cdot 0$. This implies a profit margin of 50% and a welfare triangle loss equal to one-quarter of sales. These estimates exceed those reported here, whenever the firm's profits are *less* than one-half of sales. Since this is true for all our firms, our welfare loss estimates are all smaller than under the alternative procedure.

We believe that reported costs do contain large amounts of investment-type expenditure beyond the advertising we allow for, that production costs are lower therefore, and that individual firm demand elasticities are typically lower than we implicitly estimate. We emphasise, however, that any attempt to take these costs into account, and adjust demand elasticities accordingly, while maintaining the assumption that companies do possess and exercise market power, will lead to larger estimates of welfare loss underlining again the conservative nature of our calculations.

2. Empirical Estimates

Empirical estimates of the social cost of monopoly power were obtained for both the United States and United Kingdom. We provide two sets of estimates, one based on our assumptions (ΔW_{CM}^k), the other based on Harberger-type assumptions (ΔW_H^k), both measured at the firm-level. For each approach we give a range of four estimates defined in Table 1.

Thus for $k = 1$ we define two alternative estimates of the welfare triangle, the one (ΔW_{CM}^1) based on interdependence of dp_i and dq_i, the other (ΔW_H^1) based on the Harberger methodology. This latter estimate is included for comparison with previous results especially from the viewpoint of bias due to aggregation. For $k = 2$, the same calculations are performed but in calculating dp_i advertising expenditure (A_i) is deducted from cost. For $k = 3$ we add in advertising expenditure as a social cost, and for $k = 4$ we also add in monopoly profits *after tax* as a further element of social cost. It should be noted at this point that in calculating dp_i the appropriate profit measure is *before tax* profit since the price and quantity choice of a monopolist should not be affected by a tax on profits. Thus, in contrast to most previous studies, we use before-tax profits to measure the distortion between price and costs under monopoly (the ΔW's for $k = 1, 2, 3$). However, it is *after-tax* monopoly profits which provide an inducement to additional expenditures to gain monopoly, and it is these that are added in to obtain our fourth measure of welfare loss.

To estimate monopoly profits an estimate of the return on capital of a firm in a competitive industry is needed. Any estimates based on actual returns earned in existing industries run the danger of including monopoly rents. The stock market might be regarded as coming fairly close to satisfying the free-entry and -exit requirement of a competitive industry, however. The returns on corporate stock will include monopoly rents to the extent that they become capitalised over the period for which the rate is estimated. The use of these returns for the United States is therefore equivalent to assuming that (1) all existing monopoly rents are fully capitalised at the beginning of the period, and (2) changes in monopoly rents over the period are accurately anticipated.

For the United States we use as our estimate of the competitive return on capital the Fisher–Lorie index of returns on a fully diversified portfolio of listed stocks for the same period for which our monopoly profit estimates are made (1963–6). This estimate was 12% which might be compared with the average return on capital earned by the firms in our sample of 14%.

For the United Kingdom we use the pre-tax real cost of capital as calculated by Flemming et al. (1976). These estimates avoid the newly capitalised monopoly rent

Table I *Alternative definitions of social cost*

k	ΔW_{CM}^k	ΔW_H^k
1	$\Pi/2$	$(R/2)\,(\Pi/R)^2$
2	$(\Pi + A)/2$	$(R/2)[(\Pi + A)/R]^2$
3	$A + (\Pi + A)/2$	$(R/2)[(\Pi + A)/R]^2 + A$
4	$\Pi' + A + (\Pi + A)/2$	$(R/2)[(\Pi + A)/R]^2 + A + \Pi'$

Π, before tax profit; Π', after tax profit; A, advertising; R, total revenue.

problem mentioned above entirely. For the 1968/9 period they yield an estimate of the cost of capital of 8.15 %.[13]

The firms in our samples include companies operating in both intermediate and final goods markets. To justify the addition of triangular type measures of welfare loss for final and intermediate products, we must assume that the demand schedule for an intermediate product represents a derived demand schedule as in traditional Marshallian analysis. Under this assumption, triangular measures of welfare loss calculated from intermediate product demand schedules fully capture the loss in consumer welfare monopoly distortions in the intermediate markets cause, as Wisecarver (1974) has recently demonstrated. Assuming advertising and other efforts to obtain monopoly power are as wasteful when undertaken in intermediate markets as in final goods markets, the formulae presented in Table I can be applied for both intermediate and final good producers.

2.1. *U.S. estimates*

The range of welfare loss estimates for the United States are presented in Table 2. They refer to the 1963–6 period and the sample comprises the 734 firms on the COMPUSTAT tape with useable information.[14] The firms are ranked according to the size of welfare loss as measured by ΔW_{CM}^4. General Motors leads the list with an annual welfare loss of over $1\frac{3}{4}$ billion, which alone is over $\frac{1}{4}$ of 1% of average GNP during the period, and exceeds Harberger's original welfare loss estimate for the entire economy. Most of the other members of the top 20 are names one also might have expected. One possible exception is AT&T. AT&T's gross profit rate was, in fact, less than our estimate of the cost of capital (≈ 0.12). Its advertising entry on the COMPUSTAT tape (and in this case we did have a COMPUSTAT figure, see appendix) was $\frac{3}{4}$ billion, and it is AT&T's advertising which leads to the high ΔW_{CM} estimate we have for it. Advertising also weighs heavily in the ΔW_{CM}^4 estimates for Unilever, Proctor and Gamble, Sears Roebuck, Genesco, Colgate–Palmolive, Pan Am and Pacific Tel. At first sight this might seem surprising, particularly with respect to regulated firms like AT&T and Pacific Tel. But, as Posner (1975) has argued, this is precisely what one expects to find in industries with high market power, and, as Posner himself stresses, firms under regulatory constraint can be expected to engage, if anything, in more wasteful dissipation of their monopoly rents than non-regulated firms through expenditures like advertising. It is interesting to note in this regard that 6 of the 40 largest welfare losses are accounted for by regulated firms (3 telephone companies and 3 airlines) in which advertising made up all or most of the losses.

At the bottom of Table 2 the losses are summed over the firms with positive profit margins as defined for the ΔW^1 and ΔW^2 measures (see table notes), and then expressed as a proportion of our estimate of the Gross Corporate Product originating in the 734 firms in the sample. It should be stressed here, again, that the totals do not represent the estimated gains from the simultaneous elimination of all monopoly power. The answer to this question could be obtained only via a general equilibrium analysis. What we estimate via our partial equilibrium analysis is the relative cost of monopoly for each firm, and the column totals present average estimates of these costs for our sample of firms. Note, however, that the *additions* to our cost estimates that occur in moving from the W_{CM}^2 to the W_{CM}^3 and W_{CM}^4 columns do sum across all firms, since these are estimates of the wasted expenditures made in pursuit of monopoly. If we see product market power as a ubiquitous characteristic of the

Table 2 *Monopoly welfare losses by firm (yearly averages in $ millions): U.S. 1963/6*

Company	ΔW^1_{CM}	ΔW^2_{CM}	ΔW^3_{CM}	ΔW^4_{CM}	ΔW^1_H	ΔW^2_H	ΔW^3_H	ΔW^4_H
1. General Motors	1,060.5	1,156.3	1,347.8	1,780.3	123.4	146.2	337.8	770.2
2. AT&T	0.0	257.3	1,025.0	1,025.0	0.0	13.4	781.1	781.1
3. Unilever	0.0	160.0	490.5	490.5	0.0	19.5	350.0	350.0
4. Procter & Gamble	56.7	180.1	427.0	427.0	3.3	33.0	279.9	279.2
5. Dupont	225.1	241.9	275.4	375.3	36.3	41.7	75.2	175.2
6. Ford Motor	160.4	217.5	331.7	331.7	5.2	9.3	123.5	123.5
7. IBM	251.7	264.0	288.7	319.8	36.8	40.5	65.2	96.3
8. Reynolds, R. J.	73.1	138.5	269.3	278.8	10.8	38.5	169.3	178.8
9. Sears Roebuck	36.2	115.0	272.5	272.5	0.5	4.4	162.0	162.0
10. Eastman Kodak	136.3	157.9	201.1	258.5	27.7	36.8	80.0	137.4
11. American Cyanamid Co.	27.6	98.7	240.8	240.8	1.9	23.6	165.8	165.8
12. Genesco, Inc.	0.0	67.5	202.6	292.6	0.0	14.9	150.0	150.0
13. Exxon Corp.	115.6	143.0	197.8	197.8	2.4	3.7	58.5	58.5
14. Colgate-Palmolive Co.	3.9	56.7	160.3	160.3	0.0	7.6	111.8	111.8
15. Chrysler Corp.	39.8	78.4	155.5	155.5	1.1	3.0	80.1	80.1
16. General Electric Co.	83.4	105.2	148.8	148.8	2.6	4.0	47.6	47.6
17. Pan Am Airways	1.1	49.8	147.2	147.2	0.1	7.5	104.9	104.9
18. Pacific Tel. & Tel.	0.0	18.4	138.1	138.1	0.0	0.8	128.5	128.5
19. Gillette Co.	27.8	56.0	112.3	129.2	4.7	18.9	75.3	92.2
20. Minnesota Mining & Mfg.	62.5	77.7	107.1	129.1	8.2	12.6	42.3	64.3
Totals all firms[a]	4,527.1	7,454.9	14,005.4	14,997.6[b]	448.2	897.8	7,448.3	8,440.1[b]
Total/GCP[c]	0.0396	0.0652	0.1227	0.13137	0.0040	0.0079	0.0652	0.0739

[a] The ΔW^1's for all firms having monopoly profits (Π) less than zero were set equal to zero. The ΔW^2, ΔW^3, and ΔW^4's for all firms with $(\Pi + A) < 0$ were set equal to zero. The latter was based on the assumption that these firms would not survive in the long run and hence represent no *long-run* welfare loss to society. There are 421 firms with $\Pi > 0$ and 525 firms with $(\Pi + A) > 0$ in the sample of 734 firms.

[b] When profits, after deducting taxes and the cost of capital (Π'), are less than zero, $\Delta W^4 = \Delta W^3$.

[c] The total welfare loss for all firms by each ΔW measure is first divided by the total sales of the 734 firms in the sample, and then multiplied by the ratio of corporate sales to gross corporate product over all industries (2.873) as given in Laffer (1965).

economy, then it might be reasonable to assume that this estimate of monopoly welfare loss could be generalised to the entire economy. To the extent one believes monopoly power is more (e.g. see again Posner, 1975) or less pervasive in other sectors our estimates must be raised or lowered. Assuming the social costs of monopoly are the same across all sectors, we obtain estimates for our preferred model (ΔW_{CM}^k) ranging between 4 and 13% of GCP. Thus, all losses are significant, but the range is considerable depending upon what components of social cost one includes. For the Harberger approach, the range is between 0.4 and 7%. The lowest of these follows the Harberger assumptions most closely, but nevertheless we estimate a welfare loss four times as big as he did. This difference in large part is explained by the aggregation bias incorporated into the industry level estimates.

The extent of this bias can be seen by considering Table 3. Its entries are made by assigning each firm to an industry at the appropriate level of aggregation, and aggregating over the firms in each industry. Just as negative profit firms were excluded in calculating welfare losses at the firm level, negative profit industries are excluded in calculating welfare losses across industries. For the ΔW_{CM}^k measures aggregation bias is due simply to the inclusion of losses by some firms in the calculation of each industry's profits. Table 3 shows how this bias varies with the level of aggregation and with the choice of measure. Industry estimates are between 78 and 98% of the firm level estimates in aggregate. For the ΔW_H^k estimates, a further cause of bias is introduced by the squared term, $(\Pi/R)^2$, in the formula. It can be seen from Table 3 that for the ΔW_H^1 measures, the 2-digit industry estimates aggregate to only 40% of the firm level estimates.[15] Note, however, that the biases are much smaller for the ΔW^3 and ΔW^4 measures and in the case of the ΔW_H^3 measure at the 4-digit level the bias goes slightly the other way. This comes about because of the inclusion in the industry estimates of advertising for firms earning less than normal profits. Thus in future work along these lines, when data are limited to industry level observations, the ΔW^3 and ΔW^4 measures have an additional advantage over the other two measures.

2.2. U.K. estimates

These have been calculated on the same basis as the U.S. estimates, but since no convenient computer tape was available we contended ourselves with an analysis of the top 103 firms in the United Kingdom for the periods 1968/9 and 1970/4.[16] Over the periods in question these firms were responsible for roughly one-third of the GNP and were therefore proportionally more important than the 734 firms sample from the COMPUSTAT tape for the United States. The time-periods used have been dictated by the availability of data. The basic source has been EXTEL cards but advertising expenditure was estimated by aggregating up from the brand level, using estimates of press and TV advertising contained in MEAL. We can therefore expect that our advertising expenditure figures will be biased down by the amount of non-media advertising, as is true also for the United States. Table 4 gives the results for 1968/9, with firms again being ranked by δW_{CM}^4. The two major oil companies, BP and Shell, dominate the table. The social cost associated with BP alone is roughly a quarter of 1% of GNP. The other members of the Top Ten are industry leaders plus British–American Tobacco. Two interesting features ofthe Top Twenty are the high ranking of Rank Xerox despite its size (explained presumably by its U.K. patent rights) and, in contrast to the United States, the low ranking of motor-car manufacturers (absent from the Top Twenty in 1970/4). We have

Table 3 *Comparison of firm and industry welfare loss estimates: U.S. 1963/6*

	ΔW_{CM}^1	ΔW_{CM}^2	ΔW_{CM}^3	ΔW_{CM}^4	ΔW_H^1	ΔW_H^2	ΔW_H^3	ΔW_H^4
(1) Summation over firms	4,527.1	7,454.9	14,005.4	14,997.6	448.2	897.8	7,448.3	8,440.1
(2) Summation over 4 digit industries	3,767.8	6,902.5	13,752.6	14,052.8	276.9	628.8	7,478.9	7,790.2
(3) Summation over 3 digit industries	3,619.0	6,680.5	13,355.4	13,512.8	237.4	577.7	7,252.5	7,410.4
(4) Summation over 2 digit industries	3,515.2	6,634.5	13,262.7	13,287.9	178.9	485.3	7,113.5	7,148.8
(5) (2)/(1)	0.832	0.926	0.982	0.937	0.618	0.700	1.004	0.923
(6) (3)/(1)	0.799	0.896	0.954	0.901	0.530	0.643	0.974	0.878
(7) (4)/(1)	0.776	0.890	0.947	0.886	0.399	0.541	0.955	0.847

Table 4 *Monopoly welfare losses by firm (£ million): U.K. 1968/9*

Company	ΔW_{CM}^1	ΔW_{CM}^2	ΔW_{CM}^3	ΔW_{CM}^4	ΔW_H^1	ΔW_H^2	ΔW_H^3	ΔW_H^4
1. British Petroleum	74.1	74.4	75.1	82.7	5.1	5.1	5.8	13.4
2. Shell Transport & Trading	49.4	50.8	53.6	53.6	2.2	2.3	5.1	5.1
3. British–American Tobacco	26.8	27.0	27.5	49.1	1.0	1.1	1.6	23.1
4. Unilever	2.8	11.3	28.2	29.0	0.0	0.2	17.2	18.0
5. I.C.I.	17.6	18.8	21.1	27.9	0.5	0.5	2.9	9.6
6. Rank Xerox	13.9	14.0	14.2	27.5	3.4	3.4	3.5	16.9
7. I.B.M. (U.K.)	11.1	11.2	11.3	21.9	2.2	2.2	2.4	12.9
8. Great Universal Stores	9.6	10.0	11.0	21.6	0.5	0.5	1.5	12.1
9. Beecham	6.2	8.9	14.3	20.4	0.6	1.3	6.7	12.8
10. Imperial Group	2.8	8.6	20.1	20.1	0.0	0.1	11.7	11.7
11. Marks & Spencer	9.8	9.8	9.8	18.6	0.6	0.6	0.6	9.5
12. Ford	7.2	7.8	8.8	16.6	0.2	0.2	1.3	9.1
13. F. W. Woolworth	7.3	7.4	7.8	15.9	0.3	0.4	0.7	8.9
14. J. Lyon	0.0	0.7	2.8	14.2	0.0	0.0	2.1	13.4
15. Burmah	5.3	5.5	5.9	13.9	0.2	0.3	0.7	8.7
16. Distillers	5.6	6.1	7.1	13.4	0.2	0.2	1.2	7.5
17. Rank Organisation	11.5	11.7	12.1	12.5	1.2	1.2	1.7	2.1
18. Thorn	5.6	6.1	7.1	12.5	0.3	0.3	1.4	6.7
19. Cadbury Schweppes	1.8	5.0	11.4	12.3	0.0	0.3	6.7	7.6
20. Reckitt & Coleman	2.9	4.7	8.3	10.4	0.1	0.3	3.9	6.0
Total all firms (102)	385.8	435.0	537.4	719.3	21.4	24.2	118.8	304.4
Total – GCP	0.0386	0.0436	0.0539	0.0720	0.0021	0.0024	0.0119	0.0305

No. of firms with $\Pi > 0 = 82$.
No. of firms with $\Pi + A > 0 = 86$.

computed estimates of welfare loss for the 1970/4 period, but we have not reported these results here. It is well known that the early seventies was a period of very rapid inflation in the United Kingdom and this undoubtedly raises problems such as how to account for stock appreciation and the revaluation of capital adequately. Despite these problems, it is somewhat reassuring to note that the 1970–4 results look very much like the 1968/9 results except that the oil companies become even more dominant.[17]

The aggregate estimates of welfare loss for ΔW_{CM}^k range between 3.9 and 7.2% of GCP for the 1968/9 period. The estimate for ΔW_{CM}^1 is almost identical with that for the United States but in each of the other cases the value for the United Kingdom is well below that for the United States. The obvious and important difference between the two sets of results is the apparent greater expenditure on advertising in the United States. Taking direct account of advertising quadruples the welfare loss estimate for the United States but in the case of the United Kingdom welfare loss goes up by only about 40% (compare ΔW_{CM}^1 with ΔW_{CM}^3).[18] Using the Harberger approach estimates of welfare loss vary between 0.2 and 3% of GCP for the United Kingdom in the same 1968/9 period.

Again, we must conclude that our evidence suggests significant welfare loss due to monopoly power. One other point is also brought out particularly by the U.K. results (e.g.

in the case of the oil companies) and that is the international distribution of these social costs. Monopoly power held by U.K. companies in foreign markets may be advantageous to the U.K. economy whilst being disadvantageous in the global sense. Thus the issue is a distributional one and adds an international dimension to the distributional issues already implicit in our analysis. In any national evaluation of the social costs imposed by the actions of a particular company, the international distribution of these costs would presumably gain some prominence.

3. Implications and Conclusions

Previous studies of the social costs of monopoly have generally (and often unconsciously) assumed that "monopolies" set prices as if they did not possess market power, that the only important distortions in output are brought about through the deviations in one firm's market power from the average level of market power, that the losses of some firms (perhaps incurred in unsuccessful attempts to obtain monopoly power) legitimately offset the monopoly rents of others, and that all of the expenditures made in the creation and preservation of monopoly positions are part of the normal costs which would exist in a world without monopolies. With the problem so defined, it is not surprising that most of these studies have found the welfare losses from monopoly to be small.

Since we know from general equilibrium analysis that monopoly allocation distortions may be offsetting, the conclusion that partial equilibrium analysis yields small welfare loss estimates has seemed all the more impressive. Yet each of the studies that has come up with low estimates has done so in large part because it has made assumptions (e.g. demand elasticities equal to 1.0, monopoly profits are deviations from mean profits) that can be rationalised only as *ad hoc* attempts to answer the general equilibrium question. In contrast, the present study defines a procedure for estimating the costs of monopoly that is consistent with a partial equilibrium analysis that assumes market power does (or may) exist. Our results reveal that the costs of monopoly power, calculated on an individual firm basis, are on average large. The conclusion that "even" a partial equilibrium analysis of monopoly indicates that its costs are insignificant no longer seems warranted.

This conclusion has potentially important policy implications. Antitrust policy consists typically not of a frontal attack on all existing market power, but of selective assaults on the most flagrant offenders. Our partial equilibrium estimates of monopoly welfare losses indicate the most significant contributors to these losses. The tops of our lists of the largest welfare losses by firm are logical starting points for intensified enforcement of antitrust policy. Our figures and supporting analysis further demonstrate that "the monopoly problem" is broader than traditionally suggested. A large part of this problem lies not in the height of monopoly prices and profits *per se*, but in the resources wasted in their creation and protection. These costs of monopoly should be considered when selecting targets for antitrust enforcement.

One might argue that the high profits of some firms reflect economies of scale advantages, and, therefore, these firms should not be the victims of antitrust policy. This argument points to some form of regulatory or public enterprise solution to the monopoly problem. With respect to this type of policy, our estimates of the losses from monopoly represent a still further understatement of their potential magnitude. If a policy were adopted forcing the most efficient size or organisational structure upon the entire industry, the welfare loss under the existing structure would have to be calculated using the profit margin of the most efficient *firm and the output of the entire industry*, rather than the profit margins of the individual firms and their outputs.

These considerations suggest the difficulty in estimating the social gains from the elimination of all monopoly power, since one almost has to know what form of policy is to be used (antitrust, regulation), and what the underlying cause of monopoly power is, before answering this question. Nevertheless, this has been the question that has traditionally been asked in studies of monopoly welfare losses, and the reader who has persisted to this point can justifiably ask what light our figures cast on this question. By their very nature partial equilibrium calculations cannot give very *precise* estimates of these gains, but they may establish orders of magnitude. As stressed above, we regard the Harberger-type calculations based on uniform demand elasticities of 1.0 as essentially efforts to solve the general equilibrium problem inherent in this question. As such, we regard them as the most conservative estimates of what the elimination of all monopoly would produce. Thus, we would expect the elimination of all monopoly to yield gains at least as large as the 7 and 3% of gross corporate product we estimate for the United States and United Kingdom, respectively, using ΔW_H^4. To the extent that firms sell differentiated products, and operate in separate markets, i.e. to the extent that they have and utilise market power, these gains are pushed in the direction of our ΔW_{CM}^4 estimates of 13 and 7%. Further upward pressure on these estimates is created by considering some of the other factors ignored in our calculations. We have already emphasised that reported profits understate true profits to the extent that firms compete for monopoly power by investing in excess plant capacity, advertising, patent lawyers, and so on. But much of the competition for *control* over monopoly rents may take place within the firm itself among the factor owners. Such competition will lead to an understatement of actual monopoly rents both through the inflation of costs that wasteful competition among factors owners brings about, and through the inclusion of part of the winning factor owners' shares of monopoly rents as reported costs. A large literature now exists on the variety of objectives managers have and the ways in which these objectives are satisfied through their discretionary control over company revenues. To the extent that managerial control over firm revenues is the reward for competing against other factor groups and potential managers successfully, reported profits understate the true profitability. By ignoring these possibilities we have erred in being conservative when estimating the social cost of monopoly. It is our reasoned guess that these additional costs would at least equal the "washing out" effect of the simultaneous elimination of all monopoly power on our partial equilibrium estimates and, therefore, that these latter figures are, if anything, underestimates of the true social costs of monopoly.

In this respect, it is useful to note an alternative, aggregative approach to the question. Phillips, in an appendix to Baran and Sweezy (1966), isolated several categories of expenditure dependent on the existence of "Monopoly Capitalism" (e.g. advertising, corporate profits, lawyers' fees). Their sum came to over 50% of U.S. GNP. Although the assumptions upon which these calculations were made are rather extreme, they do suggest both an alternative method of analysis and the potential magnitude of the problem. Here too it should be noted that our approach has been essentially micro-orientated and neoclassical in that we have taken the returns on corporate stocks as our cost of capital.

From a more aggregative view it could be argued that profits are not required at all to generate the savings required to sustain a given rate of growth, since alternative macro policies are available. From this perspective, all profits are excess profits and our estimates of social cost are too conservative. Still further weight would be added against the position that monopoly power is unimportant if the link with the distribution of political power were considered.

Of course, any public policy has its own sets of costs and inefficiencies. For Tullock–Posner reasons a concerted effort to apply or strengthen the anti-trust laws induces large, defensive expenditures on the part of business. Price and profit regulation leads to efforts to change, influence, or circumvent the application of the rules. The public enterprise solution raises the same sort of problems, with members of the bureaucracy participating in the competition for monopoly rents. Thus it might be that any alternative for dealing with existing monopoly power would involve higher costs than the monopolies themselves create. The present study does not answer this question. What it does do is dispel the notion that it need not even be asked, since the costs of monopoly within the present environment are necessarily small. The question of what the costs and benefits from alternative antimonopoly policies are still seems worth asking.

Notes

1 In addition to the points Bergson (1973) raises in his own defence, we have serious objections to the arguments made by Carson (1975) and Worcester (1975). Some of these are presented below in our critique of previous studies.

2 We need here an assumption of perfect competition everywhere else, of course. We shall ignore problems of the second best, along with the general equilibrium issue more generally, throughout the paper.

3 The Harberger and Schwartzman estimates are at the industry level.

4 This position is questioned by Wenders (1967) and others who attempt to show how implausible the implied η_i's are. However, their calculations are erroneous because they fail to recognise (a) that the degree of collusion is a variable – we need not assume perfect joint profit maximisation and (b) that entry is conditional on the same variables (plus others) that determine $(p_i - mc_i)/p_i$, for example η, the degree of concentration and, for differentiated products, advertising also.

5 This is true so long as the firm is in equilibrium, i.e. that the firms' expectations about the behaviour of rivals are actually borne out. If this were not the case then the elasticity on which the pricing decision was made would not correspond to the elasticity implied by the change in output. We assume firm equilibrium in our calculations.

6 But not necessarily so. Taxes and tariffs may be applied according to elasticity expectations.

7 Worcester (1975) also offers some empirical support. His collection of industry price elasticities is either irrelevant (including many agricultural products and few manufacturing ones) or suspect (no allowance having been made in the studies quoted for quality change over time), and is certainly not comprehensive.

8 Worcester (1973) makes some allowance for this bias by using 90% of the median profit rate, but this adjustment is obviously rather *ad hoc*.

9 One might believe that the losses by firms earning profits below the norm represent a form of *factor surplus loss* which must be added to the consumer surplus loss to obtain the full losses from monopoly. But, as Worcester (1973) has shown, these factor-surplus losses, if properly measured, are *an alternative way* of estimating the consumer surplus losses and should be used *instead of* the consumer surplus measure, rather than in addition to it, if used at all.

10   Harberger chose 5 years of "normal" business activity in the 1920s for his original study of the
      United States. Following his lead we have chosen 4 years in the 1960s for the U.S. estimates
      falling between a recession and the Vietnam War boom. The results reported below for the
      United Kingdom are for only two years, 1968/9. The U.K. results for 1970/4 indicate that
      averaging profits over five years does not change the nature of the outcome.
11   See Spence (1974). It is interesting to note that this type of activity generally dominates the
      entry-limiting pricing response. Entry-limiting pricing can be thought of as having extra
      capacity because of potential entry and actually using it to produce output. Thus the profits
      associated with restricting output are lost. From this viewpoint we cannot accept Posner's
      position that the elimination of entry regulation would eliminate waste. As the probability of
      entry increases so would the optimal degree of excess capacity. Monopoly pricing would be
      maintained but social waste would still occur.
12   There will always be an inherent bias in the information provided given the interests of the
      agent doing the advertising so the argument for advertising as a provider of information should
      not be taken too seriously. Even if we base our welfare measures on post-advertising preferences
      it is still possible to demonstrate that monopolies (and *a fortiori* oligopolies) invest in too much
      advertising (see Dixit and Norman, 1978).
13   It may be argued that because of inflation we are undervaluing land or capital. This should not
      be a serious problem for the United States since our data follow a period of quite modest price
      increases. Given that inflation in the United Kingdom in 1968/9 was substantial, although very
      much less than in the seventies, we have corrected our data at the company level. Using data
      from Walker (1974), we multiplied the profit figure derived from the company accounts by the
      ratio of the average rate of return at replacement cost to the average rate of return at historical
      cost and subtracted from this the estimated book value of assets times the cost of capital. The
      ratio of rates of return used was 9.4: 13.4 in 1968 and 8.2: 12.4 in 1969. We should in fact be
      using the ratio of the rate of return at replacement cost to the rate of return at book value but
      the latter rate was not available on a comparable basis (see Walker, 1974, table 3). This means
      that our measure of excess profits and therefore of welfare loss will tend to be biased down,
      given that (*a*) asset revaluations generally take place at merger, when acquired assets are given a
      current market valuation, and (*b*) revaluations, of land and buildings especially, do take place
      periodically, their frequency being related to the rate of inflation. The cost of capital measure
      used was the forward-looking, pre-tax measure which was estimated at 8.15% for the period
      1968/9 (Flemming et al., 1976).
14   The COMPUSTAT tape contains data on a sample of large firms, mostly in manufacturing, listed
      on U.S. stock exchanges. The data definitions used in making the estimates are discussed in the
      appendix.
15   Worcester (1973) plays down the extent of the bias by focusing on the *absolute* differences between
      the measures. Given that the absolute values of losses are small using ΔW_H^1, even very large relative
      biases result in small absolute distortions, as one would expect. For additional evidence on the
      importance of aggregation bias in previous studies, see Siegfried and Tiemann (1974).
16   The top 100 varies somewhat over time.
17   Indeed, comparing the results for the two periods indicates the large extent to which oil
      companies have benefited from the recent "oil crisis". However, this inference has to be
      qualified by the problems raised for the measurement of profit by stock appreciation during a
      period of rapid inflation of oil prices.
18   This does not of course mean that advertising implies no additional social costs, since profit-
      margins and the level of excess profits may both be partly determined by advertising in so far as
      elasticities of demand and entry barriers are influenced by the level of advertising in mo-
      nopolistic industries. We should also note that in some cases our direct adjustment for
      advertising is very significant (e.g. Unilever, Imperial Group and Beecham Group).

References

Baran, P. and Sweezy, P. (1966): *Monopoly Capital*. New York: Monthly Review Press.

Bergson, A. (1973): "On Monopoly Welfare Losses," *American Economic Review*, 63, December, 853–70.

Carson, R. (1975): "On Monopoly Welfare Losses: Comment," *American Economic Review*, 65, December, 1008–14.

Cubbin, J. (1975): "*Apparent Collusion, Price–Cost Margins and Advertising in Oligopoly*," mimeo, University of Warwick.

Dixit, A. and Norman, V. (1978): "Advertising and Welfare," *Bell Journal of Economics*, June, 1–17.

Flemming, J. S., Price, L. D. D. and Byers, S. A. (1976): "The Cost of Capital, Finance and Investment," *Bank of England Quarterly Bulletin*, 16, June, 193–205.

Harberger, A. C. (1954): "Monopoly and Resource Allocation," *American Economic Review*, 45, May, 77–87.

Kamerschen, D. R. (1966): "An Estimation of the Welfare Losses from Monopoly in the American Economy," *Western Economic Journal*, 4, Summer, 221–36.

Laffer, A. B. (1965): "Vertical Integration by Corporations, 1929–65," *Review of Economics and Statistics*, 51, February, 91–3.

Posner, R. A. (1975): "The Social Costs of Monopoly and Regulation," *Journal of Political Economy* 83, August, 807–27.

Scherer, F. M. (1970): *Industrial Market Structure and Market Performance*. Chicago: Rand McNally.

Schwartzman D. (1960): "The Burden of Monopoly," *Journal of Political Economy*, 68, December, 627–30.

Siegfried, J. J. and Tiemann, T. K. (1974): "The Welfare Cost of Monopoly: An Inter-Industry Analysis," *Economic Inquiry*, 12, June, 190–202.

Spence, M. (1974): "*Entry, Capacity, Investment and Oligopolistic Pricing*," technical report 131, Institute for Mathematical Studies in the Social Sciences, Stanford University.

Stigler, G. J. (1956): "The Statistics of Monopoly and Merger," *Journal of Political Economy*, 64, February, 33–40.

Tullock, G. (1967): "The Welfare Costs of Tariffs, Monopolies and Theft," *Western Economic Journal*, 5, June, 224–32.

Walker, J. L. (1974): "Estimating Companies' Rate of Return on Capital Employed," *Economic Trends*, November, xx–xxix.

Wenders, J. L. (1967): "Entry and Monopoly Pricing," *Journal of Political Economy*, 75, 755–60.

Wisecarver, D. (1974): "The Social Costs of Input-Market Distortions," *American Economic Review*, 64, June, 359–72.

Worcester Jr., D. A. (1969): "Innovations in the Calculations of Welfare Loss to Monopoly," *Western Economic Journal*, 7, September, 234–43.

—— (1973): "New Estimates of the Welfare Loss to Monopoly: U.S. 1956–69," *Southern Economic Journal*, 40, October, 234–46.

—— (1975): "On Monopoly Welfare Losses: Comment," *American Economic Review*, 65, December, 1015–23.

Appendix

Data: Definitions and Sources

United States

All data on individual firms with one exception were taken from the COMPUSTAT tape of 1969, and all definitions conform therefore to those given in the COMPUSTAT manual. The numbers in brackets {} refer to the variable numbers assigned on the COMPUSTAT annual industrial file.

The competitive return on capital used in calculating monopoly profits was 0.1197, the geometric mean of the monthly Fisher–Lorie index of returns on the market portfolio between January 1963 to December 1967. The firm's capital was measured as Total Assets/Liabilities and Net Worth less Intangibles (goodwill, patents, etc.). The latter were deducted on the grounds that they largely represent capitalised monopoly rents (see Stigler, 1956; Kamerschen, 1966). Thus, the firm's opportunity cost of capital was estimated as:

$$CC = 0.1197(DATA \{6\} - DATA \{33\})$$

Two estimates of monopoly profits were formed to compute the triangle-type measures. The first is gross profit flow (net income + interest expense + income taxes) less the cost of capital (*CC*).

$$\Pi = DATA \{18\} + DATA \{15\} + DATA \{16\} - CC$$

The second is the first plus advertising ($A = DATA \{45\}$). For roughly 85% of the sample firms the COMPUSTAT entry for advertising was missing, however. The product of the firm's Sales ($DATA \{12\}$) and the industry advertising to sales ratio for the firm's industry as given in *Advertising Age* (7 June 1965, pp. 101–3) was substituted for this entry in these cases.

To calculate the ΔW^4 measures, income taxes ($DATA \{16\}$) were subtracted from Π to obtain Π'.

United Kingdom

All the data on individual firms with the exception of advertising has its origin in the data tabulations of the Exchange Telegraph Statistics Service (EXTEL). Most of the relevant data in a summarised form was available in various issues of *The Times Review of Industry and Technology*. In the case of advertising the firm data had to be estimated via a process of aggregating estimates of press and TV advertising of the various products produced by each firm. These data were extracted from various issues of *MEAL* (*Advertisers' Annual Analysis of Media Expenditure*) and, in the case of 1968, from the *Statistical Review of Press and T.V. Advertising* (Legion Publishing Company). *Who Owns Whom* was used in the process of aggregation.

Each firm's capital was measured as total tangible assets less current liabilities (excluding bank loans, overdrafts and future tax). Profit was measured before interest and tax and then adjusted for the estimated cost of capital (taken from Flemming et al. 1976).

CHAPTER SEVEN

Rationality and Social Choice

AMARTYA SEN

Source: *American Economic Review*, 85 (1995), pp. 1–24. Reprinted with the permission of the author and the American Economic Association. ©
American Economic Association.

While Aristotle agreed with Agathon that even God could not change the past, he did think that the future was ours to make – by basing our choices on reasoning. The idea of using reason to identify and promote better – or more acceptable – societies, and to eliminate intolerable deprivations of different kinds, has powerfully moved people in the past and continues to do so now. In this lecture I would like to discuss some aspects of this question which have received attention in the recent literature in social-choice and public-choice theories. The contemporary world suffers from many new as well as old economic problems, including, among others, the persistence of poverty and deprivation despite general economic progress, the occurrence of famines and more widespread hunger, and threats to our environment and to the sustainability of the world in which we live. Rational use of the opportunities offered by modern science and technology, in line with our values and ends, is a powerful challenge today.

1. Problems and Difficulties

How are we to view the demands of rationality in social decisions? How much guidance do we get from Aristotle's general recommendation that choice should be governed by "desire and reasoning directed to some end"? There are several deep-seated difficulties here.

The first problem relates to the question: *whose* desires, *whose* ends? Different persons have disparate objects and interests, and as Horace put it, "there are as many preferences as there are people." Kenneth Arrow (1951) has shown, through his famous "General Possibility Theorem" (an oddly optimistic name for what is more commonly – and more revealingly – called Arrow's "impossibility theorem"), that in trying to obtain an integrated social preference from diverse individual preferences, it is not in general possible to satisfy even some mild-looking conditions that would seem to reflect elementary demands of reasonableness.[1] Other impossibility results have also emerged, even without using some of Arrow's conditions, but involving other elementary criteria, such as the priority of individual liberty.[2] We have to discuss why these difficulties arise, and how we can deal with them. Are the pessimistic conclusions that some have drawn from them justified?

Can we sensibly make aggregative social-welfare judgments? Do procedures for social decision making exist that reasonably respect individual values and preferences?

Second, another set of problems relates to questions raised by James Buchanan (1954a, b), which were partly a response to Arrow's results, but they are momentous in their own right.[3] Pointing to "the fundamental philosophical issues" involved in "the idea of social rationality," Buchanan (1954a) argued that "rationality or irrationality as an attribute of the social group implies the imputation to that group of an organic existence apart from that of its individual components" (p. 116). Buchanan was perhaps "the first commentator to interpret Arrow's impossibility theorem as the result of a mistaken attempt to impose the logic of welfare maximization on the procedures of collective choice" (Robert Sugden, 1993 p. 1948). But in addition, he was arguing that there was a deep "confusion surrounding the Arrow analysis" (not just the impossibility theorem but the entire framework used by Arrow and his followers) which ensued from the mistaken idea of "social or collective rationality in terms of producing results indicated by a social ordering" (Buchanan, 1960 pp. 88–9). We certainly have to examine whether Buchanan's critique negates the impossibility results, but we must also investigate the more general issues raised by Buchanan.[4]

Third, Buchanan's reasoned questioning of the idea of "social preference" suggests, at the very least, a need for caution in imposing strong "consistency properties" in social choice, but his emphasis on procedural judgments may be taken to suggest, much more ambitiously, that we should abandon altogether consequence-based evaluation of social happenings, opting instead for a procedural approach. In its pure form, such an approach would look for "right" institutions rather than "good" outcomes and would demand the priority of appropriate procedures (including the acceptance of what follows from these procedures). This approach, which is the polar opposite of the welfare-economic tradition based on classical utilitarianism of founding every decision on an ordering of different states of affairs (treating procedures just as instruments to generate good states), has not been fully endorsed by Buchanan himself, but significant work in that direction has occurred in public choice theory and in other writings influenced by Buchanan's work (most notably, in the important contributions of Robert Sugden [1981, 1986]).

This contrast is particularly important in characterizing rights in general and liberties in particular. In the social choice literature, these characterizations have typically been in terms of states of affairs, concentrating on what happens *vis-à-vis* what the person wanted or chose to do. In contrast, in the libertarian literature, inspired by the pioneering work of Robert Nozick (1974), and in related contributions using "game-form" formulations (most notably, by Wulf Gaertner, Pattanaik, and Suzumura [1992]), rights have been characterized in procedural terms, without referring to states of affairs. We have to examine how deep the differences between the disparate formulations are, and we must also scrutinize their respective adequacies.

Fourth, the prospects of rationality in social decisions must be fundamentally conditional on the nature of *individual* rationality. There are many different conceptions of rational behavior of the individual. There is, for example, the view of rationality as canny maximization of self-interest (the presumption of human beings as "*homo economicus*," used in public choice theory, fits into this framework). Arrow's (1951) formulation is more permissive; it allows social considerations to influence the choices people make. Individual preferences, in this interpretation reflect "values" in general, rather than being based only on what Arrow calls "tastes" (p. 23). How adequate are the respective characterizations of individual rationality, and through the presumption of rational behavior (shared by most economic models), the depiction of actual conduct and choices?

Another issue, related to individual behavior and rationality, concerns the role of social interactions in the development of values, and also the connection between value formation and the decision-making processes. Social choice theory has tended to avoid this issue, following Arrow's own abstinence: "we will also assume in the present study that individual values are taken as data and are not capable of being altered by the nature of the decision process itself" (Arrow, 1951 p. 7).[5] On this subject, Buchanan has taken a more permissive position – indeed emphatically so: "The definition of democracy as 'government by discussion' implies that individual values can and do change in the process of decisionmaking" (Buchanan, 1954a p. 120).[6] We have to scrutinize the importance of this difference as well.

This is a long and somewhat exacting list, but the different issues relate to each other, and I shall try to examine them briefly and also comment on some of their practical implications.

2. Social Welfare Judgments and Arrow's Impossibility Theorem

The subject of welfare economics was dominated for a long time by the utilitarian tradition, which performs interpersonal aggregation through the device of looking at the sum-total of the utilities of all the people involved. By the 1930s, however, economists came to be persuaded by arguments presented by Lionel Robbins (1938) and others (influenced by the philosophy of "logical positivism") that interpersonal comparisons of utility had no scientific basis.[7] Thus, the epistemic foundations of utilitarian welfare economics were seen as incurably defective.

Because of the eschewal of interpersonal comparability of individual utilities, the "new welfare economics" that emerged tried to rely only on one basic criterion of social improvement, the Pareto criterion. Since this confines the recognition of a social improvement only to the case in which everyone's utility goes up (or someone's goes up and no one's goes down), it does not require any interpersonal comparison, nor for that matter, any cardinality of individual utilities. However, Pareto efficiency can scarcely be an adequate condition for a good society. It is quite insensitive to the *distribution* of utilities (including inequalities of happiness and miseries), and it takes no direct note of anything *other than* utilities (such as rights or freedoms) beyond their indirect role in generating utilities. There is a need, certainly, for *further* criteria for social welfare judgments.

The demands of orderly, overall judgments of "social welfare" (or the general goodness of states of affairs) were clarified by Abram Bergson (1938, 1966) and extensively explored by Paul Samuelson (1947). The concentration was on the need for a real-valued function W of "social welfare" defined over all the alternative social states, or at least an aggregate ordering R over them, the so-called "social preference." In the reexamination that followed the Bergson–Samuelson initiative (including the development of social choice theory as a discipline), the search for principles underlying a social welfare function played a prominent part.

Arrow (1951) defined a "social welfare function" as a functional relation that specifies a social ordering R over all the social states for every set of individual preference orderings. In addition to assuming – not especially controversially – that there are at least three distinct social states and at least two (but not infinitely many) individuals, Arrow also wanted a social welfare function to yield a social ordering for every possible combination of individual preferences; that is, it must have a *universal domain*. A second condition is called *the independence of irrelevant alternatives*. This can be defined in different ways, and I shall choose an extremely simple form. The way a society ranks a pair of alternative social states x and y should depend on the individual preferences only over *that* pair – in particular, *not* on how the other ("irrelevant") alternatives are ranked.

Now consider the idea of some people being "decisive": a set G of people – I shall call them a group G – having their way no matter what others prefer. In ranking a pair x and y, if it turns out that x gets socially ranked above y *whenever* everyone in group G prefers x to y (no matter what preferences those not in G have), then G is decisive over that ordered pair (x, y). When a group G is decisive over all ordered pairs, it is simply "decisive."

Arrow required that no individual (formally, no single-member group) should be decisive (*nondictatorship*), but – following the Paretian tradition – also demanded that the group of all individuals taken together should be decisive (the *Pareto principle*). The "impossibility theorem," in this version (presented in Arrow [1963]), shows that it is impossible to have a social welfare function with *universal domain*, satisfying *independence*, the *Pareto principle*, and *nondictatorship*.

The theorem can be proved in three simple steps.[8] The first two steps are the following (with the second lemma drawing on the first).

FIELD-EXPANSION LEMMA: *If a group is decisive over any pair of states, it is decisive.*[9]

GROUP-CONTRACTION LEMMA: *If a group (of more than one person) is decisive, then so is some smaller group contained in it.*[10]

The final step uses the Group-Contraction Lemma to prove the theorem. By the Pareto principle, the group of all individuals is decisive. Since it is finite, by successive partitioning (and each time picking the decisive part), we arrive at a decisive individual, who must, thus, be a dictator. Hence the impossibility.

3. Social Preference, Social Choice, and Impossibility

The preceding discussion makes abundant use of the idea of "social preference." Should it be dropped, as suggested by Buchanan? And if so, what would remain of Arrow's impossibility theorem?

We have to distinguish between two quite different uses of the notion of "social preference," related respectively to

  (i) the operation of *decision mechanisms*, and
  (ii) the making of *social welfare judgments*.

The first notion of "social preference" is something like the "underlying preference" on which *choices* actually made for the society by prevailing mechanisms are implicitly based –

a kind of "revealed preference" of the society.[11] This "derivative" view of social preference would be, formally, a binary representation of the choices emerging from decision
mechanisms.

The second idea of "social preference" – as social welfare judgments – reflects a view of
the social good: some ranking of what would be better or worse for the society. Such
judgments would be typically made by a given person or agency. Here too an aggregation
is involved, since an individual who is making judgments about social welfare, or about the
relative goodness of distinct social states, must somehow combine the diverse interests and
preferences of different people.

Buchanan's objection is quite persuasive for the first interpretation (involving decision
mechanisms), especially since there is no *a priori* presumption that the mechanisms used
must – or even *should* – necessarily lead to choices that satisfy the requirements of binary
representation (not to mention the more exacting demands of an ordering representation).[12] On the other hand, the second interpretation does not involve this problem, and
even an individual when expressing a view about social welfare needs a concept of this
kind.[13] When applied to the making of social welfare judgments by an individual or an
agency, Arrow's impossibility theorem thus cannot be disputed on the ground that some
organic existence is being imputed to the society. The amelioration of impossibility must
be sought elsewhere (see Section 4). However, Buchanan's critique of Arrow's theorem
would apply to *mechanisms* of social decision (such as voting procedures).

Would the dropping of the requirement that social choices be based on a binary relation
– in particular a transitive ordering – negate the result in the case of social decision
mechanisms? A large literature has already established that the arbitrariness of power, of
which Arrow's case of dictatorship is an extreme example, lingers in one form or another
even when transitivity is dropped, so long as *some* regularity is demanded (such as the
absence of cycles).[14] There is, however, cause for going further, precisely for the reasons
identified by Buchanan, and to eschew not just the transitivity of social preference, but the
idea of social preference itself. All that is needed from the point of view of choice is that
the decision mechanisms determine a "choice function" for the society, which identifies
what is picked from each alternative "menu" (or opportunity set).[15]

However, provided some conditions are imposed on the "internal consistency" of the
choice function (relating decisions over one menu in a "consistent" way to decisions over
other – related – menus), it can be shown that some arbitrariness of power would still
survive.[16] But the methodological critique of James Buchanan would still apply forcefully,
as reformulated in the following way: why should *any* restriction whatever be placed *a
priori* on the choice function for the society? Why should not the decisions emerging from
agreed social mechanisms be acceptable without having to check them against some
preconceived idea of how choices made in different situations should relate to each other?

What happens, then, to Arrow's impossibility problem if no restrictions whatever are
placed on the so-called "internal consistency" of the choice function for the society?
Would the conditions relating individual preferences to social choice (i.e., the Pareto
principle, nondictatorship, and independence) then be consistent with each other? The
answer, in fact, is no, not so. If the Pareto principle and the conditions of nondictatorship
and independence are redefined to take full note of the fact that they must relate to social
choices, not to any prior notion of social *preference*, then a very similar impossibility
reemerges (see Theorem 3 in Sen [1993]).

How does this "general choice-functional impossibility theorem" work? The underlying intuition is this. Each of the conditions relating individual preferences to social decisions eliminates – either on its own or in the presence of the other conditions – the possibility of choosing *some* alternatives. And the conjunction of these conditions can lead to an empty choice set, making it "impossible" to choose anything.

For example, the Pareto principle is just such a condition, and the object of this condition in a choice context, surely, is to avoid the selection of a Pareto-inferior alternative. Therefore this condition can be sensibly redefined to demand that if everyone prefers x to y, then the social decision mechanism should be such that y should not get chosen if x is available.[17] Indeed, to eliminate any possibility that we are implicitly or indirectly using any intermenu consistency condition for social choice, we can define all the conditions for only *one given menu* (or opportunity set) S; that is, we can consider the choice problem exclusively over a given set of alternative states. The Pareto principle for that set S then only demands that if everyone prefers some x to some y in that set, then y must not be chosen from that set.

Similarly, nondictatorship would demand that there be no person such that whenever she prefers any x to any y in that set S, then y cannot be chosen from that set. What about independence? We have to modify the idea of decisiveness of a group in this choice context, related to choices over this given set S. A group would be decisive for x against y if and only if, whenever all members of this group prefer any x to any y in this set S, then y is not to be chosen from S. Independence would now demand that any group's power of decisiveness over a pair (x, y) be completely independent of individual preferences over pairs other than (x, y). It can be shown that there is no way of going from individual preferences to social choice satisfying these choice-oriented conditions of independence, the Pareto principle, nondictatorship, and unrestricted domain, even without invoking any "social preference," and without imposing any demand of "collective rationality," or any intermenu consistency condition on social choice.[18]

The morals to be drawn from all this for Buchanan's questioning of "social preference" would appear to be the following. The "impossibility" result identified in a particular form by Arrow can be extended and shown to hold even when the idea of "social preference" is totally dropped and even when no conditions are imposed on "internal consistency" of social choice. This does not, however, annul the importance of Buchanan's criticism of the idea of social preference (in the context of choices emerging from *decision mechanisms* for the society), since it is a valid criticism in its own right. But the "impossibility" problem identified by Arrow cannot be escaped by this move.

4. On Reasoned Social Welfare Judgments

How might we then avoid that impossibility? It is important to distinguish the bearing of the problem in the making of aggregative social welfare judgments, as opposed to the operation of social decision mechanisms. I start with the former.

It may be recalled that the Bergson–Samuelson analysis and Arrow's impossibility theorem followed a turn in welfare economics that had involved the dropping of interpersonal comparisons of utility. As it happens, because of its utilitarian form, traditional welfare economics had informational exclusions of its own, and it had been opposed to any basic use of nonutility information, since everything had to be judged ultimately by utility sum-totals in consequent states of affairs. To this was now added the exclusion of interpersonal comparisons of utilities, without removing the exclusion of nonutility information. This barren informational landscape makes it hard to arrive at systematic judgments of social welfare. Arrow's theorem can be interpreted, in this context, as a demonstration that even some very weak conditions relating individual preferences to social welfare judgments cannot be simultaneously satisfied given this informational privation.[19]

The problem is not just one of impossibility. Consider the Field-Expansion Lemma: decisiveness over *any* pair of alternatives entails decisiveness over *every* pair of alternatives, *irrespective of the nature of the states involved*. Consider three divisions of a given cake between two persons: (99, 1), (50, 50), and (1, 99). Let us begin with the assumption that each person – as *homo economicus* – prefers a larger personal share of the cake. So they happen to have opposite preferences. Consider now the ranking of (99, 1) and (50, 50). If it is decided that (50, 50) is better for the society than (99, 1), then in terms of preference-based information, person 2's preference is getting priority over person 1's.

A variant of the Field-Expansion Lemma would then claim that person 2's preference must get priority over all other pairs as well, so that even (1, 99) must be preferred to (50, 50).[20] Indeed, it is not possible, given the assumptions, to regard (50, 50) as best of the three; we could either have (99, 1), giving priority to person 1's preference, or (1, 99), giving priority to 2's preference. But *not* (50, 50). I am not arguing here that (50, 50) must necessarily be taken to be the best, but it is absurd that we are not even permitted to consider (50, 50) as a claimant to being the best element in this cake-division problem.

It is useful to consider what arguments there might be for considering (50, 50) as a good possibility, and why we cannot use any of these arguments in the information framework resulting from Arrow's conditions. First, it might seem good to divide the cake equally on some general *non-welfarist* ground, without even going into preferences or utilities. This is not permitted because of the exclusion of evaluative use of nonutility information, and this is what the Field-Expansion Lemma is formalizing. Second, presuming that everyone has the same strictly concave utility function, we might think that the sum-total of utilities would be maximized by an equal division of the cake. But this utilitarian argument involves comparability of cardinal utilities, which is ruled out. Third, we might think that equal division of the cake will equate utilities, and there are arguments for utility-centered egalitarianism (see James Meade, 1976). But that involves interpersonal comparison of ordinal utilities, which too is ruled out. None of the standard ways of discriminating between the alternative states is viable in this informational framework, and the only way to choose between them is to go by the preference of one person or another (since they have opposite preferences).

To try to make social welfare judgments *without* using any interpersonal comparison of utilities, and *without* using any nonutility information, is not a fruitful enterprise. We do care about the size and distribution of the overall achievements; we have reasons to want to reduce deprivation, poverty, and inequality; and all these call for interpersonal comparisons – either of utilities or of other indicators of individual advantages, such as real incomes, opportunities, primary goods, or capabilities.[21] Once interpersonal comparisons are introduced, the impossibility problem, in the appropriately redefined framework, vanishes.[22] The comparisons may have to be rough and ready and often open to disputation, but such comparisons are staple elements of systematic social welfare judgments. Even without any cardinality, ordinal interpersonal comparisons permit the use of such rules of social judgment as maximin, or lexicographic maximin.[23] This satisfies all of Arrow's conditions (and many others), though the class of permissible social welfare rules that do this is quite limited, unless cardinality is also admitted, along with interpersonal comparisons (see Louis Gevers, 1979; Kevin Roberts, 1980a). With the possibility of using interpersonal comparisons, other classes of possible rules for social welfare judgments (including *inter alia*, utilitarianism) become usable.[24]

While the axiomatic derivations of different social welfare rules in this literature are based on applying interpersonal comparisons to utilities only, the analytical problems are, in many respects, rather similar when people are compared in terms of some other feature, such as real income, holdings of primary goods, or capabilities to function. There are, thus, whole varieties of ways in which social welfare judgments can be made using richer information than in the Arrow framework.

This applies also to *procedures* specifically aimed at making social welfare judgments and other aggregative evaluations, based on institutionally accepted ways of making interpersonal comparisons: for example, in using indexes of income inequality (see Serge Kolm's [1969] and Anthony Atkinson's [1970] pioneering work on this), or in aggregate measures of distribution-corrected real national income (Sen, 1976a), or of aggregate poverty (Sen, 1976b).[25] This links the theory of social choice to some of the most intensely practical debates on economic policy.[26] While Arrow's impossibility theorem is a negative result, the challenge it provided has led, dialectically, to a great many constructive developments.

5. On Social Decision Mechanisms

Moving from the exercise of making social judgments to that of choosing social decision mechanisms, there are other difficulties to be faced. While systematic interpersonal comparisons of utilities (and other ways of seeing individual advantage) can be used by a person making a social welfare judgment, or in agreed *procedures* for social judgments (based on interpreting available statistics to arrive at, say, orderings of aggregate poverty or inequality or distribution-corrected real national income), this is not an easy thing to do in social decision mechanisms which must rely on some standard expressions of individual preference (such as voting), which do not readily lend themselves to interpersonal comparisons.

The impossibility problem, thus, has greater resilience here. While it is also the case that the critique of James Buchanan (and others) of the idea of "social rationality" and the concept of "social preference" applies particularly in this case (that of judging social *decision mechanisms*), the impossibility problem does indeed survive, as we have seen, even when the concept of social preference is eschewed and the idea of social rationality in the Arrovian form is dropped altogether (Section 3). How, then, can we respond to the challenge in this case?

We may begin by noting that the conditions formulated and used by Arrow, while appealing enough, are not beyond criticism. First, not every conceivable combination of individual preferences need be considered in devising a social decision procedure, since only some would come up in practice. As Arrow had himself noted, if the condition of unrestricted domain is relaxed, we can find decision rules that satisfy all the other conditions (and many other demands) over substantial domains of individual preference profiles. Arrow (1951), along with Duncan Black, had particularly explored the case of "single-peaked preferences," but it can be shown (Sen, 1966) that this condition can be far extended and generalized to a much less demanding restriction called "value restriction."[27]

The plausibility of different profiles of individual preferences depends on the nature of the problem and on the characteristics of individual motivations. It is readily checked that with three or more people, if everyone acts as *homo economicus* in a cake-division problem (always preferring more cake to oneself over all else), then value restriction and the related conditions would all be violated, and majority rule would standardly lead to intransitivities. It is also easy to show that in the commodity space, with each concentrating on her own commodity basket, the Arrow conditions could not be all satisfied by any decision mechanism over that domain. Majority rule and other voting procedures of this kind do cause cycles in general in what is called "the economic domain" (of interpersonal commodity space), if everyone votes in a narrowly self-interested way.

However, majority rule would be a terrible decision procedure in this case, and its intransitivity is hardly the main problem here. For example, taking the most deprived person in a community and passing on half her share of the cake divided between two richer persons would be a majority improvement, but scarcely a great welfare-economic triumph. In view of this, it is perhaps just as well that the majority rule is not only nasty and brutish, but also short in consistency.[28] The tension between social welfare judgments (of different kinds explored, for example, by Meade [1976], Arrow [1977], Mirrlees [1982], William J. Baumol [1986], or John Broome [1991]) and mechanical decision rules (like majority decision) with inward-looking, self-centered individuals is most obvious here. Also, as Buchanan (1994a, b) has argued, the acceptability of majority rule is, in fact, related to its tendency to generate cycles, and the endemic cyclicity of majority decisions is inescapable, given the endogeneity of alternative proposals that can be presented for consideration.

In practice, in facing political decisions, the choices may not come in these stark forms (there are many issues that are mixed together in political programs and proposals), and also individuals do not necessarily only look at their "own share of the cake" in taking up political positions and attitudes.[29] The "public choice" school has tended to emphasize the role of logrolling in political compromises and social decisions. While that school has also been rather wedded to the presumption of each person being *homo economicus* even in these exercises (see Buchanan and Tullock, 1962), there is a more general social process here (involving a variety of motivations) that can be fruitfully considered in examining decision mechanisms. Central to this is the role of public discussion in the formation of preferences and values, which has been emphasized by Buchanan (1954a, b).

The condition of independence of irrelevant alternatives is also not beyond disputation and, indeed, has led to debates – explicitly or by implication – for a very long time. It was one of the issues that divided J. C. Borda (1781) and Marquis de Condorcet (1785), the two French mathematicians, who had pioneered the systematic theory of voting and group decision procedures in the 18th century. One version of the rule proposed by Borda, based on adding the rank-order numbers of candidates in each voter's preference list, violates the independence condition rather robustly, but it is not devoid of other merits (and is frequently used in practice).[30] Other types of voting rules have also been shown to have different desirable properties.[31]

In examining social decision mechanisms, we have to take the Arrow conditions seriously, but not as inescapable commandments. Our intuitions vary on these matters, and Arrow's own theorem shows that not everything that appeals to us initially would really be simultaneously sustainable. There is a need for some de-escalation in the grim "fight for basic principles." The issue is not the likely absence of rationally defendable procedures for social decisions, but the relative importance of disparate considerations that pull us in different directions in evaluating diverse procedures. We are not at the edge of a precipice, trying to determine whether it is at all "possible" for us to hang on.

6. Procedures and Consequences

I turn now to the general issue, identified earlier, of the contrast between relying respectively on

   (i) the "rightness" of procedures, and
   (ii) the "goodness" of outcomes.

Social choice theory, in its traditional form, would seem to belong to the latter part of the dichotomy, with the states of affairs judged first (the subject matter of "social preference" or "social welfare judgements"), followed by identification of procedures that generate the "best" or "maximal" or "satisficing" states. There are two issues here. First, can consequences really be judged adequately without any notion of the process through which they are brought about? I shall also presently question whether this presumption of *process-independence* is the right way of seeing the claims of social choice theory. Second, can we do the converse of this, and judge procedures adequately in a *consequence-independent* way? This issue I take up first.

Sugden (1981, 1986), who has extensively analyzed this dichotomy (between procedural and consequence-based views), explains that in the public choice approach, which he supports, "the primary role of the government is not to maximize the social good, but rather to maintain a framework of rules within which individuals are left free to pursue their own ends" (Sugden, 1993 p. 1948). This is indeed so, but even in judging a "framework of rules" in this way, we do need some consequential analysis, dealing with the *effectiveness* of these frameworks in letting individuals be *actually* "free to pursue their own ends." In an interdependent world, examples of permissive rules that fail to generate the freedom to pursue the respective individual ends are not hard to find (see Sen, 1982b).

Indeed, it is not easy to believe that the public-choice approach is – or can be – really consequence-independent. For example, Buchanan's support of market systems is based on a reading of the consequences that the market mechanism tends to produce, and consequences certainly do enter substantially in Buchanan's evaluation of procedures: "To the extent that voluntary exchange among persons is valued positively while coercion is valued negatively, there emerges the implication that substitution of the former for the latter is desired, on the presumption, of course, that such substitution is technologically feasible and is not prohibitively costly in resources" (Buchanan, 1986, p. 22). While this is not in serious conflict with Buchanan's rejection of any "transcendental" evaluation of the outcomes (p. 22), nevertheless the assessment of outcomes must, in *some* form, enter this evaluative exercise.[32]

There are, however, other – more purely procedural – systems to be found in this literature. If the utilitarian tradition of judging everything by the consequent utilities is one extreme in the contrast (focusing only on a limited class of consequences), Nozick's (1974) elegant exploration of libertarian "entitlement theory" comes close to the other end (focusing on the right rules that cover personal liberties as well as rights of holding, using, exchanging, and bequeathing legitimately owned property). But the possibility of having unacceptable consequences has to be addressed by any such procedural system. What if the results are dreadful for many, or even all?

Indeed, it can be shown that even gigantic famines can actually take place in an economy that fulfills all the libertarian rights and entitlements specified in the Nozick system.[33] It is, thus, particularly appropriate that Nozick (1974) makes exceptions to consequence-independence in cases where the exercise of these rights would lead to "catastrophic moral horrors."[34] Because of this qualification, consequences are made to matter after all, and underlying this concession is Nozick's good sense (similar to Buchanan's) that a procedural system of entitlements that happens to yield catastrophic moral horrors (we have to have some consensus on what these are) would be – and should be – ethically unacceptable. However, once consequences are brought into the story, not only is the purity of a consequence-independent system lost, but also the issue of deciding on the relative importance of "right rules" and "good consequences" is forcefully reestablished.

I turn now to the other side of the dichotomy: can we have sensible outcome judgments in a totally procedure-independent way? Classical utilitarianism does indeed propose such a system, but it is hard to be convinced that we can plausibly judge any given utility distribution ignoring *altogether* the process that led to that distribution (attaching, for example, no intrinsic importance whatever to whether a particular utility redistribution is caused by charity, or taxation, or torture).[35]

This recognition of the role of processes is not, in fact, hostile to social choice theory, since there is nothing to prevent us from seeing the description of processes as a part of the consequent states generated by them.[36] If action A is performed, then "action A has been done" must be one – indeed, the most elementary – consequence of that event. If Mr. John Major were to wish not merely that he should be reelected as Prime Minister, but that he should be "reelected fairly" (I am not, of course, insinuating that any such preference has been expressed by Mr. Major), the consequence that he would be seeking would have procedural requirements incorporated within it.

This is not to claim that every process can be comfortably placed within the description of states of affairs without changing anything in social choice theory. Parts of the literature that deal with comparisons of decision mechanisms in arriving at *given* states would need modification. If, in general, processes leading to the emergence of a social state were standardly included in the characterization of that state, then we have to construct "equivalence classes" to *ignore* some differences (in this case, between some antecedent processes) to be able to discuss cogently the "same state" being brought about by different decision mechanisms. To make sense of such ideas as, say, "path independence" (on which see Plott [1973]), so that they are not rendered vacuous, equivalence classes of this type would certainly have to be constructed (on the concepts of equivalence classes and invariance conditions, see Sen [1986b]).

The contrast between the procedural and consequential approaches is, thus, somewhat overdrawn, and it may be possible to combine them, to a considerable extent, in an adequately rich characterization of states of affairs. The dichotomy is far from pure, and it is mainly a question of relative concentration.

7. Liberties, Rights, and Preferences

The need to integrate procedural considerations in consequential analysis is especially important in the field of rights and liberties. The violation or fulfillment of basic liberties or rights tends to be ignored in traditional utilitarian welfare economics not just because of its consequentialist focus, but particularly because of its "welfarism," whereby consequent states of affairs are judged exclusively by the utilities generated in the respective states.[37] While processes may end up getting some *indirect* attention insofar as they influence people's utilities, nevertheless no direct and basic importance is attached in the utililtarian framework to rights and liberties in the evaluation of states of affairs.

The initial formulation of social choice did not depart in this respect from the utilitarian heritage, but it is possible to change this within a broadly Arrovian framework (see Sen, 1970, 1982a), and a good deal of work has been done in later social choice theory to accommodate the basic relevance of rights and liberties in assessing states of affairs, and thus to evaluate economic, political, and social arrangements. If a person is prevented from doing some preferred thing even though that choice is sensibly seen to be in her "personal domain," then the state of affairs can be seen to have been worsened by this failure. The extent of worsening is not to be judged only by the magnitude of the utility loss resulting from this (to be compared with utility gains of others, if any), since something more is also at stake. As John Stuart Mill (1859 p. 140) noted, "there is no parity between the feeling of a person for his own opinion, and the feeling of another who is offended at his holding it."[38] The need to guarantee some "minimal liberties" on a priority basis can be incorporated in social choice formulations.

It turns out, however, that such unconditional priority being given even to minimal liberty can conflict with other principles of social choice, including the redoubtable Pareto principle. The "impossibility of the Paretian liberal" captures the conflict between

  (i) the special importance of a person's preferences over her own personal sphere, and
 (ii) the general importance of people's preferences over any choice, irrespective of field.

This impossibility theorem has led to a large literature extending, explaining, disputing, and ameliorating the result.[39] The "ways out" that have been sought have varied between

  (i) weakening the priority of liberties (thereby qualifying the minimal liberty condition),
 (ii) constraining the field-independent general force of preferences (thereby qualifying the Pareto principle), and
(iii) restricting the domain of permissible individual-preference profiles.

As in the case of the Arrow impossibility problem, the different ways of resolving this conflict have variable relevance depending on the exact nature of the social choice exercise involved.

There have also been attempts to redefine liberty in purely *procedural* terms. The last is an important subject on its own (quite independently of any use it might have as an attempt to resolve the impossibility), and I shall presently consider it. But as has been noted by Gaertner, Pattanaik, and Suzumura (1992), who have recently provided the most extensive recharacterization of liberty (in terms of "game forms"), the impossibility problem "persists under virtually every plausible concept of individual rights" (p. 161).[40]

The decisive move in the direction of a purely procedural view of liberty was made by Nozick (1974), responding to my social choice formulation and to the impossibility of the Paretian liberal (Sen, 1970). This has been followed by important constructive contributions by Gärdenfors (1981) and Sugden (1981), and the approach has been extended and developed into game-form formulations by Gaertner et al. (1992). In the game-form view, each of the players has a set of permissible strategies, and the outcome is a function of the combination of strategies chosen by each of the players (perhaps qualified by an additional "move" by "nature"). The liberties and rights of the different persons are defined by specifying a permissible subset from the product of the strategy sets of the different individuals. A person can exercise his rights as he likes, subject to the strategy combination belonging to the permissible set.

In defining what rights a person has, or in checking whether his rights were respected, there is, on this account, no need to examine or evaluate the resulting state of affairs, and no necessity to examine what states the individuals involved prefer. In contrasting this characterization of preference-independent, consequence-detached rights with the social choice approach to rights, perhaps the central question that is raised is the plausibility of making people's putative rights, in general, so dissociated from the effects of exercising them. This is a general issue that was already discussed at a broader level (Section 6).

In some contexts, the idea of seeing rights in the form of permission to act can be quite inadequate, particularly because of "choice inhibition" that might arise from a variety of causes. The long British discussion on the failure of millions of potential welfare recipients from making legitimate claims (apparently due to the shame and stigma of having one's penury publicized and recorded) illustrates a kind of nonrealization of rights in which permission is not the main issue at all.[41] Similarly, the inability of women in traditionally sexist societies to use even those rights that have not been formally denied to them also illustrates a type of rights failure that is not helpfully seen in terms of game forms (see Sen, 1992b pp. 148–50). Even the questions that standardly come up in this country in determining whether a rape has occurred have to go well beyond checking whether the victim in question was "free" to defy.

Leaving out such cases, it might well be plausible to argue that rights can be nicely characterized by game forms in many situations. However, even when that is the case, in deciding on what rights to protect and codify, and in determining how the underlying purpose might be most effectively achieved, there is a need to look at the likely consequences of different game-form specifications and to relate them to what people value and desire. If, for example, it appears that not banning smoking in certain gatherings (leaving the matter to the discretion of the people involved) would actually lead to unwilling victims having to inhale other people's smoke, then there would be a case for considering that the game-form be so modified that smoking is simply banned in those gatherings. Whether or not to make this move must depend crucially on consequential analysis. The object, in this case, is the prevention of the state of affairs in which nonsmokers have to inhale unwillingly other people's smoke: a situation they resent and which – it is assumed – they have a right to avoid. We proceed from there, through consequential analysis (in an "inverse" form: from consequences to antecedents), to the particular game-form formulation that would not achieve an acceptable result. The fact that the *articulation* of the game-form would be consequence-independent and preference-independent is not a terribly profound assertion and is quite consistent with the fundamental relevance of consequences and preferences.

The contrast between game-form formulations and social-choice conceptions of rights is, thus, less deep than it might first appear (see Sen, 1992b).[42] As in other fields considered earlier (Section 6), in this area too, the need to combine procedural concerns with those of actual events and outcomes is quite strong.

8. Values and Individual Choices

I have so far postponed discussing individual behavior and rationality, though the issue has indirectly figured in the preceding discussions (for example, in dealing with norms for social choice, individual interest in social welfare judgments, and determination of voting behavior). The public choice tradition has tended to rely a good deal on the presumption that people behave in a rather narrowly self-centered way – as *homo economicus* in particular, even though Buchanan (1986, p. 26) himself notes some "tension" on this issue (see also Geoffrey Brennan and Loren Lomasky, 1993). Public servants *inter alia* are to be seen as working for their own well-being and success.

Adam Smith is sometimes described as the original proponent of the ubiquity and ethical adequacy of "the economic man," but that would be fairly sloppy history. In fact, Smith (1776, 1790) had examined the distinct disciplines of "self-love," "prudence," "sympathy," "generosity," and "public spirit," among others, and had discussed not only their intrinsic importance, but also their instrumental roles in the success of a society, and also their practical influence on actual behavior. The demands of rationality need not be geared entirely to the use of only one of these motivations (such as self-love), and there is plenty of empirical evidence to indicate that the presumption of uncompromising pursuit of narrowly defined self-interest is as mistaken today as it was in Smith's time.[43] Just as it is necessary to avoid the high-minded sentimentalism of assuming that all human beings (and public servants, in particular) try constantly to promote some selfless "social good," it is also important to escape what may be called the "low-minded sentimentalism" of assuming that everyone is constantly motivated entirely by personal self-interest.[44]

This does not, however, negate an important implication of the question raised by Buchanan and others that public servants would tend to have their own objective functions; I would dissociate that point from the further claim, with which it has come mixed, that these objective functions are narrowly confined to the officials' own self-interest. The important issue to emerge is that there is something missing in a large part of the resource-allocation literature (for example, in proposals of algorithms for decentralized resource allocation, from Oscar Lange and Abba Lerner onward) which make do without any independent objective function of the agents of public action. The additional assumption of *homo economicus* is not needed to point to this general lacuna.

While this has been a somewhat neglected question in social choice theory (though partially dealt with in the related literature on implementation), there is no particular reason why such plurality of motivations cannot be accommodated within a social choice framework with more richly described social states and more articulated characterization of individual choices and behavior. In the formulation of individual preference used by Arrow (1951) and in traditional social choice theory, the nature of the objective function of each individual is left unspecified. While there is need for supplementary work here, this is a helpfully permissive framework – not tied either to ceaseless do–gooding, or to uncompromising self-centeredness.

Even with this extended framework, taking us well beyond the *homo economicus*, there remain some difficulties with the notion of individual rationality used here. There is a problem of "insufficiency" shared by this approach to rationality with other "instrumental" approaches to rationality, since it does not have any condition of critical scrutiny of the objectives themselves. Socrates might have overstated matters a bit when he proclaimed that "the unexamined life is not worth living," but an examination of what kind of life one should sensibly choose cannot really be completely irrelevant to rational choice.[45] An "instrumental rationalist" is a decision expert whose response to seeing a man engaged in slicing his toes with a blunt knife is to rush to advise him that he should use a sharper knife to better serve his evident objective.

This is perhaps more of a limitation in the normative context than in using the presumption of rationality as a device for predicting behavior, since such critical scrutiny might not be very widely practiced. However, the last is not altogether clear, since discussions and exchange, and even political arguments, contribute to the formation and revision of values. As Frank Knight (1947, p. 280) noted, "Values are established or validated and recognized through *discussion*, an activity which is at once social, intellectual, and creative." There is, in fact, much force in Buchanan's (1954a, p. 120) assertion that this is a central component of democracy ("government by discussion") and that "individual values can and do change in the process of decision making."

This issue has some real practical importance. To illustrate, in studying the fact that famines occur in some countries but not in others, I have tried to point to the phenomenon that no major famine has ever taken place in any country with a multiparty democracy with regular elections and with a reasonably free press (Sen, 1984).[46] This applies as much to the poorer democratic countries (such as India, Zimbabwe, or Botswana) as to the richer ones.[47] This is largely because famines, while killing millions, do not much affect the direct well-being of the ruling classes and dictators, who have little political incentive to prevent famines unless their rule is threatened by them. The economic analysis of famines across the world indicates that only a small proportion of the population tends to be stricken – rarely more than 5 percent or so. Since the shares of income and food of these poor groups tend normally to be no more than 3 percent of the total for the nation, it is not hard to rebuild their lost share of income and food, even in very poor countries, if a serious effort is made in that direction (see Sen, 1981; Drèze and Sen, 1989). Famines are thus easily preventable, and the need to face public criticism and to encounter the electorate provides the government with the political incentive to take preventive action with some urgency.

The question that remains is this. Since only a very small proportion of the population is struck by a famine (typically 5 percent or less), how does it become such a potent force in elections and in public criticism? This is in some tension with the assumption of universal self-centeredness, and presumably we do have the capacity – and often the inclination – to understand and respond to the predicament of others.[48] There is a particular need in this context to examine value formation that results from public discussion of miserable events, in generating sympathy and commitment on the part of citizens to do something to prevent their occurrence.

Even the idea of "basic needs," fruitfully used in the development literature, has to be related to the fact that what is taken as a "need" is not determined only by biological and uninfluencible factors. For example, in those parts of the so-called Third World in which there has been increased and extensive public discussion of the consequences of frequent childbearing on the well-being and freedom of mothers, the perception that a smaller family is a "basic need" of women (and men too) has grown, and in this value formation a combination of democracy, free public media, and basic education (especially female education) has been very potent. The implications of this finding are particularly important for rational consideration of the so-called "world population problem."[49]

Similar issues arise in dealing with environmental problems. The threats that we face call for organized international action as well as changes in national policies, particularly for better reflecting social costs in prices and incentives. But they are also dependent on value formation, related to public discussions, both for their influence on individual behavior and for bringing about policy changes through the political process. There are plenty of "social choice problems" in all this, but in analyzing them, we have to go beyond looking only for the best reflection of *given* individual preferences, or the most acceptable procedures for choices based on those preferences. We need to depart both from the assumption of given preferences (as in traditional social choice theory) and from the presumption that people are narrowly self-interested *homo economicus* (as in traditional public choice theory).

9. Concluding Remarks

Perhaps I could end by briefly returning to the questions with which I began. Arrow's impossibility theorem does indeed identify a profound difficulty in combining individual preference orderings into aggregative social welfare judgements (Section 2). But the result must not be seen as mainly a negative one, since it directly leads on to questions about how to overcome these problems. In the context of social welfare judgments, the natural resolution of these problems lies in enriching the informational base, and there are several distinct ways of doing this (Section 4). These approaches are used in practice for aggregative judgements made by individuals, but they can also be used for organized procedures for arriving at social measures of poverty, inequality, distribution-adjusted real national incomes, and other such aggregative indicators.

Second, Buchanan's questioning of the concept of social preference (and of its use as an ordering to make – or explain – social choices) is indeed appropriate in the case of social decision *mechanisms*, though less so for social welfare *judgements* (Section 3). The Arrow theorem, in its original form, does not apply once social decision making is characterized in terms of choice functions *without* any imposed requirement of intermenu consistency. However, when the natural implications of taking a choice-functional view of social decisions are worked out, Arrow's conditions have to be correspondingly restated, and then the impossibility result, returns in its entirety once again (Section 3). The idea of social preference or internal consistency of social choice is basically redundant for this impossibility result. So Buchanan's move does not negate Arrow's impossibility. On the other hand, it is an important departure in its own right.

Coming to terms with the impossibility problem in the case of social decision mechanisms is largely a matter of give and take between different principles with respective appeals. This calls for a less rigid interpretation of the role of axiomatic demands on permissible social decision rules (Section 5).

Third, Buchanan's argument for a more procedural view of social decisions has much merit. Nevertheless, there are good reasons to doubt the adequacy of a purely procedural view (independent of consequences), just as there are serious defects in narrowly consequentialist views (independent of procedures). Procedural concerns can, however, be amalgamated with consequential ones by recharacterizing states of affairs appropriately, and the evaluation of states can then take note of the two aspects together (Section 6). This combination is especially important in accommodating liberty and rights in social judgments as well as social decision mechanisms (Section 7).

Finally, there is room for paying more attention to the rationality of individual behavior as an integral component of rational social decisions. In particular, the practical reach of social choice theory, in its traditional form, is considerably reduced by its tendency to ignore value formation through social interactions. Buchanan is right to emphasize the role of public discussion in the development of preferences (as an important part of democracy). However, traditional public choice theory is made unduly narrow by the insistence that individuals invariably behave as *homo economicus* (a subject on which social choice theory is much more permissive). This uncompromising restriction can significantly misrepresent the nature of social concerns and values. But aside from this descriptive limitation, there is also an important issue of "practical reason" here. Many of the more exacting problems of the contemporary world – varying from famine prevention to environmental preservation – actually call for value formation through public discussion (Section 8).

On the rationality of social decisions, many important lessons have emerged from the discipline of social choice theory as well as the public choice approach. In fact, we can get quite a bit more by *combining* these lessons. As a social choice theorist, I had not, in fact, planned to be particularly even-handed in this paper, but need not, I suppose, apologize for ending up with rather even hands.

Notes

1   For discussions of the axioms involved and alternative formulations and proofs, see Arrow (1951, 1963), Sen (1970, 1986b), Peter C. Fishburn (1973), Robert Wilson (1975), Bengt Hansson (1976), Jerry S. Kelly (1978), Graciela Chichilnisky (1982), Chichilnisky and Geoffrey Heal (1983), Prasanta Pattanaik and Maurice Salles (1983), Kotaro Suzumura (1983), Charles Blackorby et al. (1984), and Ken Binmore (1994), among others.

2   On "the impossibility of the Paretian liberal," see Sen (1970, 1983), Kelly (1978), Suzumura (1983), John Wriglesworth (1985), and Jonathan Riley (1987), among other contributions.

Other results related to Arrow's theorem include the demonstration by Allan F. Gibbard (1973) and Mark A. Satterthwaite (1975) that "manipulability" is a ubiquitous characteristic of voting schemes; on related issues see Pattanaik (1978), Jean-Jacques Laffont (1979), Hervé Moulin (1983), Bazalel Peleg (1984), and Salvador Barberá and Bhaskar Dutta (1986), among others.

3   Dennis C. Mueller (1989) provides an excellent introduction to public choice theory and its relation to social choice theory. See also Atkinson (1987) and Sandmo (1990) on Buchanan's contributions.

4   The canonical treatise on the "public choice" approach is Buchanan and Tullock (1962), but it is important to note the differences in emphases between the appendix by Buchanan and that by Tullock.

5   Arrow (1951) himself points out "the unreality of this assumption" (p. 8).

6   The importance of politics as discussion has also been stressed in the Habermasian tradition; on this see Jon Elster and Aanund Hylland (1986) and Jürgen Habermas (1994). See also Albert Hirschman (1970) and the works inspired by his writings.

7   Robbins (1938) himself was opposed not so much to making interpersonal comparisons, but to claiming them to be "scientific."

8   The strategy of proof employed here (as in Sen [1986b]) is more direct and simpler than the versions used in Arrow (1963) and Sen (1970) and does not require defining additional concepts (such as "almost decisiveness").

9   For proof, take two pairs of alternative states (x, y) and (a, b), all distinct (the proof when they are not all distinct is quite similar). Group G is decisive over (x, y); we have to show that it is decisive over (a, b) as well. By unrestricted domain, let everyone in G prefer a to x to y to b, while all others prefer a to x, and y to b, but rank the other pairs in any way whatever. By the decisiveness of G over (x, y), x is socially preferred to y. By the Pareto principle, a is socially preferred to x, and y to b. Therefore, by transitivity, a is socially preferred to b. If this result is influenced by individual preferences over any pair other than (a, b), then the condition of independence would be violated. Thus, a must be ranked above b simply by virtue of everyone in G preferring a to b (since others can have any preference whatever over this pair). So G is indeed decisive over (a, b).

10 For proof, take a decisive group G and partition it into G_1 and G_2. Let everyone in G_1 prefer x to y and x to z, with any possible ranking of (y, z), and let everyone in group G_2 prefer x to y and z to y, with any possible ranking of (x, z). It does not matter what those not in G prefer. If, now, x is socially preferred to z then the members of group G_1 would be decisive over this pair, since they alone definitely prefer x to z (the others can rank this pair in any way). If G_1 is not to be decisive, we must have z at least as good as x for some individual preferences over (x, z) of nonmembers of G_1. Take that case, and combine this social ranking (that z is at least as good as x) with the social preference for x over y (a consequence of the decisiveness of G and the fact that everyone in G prefers x to y). By transitivity, z is socially preferred to y. But only G_2 members definitely prefer z to y. Thus G_2 is decisive over this pair (z, y). Thus, from the Field-Expansion Lemma, G_2 is decisive. So either G_1 or G_2 must be decisive – proving the lemma.

11 On some analytical problems involved in deriving "the revealed preference of a government" by observing its choices, see Kaushik Basu (1980).

12 Binariness requires a combination of two types of choice consistency: basic "contraction consistency" (α) and basic "expansion consistency" (γ). These conditions are quite exacting, and they have to be further strengthened to get transitivity and other additional properties (on this, see Sen [1971, 1977a], Rajat Deb [1983], and Isaac Levi [1986]).

13 On this, see Harsanyi (1955, p. 310): "Of course, when I speak of preferences 'from a social standpoint,' often abbreviated to 'social' preferences and the like, I always mean preferences based on a given individual's value judgments concerning 'social welfare.'"

14 This has been established in a sequence of results, presented by Gibbard, Hansson, Andreu Mas-Colell, Hugo Sonnenschein, Donald Brown, Georges Bordes, Kelly, Suzumura, Douglas Blair, Robert Pollak, Julian Blau, Deb, David Kelsey, and others; for critical overviews, see Blair and Pollak (1982), Suzumura (1983), and Sen (1986a).

15 The pioneering work on choice-functional formulations came from Hansson (1968, 1969), Thomas Schwartz (1972, 1985), Fishburn (1973), and Plott (1973). Mark Aizerman and his colleagues at the Institute of Control Sciences in Moscow provided a series of penetrating investigations of the general choice-functional features of moving from individual-choice functions to social-choice functions (see Aizerman, 1985, Aizerman and Fuad Aleskerov, 1986). On related matters see also Aizerman and A. V. Malishevski (1981).

16 A sequence of contributions on this and related issues has come from Plott, Fishburn, Hansson, Donald Campbell, Bordes, Blair, Kelly, Suzumura, Deb, R. R. Parks, John Ferejohn, D. M. Grether, Kelsey, V. Denicolo, and Yasumi Matsumoto, among others. For general overviews and critiques, see Blair et al. (1976), Suzumura (1983), and Sen (1986a).

17 See also Buchanan and Tullock (1962).

18 For exact statements of the conditions and a proof of the theorem, see Sen (1993).

19 On this issue, see Sen (1977b, 1982a).

20 Formally, person 2 is "almost decisive" over the first pair (in the sense of winning against opposition by all others – in this case, person 1), and an alternative version of the Field-Expansion Lemma shows that he will be almost decisive (indeed fully decisive) over all other pairs as well (see Lemma 3a in Sen [1970 pp. 43–4]). Note that "field expansion" is based *inter alia* on the use of the condition of "unrestricted domain," allowing the possibility that the individuals involved *could have* had other preferences as well.

21 On different types of interpersonal comparisons, and the relevance of distinct "spaces" in making efficiency and equity judgments, see Sen (1982a, 1992a), John Roemer (1986), Martha Nussbaum (1988), Richard Arneson (1989), G. A. Cohen (1989), Arrow (1991), Elster and Roemer (1991), and Nussbaum and Sen (1993).

22 On the other hand, Arrow's impossibility theorem can be generalized to accommodate cardinality of utilities without interpersonal comparisons; see Theorem 8.2 in Sen (1970).

23 Maximin gives complete priority to the interest of the worst off. It was proposed by John Rawls (1963), as a part of his "difference principle" (though the comparisons that he uses are not of utilities, but of holdings of primary goods). Lexicographic maximin, sometimes called "leximin," was proposed in Sen (1970) to make the Rawlsian approach consistent with the strong Pareto principle, and it has been endorsed and used in his *Theory of Justice* by Rawls (1971). Axiomatic derivations of leximin were pioneered by Peter J. Hammond (1976), and Claude d'Aspremont and Gevers (1977), among others. See also Edmund Phelps (1973).

24 See Harsanyi (1955), Patrick Suppes (1966), Sen (1970, 1977b), Phelps (1973), Hammond (1976, 1985), Arrow (1977), d'Aspremont and Gevers (1977), Gevers (1979), Eric Maskin (1978, 1979), Roberts (1980a, b), Roger B. Myerson (1981), James Mirrlees (1982), Suzumura (1983), Blackorby et al. (1984), d'Aspremont (1985), and Kelsey (1987), among others.

25 The literature on such measures is now quite large. Different types of exercises are illustrated by Sen (1973), Frank Cowell (1977), Blackorby and Donaldson (1978, 1980), Siddiq Osmani (1982), Sudhir Anand (1983), Atkinson (1983, 1989), S. R. Chakravarty (1983), Anthony Shorrocks (1983), Suzumura (1983), James E. Foster (1984, 1985), Ravi Kanbur (1984), Michel Le Breton and Alain Trannoy (1987), W. Eichhorn (1988), Peter J. Lambert (1989), and Martin Ravallion (1994), among many other contributions.

26 The policy discussions include those surrounding the influential *Human Development Reports*, produced by the United Nations Development Programme. Another strong force in that direction has been the sequence of UNICEF reports on *The State of the World's Children*. Policy issues related

to such social judgments have been discussed by Paul Streeten et al. (1981), Nanak Kakwani (1986), Jean Drèze and Sen (1989), Alan Hamlin and Philip Pettit (1989), Keith Griffin and John Knight (1990), Anand and Ravallion (1993), Partha Dasgupta (1993), and Meghnad Desai (1995).

27   "Value restriction" turns out to be necessary and sufficient for this class of domain conditions for consistent majority rule when individual preferences are linear orderings, though the conditions are more complex in the general case of weak orderings (see Sen and Prasanta Pattanaik, 1969; see also Ken-ichi Inada, 1969, 1970). These relations can be generalized to all Arrovian social welfare functions and for nonmanipulable voting procedures (on which see Maskin [1976] and E. Kalai and E. Muller [1977]). Other types of conditions have been proposed by Tullock (1967) (with a somewhat exaggerated title: "The General Irrelevance of the General Possibility Theorem") and in a definitive paper by Jean-Michel Grandmont (1978). Fine discussions of the issues involved in the different types of domain conditions can be found in Gaertner (1979) and Arrow and Hervé Raynaud (1986).

28   The ubiquitous presence of voting cycles in majority rule has been extensively studied by R. D. McKelvey (1979) and Norman Schofield (1983).

29   Even individual social welfare judgments (and more generally, individual views of social appropriateness) presumably have some influence on political preferences.

30   Positional rules of other kinds have been studied extensively by Peter Gärdenfors (1973) and Ben Fine and Kit Fine (1974a, b). On different versions of the Borda rule, see Sen (1977a, 1982a pp. 186–7).

31   For example, Andrew Caplin and Barry Nalebuff (1988) provide a case for 64-percent majority rule. Also see the symposium on voting procedures led by Jonathan Levin and Nalebuff (1995).

32   Buchanan (1986) expresses some basic sympathy for "libertarian socialists" (as opposed to *antilibertarian* socialists) but attributes what he sees as their well-intentioned but mistaken opposition to markets to their not having "the foggiest notion of the way the market works" and to their being "blissfully ignorant of economic theory" (pp. 4–5). *Consequential* analysis incorporated in economic theory is precisely what Buchanan is invoking here to dispute the libertarian socialist position.

33   On this see Sen (1981), linking starvation to unequal entitlements, with actual case studies of four famines. See also Ravallion (1987), Drèze and Sen (1989), and Desai (1995).

34   See also Nozick's (1974) discussion of "Locke's proviso."

35   On this question, see Sen (1982a, b).

36   On this question, see Sen (1982b), Hammond (1986), and Levi (1986).

37   Utilities can be defined in terms of choices made, desires entertained, or satisfactions received, but the point at issue applies to each of these interpretations. Utilitarian welfare economics has tended traditionally to focus on satisfactions, partly because individual choices do not immediately yield any basis for interpersonal comparisons unless some elaborately hypothetical choices are considered (on which see Harsanyi [1955]), but also because "satisfaction" had appeared to utilitarian economists as providing a more solid basis for judging individual welfare. For example, this was the reason given by A. C. Pigou (1951 pp. 288–9):

> Some economists ... have employed the term "utility" indifferently for satisfactions and for desiredness. I shall employ it here to mean satisfactions, so that we may say that a man's economic welfare is made up of his utilities.

38   The idea of "personal domains" and "protected spheres" goes back to Mill (see Riley, 1987), and more recently has found strong and eloquent expression in the writings of Friedrich Hayek (1960).

39   For general accounts of the literature, see Kelly (1978), Suzumura (1983, 1991), Wriglesworth (1985), Paul Seabright (1989), and Pattanaik and Suzumura (1994a, b). For public-choice critiques, see Sugden (1981, 1993) and Rowley (1993).

40 The belief that the problem can be resolved through Pareto-improving contracts, which has been suggested by some authors, overlooks the incentive-incompatibility of the touted solution and, perhaps more importantly, confounds the nature of the conflict itself, since the conflict in values keeps open the question as to what contracts would be offered or accepted by the persons involved. For example, in the (rather overdiscussed) case of whether the prude or the lewd should read *Lady Chatterley's Lover*, it is not at all clear that the prude, if he has any libertarian inclinations, would actually offer a contract by which he agrees to read a book that he hates to make the lewd refrain from reading a book he loves. In fact, while the prude may prefer that the lewd does not read that book, consistent with that he may not want to bring this about through an enforceable contract, and the "dilemma of the Paretian liberal" could be his dilemma too. The lewd too faces a decision problem about whether to try to alter the prude's personal life rather than minding his own business. On these issues, see Sen (1983, 1992b), Basu (1984), and Elster and Hylland (1986).

41 Stig Kanger (1985) has illuminatingly discussed "nonrealization" of rights, and the variety of ways this can occur.

42 On related matters, see also Pattanaik and Suzumura (1994a, b).

43 A set of studies on this and related issues is presented in Jane Mansbridge (1990).

44 Efforts to explain every socially motivated action as some kind of a cunning attempt at maximization of purely private gain are frequent in part of modern economics. There is an interesting question as to whether the presumption of exclusive self-interestedness is a more common general belief in America than in Europe, without being a general characteristic of *actual* behavior. Alexis de Tocqueville thought so:

> The Americans... are fond of explaining almost all the actions of their lives by the principle of self-interest rightly understood; they show with complacency how an enlightened regard for themselves constantly prompts them to assist one another and inclines them willingly to sacrifice a portion of their time and property to the welfare of the state. In this respect, they frequently fail to do themselves justice; for in the United States as well as elsewhere people are sometimes seen to give way to those disinterested and spontaneous impulses that are natural to man; but the Americans seldom admit that they yield to emotions of this kind; they are more anxious to do honor to their philosophy than to themselves.

(Tocqueville, 1840 [Book II, Chapter VIII; in the 1945 edition, p. 122]).

45 On this subject, see Nozick (1989).

46 See also Drèze and Sen (1989) and *World Disasters Report* (1994, pp. 33–7).

47 In contrast, China – despite its fine record of public health and education even before the reforms – managed to have perhaps the largest famine in recorded history, during 1959–1962, in which 23–30 million people died, while the mistaken public policies were not revised for three years through the famine. In India, on the other hand, despite its bungling ways, large famines stopped abruptly with independence in 1947 and the installing of a multiparty democracy (the last such famine, "the great Bengal famine," had occurred in 1943).

48 On this general question, see Rawls (1971) and Thomas Scanlon (1982). See also Daniel Hausman and Michael McPherson (1993).

49 See the discussion and the literature cited in Sen (1994, pp. 62–71), particularly Dasgupta (1993). See also Adam Przeworski and Fernando Limongi's (1994) international comparisons, which indicate a fairly strong association between democracy and fertility reduction. In the rapid reduction of the total fertility rate in the Indian state of Kerala from 4.4 in the 1950s to the present figure of 1.8 (a level similar to that in Britain and France and lower than in the United States), value formation related to education, democracy, and public discussion has

played a major part. While the fertility rate has also come down in China (though not as much as in Kerala), China's use of compulsion rather than consensual progress has resulted in relatively high infant-mortality rates (28 per thousand for boys and 33 per thousand for girls, compared with Kerala's 17 per thousand for boys and 16 per thousand for girls in 1991). Such public dialogues are, however, hard to achieve in many other parts of India, despite democracy, because of the low level of elementary education, especially for women. These and related issues are discussed in Drèze and Sen (1995).

References and Further Reading

Aizerman, M. A. (1985): "New Problems in the General Choice Theory," *Social Choice and Welfare*, 2 (4), December, 235–82.

Aizerman, M. A. and Aleskerov, F. (1986): "Voting Operators in the Space of Choice Functions," *Mathematical Social Sciences*, 11 (3), June, 201–42. Corrigendum, 13 (3), June 1988, 305.

Aizerman, M. A. and Malishevski, A. V. (1981): "General Theory of Best Variants Choice: Some Aspects," *IEEE Transactions on Automatic Control*, AC-26, 1031–41.

Anand, S. (1983): *Inequality and Poverty in Malaysia: Measurement and Decomposition*. New York: Oxford University Press.

Anand, S. and Ravallion, M. (1993): "Human Development in Poor Countries: On the Role of Private Incomes and Public Services," *Journal of Economic Perspectives*, 7 (1), Winter, 133–50.

Arneson, R. J. (1989): "Equality and Equal Opportunity for Welfare," *Philosophical Studies*, 56 (1), May, 77–93.

Arrow, K. J. (1951 [1963]): *Social Choice and Individual Values*. New York: Wiley.

—— (1977): "Extended Sympathy and the Possibility of Social Choice," *American Economic Review*, 67 (1), February, 219–25.

—— (ed.) (1991): *Markets and Welfare*. London: Macmillan

Arrow, K. J. and Raynaud, H. (1986): *Social Choice and Multicriterion Decision-making*. Cambridge, MA: MIT Press

Atkinson, A. B. (1970): "On the Measurement of Inequality," *Journal of Economic Theory*, 2 (3), September, 244–63.

—— (1983): *Social Justice and Public Policy*. Cambridge, MA: MIT Press.

—— (1987): "James M. Buchanan's Contributions to Economics," *Scandinavian Journal of Economics*, 89 (1), 5–15.

—— (1989): *Poverty and social security*. New York: Harvester Wheatsheaf.

Barberá, S. and Dutta, B. (1986): "General, Direct and Self-Implementation of Social Choice Functions via Protective Equilibria," *Mathematical Social Sciences*, 11 (2), April, 109–27.

Basu, Kaushik. (1980): *Revealed Preference of Government*. Cambridge: Cambridge University Press.

—— (1984): "The Right to Give Up Rights," *Economica*, 51 (204), November, 413–22.

Baumol, W. J. (1986): *Superfairness*. Cambridge, MA: MIT Press.

Bergson, A. (1938): "A Reformulation of Certain Aspects of Welfare Economics," *Quarterly Journal of Economics*, 52 (1), February, 310–34.

—— (1966): *Essays in Normative Economics*. Cambridge, MA: Harvard University Press.

Binmore, K. (1994): *Playing Fair: Game Theory and the Social Contract*, Vol. I. London: MIT Press.

Blackorby, C. and Donaldson, D. (1978): "Measures of Relative Equality and Their Meaning in Terms of Social Welfare," *Journal of Economic Theory*, 18 (1), June, 59–80.

—— (1980): "Ethical Indices for the Measurement of Poverty," *Econometrica*, 48 (4), May, 1053–60.

Blackorby, C., Donaldson, D. and Weymark, J. (1984): "Social Choice with Interpersonal Utility Comparisons: A Diagrammatic Introduction," *International Economic Review*, 25 (2), June, 325–56.

Blair, D. H. and Pollak, R. A. (1982): "Acyclic Collective Choice Rules," *Econometrica*, 50 (4), July, 931–44.

Blair, D. H., Bordes, G. A., Kelly, J. S. and Suzumura, K. (1976): "Impossibility Theorems without Collective Rationality," *Journal of Economic Theory*, 13 (3), December, 361–79.

Borda, J. C. (1781): "Mémoire sur les Élections au Scrutin," *Mémoires de l'Académie Royale des Sciences*, (Paris).

Brennan, G. and Lomasky, L. (1993): *Democracy and Decision: The Pure Theory of Electoral Preference*. Cambridge: Cambridge University Press.

Broome, J. (1991): *Weighing Goods*. Oxford: Blackwell.

Buchanan, J. M. (1954a): "Social Choice, Democracy, and Free Markets," *Journal of Political Economy*, 62 (2), April, 114–23.

——(1954b): "Individual Choice in Voting and the Market," *Journal of Political Economy*, 62 (3), August, 334–43.

——(1960): *Fiscal Theory and Political Economy*. Chapel Hill, NC: University of North Carolina Press.

——(1986): *Liberty, Market and the State*. Brighton, UK: Wheatsheaf.

——(1994a): "Foundational Concerns: A Criticism of Public Choice Theory," unpublished manuscript presented at the European Public Choice Meeting, Valencia, Spain, April.

——(1994b): "Dimensionality, Rights and Choices among Relevant Alternatives," unpublished manuscript presented at a meeting honoring Peter Bernholz, Basel, Switzerland, April.

Buchanan, J. M. and Tullock, G. (1962): *The Calculus of Consent*. Ann Arbor: University of Michigan Press.

Caplin, A. and Nalebuff, B. (1988): "On 64% Majority Rule," *Econometrica*, 56 (4), July, 787–814.

Chakravarty, S. R. (1983): "Ethically Flexible Measures of Poverty," *Canadian Journal of Economics*, 16 (1), February, 74–85.

Chichilnisky, G. (1982): "Social Aggregation Rules and Continuity," *Quarterly Journal of Economics*, 97 (2), May, 337–52.

Chichilnisky, G. and Heal, G. M. (1983): "Necessary and Sufficient Conditions for a Resolution of the Social Choice Paradox," *Journal of Economic Theory*, 31 (1), October, 68–87.

Cohen, G. A. (1989): "On the Currency of Egalitarian Justice," *Ethics*, 99 (4), July, 906–44.

Condorcet, Marquis de (1785): *Essai sur l'Application de l'Analyse à la Probabilité des Décisions Rendues à la Pluralité des Voix*. Paris: L'Imprimerie Royale.

Cowell, F. A. (1977): *Measuring Inequality*. New York: Wiley.

Dasgupta, P. (1993): *An Inquiry into Well-being and Destitution*. Oxford: Oxford University Press.

d'Aspremont, C. (1985): "Axioms for Social Welfare Ordering," in L. Hurwicz, D. Schmeidler and H. Sonnenschein (eds), *Social Goals and Social Organization*, Cambridge: Cambridge University Press, 19–76.

d'Aspremont, C. and Gevers, L. (1977): "Equity and the Informational Basis of Collective Choice," *Review of Economic Studies*, 44 (2), June, 199–209.

Deb, R. (1983): "Binariness and Rational Choice," *Mathematical Social Sciences*, 5 (1), August, 97–106.

Desai, M. (1995): *Poverty, Famine and Economic Development*. Aldershot, U.K.: Elgar.

Drèze, J. and Sen, A. (1989): *Hunger and Public Action*. Oxford: Oxford University Press.

——(1995): *India: Economic Development and Social Opportunity*. Oxford: Oxford University Press.

Eichhorn, W. (1988): *Measurement in Economics*. New York: Physica-Verlag.

Elster, J. and Hylland, A. (1986): *Foundations of Social Choice Theory*. Cambridge: Cambridge University Press.

Elster, J. and Roemer, J. (eds) (1991): *Interpersonal Comparisons of Well-being*. Cambridge: Cambridge University Press.

Fine, B. and Fine, K. (1974a): "Social Choice and Individual Ranking I," *Review of Economic Studies*, 41 (3), July, 303–22.

—— (1974b): "Social Choice and Individual Rankings II," *Review of Economic Studies*, 41 (4), October 459–75.

Fishburn, P. C. (1973): *The Theory of Social Choice*. Princeton, NJ: Princeton University Press.

Foster, J. E. (1984): "On Economic Poverty: A Survey of Aggregate Measures," *Advances in Econometrics*, 3, 215–51.

—— (1985): "Inequality Measurement," in Young, (1985), 31–68.

Gaertner, W. (1979): "An Analysis and Comparison of Several Necessary and Sufficient Conditions for Transitivity of Majority Decision Rule," in Laffont, (1979), 91–112.

Gaertner, W., Pattanaik, P. K. and Suzumura, K. (1992): "Individual Rights Revisited," *Economica*, 59 (234), May, 161–78.

Gärdenfors, P. (1973): "Positional Voting Functions," *Theory and Decision*, 4 (1), September, 1–24.

—— (1981): "Rights, Games and Social Choice," *Nous*, 15 (3), September, 341–56.

Gevers, L. (1979): "On Interpersonal Comparability and Social Welfare Orderings," *Econometrica*, 47 (1), January, 75–89.

Gibbard, A. F. (1973): "Manipulation of Voting Schemes: A General Result," *Econometrica*, 41 (4), July, 587–601.

Grandmont, J.-M. (1978): "Intermediate Preferences and the Majority Rule," *Econometrica*, 46 (2), March, 317–30.

Griffin, K. and Knight, J. (eds) (1990): *Human Development and the International Development Strategy for the 1990s*. London: Macmillan.

Habermas, J. (1994): "Three Models of Democracy," *Constellations*, 1 (1), April, 1–10.

Hamlin, A. and Pettit, P. (eds) (1989): *The Good Polity*. Oxford: Blackwell.

Hammond, P. J. (1976): "Equity, Arrow's Conditions, and Rawls' Difference Principle," *Econometrica*, 44 (4), July, 793–804.

—— (1985): "Welfare Economics," in G. Feiwel (ed.), *Issues in Contemporary Microeconomics and Welfare*, Albany: State University of New York Press, 405–34.

—— (1986): "Consequentialist Social Norms for Public Decisions," in Heller et al. (1986), 3–27.

Hansson, B. (1968): "Choice Structures and Preference Relations," *Synthese*, 18 (4), October, 443–58.

—— (1969): "Voting and Group Decision Functions," *Synthese*, 20 (4), December, 526–37.

—— (1976): "The Existence of Group Preference," *Public Choice*, 28, Winter, 89–98.

Harsanyi, J. C. (1955): "Cardinal Welfare, Individualistic Ethics, and Interpersonal Comparisons of Utility," *Journal of Political Economy*, 63 (3), August, 309–21.

Hausman, D. M. and McPherson, M. S. (1993): "Taking Ethics Seriously: Economics and Contemporary Moral Philosophy," *Journal of Economic Literature*, 31 (2), June, 671–731.

Hayek, F. A. (1960): *The Constitution of Liberty*. London: Routledge and Kegan Paul.

Heller, W. P., Starr, R. M. and Starret, D. A. (eds) (1986): *Social Choice and Public Decision-making, Vol. 1. Essays in Honor of Kenneth J. Arrow*. Cambridge: Cambridge University Press.

Hirschman, A. (1970): *Exit, Voice and Loyalty*. Cambridge, MA: Harvard University Press.

Inada, K. (1969): "On the Simple Majority Decision Rule," *Econometrica*, 37 (3), July, 490–506.

—— (1970): "Majority Rule and Rationality," *Journal of Economic Theory*, 2 (1), March, 27–40.

Kakwani, N. (1986): *Analyzing Redistribution Policies*. Cambridge: Cambridge University Press.

Kalai, E. and Muller, E. (1977): "Characterization of Domains Admitting Nondictatorial Social Welfare Functions and Nonmanipulable Voting Procedures," *Journal of Economic Theory*, 16 (2), December, 457–69.

Kanbur, S. M. (1984): "The Measurement and Decomposition of Inequality and Poverty," in F. van der Ploeg (ed.), *Mathematical Methods in Economics*, New York: Wiley, 403–32.

Kanger, S. (1985): "On Realization of Human Rights," *Acta Philosophica Fennica*, 38, May, 71–8.

Kelly, J. S. (1978): *Arrow Impossibility Theorems*. New York: Academic Press.

Kelsey, D. (1987): "The Role of Information in Social Welfare Judgments", *Oxford Economic Papers*, 39 (2), June, 301–17.

Knight, F. (1947): *Freedom and Reform: Essays in Economic and Social Philosophy*. New York: Harper. Republished in 1982, Indianapolis: Liberty.

Kolm, S. Ch. (1969): "The Optimal Production of Social Justice," in J. Margolis and H. Guitton (eds), *Public Economics*, London: Macmillan, 145–200.

Laffont, J-J. (ed.) (1979): *Aggregation and Revelation of Preferences*. Amsterdam: North-Holland.

Lambert, P. J. (1989): *The Distribution and Redistribution of Income: A Mathematical Analysis*. Oxford: Blackwell.

Le Breton, M. and Trannoy, A. (1987): "Measures of Inequalities as an Aggregation of Individual Preferences About Income Distribution: The Arrovian Case," *Journal of Economic Theory*, 41 (2), April, 248–69.

Levi, I. (1986): *Hard Choices*. Cambridge: Cambridge University Press.

Levin, J. and Nalebuff, B. (1995): "An Introduction to Vote-Counting Schemes," *Journal of Economic Perspectives*, 9 (1), 3–26.

Mansbridge, J. J. (ed.) (1990): *Beyond Self-interest*. Chicago: University of Chicago Press.

Maskin, E. (1976): "*Social Welfare Functions on Restricted Domain*," mimeo, Harvard University.

——(1978): "A Theorem on Utilitarianism," *Review of Economic Studies*, 45 (1), February, 93–6.

——(1979): "Decision-making under Ignorance with Implications for Social Choice," *Theory and Decision*, 11 (3), September, 319–37.

McKelvey, R. D. (1979): "General Conditions for Global Intransitivities in Formal Voting Models," *Econometrica*, 47 (5), September, 1085–112.

Meade, J. E. (1976): *The Just Economy*. London: Allen and Unwin.

Mill, J. S. (1859): *On Liberty*. London: Parker, 1859. Republished in 1910 in *Utilitarianism; On Liberty; Representative Government*. London: Everyman's Library.

Mirrlees, J. A. (1982): "The Economic Uses of Utilitarianism," in A. Sen and B. Williams (eds), *Utilitarianism and Beyond*, Cambridge: Cambridge University Press, 63–84.

Moulin, H. (1983): *The Strategy of Social Choice*. Amsterdam: North-Holland.

Mueller, D. C. (1989): *Public Choice II*. Cambridge: Cambridge University Press.

Myerson, R. B. (1981): "Utilitarianism, Egalitarianism, and the Timing Effect in Social Choice Problems," *Econometrica*, 49 (4), July, 883–97.

Nozick, R. (1974): *Anarchy, State, and Utopia*. New York: Basic Books.

——(1989): *The Examined Life*. New York: Simon and Schuster.

Nussbaum, M. (1988): "Nature, Function and Capability: Aristotle on Political Distribution," *Oxford Studies in Ancient Philosphy*, Supplementary volume, 145–84.

Nussbaum, M. and Sen, A. (eds) (1993): *The Quality of Life*. Oxford: Oxford University Press.

Osmani, S. R. (1982): *Economic Inequality and Group Welfare*. Oxford: Oxford University Press.

Pattanaik, P. K. (1978): *Strategy and Group Choice*. Amsterdam: North-Holland.

Pattanaik, P. K. and Salles, M. (eds) (1983): *Social Choice and Welfare*. Amsterdam: North-Holland.

Pattanaik, P. K. and Suzumura, K. (1994a): "Rights, Welfarism and Social Choice," *American Economic Review*, (Papers and Proceedings), 84 (2), May, 435–9.

——(1994b): "*Individual Rights and Social Evaluation: A Conceptual Framework*," mimeo, University of California, Riverside.

Peleg, B. (1984): *Game Theoretic Analysis of Voting in Committees*. Cambridge: Cambridge University Press.

Phelps, E. S. (ed.) (1973): *Economic Justice*. Harmondsworth, UK: Penguin.

Pigou, A. C. (1951): "Some Aspects of Welfare Economics," *American Economic Review*, 41 (3), June, 287–302.

Plott, C. (1973): "Path Independence, Rationality and Social Choice," *Econometrica*, 41 (6), November, 1075–91.

Przeworski, A. and Limongi, F. (1994): "*Democracy and Development*," mimeo, University of Chicago.

Ravallion, M. (1987): *Markets and Famines*. Oxford: Oxford University Press.

——(1994): *Poverty Comparisons*. Chur, Switzerland: Harwood.

Rawls, J. (1963): "The Sense of Justice," *Philosophical Review*, 72 (3), July, 281–305.

——(1971): *A Theory of Justice*. Cambridge, MA: Harvard University Press.

Riley, J. (1987): *Liberal Utilitarianism: Social Choice Theory and J. S. Mill's Philosophy*. Cambridge: Cambridge University Press.

Robbins, L. (1938): "Interpersonal Comparisons of Utility: A Comment," *Economic Journal*, 48 (192), December, 635–41.

Roberts, K. W. S. (1980a): "Possibility Theorems with Interpersonally Comparable Welfare Levels," *Review of Economic Studies*, 47 (2), January, 409–20.

——(1980b): "Interpersonal Comparability and Social Choice Theory," *Review of Economic Studies*, 47 (2), January 421–39.

Roemer, J. (1986): "An Historical Materialist Alternative to Welfarism," in J. Elster and A. Hylland (eds), *Foundations of Social Choice Theory*, Cambridge: Cambridge University Press, 133–64.

Rowley, C. K. (1993): *Liberty and the State*. Aldershot, UK: Elgar.

Samuelson, P. A. (1947): *Foundations of Economic Analysis*. Cambridge, MA: Harvard University Press.

Sandmo, A. (1990): "Buchanan on Political Economy: A Review Article," *Journal of Economic Literature*, 28 (1), March, 50–65.

Satterthwaite, M. A. (1975): "Strategy-proofness and Arrow's Conditions: Existence and Correspondence Theorems for Voting Procedures and Social Welfare Functions," *Journal of Economic Theory*, 10 (2), April, 187–217.

Scanlon, T. M. (1982): "Contractualism and Utilitarianism," in A. Sen and B. Williams, (eds), *Utilitarianism and Beyond*, Cambridge: Cambridge University Press, 103–28.

Schofield, N. J. (1983): "Generic Instability of Majority Rule," *Review of Economic Studies*, 50 (4), October, 695–705.

Schwartz, T. (1972): "Rationality and the Myth of the Maximum," *Nous*, 6 (2), May, 97–117.

——(1985): *The Logic of Collective Choice*. New York: Columbia University Press.

Seabright, P. (1989): "Social Choice and Social Theories," *Philosophy and Public Affairs*, 18 (4), Fall, 365–87.

Sen, A. K. (1966): "A Possibility Theorem on Majority Decisions," *Econometrica*, 34 (2), April, 491–9.

——(1970): *Collective Choice and Social Welfare*. San Francisco: Holden-Day. Reprinted in 1970. Amsterdam: North-Holland.

——(1971): "Choice Functions and Revealed Preference," *Review of Economic Studies*, 38 (3), July, 307–17 Reprinted in Sen (1982a).

——(1973): *On Economic Inequality*. Oxford: Oxford University Press.

——(1976a): "Real National Income," *Review of Economic Studies*, 43 (1), February, 19–39. Reprinted in Sen (1982a).

——(1976b): "Poverty: An Ordinal Approach to Measurement," *Econometrica*, 44 (2) March, 219–31. Reprinted in Sen (1982a).

——(1977a): "Social Choice Theory: A Reexamination," *Econometrica*, 45 (1), January, 53–89. Reprinted in Sen (1982a).

——(1977b): "On Weights and Measures: Informational Constraints in Social Welfare Analysis," *Econometrica*, 45 (7), October, 1539–72. Reprinted in Sen (1982a).

——(1981): *Poverty and Famines: An Essay on Entitlement and Deprivation*. Oxford: Oxford University Press.

——(1982a): *Choice, Welfare and Measurement*. Oxford: Blackwell.

——(1982b): "Rights and Agency," *Philosophy and Public Affairs*, 11 (2), Spring, 113–32.

—— (1983): "Liberty and Social Choice," *Journal of Philosophy*, 80 (1), January, 5–28.

—— (1984): *Resources, Values and Development*. Oxford: Blackwell.

—— (1986a): "Social Choice Theory," in K. J. Arrow and M. Intriligator (eds), *Handbook of Mathematical Economics*, Vol. III. Amsterdam: North-Holland. 1073–181.

—— (1986b): "Information and Invariance in Normative Choice," in Heller et al. (1986), 29–55.

—— (1992a): *Inequality Reexamined*. Oxford: Oxford University Press.

—— (1992b): "Minimal Liberty," *Economica*, 59 (234), May, 139–60.

—— (1993): "Internal Consistency of Choice," *Econometrica*, 61 (3), May, 495–521.

—— (1994): "Population: Delusion and Reality," *New York Review of Books*, 41 (15), 22 September, 62–71.

Sen, A. K. and Pattanaik, P. K. (1969): "Necessary and Sufficient Conditions for Rational Choice under Majority Decision," *Journal of Economic Theory*, 1 (2), August, 178–202.

Shorrocks, A. F. (1983): "Ranking Income Distributions," *Economica*, 50 (197), February, 3–17.

Smith, A. (1776): *An Inquiry into the Nature and Causes of the Wealth of Nations*. London: W. Strahan and T. Cadell. Republished, Oxford: Oxford University Press, 1976.

—— (1790): *The Theory of Moral Sentiments*, revised edn. London: T. Cadell. Republished, Oxford: Oxford University Press, 1975.

Streeten, P., Burki, S. J., Haq, M., Hicks, N. and Stewart, F. (1981): *First Things First: Meeting Basic Human Needs in Developing Countries*. London: Oxford University Press.

Sugden, R. (1981): *The Political Economy of Public Choice*. Oxford: Martin Robertson.

—— (1986): *The Economics of Rights, Co-operation and Welfare*. Oxford: Blackwell.

—— (1993): "Welfare, Resources, and Capabilities: A Review of *Inequality Reexamined* by Amartya Sen," *Journal of Economic Literature*, 31 (4), December, 1947–62.

Suppes, P. (1966): "Some Formal Models of Grading Principles," *Synthese*, 16 (3/4), December, 284–306.

Suzumura, K. (1983): *Rational Choice, Collective Decisions and Social Welfare*. Cambridge: Cambridge University Press.

—— (1991): "Alternative Approaches to Libertarian Rights," in Arrow (1991), 215–42.

Tocqueville, A. de (1840): *Democracy in America*. New York: Langley. Republished, New York: Knopf, 1945.

Tullock, G. (1967): "The General Irrelevance of the General Possibility Theorem," *Quarterly Journal of Economics*, 81 (2), May, 256–70.

Wilson, R. (1975): "On the Theory of Aggregation," *Journal of Economic Theory*, 10 (1), February, 89–99.

World Disasters Report (1994): Geneva: International Federation of Red Cross and Red Crescent Societies.

Wriglesworth, J. (1985): *Libertarian Conflicts in Social Choice*. Cambridge: Cambridge University Press.

Young, H. P. (ed.) (1985): *Fair Allocation*. Providence, RI: American Mathematical Society.

Introduction

Garrett Hardin, in the now classic article in chapter 8, brought to the attention of a broad spectrum of researchers in biological, social and moral fields a type of negative externality that arises when a resource is owned in common without restrictions on individuals' usage. More exactly, an instance of the "tragedy of the commons" arises when agents compare benefits from such usage with average private costs rather than marginal social costs. The cattle owner who placed an animal in the common pasture and thereby increased the social costs of overgrazing bore only the average costs of such action, since the damage to herds of other owners were costless externalities to the new entrant. Therefore, all owners had incentives to add their herds to the commons, ultimately destroying it through over-grazing.

A more up-to-date example is that of traffic congestion. Suppose 100 vehicles are driving over a bridge and the average time of transit is five minutes. Now, let a marginal driver – the 101st – consider entering the stream of traffic, raising the transit time to six minutes. That driver will compare the benefit of crossing the bridge with the *average* of six minutes, neglecting the marginal social cost of 100 incremental minutes inflicted on intramarginal traffic. The true marginal social cost of the 101st transit is 106 minutes, blithely ignorable by our marginal driver, and, since every driver is the marginal driver, traffic jams are the inevitable result. Efficiency requires that all such drivers be forced to compare benefits with marginal social costs – via tolls at peak hours, for example.

As a biologist, Hardin's concern is with that of overpopulation of a finite world, a favorite worry of the 1960s. Deterrence of large families is not so neatly achieved as reduction of congestion. In other contexts in the article, Hardin asserts that appeals to conscience are costly to the human consciousness in terms of the guilt feeling instilled by the id. Besides, such attempts to appeal to conscience are self-defeating because they are successful in restraining those who are susceptible to such approaches, permitting those who ignore them to have large families. Either through genetic or extra-genetic condition-ing of the offspring of the latter, over time, the population becomes increasingly non-reachable through appeals to social duty.

One is surprised, therefore, that, at the end of the chapter, when it comes time for suggesting policy measures to restrict population growth, Hardin recommends education as the policy tool, rather than the harsher measures to which his arguments seem to be building. It is difficult to see why education, even if it concentrates upon reason rather than conscience as the effective constituent, would not suffer from the self-defeating deficiency discussed in the paragraph above.

Chapter 9 deals with the problem of *adverse selection* that arises in markets with asymmetric information, or those in which buyers (sellers) possess more information about the quality of the product than sellers (buyers). Akerlof demonstrates the case where such a situation may lead to the disappearance of a market, despite the fact that, at any given price, there are buyers and sellers willing to trade. His example is that of a used car market, where sellers are better informed than buyers about the quality of a car. Cars of all qualities must sell at the same price because of consumer ignorance, but as sellers of cars whose quality is above that of the average quality established in the market withdraw their vehicles, price drifts downward toward zero and the market disappears. Akerlof discusses a wide variety of situations where uncertainty of quality on one side of the market results in such market failure, or in which minorities in labor markets are discriminated against for failure of accurate screening information, or in which venture capital is not forthcoming because of widespread fraudulent dealing. Adverse selection is a form of moral hazard in which the existence of (say) health insurance leads those in fragile health to apply for insurance in disproportionate numbers, driving up premiums and eliminating those potential customers in normal health, thereby making the insurance infeasible.

CHAPTER EIGHT

The Tragedy of the Commons

The population problem has no technical solution; it requires a fundamental extension in morality.

GARRETT HARDIN

Source: *Science*, 162 (1968), pp. 1243–8. Reprinted with the permission of The American Association for the Advancement of Science. © The American Association for the Advancement of Science.

At the end of a thoughtful article on the future of nuclear war, Wiesner and York (*1*) concluded that: "Both sides in the arms race are . . . confronted by the dilemma of steadily increasing military power and steadily decreasing national security. *It is our considered professional judgment that this dilemma has no technical solution.* If the great powers continue to look for solutions in the area of science and technology only, the result will be to worsen the situation."

I would like to focus your attention not on the subject of the article (national security in a nuclear world) but on the kind of conclusion they reached, namely that there is no technical solution to the problem. An implicit and almost universal assumption of discussions published in professional and semipopular scientific journals is that the problem under discussion has a technical solution. A technical solution may be defined as one that requires a change only in the techniques of the natural sciences, demanding little or nothing in the way of change in human values or ideas of morality.

In our day (though not in earlier times) technical solutions are always welcome. Because of previous failures in prophecy, it takes courage to assert that a desired technical solution is not possible. Wiesner and York exhibited this courage; publishing in a science journal, they insisted that the solution to the problem was not to be found in the natural sciences. They cautiously qualified their statement with the phrase, "It is our considered professional judgement . . ." Whether they were right or not is not the concern of the present article. Rather, the concern here is with the important concept of a class of human problems which can be called "no technical solution problems," and, more specifically, with the identification and discussion of one of these.

It is easy to show that the class is not a null class. Recall the game of tick-tack-toe. Consider the problem, "How can I win the game of tick-tack-toe?" It is well known that I cannot, if I assume (in keeping with the conventions of game theory) that my opponent understands the game perfectly. Put another way, there is no "technical solution" to the problem. I can win only by giving a radical meaning to the word "win." I can hit my opponent over the head; or I can drug him; or I can falsify the records. Every way in which I "win" involves, in some sense, an abandonment of the game, as we intuitively understand it. (I can also, of course, openly abandon the game – refuse to play it. This is what most adults do.)

The class of "No technical solution problems" has members. My thesis is that the "population problem," as conventionally conceived, is a member of this class. How it is conventionally conceived needs some comment. It is fair to say that most people who anguish over the population problem are trying to find a way to avoid the evils of over-population without relinquishing any of the privileges they now enjoy. They think that farming the seas or developing new strains of wheat will solve the problem – technologically. I try to show here that the solution they seek cannot be found. The population problem cannot be solved in a technical way, any more than can the problem of winning the game of tick-tack-toe.

What Shall We Maximize?

Population, as Malthus said, naturally tends to grow "geometrically," or, as we would now say, exponentially. In a finite world this means that the per capita share of the world's goods must steadily decrease. Is ours a finite world?

A fair defense can be put forward for the view that the world is infinite; or that we do not know that it is not. But, in terms of the practical problems that we must face in the next few generations with the foreseeable technology, it is clear that we will greatly increase human misery if we do not, during the immediate future, assume that the world available to the terrestrial human population is finite. "Space" is no escape (2).

A finite world can support only a finite population; therefore, population growth must eventually equal zero. (The case of perpetual wide fluctuations above and below zero is a trivial variant that need not be discussed.) When this condition is met, what will be the situation of mankind? Specifically, can Bentham's goal of "the greatest good for the greatest number" be realized?

No – for two reasons, each sufficient by itself. The first is a theoretical one. It is not mathematically possible to maximize for two (or more) variables at the same time. This was clearly stated by von Neumann and Morgenstern (3), but the principle is implicit in the theory of partial differential equations, dating back at least to D'Alembert (1717–1783).

The second reason springs directly from biological facts. To live, any organism must have a source of energy (for example, food). This energy is utilized for two purposes: mere maintenance and work. For man, maintenance of life requires about 1600 kilo-calories a day ("maintenance calories"). Anything that he does over and above merely staying alive will be defined as work, and is supported by "work calories" which he takes in. Work calories are used not only for what we call work in common speech; they are also required for all forms of enjoyment, from swimming and automobile racing to playing music and writing poetry. If our goal is to maximize population it is obvious what we must do: We must make the work calories per person approach as close to zero as possible. No gourmet meals, no vacations, no sports, no music, no literature, no art...I think that everyone will grant, without argument or proof, that maximizing population does not maximize goods. Bentham's goal is impossible.

In reaching this conclusion I have made the usual assumption that it is the acquisition of energy that is the problem. The appearance of atomic energy has led some to question this assumption. However, given an infinite source of energy, population growth still produces an inescapable problem. The problem of the acquisition of energy is replaced by the problem of its dissipation, as J. H. Fremlin has so wittily shown (*4*). The arithmetic signs in the analysis are, as it were, reversed; but Bentham's goal is still unobtainable.

The optimum population is, then, less than the maximum. The difficulty of defining the optimum is enormous; so far as I know, no one has seriously tackled this problem. Reaching an acceptable and stable solution will surely require more than one generation of hard analytical work – and much persuasion.

We want the maximum good per person; but what is good? To one person it is wilderness, to another it is ski lodges for thousands. To one it is estuaries to nourish ducks for hunters to shoot; to another it is factory land. Comparing one good with another is, we usually say, impossible because goods are incommensurable. Incommensurables cannot be compared.

Theoretically this may be true; but in real life incommensurables *are* commensurable. Only a criterion of judgment and a system of weighting are needed. In nature the criterion is survival. Is it better for a species to be small and hideable, or large and powerful? Natural selection commensurates the incommensurables. The compromise achieved depends on a natural weighting of the values of the variables.

Man must imitate this process. There is no doubt that in fact he already does, but unconsciously. It is when the hidden decisions are made explicit that the arguments begin. The problem for the years ahead is to work out an acceptable theory of weighting. Synergistic effects, nonlinear variation, and difficulties in discounting the future make the intellectual problem difficult, but not (in principle) insoluble.

Has any cultural group solved this practical problem at the present time, even on an intuitive level? One simple fact proves that none has: there is no prosperous population in the world today that has, and has had for some time, a growth rate of zero. Any people that has intuitively identified its optimum point will soon reach it, after which its growth rate becomes and remains zero.

Of course, a positive growth rate might be taken as evidence that a population is below its optimum. However, by any reasonable standards, the most rapidly growing populations on earth today are (in general) the most miserable. This association (which need not be invariable) casts doubt on the optimistic assumption that the positive growth rate of a population is evidence that it has yet to reach its optimum.

We can make little progress in working toward optimum population size until we explicitly exorcize the spirit of Adam Smith in the field of practical demography. In economic affairs, *The Wealth of Nations* (1776) popularized the "invisible hand," the idea that an individual who "intends only his own gain," is, as it were, "led by an invisible hand to promote...the public interest" (*5*). Adam Smith did not assert that this was invariably true, and perhaps neither did any of his followers. But he contributed to a dominant tendency of thought that has ever since interfered with positive action based on rational analysis, namely, the tendency to assume that decisions reached individually will, in fact, be the best decisions for an entire society. If this assumption is correct it justifies the continuance of our present policy of *laissez-faire* in reproduction. If it is correct we can assume that men will control their individual fecundity so as to produce the optimum population. If the assumption is not correct, we need to reexamine our individual freedoms to see which ones are defensible.

Tragedy of Freedom in a Commons

The rebuttal to the invisible hand in population control is to be found in a scenario first sketched in a little-known pamphlet (*6*) in 1833 by a mathematical amateur named William Forster Lloyd (1794–1852). We may well call it "the tragedy of the commons," using the word "tragedy" as the philosopher Whitehead used it (*7*). "The essence of dramatic tragedy is not unhappiness. It resides in the solemnity of the remorseless working of things." He then goes on to say, "This inevitableness of destiny can only be illustrated in terms of human life by incidents which in fact involve unhappiness. For it is only by them that the futility of escape can be made evident in the drama."

The tragedy of the commons develops in this way. Picture a pasture open to all. It is to be expected that each herdsman will try to keep as many cattle as possible on the commons. Such an arrangement may work reasonably satisfactorily for centuries because tribal wars, poaching, and disease keep the numbers of both man and beast well below the carrying capacity of the land. Finally, however, comes the day of reckoning, that is, the day when the long-desired goal of social stability becomes a reality. At this point, the inherent logic of the commons remorselessly generates tragedy.

As a rational being, each herdsman seeks to maximize his gain. Explicitly or implicitly, more or less consciously, he asks, "What is the utility *to me* of adding one more animal to my herd?" This utility has one negative and one positive component.

1 The positive component is a function of the increment of one animal. Since the herdsman receives all the proceeds from the sale of the additional animal, the positive utility is nearly +1.

2 The negative component is a function of the additional overgrazing created by one more animal. Since, however, the effects of overgrazing are shared by all the herdsmen, the negative utility for any particular decision-making herdsman is only a fraction of −1.

Adding together the component partial utilities, the rational herdsman concludes that the only sensible course for him to pursue is to add another animal to his herd. And another; and another.... But this is the conclusion reached by each and every rational herdsman sharing a commons. Therein is the tragedy. Each man is locked into a system that compels him to increase his herd without limit – in a world that is limited. Ruin is the destination toward which all men rush, each pursuing his own best interest in a society that believes in the freedom of the commons. Freedom in a commons brings ruin to all.

Some would say that this is a platitude. Would that it were! In a sense, it was learned thousands of years ago, but natural selection favors the forces of psychological denial (*8*). The individual benefits as an individual from his ability to deny the truth even though society as a whole, of which he is a part, suffers. Education can counteract the natural tendency to do the wrong thing, but the inexorable succession of generations requires that the basis for this knowledge be constantly refreshed.

A simple incident that occurred a few years ago in Leominster, Massachusetts, shows how perishable the knowledge is. During the Christmas shopping season the parking meters downtown were covered with plastic bags that bore tags reading: "Do not open until after Christmas. Free parking courtesy of the mayor and city council." In other words, facing the prospect of an increased demand for already scarce space, the city fathers reinstituted the system of the commons. (Cynically, we suspect that they gained more votes than they lost by this retrogressive act.)

In an approximate way, the logic of the commons has been understood for a long time, perhaps since the discovery of agriculture or the invention of private property in real estate. But it is understood mostly only in special cases which are not sufficiently general-ized. Even at this late date, cattlemen leasing national land on the western ranges demonstrate no more than an ambivalent understanding, in constantly pressuring federal authorities to increase the head count to the point where over-grazing produces erosion and weed-dominance. Likewise, the oceans of the world continue to suffer from the survival of the philosophy of the commons. Maritime nations still respond automatically to the shibboleth of the "freedom of the seas." Professing to believe in the "inexhaustible resources of the oceans," they bring species after species of fish and whales closer to extinction (9).

The National Parks present another instance of the working out of the tragedy of the commons. At present, they are open to all, without limit. The parks themselves are limited in extent – there is only one Yosemite Valley – whereas population seems to grow without limit. The values that visitors seek in the parks are steadily eroded. Plainly, we must soon cease to treat the parks as commons or they will be of no value to anyone.

What shall we do? We have several options. We might sell them off as private property. We might keep them as public property, but allocate the right to enter them. The allocation might be on the basis of wealth, by the use of an education system. It might be on the basis of merit, as defined by some agreed-upon standards. It might be by lottery. Or it might be on a first-come, first-served basis, administered to long queues. These, I think, are all the reasonable possibilities. They are all objectionable. But we must choose – or acquiesce in the destruction of the commons that we call our National Parks.

Pollution

In a reverse way, the tragedy of the commons reappears in problems of pollution. Here it is not a question of taking something out of the commons, but of putting something in – sewage, or chemical, radioactive, and heat wastes into water; noxious and dangerous fumes into the air; and distracting and unpleasant advertising signs into the line of sight. The calculations of utility are much the same as before. The rational man finds that his share of the cost of the wastes he discharges into the commons is less than the cost of purifying his wastes before releasing them. Since this is true for everyone, we are locked into a system of "fouling our own nest," so long as we behave only as independent, rational, free-enterprisers.

The tragedy of the commons as a food basket is averted by private property, or something formally like it. But the air and waters surrounding us cannot readily be fenced, and so the tragedy of the commons as a cesspool must be prevented by different means, by coercive laws or taxing devices that make it cheaper for the polluter to treat his pollutants than to discharge them untreated. We have not progressed as far with the solution of this problem as we have with the first. Indeed, our particular concept of private property, which deters us from exhausting the positive resources of the earth, favors pollution. The owner of a factory on the bank of a stream – whose property extends to the middle of the stream – often has difficulty seeing why it is not his natural right to muddy the waters flowing past his door. The law, always behind the times, requires elaborate stitching and fitting to adapt it to this newly perceived aspect of the commons.

The pollution problem is a consequence of population. It did not much matter how a lonely American frontiersman disposed of his waste. "Flowing water purifies itself every 10 miles," my grandfather used to say, and the myth was near enough to the truth when he was a boy, for there were not too many people. But as population became denser, the natural chemical and biological recycling processes became overloaded, calling for a redefinition of property rights.

How to Legislate Temperance?

Analysis of the pollution problem as a function of population density uncovers a not generally recognized principle of morality, namely: *the morality of an act is a function of the state of the system at the time it is performed* (*10*). Using the commons as a cesspool does not harm the general public under frontier conditions, because there is no public; the same behavior in a metropolis is unbearable. A hundred and fifty years ago a plainsman could kill an American bison, cut out only the tongue for his dinner, and discard the rest of the animal. He was not in any important sense being wasteful. Today, with only a few thousand bison left, we would be appalled at such behavior.

In passing, it is worth noting that the morality of an act cannot be determined from a photograph. One does not know whether a man killing an elephant or setting fire to the grassland is harming others until one knows the total system in which his act appears. "One picture is worth a thousand words," said an ancient Chinese; but it may take 10,000 words to validate it. It is as tempting to ecologists as it is to reformers in general to try to persuade others by way of the photographic shortcut. But the essence of an argument cannot be photographed: it must be presented rationally – in words.

That morality is system-sensitive escaped the attention of most codifiers of ethics in the past. "Thou shalt not..." is the form of traditional ethical directives which make no allowance for particular circumstances. The laws of our society follow the pattern of ancient ethics, and therefore are poorly suited to governing a complex, crowded, change-able world. Our epicyclic solution is to augment statutory law with administrative law. Since it is practically impossible to spell out all the conditions under which it is safe to burn trash in the back yard or to run an automobile without smog-control, by law we delegate the details to bureaus. The result is administrative law, which is rightly feared for an ancient reason – *Quis custodiet ipsos custodes?* – "Who shall watch the watchers themselves?" John Adams said that we must have "a government of laws and not men." Bureau administrators, trying to evaluate the morality of acts in the total system, are singularly liable to corruption, producing a government by men, not laws.

Prohibition is easy to legislate (though not necessarily to enforce); but how do we legislate temperance? Experience indicates that it can be accomplished best through the mediation of administrative law. We limit possibilities unnecessarily if we suppose that the sentiment of *Quis custodiet* denies us the use of administrative law. We should rather retain the phrase as a perpetual reminder of fearful dangers we cannot avoid. The great challenge facing us now is to invent the corrective feedbacks that are needed to keep custodians honest. We must find ways to legitimate the needed authority of both the custodians and the corrective feedbacks.

Freedom to Breed is Intolerable

The tragedy of the commons is involved in population problems in another way. In a world governed solely by the principle of "dog eat dog" – if indeed there ever was such a world – how many children a family had would not be a matter of public concern. Parents who bred too exuberantly would leave fewer descendants, not more, because they would be unable to care adequately for their children. David Lack and others have found that such a negative feedback demonstrably controls the fecundity of birds (*11*). But men are not birds, and have not acted like them for millenniums, at least.

If each human family were dependent only on its own resources; *if* the children of improvident parents starved to death; *if*, thus, overbreeding brought its own "punishment" to the germ line – *then* there would be no public interest in controlling the breeding of families. But our society is deeply committed to the welfare state (*12*), and hence is confronted with another aspect of the tragedy of the commons.

In a welfare state, how shall we deal with the family, the religion, the race, or the class (or indeed any distinguishable and cohesive group) that adopts overbreeding as a policy to secure its own aggrandizement (*13*)? To couple the concept of freedom to breed with the belief that everyone born has an equal right to the commons is to lock the world into a tragic course of action.

Unfortunately this is just the course of action that is being pursued by the United Nations. In late 1967, some 30 nations agreed to the following (*14*)

> The Universal Declaration of Human Rights describes the family as the natural and funda-mental unit of society. It follows that any choice and decision with regard to the size of the family must irrevocably rest with the family itself, and cannot be made by anyone else.

It is painful to have to deny categorically the validity of this right; denying it, one feels as uncomfortable as a resident of Salem, Massachusetts, who denied the reality of witches in the 17th century. At the present time, in liberal quarters, something like a taboo acts to inhibit criticism of the United Nations. There is a feeling that the United Nations is "our last and best hope," that we shouldn't find fault with it; we shouldn't play into the hands of the archconservatives. However, let us not forget what Robert Louis Stevenson said: "The truth that is suppressed by friends is the readiest weapon of the enemy." If we love the truth we must openly deny the validity of the Universal Declaration of Human Rights, even though it is promoted by the United Nations. We should also join with Kingsley Davis (*15*) in attempting to get Planned Parenthood-World Population to see the error of its ways in embracing the same tragic ideal.

Conscience is Self-Eliminating

It is a mistake to think that we can control the breeding of mankind in the long run by an appeal to conscience. Charles Galton Darwin made this point when he spoke on the centennial of the publication of his grandfather's great book. The argument is straight-forward and Darwinian.

People vary. Confronted with appeals to limit breeding, some people will undoubtedly respond to the plea more than others. Those who have more children will produce a larger fraction of the next generation than those with more susceptible consciences. The difference will be accentuated, generation by generation.

In C. G. Darwin's words: "It may well be that it would take hundreds of generations for the progenitive instinct to develop in this way, but if it should do so, nature would have taken her revenge, and the variety *Homo contracipiens* would become extinct and would be replaced by the variety *Homo progenitivus*" (*16*).

The argument assumes that conscience or the desire for children (no matter which) is hereditary – but hereditary only in the most general formal sense. The result will be the same whether the attitude is transmitted through germ cells, or exosomatically, to use A. J. Lotka's term. (If one denies the latter possibility as well as the former, then what's the point of education?) The argument has here been stated in the context of the population problem, but it applies equally well to any instance in which society appeals to an individual exploiting a commons to restrain himself for the general good – by means of his conscience. To make such an appeal is to set up a selective system that works toward the elimination of conscience from the race.

Pathogenic Effects of Conscience

The long-term disadvantage of an appeal to conscience should be enough to condemn it; but has serious short-term disadvantages as well. If we ask a man who is exploiting a commons to desist "in the name of conscience," what are we saying to him? What does he hear? – not only at the moment but also in the wee small hours of the night when, half asleep, he remembers not merely the words we used but also the nonverbal communication cues we gave him unawares? Sooner or later, consciously or subconsciously, he senses that he has received two communications, and that they are contradictory:

   (i) (intended communication) "If you don't do as we ask, we will openly condemn you for not acting like a responsible citizen";
   (ii) (the unintended communication) "if you *do* behave as we ask, we will secretly condemn you for a simpleton who can be shamed into standing aside while the rest of us exploit the commons."

Everyman then is caught in what Bateson has called a "double bind." Bateson and his co-workers have made a plausible case for viewing the double bind as an important causative factor in the genesis of schizophrenia (*17*). The double bind may not always be so damaging, but it always endangers the mental health of anyone to whom it is applied. "A bad conscience," said Nietzsche, "is a kind of illness."

To conjure up a conscience in others is tempting to anyone who wishes to extend his control beyond the legal limits. Leaders at the highest level succumb to this temptation. Has any President during the past generation failed to call on labor unions to moderate voluntarily their demands for higher wages, or to steel companies to honor voluntary guidelines on prices? I can recall none. The rhetoric used on such occasions is designed to produce feelings of guilt in noncooperators.

For centuries it was assumed without proof that guilt was a valuable, perhaps even an indispensable, ingredient of the civilized life. Now, in this post-Freudian world, we doubt it.

Paul Goodman speaks from the modern point of view when he says: "No good has ever come from feeling guilty, neither intelligence, policy, nor compassion. The guilty do not pay attention to the object but only to themselves, and not even to their own interests, which might make sense, but to their anxieties" (*18*).

One does not have to be a professional psychiatrist to see the consequences of anxiety. We in the Western world are just emerging from a dreadful two-centuries-long Dark Ages of Eros that was sustained partly by prohibition laws, but perhaps more effectively by the anxiety-generating mechanisms of education. Alex Comfort has told the story well in *The Anxiety Makers* (*19*); it is not a pretty one.

Since proof is difficult, we may even concede that the results of anxiety may sometimes, from certain points of view, be desirable. The larger question we should ask is whether, as a matter of policy, we should ever encourage the use of a technique the tendency (if not the intention) of which is psychologically pathogenic. We hear much talk these days of responsible parenthood; the coupled words are incorporated into the titles of some organizations devoted to birth control. Some people have proposed massive propaganda campaigns to instill responsibility into the nation's (or the world's) breeders. But what is the meaning of the word responsibility in this context? Is it not merely a synonym for the word conscience? When we use the word responsibility in the absence of substantial sanctions are we not trying to browbeat a free man in a commons into acting against his own interest? Responsibility is a verbal counterfeit for a substantial *quid pro quo*. It is an attempt to get something for nothing.

If the word responsibility is to be used at all, I suggest that it be in the sense Charles Frankel uses it (*20*). "Responsibility," says this philosopher, "is the product of definite social arrangements." Notice that Frankel calls for social arrangements – not propaganda.

Mutual Coercion Mutually Agreed Upon

The social arrangements that produce responsibility are arrangements that create coercion, of some sort. Consider bank-robbing. The man who takes money from a bank acts as if the bank were a commons. How do we prevent such action? Certainly not by trying to control his behavior solely by a verbal appeal to his sense of responsibility. Rather than rely on propaganda we follow Frankel's lead and insist that a bank is not a commons; we seek the definite social arrangements that will keep it from becoming a commons. That we thereby infringe on the freedom of would-be robbers we neither deny nor regret.

The morality of bank-robbing is particularly easy to understand because we accept complete prohibition of this activity. We are willing to say "Thou shalt not rob banks," without providing for exceptions. But temperance also can be created by coercion. Taxing is a good coercive device, To keep downtown shoppers temperate in their use of parking space we introduce parking meters for short periods, and traffic fines for longer ones. We need not actually forbid a citizen to park as long as he wants to; we need merely make it increasingly expensive for him to do so. Not prohibition, but carefully biased options are what we offer him. A Madison Avenue man might call this persuasion; I prefer the greater candor of the word coercion.

Coercion is a dirty word to most liberals now, but it need not forever be so. As with the four-letter words, its dirtiness can be cleansed away by exposure to the light, by saying it over and over without apology or embarrassment. To many, the word coercion implies arbitrary decisions of distant and irresponsible bureaucrats; but this is not a necessary part of its meaning. The only kind of coercion I recommend is mutual coercion, mutually agreed upon by the majority of the people affected.

To say that we mutually agree to coercion is not to say that we are required to enjoy it, or even to pretend we enjoy it. Who enjoys taxes? We all grumble about them. But we accept compulsory taxes because we recognize that voluntary taxes would favor the conscienceless. We institute and (grumblingly) support taxes and other coercive devices to escape the horror of the commons.

An alternative to the commons need not be perfectly just to be preferable. With real estate and other material goods, the alternative we have chosen is the institution of private property coupled with legal inheritance. Is this system perfectly just? As a genetically trained biologist I deny that it is. It seems to me that, if there are to be differences in individual inheritance, legal possession should be perfectly correlated with biological inheritance – that those who are biologically more fit to be the custodians of property and power should legally inherit more. But genetic recombination continually makes a mockery of the doctrine of "like father, like son" implicit in our laws of legal inheritance. An idiot can inherit millions, and a trust fund can keep his estate intact. We must admit that our legal system of private property plus inheritance is unjust – but we put up with it because we are not convinced, at the moment, that anyone has invented a better system. The alternative of the commons is too horrifying to contemplate. Injustice is preferable to total ruin.

It is one of the peculiarities of the warfare between reform and the status quo that it is thoughtlessly governed by a double standard. Whenever a reform measure is proposed it is often defeated when its opponents triumphantly discover a flaw in it. As Kingsley Davis has pointed out (15), worshippers of the status quo sometimes imply that no reform is possible without unanimous agreement, an implication contrary to historical fact. As nearly as I can make out, automatic rejection of proposed reforms is based on one of two unconscious assumptions:

(i) that the status quo is perfect; or
(ii) that the choice we face is between reform and no action;

if the proposed reform is imperfect, we presumably should take no action at all, while we wait for a perfect proposal.

But we can never do nothing. That which we have done for thousands of years is also action. It also produces evils. Once we are aware that the status quo is action, we can then compare its discoverable advantages and disadvantages with the predicted advantages and disadvantages of the proposed reform, discounting as best we can for our lack of experience. On the basis of such a comparison, we can make a rational decision which will not involve the unworkable assumption that only perfect systems are tolerable.

Recognition of Necessity

Perhaps the simplest summary of this analysis of man's population problems is this: the commons, if justifiable at all, is justifiable only under conditions of low-population density. As the human population has increased, the commons has had to be abandoned in one aspect after another.

First we abandoned the commons in food gathering, enclosing farm land and restricting pastures and hunting and fishing areas. These restrictions are still not complete throughout the world.

Somewhat later we saw that the commons as a place for waste disposal would also have to be abandoned. Restrictions on the disposal of domestic sewage are widely accepted in the Western world; we are still struggling to close the commons to pollution by automobiles, factories, insecticide sprayers, fertilizing operations, and atomic energy installations.

In a still more embryonic state is our recognition of the evils of the commons in matters of pleasure. There is almost no restriction on the propagation of sound waves in the public medium. The shopping public is assaulted with mindless music, without its consent. Our government is paying out billions of dollars to create supersonic transport which will disturb 50,000 people for every one person who is whisked from coast to coast 3 hours faster. Advertisers muddy the airwaves of radio and television and pollute the view of travelers. We are a long way from outlawing the commons in matters of pleasure. Is this because our Puritan inheritance makes us view pleasure as something of a sin, and pain (that is, the pollution of advertising) as the sign of virtue?

Every new enclosure of the commons involves the infringement of somebody's personal liberty. Infringements made in the distant past are accepted because no contemporary complains of a loss. It is the newly proposed infringements that we vigorously oppose; cries of "rights" and "freedom" fill the air. But what does "freedom" mean? When men mutually agreed to pass laws against robbing, mankind became more free, not less so. Individuals locked into the logic of the commons are free only to bring on universal ruin; once they see the necessity of mutual coercion, they become free to pursue other goals. I believe it was Hegel who said, "Freedom is the recognition of necessity."

The most important aspect of necessity that we must now recognize, is the necessity of abandoning the commons in breeding. No technical solution can rescue us from the misery of overpopulation. Freedom to breed will bring ruin to all. At the moment, to avoid hard decisions many of us are tempted to propagandize for conscience and responsible parenthood. The temptation must be resisted, because an appeal to independently acting consciences selects for the disappearance of all conscience in the long run, and an increase in anxiety in the short.

The only way we can preserve any nurture other and more precious freedoms is by relinquishing the freedom to breed, and that very soon. "Freedom is the recognition of necessity" – and it is the role of education to reveal to all the necessity of abandoning the freedom to breed. Only so, can we put as end to this aspect of the tragedy of the commons.

References

 1. Wiesner, J. B. and York, H. F. (1964): *Scientific American*, 211 (4), 27.
 2. Hardin, G. (1959): *Journal of Heredity*, 150, 68; [von Hoernor, S. (1962)]: *Science*, 137, 18.
 3. Neumann, J. von and Morgenstern, O. (1947): *Theory of Games and Economic Behavior*. Princeton, NJ: Princeton University Press, 11.
 4. Fremlin, J. H. (1964): *New Scientist*, 415, 285.
 5. Smith, A. (1937): *The Wealth of Nations*. New York: Modern Library, 423.
 6. Lloyd, W. F. (1833): *Two Lectures on the Checks of Population*. Oxford, England: Oxford University Press. Reprinted (in part) in G. Hardin (ed.), (1964): *Population, Evolution and Birth Control*, San Francisco: Freeman, 37.
 7. Whitehead, A. N. (1948): *Science and the Modern World*. New York: Mentor, 17.
 8. Hardin, G. (ed.) (1964): *Population Evolution, and Birth Control*. San Francisco: Freeman, 56.
 9. McVay, S. (1966): *Scientific American*, 216 (8), 13.
10. Fletcher, J. (1966): *Situation Ethics*. Philadelphia: Westminster.
11. Lack, D. (1954): *The Natural Regulation of Animal Numbers*. Oxford: Clarendon Press.
12. Giryetz, H. (1950): *From Wealth to Welfare*. Stanford, CA: Stanford University Press.
13. Hardin, G. (1963): *Perspectives in Biology and Medicine*, 6, 366.
14. Thant, U. (1968): *International Planned Parenthood News*, 168, February, 3.
15. Davis, K. (1967): *Science*, 158, 730.
16. Tax, S. (ed.) (1960): *Evolution after Darwin*. Chicago: University of Chicago Press, vol. 2. 469.
17. Bateson, G., Jackson, D. D., Haley, J. and Weakland, J. (1956): *Behavioral Science*, 1, 251.
18. Goodman, P. (1968): *New York Rev. Books*, 10 (8), May, 23, 22.
19. Comfort, A. (1967): *The Anxiety Makers*. London: Nelson.
20. Frankel, C. (1955): *The Case for Modern Man*. New York: Harper, 203.
21. Roslansky, J. D. (1966): *Genetics and the Future of Man*. New York: Appleton-Century-Crofts, 177.

CHAPTER NINE

The Market for "Lemons": Quality Uncertainty and the Market Mechanism

GEORGE A. AKERLOF

Source: *Quarterly Journal of Economics*, 84 (1970), pp. 488–500. Reprinted with the permission of The MIT Press. © The MIT Press.

1. Introduction

This paper relates quality and uncertainty. The existence of goods of many grades poses interesting and important problems for the theory of markets. On the one hand, the interaction of quality differences and uncertainty may explain important institutions of the labor market. On the other hand, this paper presents a struggling attempt to give structure to the statement: "Business in under-developed countries is difficult"; in particular, a structure is given for determining the economic costs of dishonesty. Additional applications of the theory include comments on the structure of money markets, on the notion of "insurability," on the liquidity of durables, and on brand-name goods.

There are many markets in which buyers use some market statistic to judge the quality of prospective purchases. In this case there is incentive for sellers to market poor quality merchandise, since the returns for good quality accrue mainly to the entire group whose statistic is affected rather than to the individual seller. As a result there tends to be a reduction in the average quality of goods and also in the size of the market. It should also be perceived that in these markets social and private returns differ, and therefore, in some cases, governmental intervention may increase the welfare of all parties. Or private institutions may arise to take advantage of the potential increases in welfare which can accrue to all parties. By nature, however, these institutions are nonatomistic, and therefore concentrations of power – with ill consequences of their own – can develop.

The automobile market is used as a finger exercise to illustrate and develop these thoughts. It should be emphasized that this market is chosen for its concreteness and ease in understanding rather than for its importance or realism.

2. The Model with Automobiles as an Example

2.1. The automobiles market

The example of used cars captures the essence of the problem. From time to time one hears either mention of or surprise at the large price difference between new cars and those which have just left the showroom. The usual lunch table justification for this phenomenon is the pure joy of owning a "new" car. We offer a different explanation. Suppose (for the sake of clarity rather than reality) that there are just four kinds of cars. There are new cars and used cars. There are good cars and bad cars (which in America are known as "lemons"). A new car may be a good car or a lemon, and of course the same is true of used cars.

The individuals in this market buy a new automobile without knowing whether the car they buy will be good or a lemon. But they do know that with probability q it is a good car and with probability $(1 - q)$ it is a lemon; by assumption, q is the proportion of good cars produced and $(1 - q)$ is the proportion of lemons.

After owning a specific car, however, for a length of time, the car owner can form a good idea of the quality of this machine; i.e., the owner assigns a new probability to the event that his car is a lemon. This estimate is more accurate than the original estimate. An asymmetry in available information has developed: for the sellers now have more knowledge about the quality of a car than the buyers. But good cars and bad cars must still sell at the same price – since it is impossible for a buyer to tell the difference between a good car and a bad car. It is apparent that a used car cannot have the same valuation as a new car – if it did have the same valuation, it would clearly be advantageous to trade a lemon at the price of new car, and buy another new car, at a higher probability q of being good and a lower probability of being bad. Thus the owner of a good machine must be locked in. Not only is it true that he cannot receive the true value of his car, but he cannot even obtain the expected value of a new car.

Gresham's law has made a modified reappearance. For most cars traded will be the "lemons," and good cars may not be traded at all. The "bad" cars tend to drive out the good (in much the same way that bad money drives out the good). But the analogy with Gresham's law is not quite complete: bad cars drive out the good because they sell at the same price as good cars; similarly, bad money drives out good because the exchange rate is even. But the bad cars sell at the same price as good cars since it is impossible for a buyer to tell the difference between a good and a bad car; only the seller knows. In Gresham's law, however, presumably both buyer and seller can tell the difference between good and bad money. So the analogy is instructive, but not complete.

2.2. Asymmetrical information

It has been seen that the good cars may be driven out of the market by the lemons. But in a more continuous case with different grades of goods, even worse pathologies can exist. For it is quite possible to have the bad driving out the not-so-bad driving out the medium driving out the not-so-good driving out the good in such a sequence of events that no market exists at all.

One can assume that the demand for used automobiles depends most strongly upon two variables – the price of the automobile p and the average quality of used cars traded, μ, or $Q^d = D(p, \mu)$. Both the supply of used cars and also the average quality μ will depend upon the price, or $\mu = \mu(p)$ and $S = S(p)$. And in equilibrium the supply must equal the demand for the given average quality, or $S(p) = D(p, \mu(p))$. As the price falls, normally the quality will also fall. And it is quite possible that no goods will be traded at any price level.

Such an example can be derived from utility theory. Assume that there are just two groups of traders: groups one and two. Give group one a utility function

$$U_1 = M + \sum_{i=1}^{n} x_i$$

where M is the consumption of goods other than automobiles, x_i is the quality of the ith automobile, and n is the number of automobiles.

Similarly, let

$$U_2 = M + \sum_{i=1}^{n} \frac{3}{2} x_i$$

where M, x_i and n are defined as before.

Three comments should be made about these utility functions:

1 Without linear utility (say with logarithmic utility) one gets needlessly mired in algebraic complication.
2 The use of linear utility allows a focus on the effects of asymmetry of information; with a concave utility function we would have to deal jointly with the usual risk-variance effects of uncertainty and the special effects we wish to discuss here.
3 U_1 and U_2 have the odd characteristic that the addition of a second car, or indeed a kth car, adds the same amount of utility as the first. Again realism is sacrificed to avoid a diversion from the proper focus.

To continue, it is assumed

1 that both type one traders and type two traders are von Neumann–Morgenstern maximizers of expected utility;
2 that group one has N cars with uniformly distributed quality x, $0 \leq x \leq 2$, and group two has no cars;
3 that the price of "other goods" M is unity.

Denote the income (including that derived from the sale of automobiles) of all type one traders as Y_1 and the income of all type two traders as Y_2. The demand for used cars will be the sum of the demands by both groups. When one ignores indivisibilities, the demand for automobiles by type one traders will be

$$D_1 = \frac{Y_1}{p} \qquad \frac{\mu}{p} > 1$$

$$D_1 = 0 \qquad \frac{\mu}{p} < 1$$

And the supply of cars offered by type one traders is

$$S_2 = \frac{pN}{2} \qquad p \leqq 2 \qquad\qquad (1)$$

with average quality

$$\mu = \frac{p}{2} \qquad\qquad (2)$$

(To derive (1) and (2), the uniform distribution of automobile quality is used.)
Similarly the demand of type two traders is

$$D_2 = \frac{Y_2}{p} \qquad \frac{3\mu}{2} > p$$

$$D_2 = 0 \qquad \frac{3\mu}{2} < p$$

and

$$S_2 = 0$$

Thus total demand $D(p, \mu)$ is

$$D(p, \mu) = \frac{(Y_2 + Y_1)}{p} \qquad \text{if } p < \mu$$

$$D(p, \mu) = \frac{Y_2}{p} \qquad \text{if } \mu < p < \frac{3\mu}{2}$$

$$D(p, \mu) = 0 \qquad \text{if } p > \frac{3\mu}{2}$$

However, with price p, average quality is $p/2$ and therefore at no price will any trade take place at all: in spite of the fact that *at any given price* between 0 and 3 there are traders of type one who are willing to sell their automobiles at a price which traders of type two are willing to pay.

2.3. Symmetric information

The foregoing is contrasted with the case of symmetric information. Suppose that the quality of all cars is uniformly distributed, $0 \leq x \leq 2$. Then the demand curves and supply curves can be written as follows:

Supply

$$S(p) = N \qquad p > 1$$
$$S(p) = 0 \qquad p < 1$$

And the demand curves are

$$D(p) = \frac{(Y_2 + Y_1)}{p} \qquad p < 1$$

$$D(p) = \left(\frac{Y_2}{p}\right) \qquad 1 < p < \frac{3}{2}$$

$$D(p) = 0 \qquad p > \frac{3}{2}$$

In equilibrium

$$p = 1 \qquad\qquad \text{if } Y_2 < N \qquad\qquad\qquad (3)$$

$$p = \frac{Y_2}{N} \qquad\qquad \text{if } \frac{2Y_2}{3} < N < Y_2 \qquad\qquad (4)$$

$$p = \frac{3}{2} \qquad\qquad \text{if } N > \frac{2Y_2}{3} \qquad\qquad\qquad (5)$$

If $N < Y_2$ there is a gain in utility over the case of asymmetrical information of $N/2$. (If $N < Y_2$, in which case the income of type two traders is insufficient to buy all N automobiles, there is a gain in utility of $Y_2/2$ units.)

Finally, it should be mentioned that in this example, if traders of groups one and two have the same probabilistic estimates about the quality of individual automobiles – though these estimates may vary from automobile to automobile – (3), (4), and (5) will still describe equilibrium with one slight change: p will then represent the expected price of one quality unit.

3. Examples and Applications

3.1. Insurance

It is a well-known fact that people over 65 have great difficulty in buying medical insurance. The natural question arises: why doesn't the price rise to match the risk?

Our answer is that as the price level rises the people who insure themselves will be those who are increasingly certain that they will need the insurance; for error in medical check-ups, doctors' sympathy with older patients, and so on make it much easier for the applicant to assess the risks involved than the insurance company. The result is that the average medical condition of insurance applicants deteriorates as the price level rises –

with the result that no insurance sales may take place at any price.[1] This is strictly analogous to our automobiles case, where the average quality of used cars supplied fell with a corresponding fall in the price level. This agrees with the explanation in insurance textbooks (Dickerson, 1959, p. 333):

> Generally speaking policies are not available at ages materially greater than sixty-five.... The term premiums are too high for any but the most pessimistic (which is to say the least healthy) insureds to find attractive. Thus there is a severe problem of adverse selection at these ages.

The statistics do not contradict this conclusion. While demands for health insurance rise with age, a 1956 national sample survey of 2,809 families with 8,898 persons (Anderson with Feldman, 1956) shows that hospital insurance coverage drops from 63 per cent of those aged 45 to 54, to 31 per cent for those over 65. And surprisingly, this survey also finds average medical expenses for males aged 55 to 64 of $88, while males over 65 pay an average of $77. While noninsured expenditure rises from $66 to $80 in these age groups, insured expenditure declines from $105 to $70. The conclusion is tempting that insurance companies are particularly wary of giving medical insurance to older people.

The principle of "adverse selection" is potentially present in all lines of insurance. The following statement appears in an insurance textbook written at the Wharton School (Denenberg et al., 1964, p. 446):

> There is potential adverse selection in the fact that healthy term insurance policy holders may decide to terminate their coverage when they become older and premiums mount. This action could leave an insurer with an undue proportion of below average risks and claims might be higher than anticipated. Adverse selection "appears (or at least is possible) whenever the individual or group insured has freedom to buy or not to buy, to choose the amount or plan of insurance, and to persist or to discontinue as a policy holder."

Group insurance, which is the most common form of medical insurance in the United States, picks out the healthy, for generally adequate health is a precondition for employment. At the same time this means that medical insurance is least available to those who need it most, for the insurance companies do their own "adverse selection."

This adds one major argument in favor of medicare.[2] On a cost benefit basis medicare may pay off: for it is quite possible that every individual in the market would be willing to pay the expected cost of his medicare and buy insurance, yet no insurance company can afford to sell him a policy – for at any price it will attract too many "lemons." The welfare economics of medicare, in this view, is *exactly* analogous to the usual classroom argument for public expenditure on roads.

3.2. The employment of minorities

The Lemons Principle also casts light on the employment of minorities. Employers may refuse to hire members of minority groups for certain types of jobs. This decision may not reflect irrationality or prejudice – but profit maximization. For race may serve as a good *statistic* for the applicant's social background, quality of schooling, and general job capabilities.

Good quality schooling could serve as a substitute for this statistic; by grading students the schooling system can give a better indicator of quality than other more superficial characteristics. As T. W. Schultz (1964, p. 42) writes, "The educational establishment *discovers* and cultivates potential talent. The capabilities of children and mature students can never be known until *found* and cultivated." (Italics added.) An untrained worker may have valuable natural talents, but these talents must be certified by "the educational establishment" before a company can afford to use them. The certifying establishment, however, must be credible; the unreliability of slum schools decreases the economic possibilities of their students.

This lack may be particularly disadvantageous to members of already disadvantaged minority groups. For an employer may make a rational decision not to hire any members of these groups in responsible positions – because it is difficult to distinguish those with good job qualifications from those with bad qualifications. This type of decision is clearly what George Stigler (1962, p. 104) had in mind when he wrote, "in a regime of ignorance Enrico Fermi would have been a gardener, Von Neumann a checkout clerk at a drugstore."

As a result, however, the rewards for work in slum schools tend to accrue to the group as a whole – in raising its average quality – rather than to the individual. Only insofar as information in addition to race is used is there any incentive for training.

An additional worry is that the Office of Economic Opportunity is going to use cost–benefit analysis to evaluate its programs. For many benefits may be external. The benefit from training minority groups may arise as much from raising the average quality of the group as from raising the quality of the individual trainee; and, likewise, the returns may be distributed over the whole group rather than to the individual.

3.3. The costs of dishonesty

The Lemons model can be used to make some comments on the costs of dishonesty. Consider a market in which goods are sold honestly or dishonestly; quality may be represented, or it may be misrepresented. The purchaser's problem, of course, is to identify quality. The presence of people in the market who are willing to offer inferior goods tends to drive the market out of existence – as in the case of our automobile "lemons." It is this possibility that represents the major costs of dishonesty – for dishonest dealings tend to drive honest dealings out of the market. There may be potential buyers of good quality products and there may be potential sellers of such products in the appropriate price range; however, the presence of people who wish to pawn bad wares as good wares tends to drive out the legitimate business. The cost of dishonesty, therefore, lies not only in the amount by which the purchaser is cheated; the cost also must include the loss incurred from driving legitimate business out of existence.

Dishonesty in business is a serious problem in underdeveloped countries. Our model gives a possible structure to this statement and delineates the nature of the "external" economies involved. In particular, in the model economy described, dishonesty, or the misrepresentation of the quality of automobiles, costs $\frac{1}{2}$ unit of utility per automobile; furthermore, it reduces the size of the used car market from N to 0. We can, consequently, directly evaluate the costs of dishonesty – at least in theory.

There is considerable evidence that quality variation is greater in underdeveloped than in developed areas. For instance, the need for quality control of exports and State Trading

Corporations can be taken as one indicator. In India, for example, under the Export Quality Control and Inspection Act of 1963, "about 85 per cent of Indian exports are covered under one or the other type of quality control" *The Times of India*, November 10, 1967, p. 1. Indian housewives must carefully glean the rice of the local bazaar to sort out stones of the same color and shape which have been intentionally added to the rice. Any comparison of the heterogeneity of quality in the street market and the canned qualities of the American supermarket suggests that quality variation is a greater problem in the East than in the West.

In one traditional pattern of development the merchants of the pre-industrial generation turn into the first entrepreneurs of the next. The best-documented case is Japan,[3] but this also may have been the pattern for Britain and America (Kindleberger, 1958, p. 86). In *our* picture the important skill of the merchant is identifying the quality of merchandise; those who can identify used cars in our example and can guarantee the quality may profit by as much as the difference between type two traders' buying price and type one traders' selling price. These people are the merchants. In production these skills are equally necessary – both to be able to identify the quality of inputs and to certify the quality of outputs. And this is one (added) reason why the merchants may logically become the first entrepreneurs.

The problem, of course, is that entrepreneurship may be a scarce resource; no development text leaves entrepreneurship unemphasized. Some treat it as central.[4] Given, then, that entrepreneurship is scarce, there are two ways in which product variations impede development. First, the pay-off to trade is great for would-be entrepreneurs, and hence they are diverted from production; second, the amount of entrepreneurial time per unit output is greater, the greater are the quality variations.

3.4. Credit markets in underdeveloped countries

Credit markets in underdeveloped countries often strongly reflect the operation of the Lemons Principle. In India a major fraction of industrial enterprise is controlled by managing agencies (according to a recent survey (Government of India, 1964, p. 44) these "managing agencies" controlled 65.7 per cent of the net worth of public limited companies and 66 per cent of total assets). Here is a historian's account of the function and genesis of the "managing agency system" (Tinker, 1966, p. 134):

> The management of the South Asian commercial scene remained the function of merchant houses, and a type of organization peculiar to South Asia known as the Managing Agency. When a new venture was promoted (such as a manufacturing plant, a plantation, or a trading venture), the promoters would approach an established managing agency. The promoters might be Indian or British, and they might have technical or financial resources or merely a concession. In any case they would turn to the agency because of its reputation, which would encourage confidence in the venture and stimulate investment.

In turn, a second major feature of the Indian industrial scene has been the dominance of these managing agencies by caste (or, more accurately, communal) groups. Thus firms can usually be classified according to communal origin.[5] In this environment, in which outside investors are likely to be bilked of their holdings, either

  1 firms establish a reputation for "honest" dealing, which confers upon them a monopoly rent insofar as their services are limited in supply, or

2 the sources of finance are limited to local communal groups which can use communal
   – and possibly familial – ties to encourage honest dealing *within* the community.

It is, in Indian economic history, extraordinarily difficult to discern whether the savings
of rich landlords failed to be invested in the industrial sector

1 because of a fear to invest in ventures controlled by other communities,
2 because of inflated propensities to consume, or
3 because of low rates of return.[6]

At the very least, however, it is clear that the British-owned managing agencies tended
to have an equity holding whose communal origin was more heterogenous than the Indian-
controlled agency houses, and would usually include both Indian and British investors.

A second example of the workings of the Lemons Principle concerns the extortionate
rates which the local moneylender charges his clients. In India these high rates of interest
have been the leading factor in landlessness; the so-called "Cooperative Movement" was
meant to counteract this growing landlessness by setting up banks to compete with the
local moneylenders.[7] While the large banks in the central cities have prime interest rates of
6, 8, and 10 per cent, the local moneylender charges 15, 25, and even 50 per cent. The
answer to this seeming paradox is that credit is granted only where the granter has

1 easy means of enforcing his contract or
2 personal knowledge of the character of the borrower.

The middleman who tries to arbitrage between the rates of the moneylender and the
central bank is apt to attract all the "lemons" and thereby make a loss.

This interpretation can be seen in Sir Malcolm Darling's (1932, p. 204) interpretation
of the village moneylender's power:

> It is only fair to remember that in the Indian village the money-lender is often the one thrifty
> person amongst a generally thriftless people; and that his methods of business, though
> demoralizing under modern conditions, suit the happy-go-lucky ways of the peasant. He is
> always accessible, even at night; dispenses with troublesome formalities, asks no inconvenient
> questions, advances promptly, and if interest is paid, does not press for repayment of
> principal. He keeps in close personal touch with his clients, and in many villages shares
> their occasions of weal or woe. *With his intimate knowledge of those around him he is able,
> without serious risk, to finance those who would otherwise get no loan at all.* [Italics added.]

Or look at Barbara Ward's (1960, p. 142) account:

> A small shopkeeper in a Hong Kong fishing village told me: "I give credit to anyone who
> anchors regularly in our bay; but if it is someone I don't know well, then I think twice about it
> unless I can find out all about him."

Or, a profitable sideline of cotton ginning in Iran is the loaning of money for the next
season, since the ginning companies often have a line of credit from Teheran banks at the
market rate of interest. But in the first years of operation large losses are expected from
unpaid debts – due to poor knowledge of the local scene.[8]

4. Counteracting Institutions

Numerous institutions arise to counteract the effects of quality uncertainty. One obvious institution is guarantees. Most consumer durables carry guarantees to ensure the buyer of some normal expected quality. One natural result of our model is that the risk is borne by the seller rather than by the buyer.

A second example of an institution which counteracts the effects of quality uncertainty is the brand-name good. Brand names not only indicate quality but also give the consumer a means of retaliation if the quality does not meet expectations. For the consumer will then curtail future purchases. Often too, new products are associated with old brand names. This ensures the prospective consumer of the quality of the product.

Chains – such as hotel chains or restaurant chains – are similar to brand names. One observation consistent with our approach is the chain restaurant. These restaurants, at least in the United States, most often appear on interurban highways. The customers are seldom local. The reason is that these well-known chains offer a better hamburger than the *average* local restaurant; at the same time, the local customer, who knows his area, can usually choose a place he prefers.

Licensing practices also reduce quality uncertainty. For instance, there is the licensing of doctors, lawyers, and barbers. Most skilled labor carries some certification indicating the attainment of certain levels of proficiency. The high school diploma, the baccalaureate degree, the Ph.D., even the Nobel Prize, to some degree, serve this function of certification. And education and labor markets themselves have their own "brand names."

5. Conclusion

We have been discussing economic models in which "trust" is important. Informal unwritten guarantees are preconditions for trade and production. Where these guarantees are indefinite, business will suffer – as indicated by our generalized Gresham's law. This aspect of uncertainty has been explored by game theorists, as in the Prisoner's Dilemma, but usually it has not been incorporated in the more traditional Arrow–Debreu approach to uncertainty (Radner, 1967). But the difficulty of distinguishing good quality from bad is inherent in the business world; this may indeed explain many economic institutions and may in fact be one of the more important aspects of uncertainty.

Notes

1   Arrow's (1963) fine article, does not make this point explicitly. He emphasizes "moral hazard" rather than "adverse selection." In its strict sense, the presence of "moral hazard" is equally disadvantageous for both governmental and private programs; in its broader sense, which includes "adverse selection," "moral hazard" gives a decided advantage to government insurance programs.

2   The following quote, again taken from an insurance textbook, shows how far the medical insurance market is from perfect competition:

> "... insurance companies must screen their applicants. Naturally it is true that many people will voluntarily seek adequate insurance on their own initiative. But in such lines as

accident and health insurance, companies are likely to give a second look to persons who voluntarily seek insurance without being approached by an agent." (1957, pp. 8–9.)

This shows that insurance is *not* a commodity for sale on the open market.

3 See Levy (1955).
4 For example, see Lewis (1955, p. 196).
5 The existence of the following table (and also the small per cent of firms under mixed control) indicates the communalization of the control of firms. Also, for the cotton industry see Fukuzawa (1965).

Distribution of industrial control by community

	1911	1931	1951
		(number of firms)	
British	281	416	382
Parsis	15	25	19
Gujartis	3	11	17
Jews	5	9	3
Muslims	—	10	3
Bengalis	8	5	20
Marwaris	—	6	96
Mixed control	28	28	79
Total	341	510	619

Source: Mehta (1955, p. 314)

6 For the mixed record of industrial profits, see Buchanan (1966).
7 The leading authority on this is Sir Malcolm Darling. See his (1932) *Punjabi Peasant in Prosperity and Debt*. The following table may also prove instructive:

	Secured loans (per cent)	Commonest rates for unsecured loans (per cent)	Grain loans (per cent)
Punjab	6 to 12	12 to 24 ($18\frac{3}{4}$ commonest)	25
United Provinces	9 to 12	24 to $37\frac{1}{2}$	25 (50 in Oudh)
Bihar		18 3/4	50
Orissa	12 to $18\frac{3}{4}$	25	25
Bengal	8 to 12	9 to 18 for "respectable clients" 18 3/4 to $37\frac{1}{2}$ (the latter common to agriculturalists)	25
Central Provinces	6 to 12	15 for proprietors 24 for occupancy tenants $37\frac{1}{2}$ for ryots with no right of transfer	25
Bombay	9 to 12	12 to 25 (18 commonest)	
Sind		36	
Madras	12	15 to 18 (in insecure tracts 24 not uncommon)	20 to 50

Source: Darling (1932, p. 190).

8 Personal conversation with mill manager, April 1968.

References

Anderson, O. W. (with Feldman, J. J.) (1956): *Family Medical Costs and Insurance*. New York: McGraw-Hill.

Angell, F. J. (1957): *Insurance, Principles and Practices*. New York: The Ronald Press.

Arrow, K. (1963): "Uncertainty and the Welfare Economics of Medical Care," *American Economic Review*, 53 (5), 941–73.

Buchanan, D. H. (1966): *The Development of Capitalist Enterprise in India*. New York: Kelley (reprinted).

Darling, Sir M. (1932): *Punjabi Peasant in Prosperity and Debt*, 3rd edn. London: Oxford University Press.

Denenberg, H. S., Eilers, R. D., Hoffman, G. W., Kline, C. A., Melone, J. J. and Snider, H. W. (1964): *Risk and Insurance*. Englewood Cliffs, New Jersey: Prentice Hall.

Dickerson, O. D. (1959): *Health Insurance*. Homewood, Ill.: Irwin.

Fukuzawa, H. (1965): "Cotton Mill Industry," in V. B. Singh (ed.), *Economic History of India, 1857– 1956*, Bombay: Allied Publishers, 223–59.

Government of India, Planning Commission (1964): *Report of the Committee on the Distribution of Income and Levels of Living, Part 1*. February, 44.

Kindleberger, C. P. (1958): *Economic Development*. New York: McGraw-Hill.

Levy, M. J., Jr. (1955): "Contrasting Factors in the Modernization of China and Japan," in S. Kuznets, W. E. Moore and J. J. Spengler (eds), *Economic Growth: Brazil, India, Japan*, Durham, N.C.: Duke University Press, 496–536.

Lewis, W. A. (1955): *The Theory of Economic Growth*. Homewood, Ill.: Irwin.

Mehta, M. M. (1955): *Structure of Indian Industries*. Bombay: Popular Book Depot.

Radner, R. (1967): "Équilibre de Marchés à Terme et au Comptant en Cas d'Incertitude," *Cahiers d'Econometrie*, 12, November. Paris: Centre National de la Recherche Scientifique.

Schultz, T. W. (1964): *The Economic Value of Education*. New York: Columbia University Press.

Stigler, G. J. (1962): "Information in the Labor Market," *Journal of Political Economy*, 70, October, Supplement, 94–105.

The Times of India (1967): November 10, 1.

Tinker, H. (1966): *South Asia: A Short History*. New York: Praeger.

Ward, B. (1960): "Cash or Credit Crops," *Economic Development and Cultural Change*, 8 (12), January, 148–63. Reprinted in G. Foster, J. M. Potter and M. N. Diaz (eds) 1967: *Peasant Society, A Reader*, Boston: Little Brown and Company, 142.

PART IV

Social Regulation

Introduction

The classic regulatory regime for a public utility was to permit such companies to earn a "fair return on a fair value", which meant a rate of return, taking into account the reduced risk of public utility sales fluctuations, that was in line with market requirements for attracting capital, applied to the depreciated value of the firm's capital base value. Needless to say, utility regulatory commissions found it extremely difficult to determine both of these magnitudes. One social drawback from such a criterion, even when both variables were settled to the satisfactions of all parties, was that it discouraged innovation by the company. Were a firm to install new capital equipment to institute economies, its actual rate of return would rise above the allowed level and the regulatory commission would force it to reduce its charges to the public in order to earn the allowed return.

Chapter 10 highlights a more profound difficulty with this regime. The utility has a vested interest in increasing the size of its capital base as long as the allowed rate of return on capital is above its actual cost of borrowing (but below the rate of return it could earn were it to function as an unregulated monopoly). Quarrels with the commission about the true depreciation of its capital base or which components of the base were actually necessary for serving the designated public aside, the firm would treat the difference between the fair return and the actual interest rate paid as a reduction in the cost of its capital. This would lead it to substitute capital for labor beyond the cost-minimizing mix and to increase its output beyond the socially efficient point. Averch and Johnson also show that, if the firm is allowed to function in more than one regulated market, it might actually be to the firm's advantage to function at a loss in some markets to permit the capital bases of those markets to enter the combined base on which a fair rate of return was applied.

The analysis of the telephone and telegraph industries as they existed at the time the article was written is outdated, and the existing data of the time could only permit the authors to assert that the operation of AT&T and Western Union were consistent with their theories. However, the article was one of the forces leading more and more public utility regulatory authorities to establish prices – adjusted for inflation and expected technological progress – as regulatory targets rather than the "fair return on a fair value" tool.

In Chapter 11, Posner poses a question of monumental ambition: Is it possible to construct a unifying theory of the genesis and functioning of governmental economic regulation that can be verified empirically? He investigates what he identifies as three (not wholly independent) current theories – in their present state, rather fuzzy in their structure and, in large part, intuitive and anecdotal in primitive attempts at their realistic verification. The first is *public interest* theory which argues that the origin of such intervention is to serve a legitimate public interest in correcting a market inefficiency or inequity, and whose frequent lack of success originates in bureaucratic inefficiency. Posner proceeds to give the theory a firmer reformulative theoretical backbone, but even then finds its deficiencies too great to provide a basis for the unifying theory he is seeking.

The second theory is the *capture theory*, which asserts that regulative commissions are formed to promote the interests of the industries they oversee, or become their effective protectors as the body of administrative law grows. Posner finds such theories overly simplistic and self-contradictory in their assertions, and dismisses them rather summarily.

The third theory, on which Posner places the greatest hope for the Grail, is the *economic theory*, which views regulatory activity as the result of the demands and supplies that economic agents and public officials with economic interests at stake reach in a kind of market equilibrium. The path is recognizable as that blazed by the Chicago school in its attempt to extend the explanatory power of economic theory beyond its narrow economic precincts. Posner's formulation of its nucleus is extremely interesting, but even more commendable is his candor in pointing out to the reader its shortcomings as well as its strengths. The entire article throws off considered refutations of the simplistic canons of the folk wisdom that permeate debate in this important social field. That Posner does not succeed in his ambitious search does not surprise us – even less, himself – but its clearing of the progress-impeding thorny underbrush makes his effort a valuable one.

The abrupt deregulation of the airline industry in 1997–98, which converted it from a tightly hobbled industry in which the Civil Aeronautics Board microregulated route and rate competition to one in which free competition reigned almost without restraints, has been the most dramatic experiment in deregulation in US history. In chapter 12, Kahn, as one of the prime movers behind the deregulatory effort, discusses some of the unforeseen consequences over the first ten years of the industry's reactions to its newfound freedoms. It was expected at the outset that, because of the mobility of the major capital investment of the industry – the aircraft – small airlines would move in rapidly to compete with the oligopolistic incumbents. This did indeed happen, but the barriers to entry that inhered in infrastructure and brand names were not clearly enough foreseen, and the importance of economies of scale was underestimated. Kahn discusses the "hubification" of the industry with dominant incumbents at major hubs, the development of biased computer reservation systems by major airlines, the birth of frequent flyer programs, the squeezing of labor monopoly rents that resulted from years of regulation, and other developments that were unforeseen results of deregulation and the competition that followed. Finally, Kahn makes judgments about the overall social welfare changes – overwhelmingly positive – that resulted from the move.

Chapter 13 discusses the desirability of deregulation in a considerably more controversial area: that of drug prohibition. Miron and Zwiebel present an economically based case for eliminating the current policies of drug enforcement authorities, with an argument that they lead to socially more harmful effects, both directly and in generating externalities, than a free market (with some restrictions) would bring about. Using statistical and historical data, they argue that moderate usage of marijuana, opiates and cocaine is much more widespread than is recognized in the "education" literature, with negligible effects on health or efficiency, and with cases of overdose or addiction overplayed. Regulatory activity increases the price of narcotics, raising the level of personal and property crime, because the price inelasticity of heavy users leads to such activity, while recreational users switch quickly to alcohol or other stimulants. It also aids the formation of black markets in such products, and to the formation of cartels with violent protections of turf, as well as potentially fatal adulteration of quality.

Perhaps the most controversial part of their argument is to assert that the narcotics user determines his or her usage in the economically rational way of weighing costs and benefits, and that government interference with such decision making on the basis of protecting buyers from imperfect information on the possibility of addition or harmful health consequences is not provably necessary. The "custodial" function of government with respect to those with high rates of discounting the future is too costly, given its benefits as compared with the many direct and indirect costs of such policies.

The application of an economic framework within which to examine drug policy leads to a cogent argument against government regulation, drawing upon a now large body of research and the historic experiments with alcohol and tobacco. The reader may disagree with some of the arguments, but no doubt his or her "certainties" about the subject will be seriously challenged.

Chapter 14 deals with the more subtle problems that arise with the recent interest of Congress and the executive in matters of risk and uncertainty as they pertain to the environment, job safety and product safety. Congress passed rather loose and vague guidelines for such policies, passing their more exact definition and execution to executive agencies such as the Occupational Health and Safety Administration, National Highway and Traffic Safety Administration, and the Environmental Protection Agency. Recently, in recognition of the varied manners in which these agencies have interpreted their mandates, the Office of Management and Budget was given some oversight of these agency decisions, but the experiment has not been fruitful in injecting uniform economic benefit–cost approaches into the regulatory process.

Viscusi discusses the lack of benefit–cost analyses, the difficulty of incorporating non-monetizable considerations into them, the varied implicit or explicit valuations of saving a statistical life used by the various agencies, the hesitancy of the courts to interfere with agency standards, and some alternative, if less rigorous, techniques of introducing efficiency calculations into this growing body of government custodial concerns. After reading his analysis, one is left with the belief that this area is in great need of a body of standards, analytical techniques and statistical parameters that are broadly applicable over the spectrum of administrative agencies with regulatory powers, with their application monitored by a Congressional office with enforcement power.

CHAPTER TEN

Behavior of the Firm Under Regulatory Constraint

HARVEY AVERCH AND LELAND L. JOHNSON

Source: *American Economic Review*, 52 (1962), pp. 1052–69. Reprinted with the permission of the authors and the American Economic Association. © American Economic Association.

In judging the level of prices charged by firms for services subject to public control, government regulatory agencies commonly employ a "fair rate of return" criterion: After the firm subtracts its operating expenses from gross revenues, the remaining net revenue should be just sufficient to compensate the firm for its investment in plant and equipment. If the rate of return, computed as the ratio of net revenue to the value of plant and equipment (the rate base), is judged to be excessive, pressure is brought to bear on the firm to reduce prices. If the rate is considered to be too low, the firm is permitted to increase prices.

The purpose here is

(a) to develop a theory of the monopoly firm seeking to maximize profit but subject to such a constraint on its rate of return, and

(b) to apply the model to one particular regulated industry – the domestic telephone and telegraph industry.

We conclude in the theoretical analysis that a "regulatory bias" operates in the following manner:

1 The firm does not equate marginal rates of factor substitution to the ratio of factor costs; therefore the firm operates inefficiently in the sense that (social) cost is not minimized at the output it selects.

2 The firm has an incentive to expand into other regulated markets, even if it operates at a (long-run) loss in these markets; therefore, it may drive out other firms, or discourage their entry into these other markets, even though the competing firms may be lower-cost producers.

Applying the theoretical analysis to the telephone and telegraph industry, we find that the model does raise issues relevant to evaluating market behavior.

1. The Single-Market Model

First we shall consider a geometrical and a mathematical framework showing the effect of the regulatory constraint on the cost curves of the firm employing two factors. The essential characteristic to be demonstrated is: if the rate of return allowed by the regulatory agency is greater than the cost of capital but is less than the rate of return that would be enjoyed by the firm were it free to maximize profit without regulatory constraint, then the firm will substitute capital for the other factor of production and operate at an output where cost is not minimized.

Figure 1 denotes the firm's production where capital x_1 is plotted on the horizontal axis and labor x_2 on the vertical axis. The market or "social" cost of capital and labor generates the isocost curve A and the *unregulated* firm would move along expansion path 1 where market cost is minimized for any given output. With regulation, however, the cost of capital to the firm – the "private" cost – is no longer equal to market cost. For each additional unit of capital input, the firm is permitted to earn a profit (equal to the difference between the market cost of capital and rate of return allowed by the regulatory agency) that it otherwise would have to forego. Therefore, private cost is less than market cost by an amount equal to this difference. The effect of regulation is analogous to that of changing the relative prices of capital x_1 and labor x_2: isocost curve B becomes relevant and the firm moves along expansion path 2 – a path along which market cost is not minimized for any given output. The firm finds path 2 advantageous simply because it is along that path that the firm is able to maximize total profit given the constraint on its rate of return.

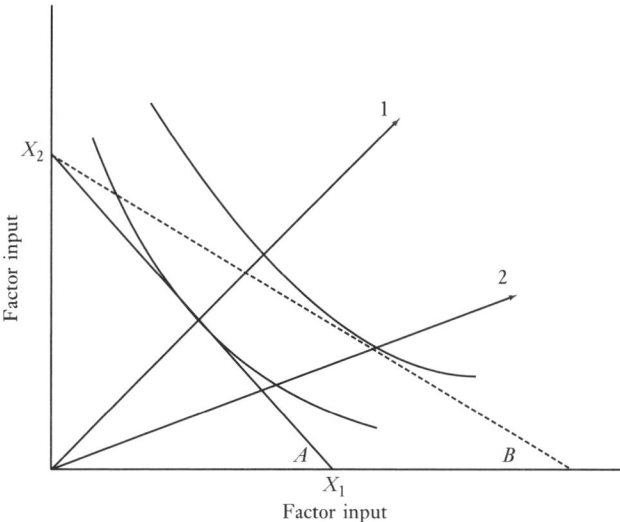

Figure 1

Treating the problem mathematically, we now consider a monopoly producing a single homogeneous product using two inputs. Define

$$z = z(x_1, x_2) \qquad x_1 \geq 0 \qquad x_2 \geq 0$$
$$\frac{\partial z}{\partial x_1} > 0 \qquad \frac{\partial z}{\partial x_2} > 0 \tag{1}$$
$$z(0, x_2) = z(x_1, 0) = 0$$

as the firm's production function. That is, marginal products are positive, and production requires both inputs.

We write the inverse demand function as

$$p = p(z) \tag{2}$$

Profit is defined by

$$\pi = pz - r_1 x_1 - r_2 x_2 \tag{3}$$

where the $r_i (i = 1, 2)$ are factor costs presumed constant for all levels of factor input.

Let x_1 denote the physical quantity of plant and equipment in the rate base, c_1 the acquisition cost per unit of plant and equipment in the rate base, u_1 the value of depreciation of plant and equipment during a time period in question, and U_1 the cumulative value of depreciation. Let x_2 denote the quantity of labor input and r_2 the labor wage rate. The regulatory constraint is:

$$\frac{pz - r_2 x_2 - u_1}{c_1 x_1 - U_1} \leq s_1 \tag{4}$$

where the profit net of labor cost and capital depreciation constitutes a percentage of the rate base (net of depreciation) no greater than a specified maximum s_1.

For simplicity, we assume that depreciation (u_1 and U_1) is zero and we define capital so that its acquisition cost or value c_1 is equal to 1, i.e., the value of the rate base is equal to the physical quantity of capital.[1] The "cost of capital" r_1 (to be distinguished from the acquisition cost of plant and equipment measured by c_1) is the interest cost involved in holding plant and equipment. The allowable rate of return s_1 is the rate of return allowed by the regulatory agency on plant and equipment in order to compensate the firm for the cost of capital – the interest cost – involved in holding plant and equipment. Therefore, the constraint may be rewritten as

$$\frac{pz - r_2 x_2}{x_1} \leq s_1 \tag{5}$$

or

$$pz - s_1 x_1 - r_2 x_2 \leq 0 \tag{6}$$

For $s_1 < r_1$ the allowable rate of return is less than the actual cost of capital, and the firm withdraws from the market. For, from (6), if $x_1 > 0$,

$$pz - r_1 x_1 - r_2 x_2 = pz - s_1 x_1 + (s_1 - r_1)x_1 - r_2 x_2 \leq (s_1 - r_1)x_1 < 0$$

If $x_1 = 0$, $\pi = -r_2 x_2$ from (3), and the firm can further reduce its loss by setting $x_2 = 0$. Then $\pi = 0$. Therefore, $s_1 \geq r_1$; the allowable rate of return must at least cover the actual cost of capital.

The problem then is to maximize (3) subject to (6).[2] Define the Lagrangian expression:

$$L(x_1, x_2, \lambda) = pz - r_1 x_1 - r_2 x_2 - \lambda[pz - s_1 x_1 - r_2 x_2] \tag{7}$$

The Kuhn–Tucker necessary conditions[3] for a maximum at $\bar{x}_1, \bar{x}_2, \bar{\lambda}$ are

$$r_1 \geq (1 - \lambda)\left[p + z\frac{dp}{dz}\right]\frac{\partial z}{\partial x_1} + \lambda s_1 \qquad x_1 \geq 0 \tag{8.1}$$

$$r_1 > (1 - \lambda)\left[p + z\frac{dp}{dz}\right]\frac{\partial z}{\partial x_1} + \lambda s_1 \qquad \text{implies} \quad \bar{x}_1 = 0 \tag{8.2}$$

$$(1 - \lambda)r_2 \geq (1 - \lambda)\left[p + z\frac{dp}{dz}\right]\frac{\partial z}{\partial x_2} \qquad \bar{x}_2 \geq 0 \tag{8.3}$$

$$(1 - \lambda)r_2 > (1 - \lambda)\left[p + z\frac{dp}{dz}\right]\frac{\partial z}{\partial x_2} \qquad \text{implies} \quad \bar{x}_2 = 0 \tag{8.4}$$

$$pz - s_1 x_1 - r_2 x_2 \leq 0 \qquad\qquad \bar{\lambda} \geq 0 \tag{8.5}$$

$$pz - r_2 x_2 < s_1 x_1 \qquad\qquad \text{implies} \quad \bar{\lambda} = 0 \tag{8.6}$$

Assuming $\bar{\lambda} > 0$, it is clear from (8.1) that $\lambda = 1$ if and only if $r_1 = s_1$. If $\lambda = 1, r_1 = s_1$. This does not involve any variables, and it follows that any x_1, x_2 which satisfies (8.5) is a solution.

For $s_1 > r_1$, which is the interesting case, it follows that $0 \leq \lambda < 1$: From (8.6), s_1 may be chosen large enough so that $\lambda = 0$ (i.e., at some high level of allowable rate of return s_1, the value $x_1(s_1 - r_1)$ exceeds the level of unconditionally maximized profit, and the constraint is ineffective). If we now let $s_1 \to r_1$, λ varies continuously, and since $\lambda \neq 1$, we have $0 < \lambda < 1$. For the unregulated monopoly, the marginal conditions are:

$$r_i = \left[p + z\frac{dp}{dz}\right]\frac{\partial z}{\partial x_i} \qquad (i = 1, 2) \tag{9}$$

Under conditions of effective regulatory constraint ($\lambda > 0$) equations (8.3) and (9) disclose that, as in the case of unregulated monopoly, the input of x_2 is such that its marginal cost r_2 is equal to its marginal value product. In contrast, equations (8.1) and (9) disclose that the input of x_1 is such that its marginal cost r_1 is greater than its marginal value product,[4] i.e., its use is expanded beyond the point at which its marginal cost would be equal to its marginal value product.

From equations (8.1) and (8.3) when the equalities hold, the marginal rate of substitution of factor 1 for factor 2 is:

$$\frac{-dx_2}{dx_1} = \frac{r_1}{r_2} - \frac{\lambda}{(1-\lambda)} \frac{(s_1 - r_1)}{r_2} \tag{10}$$

Since

$$\frac{\lambda}{(1-\lambda)} \frac{(s_1 - r_1)}{r_2} > 0 \qquad \lambda > 0 \qquad s_1 > r_1$$

then

$$\frac{-dx_2}{dx_1} < \frac{r_1}{r_2} \tag{11}$$

The firm adjusts to the constraint, then, by substituting capital for the cooperating factor and by expanding total output. Comparative equilibrium outputs are shown in

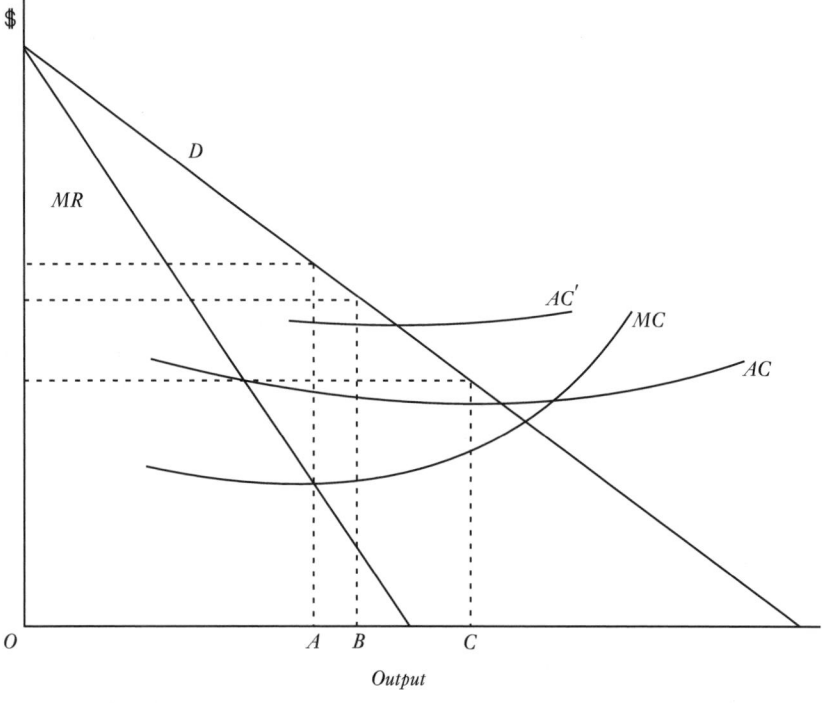

Figure 2

Figure 2. If the regulated firm were constrained to move along the socially efficient expansion path 1 in Figure 1, it would operate at OC in Figure 2. Here price is slightly above average cost AC to reflect the fact that $s_1 > r_1$ (profit is not entirely eliminated). Since the regulated firm moves along path 2, the social cost curve rises from AC to AC', and the regulatory constraint is satisfied at the lower output OB. The effect of regulation is to force the firm to expand output from the unregulated position OA, but output does not expand to C because a portion of what would otherwise be profit is absorbed by cost. The extent to which regulation affects output depends upon the nature of the production function. If it involves fixed proportions, i.e., min $(x_1/a, x_2/b)$, the regulated firm is constrained to the efficient expansion path and it moves all the way to OC. If the production function is linear and if the iso-output curves have a slope equal to $-r_1/r_2$, the firm could substitute x_1 for x_2 and, with no change in marginal rate of substitution, hold output constant. In this case it could remain at OA, the unregulated monopoly output, under the condition that at output OA

$$pz - s_1x_1 - r_2x_2 \leq 0 \qquad x_2 = 0$$

2. The Multimarket Case

Suppose that in addition to operating in a single market, the firm can also enter other regulated markets, and that the regulatory agency bases its "fair rate of return" criterion on the firm's overall value of plant and equipment for all markets taken together rather than computing a separate rate of return for each market. In this case the firm may have an incentive (that it would not have in the absence of regulation) to enter these other markets, even if the cost of so doing exceeds the additional revenues. Expanding into other markets may enable the firm to inflate its rate base to satisfy the constraint and permit it to earn a greater total constrained profit than would have been possible in the absence of second markets.

A noteworthy implication is that the firm operating in oligopolistic second markets may have an advantage over competing firms. The regulated firm can "afford" to take (long-run) losses in these second markets while competing firms cannot. Under these circumstances, it is conceivable that the firm could drive out lower-cost producers – the loss it willingly takes in second markets could exceed the difference between its costs and the lower costs of other firms. It may succeed, therefore, in either driving lower cost firms out of these markets or of discouraging their entry into them. This is unlike the textbook case of "predatory price-cutting" where the regulated monopolist may temporarily cut prices in outside competitive markets to drive out rivals and subsequently raise prices to monopoly levels. The monopolist would ordinarily engage in such a practice only if he had the expectation that in the long run he would make a positive profit in these additional markets; but here even in the case of a long-run loss the regulated firm may find operations in such markets to be advantageous as long as the firm is permitted to include its capital input in these markets in its rate base.

Moving to a mathematical treatment, let us consider an extreme example where operating in a second market permits the firm to act as an unconstrained monopoly in the first market, i.e., operating in the second market permits satisfaction of the regulatory constraint such that the firm can operate in the first market at output OA in Figure 2. We shall assume that for any combination of factors along the socially optimal expansion path in market 2 the firm is just able to break even in that market. That is, for any equilibrium x_{12}, x_{22}

$$p_2 z_2 - r_1 x_{12} - r_2 x_{22} = 0 \qquad (12)$$

The constraint for n markets is written:

$$\sum_{i=1}^{n} p_i z_i - s_1 \sum_{i=1}^{n} x_{1i} - r_2 \sum_{i=1}^{n} x_{2i} \leq 0 \qquad (13)$$

Denoting output and factor inputs in market 1 as $\bar{z}_{11}$ and $\bar{x}_{11}$, $\bar{x}_{21}$ respectively at the output at which profit is unconditionally maximized in market 1, we have

$$p_1 \bar{z}_1 - s_1 \bar{x}_{11} - r_2 \bar{x}_{21} = m \qquad m > 0 \qquad (14)$$

where m is the value of "excess" profit in market 1 that would violate the constraint (13) if the firm operated only in market 1. However, by moving along its expansion path in market 2 the firm can choose a level of capital input such that

$$p_2 \bar{z}_2 - s_1 \bar{x}_{12} - r_2 \bar{x}_{22} = -m \qquad (15)$$

Adding (14) and (15) we see that the firm can now satisfy constraint (13) without foregoing any profit in market 1. While the unregulated firm would be indifferent about operating in market 2, the regulated firm in this example finds market 2 attractive because it can add capital to the rate base at "no loss"; i.e., for any capital input in market 2 the output generates revenues just equal to factor cost. Since in market 2 the actual cost of capital is below the allowed rate of return, the firm can apply the difference in satisfying the constraint in market 1 and thereby enjoy additional profit equal to $s_1 - r_1$ for each unit of capital in market 2.

This analysis suggests that even if the firm suffers a loss in market 2 (measured in terms of social costs r_1 and r_2) it may still operate there provided the value of $x_{12}(s_1 - r_1)$ exceeds this level of loss. If it suffers a loss it would no longer operate in market 1 at the profit-maximizing output OA in Figure 1; seeking to equate the marginal value product of capital in both markets, it would move toward OB.

In the literature on public utility economics, concern is frequently expressed that the firm will attempt to inflate its rate base to increase its profit. However, the problem is generally viewed as one of proper valuation of rate base, i.e., the firm would always have an incentive to have its property stated at a value higher than its cost. The problem has given rise to a great deal of controversy about proper valuation, especially concerning original versus reproduction cost, and depreciation policy.[5] In the present study the problem of rate-base inflation is not viewed as one of valuation but rather as one of *acquisition* − quite apart from the problem of placing a valuation upon the rate base, the firm has an incentive to acquire additional capital if the allowable rate of return exceeds the cost of capital.

3. The Telephone and Telegraph Industry

Turning to the domestic telephone and telegraph industry, we find that the market structure and the regulatory setting are consistent with those described in the model. And the implications drawn from the model, concerning relative factor inputs and incentives to operate in some markets even at a loss, raise issues relevant to assessing market behavior of firms in the industry.

For our purposes, the notable feature of the industry's market structure is that the degree of competition does vary from one subsector to another. Common carriers have monopoly positions with regard to public message telephone and telegraph services, while they compete with each other in supplying private line services to customers who, in addition, are free to construct private wire facilities for their own use as an alternative to purchasing from the common carriers.

The principal supplier of public message telephone service is the Bell Telephone System. Besides the parent corporation, American Telephone and Telegraph Company, the Bell system includes 22 subsidiary "associated" companies of which 20 are primarily or wholly owned by AT&T. Each of the associated carriers provides local exchange and toll service within the state or group of (contiguous) states that comprises its "operating territory".[6] The Bell system holds about 98 per cent of all facilities employed in long-distance message toll telephone service in the United States, and about 85 per cent of all facilities employed in local telephone service. The remaining 15 per cent of local exchange facilities are in the hands of about 3,200 "independent" telephone firms, most of which are very small. These carriers connect with the Bell system, under service- and revenue-sharing agreements, and provide an integrated nationwide network. Competition does not exist among firms in the public message telephone business. Although many firms are in the industry, each has its own exclusive local marketing area.[7]

In the telegraph field, in contrast to telephone, public message telegraph service is offered only by the Western Union Telegraph Company. This is a much smaller subsector in terms of revenues than public message telephone service. In 1959 Western Union revenues for the former were about $170 million, while Bell and independent connecting carrier revenues for the latter were $7 billion.

Bell and Western Union compete in common markets in providing other services. Until recently Bell (together with independent connecting carriers) was sole supplier of private-line telephone service. However, in 1961 Bell and Western Union negotiated facilities contracts[8] that enable Western Union to offer private-line telephone service in competition with Bell. Western Union and Bell both provide telegraph exchange service and private-line telegraph service – Bell's teletypewriter or TWX service is similar to Western Union's Telex, and Bell's teletype private-wire service is similar to Western Union's leased circuit teleprinter offering. In addition, a new competitive element has recently been introduced: as an alternative to purchasing private-line telephone and telegraph services from the common carriers, firms outside the communications industry may now operate their own microwave facilities to provide communication among their geographically separated plants.[9]

Intrastate services of the common carriers are regulated by individual state regulatory commissions; interstate operations are regulated by the Federal Communications

Commission. These agencies use a "fair rate of return" criterion in regulating prices within their respective jurisdictions. The services of each common carrier are generally lumped together in computing the rate of return to be regulated. For example, in regulating Bell's service the FCC routinely considers together all revenues, plant invest-ment, and operating costs of Bell's interstate services in computing a rate of return to serve as the basis for decisions about price adjustments.[10] Likewise, most state agencies compute an overall rate of return for each carrier for all of its intrastate operations within the state in question.

Since the interesting implications of the model rest on the assumption that the allowable rate of return exceeds the actual cost of capital, the question arises as to whether revenues of the industry do exceed factor costs. While it is impossible to treat this question exhaustively here, there is some reason to believe that revenues are generally in excess of costs. We have been told by representatives in both the industry and in regulatory agencies that justification exists for allowing a return in excess of cost to give firms an incentive to develop and adopt cost-saving techniques. If the firm is left only indifferent as among a wide range of activities it has no positive incentive to minimize costs for any given activity. Consequently, regulatory agencies do not typically view with disfavor rates of return which are (within broad limits) somewhat in excess of rates they would judge to reflect cost. Positive profit is sometimes generated by the "regulatory lag" phenomenon: As the firm adopts new cost-saving technology or as its business volume rises for output subject to decreasing costs, its rate of return rises. However, the regulatory agency does not react immediately to force prices down. Rather, a lag of years may be involved. An example of this can be drawn from the interstate telephone operations of the Bell System. In its overall interstate operations Bell experienced a decline in its rate of return from 7.5 per cent to 5.2 per cent from 1950 to 1953. Reasoning that a rate in the neighborhood of 5 per cent was too low, it filed revised tariff schedules increasing interstate message toll rates by about 8 per cent – an increase expected to bring the rate of return up to about 6.5 per cent. The FCC, agreeing that earnings under the old tariff were inadequate, allowed the new tariff to go into effect. There is a strong implication in the FCC staff memoranda written at the time that a fair rate of return was considered to be in the neighborhood of 6 per cent.[11] After the increase went into effect in 1953, the rate of return rose to 6.6 per cent in 1954, 7.7 per cent in 1955, reached a peak of 8.5 per cent in early 1956, and continued in excess of 7 per cent during 1957 and 1958. Despite an interstate toll rate reduction in 1959, the rate of return amounted to almost 8 per cent in 1959 and 1960. The fact that the rate of return remained above a 6 per cent level during most of the decade meant that for a number of years revenues in interstate operations exceeded the FCC Staff estimate of cost.[12]

One implication drawn from the model is that the firm increases its ratio of capital input to cooperating factor input in a manner that increases social costs at the equilibrium output. Do the common carriers in this industry overinvest in this fashion? Unfortunately, empirical evidence is not available to us on the issue of bias in favor of investment in plant and equipment. However, one point should be made: the regulatory agencies exert little direct control over investment decisions that would force the firm to follow the socially optimal expansion path. The FCC, for example, follows a "used and useful" criterion in judging whether a given item is to be included in the rate base of plant and equipment. If the item is being employed in operations, and if it is useful (judged partially on subjective grounds), it is included. While common carriers are required routinely to provide a formidable list of reports concerning current operations, the relatively small staffs of the regulatory agencies available for research and investigative tasks, the lack of satisfactory criteria upon which to make judgments, and the heterogeneity of both factor inputs and service outputs would make extremely difficult if not impossible the task of detecting such bias.

The second implication drawn from the model is that due to the nature of regulation that firm has an incentive to operate in some markets even at a loss. Again, there is no clear-cut evidence which shows whether common carriers in this industry do, in fact, operate at a loss in some markets. However, evidence is available disclosing that

1 fears of "unfair" competition based on operations at "noncompensating" prices play a prominent role as a source of conflict between the carriers themselves and between the carriers and the FCC; and
2 in attempting to establish a commercial communications satellite system, the federal government has enacted a law containing provisions that (to serve "public ends") appear to exploit the willingness of common carriers to operate in markets at a loss.

We shall now discuss some of this evidence.

The FCC undertook a study in 1956 of interstate private-line services offered by the common carriers in order to determine the relationship between price and cost for these services on a more precise basis than is possible by considering only the overall rate of return for each carrier on all its interstate services. In the course of the study Bell submitted data (based on 1955 operations) showing that its telephone grade services were earning at a rate of 11.7 per cent, and its teletypewriter (telegraph) grade services at 2.6 per cent.[13] On the basis of this evidence, the FCC ordered interim price reductions in telephone grade services (in which Bell at the time was sole supplier) and permitted an increase for both Bell and Western Union for telegraph services (in which the two carriers do compete). The FCC expected the price adjustments to reduce substantially the spread between Bell's rates of return on telephone and telegraph grade services and to increase Western Union's rate of return on telegraph services.

During the study Western Union criticized Bell's behavior that allegedly resulted in Bell's relatively low rate of return on the telegraph services competitive with Western Union's own offerings. In the words of the FCC staff [6, p. 54]:

Western Union refers to evidence of record indicating that during the twenty-year period preceding this investigation, all principal private line telegraph rate adjustments were initiated by AT&T and, with one exception, all were rate reductions. Western Union alleges that AT&T has received a noncompensatory return on its private line telegraph service while enjoying a substantial return from services not competitive with Western Union.... According to Western Union, it follows that AT&T has engaged in unfair competition by maintaining unreasonably low rates for a competitive service and shifting the resulting financial burden to other services.[14]

Western Union's allegations, if true, would indicate that in conformity with the model, Bell is operating in private-line telegraph at a loss. However, it is impossible, for two reasons, to determine from the evidence in the FCC study whether this is in fact the case. First, the evidence in the record is simply not sufficient to determine what earnings level is "proper", i.e., what earnings level would just cover the cost of capital.[15] Second, the rates of return quoted above are based on "fully allocated cost" as opposed to marginal cost. In our model, the firm operates at a loss in a market only if the additional revenues it receives by operating in that market are below the additional costs it incurs. And whether operations in that market impose a "financial burden" (to use Western Union's words) on the other services depends on whether additional revenues do cover the additional costs.[16] But fully allocated costs are something else again. These include the costs of facilities used solely for the service in question and, in addition, they include an allocation of the "common" costs incurred by the carrier. For example, the telephone instrument itself is necessary in providing both intrastate and interstate message toll service as well as local exchange service; a transcontinental microwave system carries both public message toll and private-line traffic. In computing a rate of return for each of these services, it is necessary to allocate the costs of facilities having multiple uses. In general, the FCC allocates these costs in accordance with relative time of use. If a given facility is employed by service A 50 per cent of the time and by service B 50 per cent of the time, the cost of the facility is split equally between A and B. For our purposes, however, the crucial question is whether the cost of the facility could have been cut in half if either service A or service B had not been offered.[17] Is allocation on the basis of relative time in use an accurate reflection of marginal costs generated by each service? We may presume an affirmative answer only if the industry is subject to constant costs. However, the available evidence is not sufficient to determine whether the industry is, in general, subject to constant costs in the relevant range of output. If, on the contrary, it is subject either to decreasing or to increasing costs, use of the conventional cost allocation procedures would tend either to overstate or to understate marginal costs for particular services. Because of these possibilities, the rates of return commonly quoted for a particular communications service cannot be used as a reliable guide in determining whether a loss, in the relevant sense, is being incurred in providing that service and whether a financial burden is thereby being imposed upon the other services.

Competition between Bell and Western Union will probably continue to be a lively issue in future FCC investigations. In February 1962, the FCC was reported to have had "under consideration for some time an overall study of telephone vs. telegraph competition"; in the same month the American Communications Association (a union representing Western Union employees) "formally petitioned for an investigation into the extent and effect of participation by the American Telephone and Telegraph Co. in domestic and international telegraph communications." [9, February 26, 1962, p. 1].

Our model suggests that apprehension about the nature of competition in the industry is justified since a common carrier, regulated as described above, would (under certain conditions) have an incentive to operate at a loss in competitive markets and to shift the financial burden to its other services. In this sense, it would have an "unfair" advantage over other firms which do not have other markets sufficiently profitable to bear the loss of competing with it.[18] Unfortunately, however, the FCC and other regulatory bodies are so wedded to the fully allocated cost criteria rather than to marginal cost criteria in judging the "fairness" of competition, that evidence drawn from future hearings and investigations will probably not throw much light on the question whether common carriers in some markets do, in fact, operate at a loss measured in the relevant economic sense.

Finally, the model appears useful in treating economic implications of the Communications Satellite Act passed by Congress in August 1962, after long and bitter debate [13]. The Act specifies establishment of a new, private corporation regulated as a separate entity by the FCC to develop and operate the satellite system. The corporation is to be financed in two ways:

1 It may issue capital stock, carrying voting rights and eligible for dividends, to be sold "in a manner to encourage the widest distribution to the American public [13, Sec. 304 (a)]. Purchase of this stock is also permitted by "authorized" communications common carriers[19] subject to the constraint that the aggregate of shares held by these carriers together not exceed 50 percent of the total shares issued and outstanding. This stock is *not* eligible for inclusion in the carrier's rate base. For convenience in subsequent analysis we shall refer to these securities as "type I securities."

2 The Corporation may issue "nonvoting securities, bonds, debentures and other certificates of indebtedness as it may determine." Communications common carriers are permitted to hold these securities without specified limit, and these securities *are* eligible for inclusion in the rate base of the carrier "to the extent allowed by the Commission [FCC]" [13, Sec. 304 (b)]. For convenience we shall refer to these as "type II securities."

The model suggests that, given the provisions of the Act, communications common carriers would have a special incentive to invest in type II securities, and that their financial support might constitute a partial subsidy for the satellite corporation. By holding type II securities the common carrier incurs an interest cost (r_1) and collects whatever interest or dividends are forthcoming on type II securities (r'_1). Were the carrier unregulated or were the securities not eligible for inclusion in its rate base it would purchase securities only under the condition that $r'_1 \geq r_1$. Since, however, the investment in type II securities can be included in the overall rate base of the carrier, the carrier has an incentive (again under certain conditions) to invest more than would otherwise be the case.

Consider the example where the carrier receives a zero return on its investment in type II securities, i.e., $r'_1 = 0$ at all levels of investment; therefore, the carrier suffers a loss of r_1 for each dollar of investment. If, however, the allowable rate of return (s_1) is greater than the interest cost (r_1) the regulatory constraint on the carrier's other services is relaxed, permitting prices and profits to be raised in the other sectors. For each dollar in type II securities, the carrier's overall profit would *rise* by the value ($s_1 - r_1$): The loss involved in the investment in type II securities would be more than offset by the increased profits elsewhere resulting from inflation of the rate base and relaxation of the regulatory constraint. The carrier, then, may have an incentive to hold type II securities even if a direct loss is involved.

Two closely related implications arise from this analysis: First, the costs to the satellite corporation of obtaining money capital will fall if it can sell type II securities to common carriers at a return that is below their own interest cost (and if their own rate of interest is no higher than that which the satellite corporation would otherwise have to pay). To the extent that these funds provided at reduced cost to the satellite corporation permit a shift downward in its cost curves, the communications toll rates it charges to users of satellite services would also fall below the level that would have been established had the satellite corporation been forced to resort to conventional financing.[20]

Interestingly, a reduction in satellite communications toll rates by reducing financing costs to the satellite corporation, shifting the burden to other services, was intended by the sponsors of the bill that led to the Satellite Act. Senator Kerr, when introducing the bill to the Senate in February 1962, stated [11, p. 1670]:

> [This bill strives for]...a privately owned corporation in which the existing American companies engaged in the international communications business would be able to invest, with their investments treated the same as the acquisition of new equipment and thus includable in their rate bases. This important feature permitting the rate of return for all communication services to be spread over a broad base would insure lower charges for communication satellite services.

Second, inclusion of type II securities in the carrier's rate base may permit the satellite corporation to operate even if its total revenues do not cover total market costs. In this case type I securities issues may be small, since little if any dividends would be earned, and the bulk of financial support might come from common carriers holding type II securities at a return below the market rate of interest.[21] Again, the losses in satellite operations would be covered by revenues from telephone and telegraph services provided by the carriers.

5. Conclusions

The preceding analysis discloses that a misallocation of economic resources may result from the use by regulatory agencies of the rate-of-return constraint for price control. The firm has an incentive to substitute between factors in an uneconomic fashion that is difficult for the regulatory agency to detect. Moreover, if a large element of common costs exists for the firm's outputs in the various markets, the widely used "fully allocated" cost basis for rate-of-return computation is likely to prove unsatisfactory in determining whether the firm is operating at a loss in any given market, or whether its activities in some markets tend to restrict competition in an undesirable manner. At the same time, regulatory practices that provide an incentive for the firm to operate in some markets even at a loss may constitute a convenient mechanism through which certain activities of the firm judged to be in the "public interest" can be subsidized.

Our analysis suggests lines of further inquiry: We have considered only the telephone and telegraph industry, but the issues raised by the model may be relevant to evaluating market behavior in other industries as well. It is notable that Gardner Means in a recent study [7] has advocated that certain large nonregulated firms judged to be "collective enterprises" be encouraged, by tax incentive, to engage in "target pricing" where they aim for a profit equal to a fair rate of return on investment. By following this approach to pricing, which is similar to that employed in public utilities, the danger exists (which he does not recognize) that these firms would be exposed to the same pressures discussed above of inflating their rate bases by substituting capital for labor and by expanding into unprofitable new lines in order to satisfy the authorities that they were using "proper" target pricing. It might prove worthwhile to examine the effect of target pricing in steel and other industries discussed by Means in the light of the preceding analysis. Furthermore, it might be interesting to explore alternative forms of government control that, by avoiding the return-on-investment criterion for price regulation, do not generate the bias disclosed here.

Notes

1 Alternatively, one could construct a dynamic rather than a static model and consider positive values for depreciation; but to do so would complicate the results without contributing much additional insight into the behavior of the firm.
2 Since (6) is an inequality, we are faced with a nonlinear programming problem. However, the similarity of the results to ordinary marginal conditions is obvious.
3 If the total revenue function, pz, is concave in the relevant range of operation, it is clear that the Kuhn – Tucker conditions in this case are also sufficient. Given a concave pz, it is possible to define the dynamic gradient process corresponding to the static Kuhn–Tucker conditions showing the firm's input variation over time. But we do not do this here since we are primarily interested in equilibrium and the optimal inputs under regulation.
4 Clearly

$$\frac{r_1 - \lambda s_1}{1 - \lambda} = r_1 - \frac{\lambda}{1 - \lambda}(s_1 - r_1) \geq \left[p + z\frac{dp}{dz}\right]\frac{\partial z}{\partial x_1}$$

Since $0 < \lambda < 1, s_1 > r_1$, it follows immediately that:

$$r_1 > \left[p + s\frac{dp}{dz}\right]\frac{\partial z}{\partial x_1}$$

5 For examples of the manner in which the problem has previously been treated see [5, Ch. 19, 20] [10, Ch. 12, 17] [14, pp. 515–16].
6 AT&T, through its Long Lines Department, provides interstate line and radio facilities to connect the separate operating territories of the associated companies; in addition, in some cases Long Lines participates in providing interstate service internally within the territories of the multistate associated companies.
7 A good description of the industry and its present-day market structure is contained in [8, pp. 4–34].
8 These contracts permit Western Union to lease Bell communications facilities in order to enter markets that it could not feasibly serve if confined to its own facilities.
9 While railroads and public utilities, the so-called "right-of-way" companies, have historically been permitted by law to employ privately owned radio communications facilities for their internal needs, it was not until 1960 that the way was cleared (by a final decision of the Federal Communications Commission in Docket 11866) for other firms to provide their own communications facilities.
10 It is true that special studies of the separate services are occasionally made by the FCC in order to determine individual rates of return. Evidence from one such study will be presented below.
11 A clear, concise account of the manner in which the FCC regulates interstate telephone and telegraph services is contained in [12, pp. 3427–45].
12 The rise in Bell's rate of return is partly attributable to Bell's striking success in developing and adopting new cost-saving technology. The average book cost per circuit mile of Long Lines plant declined from roughly $230 in 1925 to $30 in 1960. The strong long-run incentives

apparent in Bell's activities to cut costs may be construed as prima-facie evidence that it enjoys positive profits. Of course, one could argue that another factor is present – entrepreneurship – whose cost would more or less offset the positive profit; i.e., in the economic sense (in contrast to the accounting sense) revenue may just cover cost and the firm still has incentive to minimize cost. But here we are concerned with the *marginal* cost of capital to the firm compared to the *marginal* return to capital allowed by the regulatory agency. If the latter exceeds the former, the "regulatory bias" emerges regardless of whether total cost includes a fixed charge attributable to an additional factor.

13   The initial decision of the FCC staff in this study (not adopted by the Commission at this writing) is contained in [6].

14   For AT&T's reply see [4, pp. 14–18].

15   The FCC staff concluded that AT&T's proper earnings levels in $7\frac{1}{4}$ per cent and for Western Union 9 per cent [3]. This conclusion was contested by Bell in its reply brief: "These [FCC staff] findings are made despite the fact that there is not a word of testimony in the record concerning the over-all costs of capital to either carrier, much less the costs of capital for their private line services" [4, p. 3]. See also [2, p. 27].

16   A good statement of this point is contained in [1, pp. 7–10].

17   For purposes of this simple illustration, we are assuming a zero elasticity of demand substitution between A and B.

18   That is, the unconditionally maximized profits of the other regulated firms may be sufficiently low so that imposition of the regulatory constraint does not induce them to operate at a loss in competitive markets.

19   Authorized common carriers presumably would include AT&T, Western Union and eight U.S. overseas radio and cable telegraph companies.

20   These users include both U.S. and foreign international common carriers who would employ the satellite relays primarily for transoceanic communications links in combination with or as a substitute for submarine cable and radio. To the extent that users of the satellite system are the same carriers which invest in type II securities, their subsidy to the satellite corporation would be more or less offset by the reduction in toll rates they pay to the satellite corporation. However the Act specifies no particular relationship between the amount of type II securities they respectively hold and their relative use of the satellite system.

21   In this case type I securities would be attractive primarily because of the voting rights they confer.

References

1. American Telephone and Telegraph Co. (1961): *Brief of Bell System Respondents in Support of Lawfulness of Revised Telpak Tariff under Section 202 (a) of the Communications Act*, regarding FCC Docket No. 14251.
2. ——(1961): *Exceptions of Bell System Companies to the Initial Decision Released July 14, 1961*, regarding FCC Docket Nos. 11645, 11646, 12194.
3. ——(1960): *Proposed Findings and Conclusions of the Bell System Companies*, regarding FCC Docket Nos. 11645, 11646.
4. ——(1961): *Reply Brief of the Bell System Companies*, regarding FCC Docket Nos. 11645, 11646, 12194.
5. Clark, J. M. (1939): *Social Control of Business*, 2nd edn. New York: McGraw-Hill.
6. Federal Communications Commission, (1961): *Initial Decision* (adopted July 6, 1961), regarding Docket Nos. 11645, 11646, 12194.
7. Means, G. C. (1962): *Pricing Power and the Public Interest*. New York: Harper.

8. National Association of Railroad and Utilities Commissioners (1951): *Message Toll Telephone Rates and Disparities*. Washington.

9. *Telecommunications Reports* (Washington), weekly news service covering telephone, telegraph and radio communications.

10. Troxel, E. (1947): *Economics of Public Utilities*. New York: Reinhart & Co.

11. U.S. Congress (1962): *Congressional Record* (Senate), February 7, 87th congress, 2nd session Washington.

12. —— (1958): *Consent Decree Program of the Department of Justice*. Hearings before the Anti-Trust Subcommittee of the House Committee on the Judiciary, 85th congress, 2nd session Washington 1958. Pt. 2, American Telephone and Telegraph Co. (3 vols).

13. U.S. Public Law (1962): *Communications Satellite Act of 1962*, 87th congress August 31, 87–624.

14. Wilcox, C. (1955): *Public Policies toward Business*, 5th Edn. Homewood, Illinois: R. Irwin.

CHAPTER ELEVEN

Theories of Economic Regulation

RICHARD A. POSNER

Source: *Bell Journal of Economics*, 5 (1974), pp. 335–58. Reprinted with the permission of The RAND Corporation. © The RAND Corporation.

1. Introduction

A major challenge to social theory is to explain the pattern of government intervention in the market – what we may call "economic regulation." Properly defined, the term refers to taxes and subsidies of all sorts as well as to explicit legislative and administrative controls over rates, entry, and other facets of economic activity. Two main theories of economic regulation have been proposed. One is the "public interest" theory, bequeathed by a previous generation of economists to the present generation of lawyers.[1] This theory holds that regulation is supplied in response to the demand of the public for the correction of inefficient or inequitable market practices. It has a number of deficiencies that we shall discuss. The second theory is the "capture" theory – a poor term but one that will do for now. Espoused by an odd mixture of welfare state liberals, muckrakers, Marxists, and free-market economists, this theory holds that regulation is supplied in response to the demands of interest groups struggling among themselves to maximize the incomes of their members. There are crucial differences among the capture theorists. I shall argue that the economists' version is the most promising, but shall also point out the significant weaknesses in both the theory and the empirical research that is alleged to support the theory.

2. The Public Interest Theory of Regulation

The original theory

Two assumptions seem to have typified thought about economic policy (not all of it by economists) in the period roughly from the enactment of the first Interstate Commerce Act in 1887 to the founding of the *Journal of Law and Economics* in 1958. One assumption was that economic markets are extremely fragile and apt to operate very inefficiently (or inequitably) if left alone; the other was that government regulation is virtually costless. With these assumptions, it was very easy to argue that the principal government interventions in the economy – trade union protection, public utility and common carrier regulation, public power and reclamation programs, farm subsidies, occupational licensure, the minimum wage, even tariffs – were simply responses of government to public demands for the rectification of palpable and remediable inefficiencies and inequities in the operation of the free market. Behind each scheme of regulation could be discerned a market imperfection, the existence of which supplied a complete justification for some regulation assumed to operate effectively and without cost.

Were this theory of regulation correct, we would find regulation imposed mainly in highly concentrated industries (where the danger of monopoly is greatest) and in industries that generate substantial external costs or benefits. We do not. Some fifteen years of theoretical and empirical research, conducted mainly by economists, have demonstrated that regulation is not positively correlated with the presence of external economies or diseconomies or with monopolistic market structure. Few, if any, responsible students of the airline industry, for example, believe that there is some intrinsic peculiarity about the market for air transportation that requires prices and entry to be fixed by the government. The same may be said for trucking, taxi service, stock brokerage, ocean shipping, and many other heavily regulated industries. Even the danger of "market failure" in such traditionally unquestioned areas of regulation as health care, the legal profession, and the safety of drugs and other products is increasingly discounted. The conception of government as a costless and dependably effective instrument for altering market behavior has also gone by the boards.[2] Theoretical revision has both stimulated and been reinforced by a growing body of case studies demonstrating that particular schemes of government regulation – whether of taxicabs, or producers of natural gas, or truckers, or airlines, or stock brokers, or new drugs, or electricity rates, or broadcasting – cannot be explained on the ground that they increase the wealth or, by any widely accepted standard of equity or fairness, the justice of the society.[3]

A reformulation

The empirical evidence is sometimes challenged on the ground that the disappointing performance of the regulatory process is the result not of any unsoundness in the basic goals or nature of the process but of particular weaknesses in personnel or procedures that can and will be remedied (at low cost) as the society gains experience in the mechanics of public administration.[4] Thus reformulated, the public interest theory of regulation holds that regulatory agencies are created for bona fide public purposes, but are then mismanaged, with the result that those purposes are not always achieved.

This reformulation is unsatisfactory on two grounds. First, it fails to account for a good deal of evidence that the socially undesirable results of regulation are frequently desired by groups influential in the enactment of the legislation setting up the regulatory scheme. The railroads supported the enactment of the first Interstate Commerce Act, which was designed to prevent railroads from practicing price discrimination, because discrimination was undermining the railroads' cartels. American Telephone and Telegraph pressed for state regulation of telephone service because it wanted to end competition among telephone companies. Truckers and airlines supported the extension of common carrier regulation to their industries because they considered unregulated competition "excessive." Sometimes the regulatory statute itself reveals an unmistakable purpose of altering the operation of markets in directions inexplicable on public interest grounds, as in the reference in the ICC's statutory mandate to the desirability of maintaining "balance" among competing modes of transporta-tion.[5] None of this evidence is decisive against the public interest theory – in each case other groups besides the industry directly regulated supported the legislation. Whether the other groups were also interest groups is discussed later on.

Second, the evidence that has been offered to show mismanagement by the regulatory agency is surprisingly weak. Much of it is consistent with the rival theory (which is considered more closely in Section 3) that the typical regulatory agency operates with reasonable efficiency to attain deliberately inefficient or inequitable goals set by the legislature that created it. The proclivity of some agencies for concentrating their resources heavily on cases of small individual consequence – a proclivity often thought to be convincing evidence of mismanagement – is in fact consistent with an efficient allocation of resources within the agency [33]. The frequent criticisms of agencies for relying on case-by-case adjudication to make policy, rather than engaging in elaborate planning exercises, are extremely superficial since they ignore, first, the intrinsic difficulty of forecasting the future and, second, the disastrous consequences for agencies, notably the Federal Communications Commission, that have engaged in such planning [8, 32]. The common argument that the employees of regulatory agencies must be less able than their counterparts in the private sector, since they are paid lower salaries,[6] ignores the fact that service with an agency frequently increases the later earning capacity of the employee in the private sector. The agency makes a contribution to the employee's human capital. This contribution, when added to his salary, may equal the value of the salary (plus contribu-tions of human capital) that he would have received in the private sector [11, 34]. In sum, one is left puzzled as to why such failures of regulation in the public interest as one observes should be ascribed so confidently to bureaucratic ineptitude.

Third, no persuasive theory has yet been proposed as to why agencies should be expected to be less efficient than other organizations. The motivation of the agency employee to work diligently and honestly is similar to that of the employee of a business firm. Both want to obtain advancement (not necessarily within the employing firm or agency) and to avoid being fired, demoted, or humiliated. To some extent, these motiva-tions are independent of the incentive of the agency's head to enforce standards of diligence and honesty against the employees. Many employees will want to demonstrate the possession of excellent qualities in order to improve their prospects for superior private employment anyway. In any event, the agency head's incentive is clear. He derives few benefits from the slackness of his staff – not even the famous "quiet life." His life would not be so quiet, for many employees would be restless and dissatisfied, knowing that their opportunities for private employment were being impaired by the agency's reputation for laxity and sloth.

Furthermore, the agency's head is answerable both to the legislative and (if he desires promotion or reappointment) to the executive branches. Legislative oversight of agencies is too little emphasized. Unlike business firms, government agencies must go to *their* capital markets – the legislative appropriations committees – every year. There is compe-tition among agencies for the largest possible slice of the appropriations pie, and the agency that has a reputation for economy and hard work enjoys an advantage in the competition, for only in the exceptional case will it be to the legislators' advantage that the agency's personnel be lining *their* pockets (whether with pecuniary income or with nonpecuniary income such as leisure).[7]

One objection to the foregoing argument is that the agency differs from the private firm in not competing in any product market. But that is to say only that the agency is like a private monopolist, and there is no convincing theoretical or empirical support for the proposition that the internal management of monopolistic firms is any laxer than that of competitive firms. Another objection is that the agency has little incentive to minimize costs because, unlike a business firm, it cannot keep the profits generated by its cost savings. Yet most employees of business firms do not share in the profits of the enterprise, and they are somehow motivated to work efficiently. Moreover, I have suggested several ways in which agency employees, from the head of the agency down, do "profit" from efficient management, and lose if the agency is managed inefficiently.

A further reformulation of the public interest theory

The idea that regulation is an honest but frequently an unsuccessful attempt to promote the public interest becomes somewhat more plausible if we introduce two factors often ignored. The first is the intractable character of many of the tasks that have been assigned to the regulatory agencies. The clearest example is the regulation of price levels under public utility and common carrier statues. These statutes require the agencies to determine the costs of the regulated firms and to hold their prices to those costs, and there are good grounds for believing that the necessary instruments of measurement and control simply do not exist [35]. The agencies are asked to do the impossible and it is not surprising that they fail, and in attempting to succeed distort the efficient functioning of the regulated markets. But this does not explain why legislatures assign such tasks to agencies.

The second factor is the cost of effective legislative supervision of the agencies' performance. In a recent article on legal rule-making, Isaac Ehrlich and I point out that legislative bodies are a type of firm in which the costs of production are extremely high and, moreover, rise very sharply with increases in output [12]. The reason is that legislative "production" is a process of negotiation among a large group, the legislators, and the analysis of transaction costs in other contexts suggests that bargaining among a number of individuals is a costly process (and explains why legislatures require only a majority and not a unanimous vote in the conduct of their business). Because costs of bargaining rise rapidly with the number of bargainers, a legislature cannot respond efficiently to a growth in workload by increasing the number of its members. Hence, as the business of a legislature rises, it can be expected to delegate more and more of its work to agencies, and to exercise progressively less control over those agencies. This theory has various testable implications. It suggests, for example, a "life cycle" theory of administrative regulation. The agency is created at a time when the legislature has a strong interest in the problem to be dealt with by the agency. But as time passes, and other problems come before the legislature, the legislature finds itself unable at reasonable cost to continue to devote time to properly monitoring the agencies created previously. The theory also implies that administrative failure will become, on average, a more serious problem over time, with the growth of the size and complexity of the economy. As we shall see shortly, however, the inquiries suggested by these hypotheses might not discriminate adequately between the version of the public interest theory suggested here and some versions of the capture theory of regulation.

Behavioral assumptions of the public interest theory

A serious problem with any version of the public interest theory is that the theory contains no linkage or mechanism by which a perception of the public interest is translated into legislative action. In the theory of markets, it is explained how the efforts of individuals to promote their self-interest through transacting bring about an efficient allocation of resources. There is no comparable articulation of how a public perception as to what legislative policies or arrangements would maximize public welfare is translated into legislative action. It is not enough to say that a voter will vote for the candidate who promises to carry out the policies that the voter perceives to be in the public interest; other policies might benefit the particular voter more. Policies that benefitted 51 percent of the voters might impose much greater costs on the other 49 percent, in which event the majority would be confronted with a conflict between principle and interest – and no body of theory or of evidence suggests that they would be likely to vote the former.

There are two possible ways around this problem. One, suggested by Ronald Coase, emphasizes the moral differences between private and political action. The assumption that market behavior is normally motivated by fairly narrow considerations of self-interest is plausible, because most market decisions are social goods rather than bads. To be sure, a decision to sell a new product may harm a competitor or a locality or a group of workers or of customers, but the decision makers can be reasonably confident that these harms are more than offset by the gains to others. Where, however, an individual votes for policies designed to exploit his fellows, he can hardly avoid confronting the moral implications of his action and the moral code may constrain him from voting in that manner.

A second approach is to observe the potentiality for collusion among politicians. There are only two important political parties in this country, and there are barriers not only to the formation of additional parties but to the takeover of either of the major parties by disgruntled members or outsiders. Thus, there would appear to be opportunities for the politicians who dominate the parties to agree to impose some of their own policy preferences on the electorate. They could also use their monopoly power to obtain pecuniary income – and doubtless do – but I am assuming that they take at least some of their monopoly profits in the form of satisfaction from imposing on the public their conception of the public interest (which might differ from the conception held by the electorate and from the desires of any particular interest group). If this analysis is accepted, it becomes plausible to suppose that some policies are adopted because they conform to the public interest – as conceived by the politicians.

3. Some Versions of the Capture Theory

The Marxists and the muckrakers

The theory that economic regulation is not about the public interest at all, but is a process by which interest groups seek to promote their (private) interests, takes several distinct forms. One, which is put forward by Marxists and by Ralph Nader-type muckrakers, can be crudely summarized in the following syllogism. Big business – the capitalists – control the institutions of our society. Among those institutions is regulation. The capitalists must therefore control regulation. The syllogism is false. A great deal of economic regulation serves the interests of small-business – or nonbusiness – groups, including dairy farmers, pharmacists, barbers, truckers, and, in particular, union labor. Such forms of regulation are totally unexplained (and usually either ignored or applauded) in this version of the interest-group or "capture" theory.

The political scientists' formulations

A more interesting version of the "capture" theory derives from political science, and in particular from Bentley and Truman and their followers, who emphasize the importance of interest groups in the formation of public policy.[8] The political scientists have developed some evidence of the importance of interest groups in legislative and administrative processes, but unfortunately their work is almost entirely devoid of theory. They do not tell us why some interests are effectively represented in the political process and others not, or under what conditions interest groups succeed or fail in obtaining favorable legislation.[9]

A few political scientists have proposed the rudiments, at least, of a usable theory. This theory – which the term "capture" describes particularly well – is that over time regulatory agencies come to be dominated by the industries regulated [3, 17, 23, 46].[10] This formulation is more specific than the general interest group theory. It singles out a particular interest group – the regulated firms – as prevailing in the struggle to influence legislation, and it predicts a regular sequence, in which the original purposes of a regulatory program are later thwarted through the efforts of the interest group.

Unfortunately, the theory is still unsatisfactory. First, it is confusingly similar to, and in practice probably indistinguishable from, some versions of the public interest theory discussed in Section 2. Second, while I have generously called it a "theory," it is actually a hypothesis that lacks any theoretical foundation. No reason is suggested for characterizing the interaction between the regulatory agency and the regulated firm by a metaphor of conquest, and surely the regulatory process is better viewed as the outcome of implicit (sometimes explicit) bargaining between the agency and the regulated firms. No reason is suggested as to why the regulated industry should be the only interest group able to influence an agency. Customers of the regulated firm have an obvious interest in the outcome of the regulatory process – why may they not be able to "capture" the agency as effectively as the regulated firms, or more so? No reason is suggested as to why industries are able to capture only existing agencies – never to procure the creation of an agency that will promote their interests – or why an industry strong enough to capture an agency set up to tame it could not prevent the creation of the agency in the first place.

The "theory" answers none of these questions. In addition, it is contradicted by three important bodies of evidence. First, not every agency is characterized by a pristine virtue; often there is no occasion for conquest. As mentioned earlier, there is now considerable evidence that a major purpose (in fact) of the original Interstate Commerce Act was to shore up the railroads' cartels [15, 22, 24]. Later amendments, typically passed at the behest of the Commission itself, seem to have been less rather than more favorable to railroads (an example is the Hepburn Act which gave the ICC the power to fix maximum rates). The sequence is opposite to what the capture hypothesis predicts.

Second, the theory has no predictive or explanatory power at all when a single agency regulates separate industries having conflicting interests. The ICC is again a conspicuous example. It regulates competing modes of transportation – truckers, railroads, and barge lines – and the theory does not tell us which one the ICC can be expected to favor. This difficulty is not limited to the agency with a multiindustry "clientele." There are always competing groups within an industry. The interests of the trunk airlines are not identical to those of the regional or of the local service lines: which will the CAB decide to promote? The interests of the telephone companies, primarily AT&T, are in conflict with those of Western Union and other "record" carriers: which competing group will the Federal Communications Commission promote?

Third, the capture theory ignores a good deal of evidence that the interests promoted by regulatory agencies are frequently those of customer groups rather than those of the regulated firms themselves. Indeed, not only many examples of specific regulatory policies, but some of the structural characteristics of the regulatory process, seem best explained by reference to the influence on the regulatory process of interest groups consisting of customers of the regulated industry [40].

The economic theory of regulation

What I shall call "the economic theory of regulation" was proposed by George Stigler in a path breaking article.[10] The theory seems at first glance merely a refined version of the capture theory just discussed. It discards the unexplained, and frequently untrue, assumption of pristine legislative purpose; it admits the possibility of "capture" by interest groups other than the regulated firms; and it replaces the "capture" metaphor, with its inappropriately militaristic flavor, by the more neutral terminology of supply and demand. But it insists with the political scientists that economic regulation serves the private interests of politically effective groups.

More is involved, however, than merely a recasting of the work of the political scientists. The economic theory is more precise and hard-edged – easier to confront and test with a body of data – than the political theory (which, as I pointed out, is not really a theory at all). Moreover, the economic theory is committed to the strong assumptions of economic theory generally, notably that people seek to advance their self-interest and do so rationally. A political scientist can argue that regulation is more likely to be imposed in a declining industry because adversity is a greater spur to effort than opportunity [45] (an example that assumes that regulation is normally obtained for the benefit of the regulated firms). The economist is reluctant to accept such an explanation. He does not distinguish between a profit foregone and a loss incurred – the former is a cost too, indeed the same kind of cost.[11] (I note parenthetically that the hypothesis is contradicted by a good deal of evidence.[12])

It is, of course, a weakness rather than a strength in a theory that it is so elastic as to fit any body of data with which it is likely to be confronted. The political science theory of regulation is such a theory. Exceptions to the general rule that regulatory agencies are captured by the regulated firms are explained away by facile references to the personality of the legislators, public opinion, ignorance, folk wisdom, [44, p. 512] etc. The economic theory insists that regulation be explained as the outcome of the forces of demand and supply. Outcomes that cannot be so explained count as evidence against the theory.

4. A Closer Look at the Economic Theory of Regulation

The theory

I shall now try to describe the economic theory more precisely and to state what I believe to be its strengths and weaknesses. The theory is based on two simple but important insights. The first is that since the coercive power of government can be used to give valuable benefits to particular individuals or groups, economic regulation – the expression of that power in the economic sphere – can be viewed as a product whose allocation is governed by laws of supply and demand. The second insight is that the theory of cartels may help us locate the demand and supply curves.

Viewing regulation as a product allocated in accordance with basic principles of supply and demand directs attention to factors bearing on the value of regulation to particular individuals or groups, since, other things being equal, we can expect a product to be supplied to those who value it the most. It also directs our attention to the factors bearing on the cost of obtaining regulation. The theory of cartels illuminates both the benefit and the cost side. The theory teaches that the value of cartelization is greater, the less elastic the demand for the industry's product and the more costly, or the slower, new entry into the industry (or cartelized markets within the industry) is. The theory identifies two major costs of cartelization (besides punishment costs, which are relevant only where cartelization is forbidden by law). The first is the cost to the sellers of arriving at an agreement on the price to be charged by and the output of each seller. This agreement determines the profits of each cartel member. The second cost is the cost of enforcing the cartel agreement against nonparticipants or defectors. Cartels are plagued by "free rider" problems. After the sellers agree to charge the price that maximizes their joint profits, each seller has an incentive to sell at a slightly lower price, because his profits are likely to be higher at the much greater sales volume that a slightly lower price will enable him to obtain. If enough sellers submit to the temptation, the cartel will collapse. A cartel is particularly fragile if members are able to conceal price cuts from one another; then each has the hope of being able to obtain substantial short-term profits before the other members realize that he is cutting price and match him.[13]

Since the effect of typical regulatory devices (entry control, minimum rates, exemption from the antitrust laws) is the same as that of cartelization – to raise prices above competitive levels – the benefit side of cartel theory is clearly relevant. The cost side also seems relevant. The members of the industry must agree on the form of regulation. And just as the individual seller's profits are maximized if he remains outside of the cartel (as long as his competitors remain inside), so any individual or firm that would be benefitted by a type of regulation will have some incentive to avoid joining in the efforts of his group to obtain the regulation. If the regulation is forthcoming, he will benefit from it – he cannot be excluded from the protection of a general regulation, just as a seller cannot be excluded from the benefits of his competitors' charging a monopoly price – but, unlike the active participants in the coalition, he will benefit at no cost.

The theory of cartels teaches that the reluctance to cooperate in maintaining a monopoly price is most likely to be overcome if the number of sellers whose actions must be coordinated is small, which tends to reduce the costs of coordination and of policing, and if the interests of the sellers are identical or nearly so, which should reduce the cost of securing agreement.[14] Likewise in the regulatory sphere, the fewer the prospective beneficiaries of a regulation, the easier it will be for them to coordinate their efforts to obtain the regulation. Also, it will be more difficult for one of them to refuse to participate in the cooperative effort without causing the effort to collapse. Thus, all will tend to participate, knowing that any defection is likely to be followed promptly by the defection of the remaining members of the group, leaving the original defector worse off than if he had not cooperated. The homogeneity of the interests of the members is also significant. The more homogeneous their interest in the regulation in question, the easier (cheaper) will it be for them to arrive at a common position and the more likely will it be that the common position does not so disadvantage one or more members as to cause them to defect from the group.[15]

The analysis of cartels is plainly relevant to the development of an economic theory of regulation, but it is not that theory. If it were, we would observe the same industries obtaining regulatory protection as form durable cartels. We do not. Many industries, such as agriculture, certain occupations, many branches of retail trade, and some manufacturing industries such as textiles, which have obtained favorable regulation, lack the characteristics that predispose a market to cartelization, in particular fewness of sellers. Casual observation suggests that highly concentrated industries are actually *less* likely to obtain favorable regulation than less concentrated industries,[16] reversing the usual expectation with regard to the incidence of cartelization.

There are two reasons why the pattern of regulation and the pattern of private cartelization are different. First, the demand for regulation (derived from its value in enhancing the profits of the regulated firms) is greater among industries for which private cartelization is an unfeasible or very costly alternative – industries that lack high concentration and other characteristics favorable to cartelizing. They lack good substitutes for regulation. (This point suggests, incidentally, a testable – in principle anyway – hypothesis of the economic theory of regulation: among randomly selected unconcentrated industries the presence of cartel-like regulation will be negatively related to the price elasticity of demand for the industry's product *at the competitive price*. The qualification, which is critical, makes the test difficult to carry out in practice.)

Second, whereas cartelization is the product purely of the cooperative action of the firms, favorable regulation requires, in addition, the intervention of the political process. Some industries may be able to influence that process at lower cost than others and these may not be the same industries that are able to cartelize at low cost. In particular, the political dimension of regulation requires two modifications of the theory of cartels as applied to regulation. First, as Stigler proposes in his paper on the free-rider problem, which is appropriate as an appendix to this article, each member will have an interest in participating in the coalition seeking protective regulation when there is significant asymmetry among the positions of industry members. Protective regulation can take a variety (greater than in the case of private cartelization) of forms – limitation of entry, cash subsidy, tariff, etc. – and the choice of the form may, assuming asymmetry among the positions of the industry's members, affect differentially the welfare of those members. If so, each will want to participate in the industry campaign for regulation so that the choice of the form of regulation to seek will reflect his views. The free-rider problem will still be easiest to overcome where the number of firms in an industry is small, but if the asymmetry condition is fulfilled, even the presence of many firms may not erect an insurmountable obstacle to the formation of an effective coalition. This suggests that it may be cheaper for large-number industries to obtain public regulation than to cartelize privately.

Second, the determinants of political influence must be worked into the supply side of the market in regulation. But before this can be done it is necessary to specify the character of the political system under discussion: the political system of the Soviet Union – or of the City of Chicago – is not identical to that of the United States.

One can distinguish three distinct forms of political system, all of which play some role in the actual political systems of democratic countries such as the United States. One system I shall call "entrepreneurial:" favorable legislation is sold[17] to the industries that value it most. For the reason just mentioned, these would not be the same industries that form private cartels. The costs of cooperative action are irrelevant under this system: the government can use its taxing or other powers of coercion to enable the industry to overcome any free-rider problem it might have, in order that the industry can raise the maximum purchase price for the legislation.

The next system to be considered is the "coercive:" legislation is awarded to groups that are able to make credible threats to retaliate with violence (or disorder, or work stoppages, or grumbling) if society does not give them favorable treatment. We lack good theories of threats or violence but as a first approximation it would seem that the number of people in the group would be an important determinant of its ability to make credible threats of *serious* disorder or violence (as opposed to threats of minor sabotage, annoying and costly but not deeply threatening).

The third system is the "democratic:" legislation is awarded by the vote of elected representatives of the people. This system, like the coercive, emphasizes the importance of numbers: not of threateners but of voters. The groups are not identical, but there is great overlap, so we are led to predict that the economic legislation of dictatorial regimes will broadly resemble that of democratic ones – as seems on casual observation to be the case. Willingness to pay is also important in the democratic as in the entrepreneurial political system, since legislators are elected in campaigns in which the amount of money expended on behalf of a candidate exerts great influence on the outcome. However, unlike the case of an entrepreneurial system, in a democratic system the free-rider problem remains a serious one: it may limit the ability of an industry or other interest group to make substantial campaign contributions.

The foregoing analysis suggests that while the characteristics that predispose an industry to successful cartelization may also help it to obtain favorable government regulation, one characteristic that discourages cartelization – a large number of parties whose cooperation is necessary to create and maintain the cartel – encourages regulation. Large numbers have voting (and, potentially, coercive) power and also increase the likelihood of an asymmetry of interests that will encourage broad participation in the coalition seeking regulation. In addition, large numbers, and other factors that discourage private cartelization, increase the demand for protective legislation.

The economic theory can thus be used to explain why we so often observe protective legislation in areas like agriculture, labor, and the professions, where private cartelization would hardly be feasible. This is an important advance over the other theories that we have examined. However, the economic theory has not been refined to the point where it enables us to predict specific industries in which regulation will be found. That is because the theory does not tell us what (under various conditions) is the number of members of a coalition that maximizes the likelihood of regulation. Formally, this is the number beyond which the loss of group cohesiveness caused by adding another member would outweigh the increase in the feasibility and attractiveness of becoming regulated produced by greater voting power and by greater demand for regulation due to greater difficulty of cartelizing privately.

I used to think that there was one case in which the theory yielded an unequivocal and testable prediction. That is where the number of *firms* in the industry is small, thereby facilitating the organization of the industry for effective political action,[18] but the number of *employees* in the industry is great.[19] Since the profits from protective regulation can be divided between the employees and the firms through collective bargaining, it should be possible for the firms to induce the employees to "lend" their voting power to obtaining such regulation. The industry does not quite have the best of both worlds, because the firms' profits from favorable legislation, and hence their incentive to seek it, will be diminished by the amount of the payoff to the employees. This may be considerable. Legislation favorable to the industry, by raising prices, will reduce output and hence the industry's demand for inputs, including labor. The reduction in demand will harm not only the employees who are laid off but the remaining employees as well, since the diminution in the number of employees will reduce their voting power, which they might want to exercise in other areas. These costs will presumably be considered by the union when it negotiates for its share of the profits conferred by the regulation being sought by the firms.

The major problem with this hypothesis is that the small number of firms is a factor that, by reducing the costs of private collusion, reduces the industry's demand for favorable legislation. So the economic theory is not refuted by observing that the most conspicuous example of such an industry – the automobile industry – seems to have been unsuccessful either in obtaining favorable regulation or in warding off unfavorable regulation (such as safety and emission controls). Anyway, the automobile example – like so many in this field – is ambiguous.[20]

As this example suggests, the economic theory is still so spongy that virtually any observations can be reconciled with it. Consider, as a further example, the apparent paradox that so many regulated industries appear to be either extremely atomistic (like agriculture) or extremely concentrated (like local telephone or electrical service). The former would appear to encounter substantial free-rider problems in organizing a politically effective group; the latter would appear to have little demand for regulation. The moderately concentrated industry would seem to have the optimal structure in terms of the costs of obtaining legislation and the benefits to be derived from it. But theory can worm its way out of this hole, too. For the small-number case, we can point out:

1 even a naturally monopolistic industry would gain from legislation that increased the demand for its product (e.g., by suppressing substitutes) or prevented entry;[21]
2 even if the members of the regulated industry do not gain from regulation, other groups, for example groups of customers, may [40]; and
3 concentration or monopoly may itself be the result of regulation.

In the large-number case, we can point out that the reluctance of each member of a coalition to participate substantially in it may be dominated by the number of members who participate, albeit very modestly. Is industry X, having 10 members, likely to spend more money on trade association activities than industry Y, which differs only in that it has 10,000 members? Free-rider problems are presumably not serious in the case of industry X. Let us assume that each member of that industry contributes $1,000 for a total of $10,000 and that this approximates the optimal expenditure for the industry. Free-rider problems may be serious in industry Y, so serious that it would be impossible for the industry to raise $1,000 from each member were that necessary to reach an optimal level of expenditures. But the industry does not have to raise that amount from each member in order to match industry X – to do that it need only raise $1 from each member.

As part of the search for a harder-edged theory of regulation, it has been suggested that the geographic concentration of the people who would benefit from favourable regulation is an important element since a legislator will exert greater efforts on behalf of a voter bloc large enough to influence the outcome of an election materially. But it has not been demonstrated that this is a generally valid proposition. If the same number of voters are more widely dispersed, no legislator will pay as much attention to their demands, but more legislators will pay some attention, and the net effectiveness of the interest group in the legislature *may* (it is an empirical question whether it *will*) be greater. The proposition also ignores the importance of the President in the legislative process. A Presidential candidate has little reason to respond to the desires of voter blocs concentrated in states in which the vote is not expected to be close. Thus we are at a loss to say whether observing a geographically concentrated – or dispersed – group obtaining – or failing to obtain – regulation confirms or refutes the economic theory of regulation. And this illustrates the essential deficiency of the economic theory of regulation in its present form. At best it is a list of criteria relevant to predicting whether an industry will obtain favorable legislation. It is not a coherent theory yielding unambiguous and therefore testable hypotheses.

Another sort of weakness is that the theory, pushed to its logical extreme, becomes rather incredible, because it excludes the possibility that a society concerned with the ability of interest groups to manipulate the political process in their favor might establish institutions that enabled genuine public interest considerations to influence the formation of policy. One can certainly argue that the U.S. Constitution, in establishing an independent judiciary, did just this (and this point is discussed further below). The constitutional requirement of payment of compensation in eminent domain cases is a similar example [34, p. 22n2]. More generally, the many features of law and public policy designed to maintain a market system are more plausibly explained by reference to a broad social interest in efficiency than by reference to the designs of narrow interest groups.[22] One can of course say that on some issues the relevant interest group consists of everyone, or almost everyone, in the society. But this usage robs the interest group concept of its utility by collapsing it into the public interest theory.

The evidence

Let us turn now to the empirical evidence bearing on the economic theory of regulation. There are a fair number of case studies – of trucking, airlines, railroads, and many other industries – that support the view that economic regulation is better explained as a product supplied to interest groups than as an expression of the social interest in efficiency or justice.[3] I shall discuss in a moment the question just how much support for the economic theory of regulation do these studies really provide. But first I want to discuss another type of empirical evidence, so far largely neglected, that provides additional support for the economic interest group approach. This is evidence concerning the procedures employed in the regulatory process.

A corollary of the economic theory of regulation is that the regulatory process can be expected to operate with reasonable efficiency to achieve its ends. The ends are the product of the struggle between interest groups, but, as suggested earlier, it would be contrary to the usual assumptions of economics to argue that wasteful or inappropriate means would be chosen to achieve those ends. We saw that the evidence traditionally adduced to show that regulatory agencies are inefficient is highly ambiguous. I want to go beyond that evidence and note some general features of the regulatory process that suggest it is well designed to achieve the ends posited by the economic theory of regulation.

One is the delegation of regulatory authority by legislatures to administrative agencies. As mentioned earlier, legislatures cannot continuously regulate a complex area; they must delegate much of the regulatory function either to the courts or to administrative agencies. In the area of economic regulation the legislative choice has generally been the administrative agency rather than the court. Lawyers defend this choice on the ground that the public interest purposes assumed to lie behind the legislation can be achieved more efficiently due to

1 the agency's specialization and
2 its independence from political control.

The first reason seems specious. Courts have long handled highly complex economic questions, such as those which arise in antitrust cases, no less efficiently (or more inefficiently) than the agencies. Is a merger case tried before a federal district court likelier to be mishandled than one tried before the FTC, or the ICC?[23] The second reason is illogical. The choice is not between agency and direct legislative regulation – the latter is assumed to be impracticable. The choice is between agency and court, and the court is more insulated from political control than the agency. The terminal character of many judicial appointments, the general jurisdiction of most courts, the procedural characteristics of the judicial process, and the freedom of judges from close annual supervision by appropriations committees, all operate to make the courts freer from the interest group pressures operating through the legislative process, and more disposed to decide issues of policy on grounds of efficiency, than any other institution of government – specifically the administrative agency, where these features are absent or attenuated.[24] If I am correct in suggesting that the judicial process is designed to resist interest group pressures, it would seem to follow that the delegation phenomenon should count as evidence in support of the interest group theory of regulation.

My article [40], "Taxation by Regulation," presented some additional evidence of the influence of interest group pressures on the structure and procedures (as distinct from the substantive outcomes) of the regulatory process. The article suggests that a number of standard features of public utility and common carrier regulation, including controls over construction of new plant and over abandonment of service, the duty of the common carrier to serve all comes, and the tendency to impose public utility and common carrier controls on industries that sell services rather than goods, are best explained on the theory that regulation is designed in significant part to confer benefits on politically effective customer groups. Much regulation, I argued, may be the product of coalitions between the regulated industry and customer groups, the former obtaining some monopoly profits from regulation, the latter obtaining lower prices (or better service) than they would in an unregulated market – all at the expense of unorganized, mostly consumer, groups.[25]

Since that article was written, an example has occurred to me where regulation may be the product of an alliance between the industry and a supplier group. A perplexing feature of airline regulation is that although the CAB has evidently been effective in facilitating cartel pricing by the airlines, it has (until very recently[26]) exercised no control whatever over nonprice competition. The effect of unrestricted nonprice competition when price competition is constrained is to increase the costs of the competing firms and thereby reduce their profits, but, under plausible assumptions, by less than if they competed in price [41]. It seems that the airline industry has incurred additional costs largely from equipment purchases. The airlines compete with one another by purchasing newer and more comfortable aircraft and by offering more flights and therefore greater convenience to travelers. The airlines may have purchased *more* equipment than they would if they were competing in price as well as in service (although a possibly offsetting fact is that the demand-for air travel is less than it would be if the industry's prices were lower). If so, this would suggest that an apparently inexplicable omission in the regulatory scheme may actually be the calculated result of a coalition of interest groups.

The body of empirical evidence supporting the economic theory of regulation has, however, several shortcomings.

First, most of the evidence is consistent with *any version* of the interest group theory. The evidence relating to the internal efficiency of regulatory agencies does not enable one to discriminate among any specific such theories (such as the economic theory), because none asserts that regulatory agencies are inept.[27] Only the public interest theory is damaged by such evidence. The case studies on the substance of regulatory policy suffer from the same inadequacy. To show that the Interstate Commerce Act was enacted to benefit the railroads, or the Civil Aeronautics Act the airlines, or that the licensure of physicians benefits them rather than their patients, or that much regulation seems sub-servient to special-interest customer groups, is to show only that interest groups influence public policy. For these case studies to support the economic theory of regulation they would have to demonstrate that the characteristics and circumstances of the interest groups were such that the economic theory would have predicted that they, and not some other groups, would obtain the regulation that we observe them enjoying. Otherwise *any* legislation that benefitted some group at the expense of the general public would count as support for the economic theory of regulation.

I am aware of only three studies that have tried to test the economic theory of regulation, as distinct from the general interest group theory: two by Stigler (of highway weight limitations for trucks and of occupational licensure) [41, 42] and one by McPher-son (of tariffs) [26]. Only the results of one of the studies (trucks) clearly support the theory.[28]

Second, the empirical research has not been systematic. The researcher does not draw a random sample of, say, the economic legislation passed in the last ten years and ask how

much of that legislation can be explained by the economic theory of regulation. Instead, he
picks the cases that seem from a distance to support the theory[29] and seeks to determine
whether that initial impression was correct. I am not criticizing these studies. Had they
shown that trucking, and airline, and railroad regulation could *not* be explained by
reference to the operation of interest groups, the significance for scholarship would have
been immense. But even a lengthy series of case studies cannot provide much support for
the economic theory of regulation, given that the industries studied do not appear to be –
and were not selected as – typical and that apparent counterexamples abound. The
"consumerist" measures of the last few years – truth in lending and in packaging,
automobile safety and emission controls, other pollution and safety regulations, the
aggressiveness recently displayed by the previously lethargic Federal Trade Commission
– are not an obvious product of interest group pressures,[30] and the proponents of the
economic theory of regulation have thus far largely ignored such measures. Nor have there
been case studies of industries that fail (or never try) to obtain favorable regulation.
Furthermore, there is a serious question whether it is proper to define the subject of
study as "economic" regulation. Criminal laws, civil rights legislation, legislative reappor-
tionment, and other "noneconomic" regulations affect economic welfare no less than the
conventional forms of economic regulation, and it seems arbitrary to exclude them from
the analysis: presumably they obey the same laws of social behavior that we think explain
economic regulation.

Third, some of the case studies of regulation have produced evidence difficult to
reconcile with the economic theory. I refer in particular to studies which indicate that
maximum-price regulation has little or no effect on the price levels of public utilities [18,
27, 43] and that some forms of regulation generate costs in resource misallocation that
seem large in relation to the benefits to the favored interest group.[31] Both sorts of evidence
may seem to confirm the influence of interest groups in the regulatory process but it is
only the crudest form of interest group analysis that they support. There is no basis in the
economic theory of regulation for ineffectual regulation – for trying and failing to limit the
prices of the regulated firms. The obvious explanation is that maximum price controls are
a fig leaf which the regulatory agency dons to conceal from the public its domination by an
interest group. But the economic theory of regulation – as thus far developed – does not
predict that regulatory agencies will practice fraud on the general public.[32]

Nor does the theory predict that legislatures will choose unnecessarily expensive
methods of conferring benefits upon effective political groups. Perhaps they do not. It
has been estimated that hundreds of millions of dollars a year could have been saved had
oil companies received outright grants from the Treasury rather than oil import quotas
which, in the process of enriching the companies and the owners of domestic oil–producing property, induce consumers to make inefficient substitutions for oil [6]. But the
underlying assumption – that there is a large avoidable deadweight loss – may well be
incorrect. An increase in income tax rates to finance an outright grant to the oil companies
could have costly substitution effects (e.g., leisure for work) of its own. If the assumption
is correct, the implications for the economic theory of regulation are disturbing. It is in
everyone's interest to use a more rather than a less efficient way of transferring money to
the oil companies. Stigler, in his search for a rational explanation of the quotas, has argued
that it would be impracticable to give money to the oil companies directly, because then
firms would have an incentive to create oil-company affiliates in order to be entitled to the

subsidy [42, pp. 4–5]. However, that danger could be averted by limiting the subsidy to oil companies in existence as of the date of the grant. The CAB gave cash subsidies to the airlines for many years: its control over entry prevented the subsidies from attracting new entrants. Nor are entry controls strictly necessary: the cash grant can be limited to the firms in the industry at the date of the grant (or some earlier date to prevent entry in anticipation of the grant).

Fourth, the empirical evidence depends heavily on a confident rejection of the public interest rationales in which all legislation is – for reasons not yet illuminated by the economic theory of regulation – cloaked. Sometimes these rationales have just enough plausibility to make such rejection questionable. The oil import quota case is again an interesting one. The recent Arab oil embargo suggests that it is not palpably absurd to adopt governmental policies designed to reduce U.S. dependence on the oil produced by the Arabs. Stigler has argued that if this were the actual purpose behind the oil import quota system, it would have been carried out not by a quota system but by a tariff, since the revenues generated by a tariff would go to the taxpayers rather than to the oil companies' stockholders [42, p. 4]. (Another alternative would be stockpiling imported oil.) But the argument proves only that the purpose behind the system may have been a mixture of public interest considerations and interest group pressures.[33]

Fifth, the effects of economic regulation are difficult to trace. A tax on gasoline might help the railroad industry. The cartelization of the airline industry under the CAB's aegis benefits surface transportation (the demand for which is increased by anything that increases the price of a substitute service). These complications make it difficult to identify the industries that benefit from and those that are injured by regulation. It is superficial to point to an industry as an example of an effective political group because it enjoys a high tariff without considering the impact on it of other governmental policies, including many ostensibly imposed on different industries. We do not know whether to regard automobile emission controls as a sign of the industry's inability to ward off adverse regulation or as a token of how limited, and late, government regulation of the automobile industry has been.

Sixth, an important, but as yet unexplained, datum is the characteristic public interest rhetoric in which discussions of public policy are conducted and the policies themselves framed. The use of language that, if the economic theory of regulation is correct, is utterly uninformative and indeed misleading is not costless; presumably it is employed only because there are offsetting benefits. These benefits must have to do with increasing the costs to members of the public of obtaining accurate information about the effect of the actions of their legislative representatives on their welfare.

Recent developments in the economic theory of fraud may prove helpful in explaining the prevalence of misleading rhetoric in discussions of public policy. The propensity to engage in fraud seems to be related to such factors as the difficulty (cost) of the buyer's determining the performance characteristics of the product (by inspection, use, or what-ever) and the value of the buyer's time. The greater the cost of determining the product's performance characteristics, or of the time spent by the buyer in trying to ascertain those characteristics, the more fraud we can expect to find. Where the product is legislation, the cost of determining its quality is often extremely high. With respect to the value of the buyer's time, it is important to note that a legislative proposal must be "sold" to two groups: the legislators and the electorate. Our earlier discussion of the costs of legislation implied that the cost of a legislator's time is very high, which in turn implies that the amount of time he can efficiently devote to appraising the merits of proposed legislation is small.

The introduction of considerations based on the economic analysis of fraud, or more broadly of the costs of information, suggests that it may be possible to revive the public-interest-miscarried theory of regulation in a form that it can be made rigorous and empirically testable.

5. Conclusion

This article has offered a number of criticisms of both the traditional public interest theory of regulation and the newer economic theory which conceives regulation as a service supplied to effective political interest groups. Neither theory can be said to have, as yet, substantial empirical support. Indeed, neither theory has been refined to the point where it can generate hypotheses sufficiently precise to be verified empirically. However, the success of economic theory in illuminating other areas of nonmarket behavior leads one to be somewhat optimistic that the economic theory will eventually jell: the general assumption of economics that human behavior can best be understood as the response of rational self-interested beings to their environment must have extensive application to the political process.

Notes

1   The theory is more often assumed than articulated. Some representative works embodying it are Bonbright [4], Davis [9], and Friendly [13].

2   Some examples of the emerging theory of "government failure" are Hirshleifer, DeHaven, and Milliman [16], pp. 74–82, and Posner [39] and [35].

3   See, for example, Baxter [1], Cabinet Task Force on Oil Import Control [6], Coase [7], Hilton [15], Jordan [19], Kitch, Isaacson, and Kasper [21], MacAvoy [25], Peltzman [30, 31], and, for a general summary of the literature, Jordan [20].

4   An interesting example of this point of view is provided by Herring in [14], which argues that the challenge to public administration is to develop techniques of overcoming the interest group pressures that threaten to deflect legislative programs from serving the public interest. He may underestimate the difficulties of doing this because of a certain economic naivete that leads him to suggest that opposing group interests can often be harmonized in a way that vindicates the public interest. Ordinarily harmony is achieved at the expense of the public interest. See pages 208–9 *infra*.

5   National Transportation Policy, 49 U.S.C. preceding §1.

6   The question is never asked whether their jobs might be less risky or require less skill than the private-sector jobs with which they are compared.

7   One could argue that the legislator may not have much incentive to ride herd on the agency: he will not get paid more and his popularity with the voters will be increased only marginally. But this ignores the fact that the actual audit will be conducted by an employee of the legislative body, who will have the same incentive to conduct a searching audit as any privately employed auditor.

8   See Bentley [2] and Truman [44]. For a specific application of the approach to regulatory agencies, see Truman [44], pp. 416–21. For the position of Herring on the role of interest

groups in regulation see endnote 4. It is interesting to note that "interest group" is not a pejorative term for most of the political scientists, since they are either indifferent to or unaware of the fact that the economic costs of regulation procured by an interest group normally exceed the economic benefits.

9   The vagueness of the theorizing in Truman's book [44], especially pp. 506–7 and 515, is typical.

10   Stigler [42]. For an attempt to marshal empirical support for the theory see Jordan [20]. Stigler, it should be noted, builds on earlier work by economists on the political system. See Buchanan and Tullock [5], Downs [10], and Olson [28].

11   Coase, however, suggests the interesting possibility that when a business is in decline, managers may find it profitable to shift their attention from improving their business operations to improving the political environment, another potential source of profits. There is a further point: the costs of becoming informed about opportunities for enhanced profits through government regulation may be greater than the costs of perceiving losses that regulation might reduce.

12   For example, the airline industry was not declining in 1938 when the Civil Aeronautics Act was passed, nor the railroad industry in 1887 when the first Interstate Commerce Act was passed. One tends to associate regulation with declining industries primarily because so many regulatory programs were instituted during the depression of the 1930s.

13   For a summary of the theory of cartels, see Posner [36].

14   The characteristics that predispose a market to cartelization are discussed in Posner [34], pp. 116–17.

15   On the other hand, the more successful and profitable the cartel, the greater the costs to consumers, and so the greater the incentive of consumers to organize against the cartel. Stigler has suggested that the role of the "outsider" (e.g., the consumer) is greater in the public regulation than in the private cartelization context (see [42], p. 16), but it is not clear why a cohesive group of customers would not be equally effective in exacting concessions from a private cartel.

16   For some evidence in support of this hunch, see MacPherson [26].

17   At what price? The government has a monopoly of the sale of regulation so presumably it will be able to charge a positive price even if the cost of supplying regulation is zero. In fact the cost is greater than zero, both because the production of legislation is costly (see page 199) and because regulation that favors one group imposes costs on others.

18   I assume that the free-rider problem is least serious when the number of parties is very few, albeit larger coalitions might also be able to overcome the problem.

19   The fundamental distinction between number of firms and number of voters undermines Stigler's hypothesis [42], p. 7) that small firms will enjoy disproportionate political influence. If the number of employees is proportional to sales, it is not obvious why small firms should be any more important in obtaining favorable regulation than in the formation of a private cartel.

20   Conceivably safety and emission controls hurt foreign manufacturers more than domestic ones. Without evidence, I find this suggestion somewhat implausible, however. For example, the emission controls reduce engine performance – always a big selling point for American cars – which would seem to hurt the domestic manufacturer more. Also, the argument ignores the fact that many imported cars are manufactured by foreign subsidiaries of domestic manufacturers. The foreign entanglements of the domestic companies may explain, however, why the industry does not enjoy tariff protection. Also to be considered is the fact that while the gasoline tax would seem to reduce the demand for automobiles, the proceeds of the tax are largely earmarked for highway construction – and highways are complementary to automobiles – so the tax may have little adverse effect on the industry after all. The need for further research in this area is dramatically apparent.

21   Even under conditions of natural monopoly, the profit-maximizing monopoly price will induce
     entry, albeit of firms having higher costs than the monopolist.
22   The role of legal institutions in supporting the market system is a major theme is Posner [34].
23   For some evidence that it is not, see Posner [39].
24   See Posner [34], chapters 23, 27. An interesting point here is the traditional reluctance of the
     courts to permit groups to litigate, which is manifested in requirements of "standing" to sue
     and in prohibitions against "lay intermediaries" between client and lawyer. A trade association
     cannot bring a lawsuit seeking a legal rule favorable to its members. The member must sue on
     his own behalf. This reduces the influence of interest groups in the litigation process. But see
     NAACP v. *Button*, 371 U.S. 415 (1963).
25   This extension of the economic theory of regulation helps explain, for example, why the original
     Interstate Commerce Act was supported by (some) shippers as well as the railroads themselves:
     the railroads' discriminatory pricing – the target of the Act – both undermined the railroads'
     cartels and harmed shippers competing with favored purchasers.
26   When it approved capacity-limitation agreements among airlines in certain markets.
27   The theory, discussed in Section 3, that regulatory agencies eventually knuckle under to the
     regulated firms comes close to implying that regulatory agencies are ineptly managed (otherwise
     they would not be so easily conquered). This is an example of the confusing overlap, noted
     earlier, between this version of the capture theory and the public interest theory.
28   Stigler's tests of occupational licensure produced mixed results. A partial test of the theory is
     also attempted in Pashigian [29], again without successful results.
29   However, this does not appear to be true of Stigler's study of state limitations on truck weights.
30   See Peltzman's recent study of the regulation of new drugs by the Food and Drug Adminis-
     tration in [31]; cf. Posner [37].
31   The oil import quota program is a notable example. See Cabinet Task Force on Oil Import
     Control [6], pp. 28–30.
32   Such a prediction would be a logical extension of Stigler's remarks on the relevance of
     information costs in the analysis of the political process (in [42], pp. 11–12), but the extension
     has not been made. On the economics of fraud, see Posner [38], pt. 1, and references cited
     therein. The possible application of the economic theory of fraud to the theory of regulation is
     discussed in the text below.
33   Another consideration is that the oil import quota program could be and was established by
     Executive Order rather than by statute, whereas imposition of a tariff would have required
     congressional action.

References

1. Baxter, W. F. (1970): "NYSE Fixed Commission Rates: A Private Cartel Goes Public," *Stanford Law Review*, 22, April, 675–712.
2. Bentley, A. F. (1908): *The Process of Government*. Chicago: University of Chicago Press.
3. Bernstein, M. (1955): *Regulating Business by Independent Commission*. Princeton: Princeton University Press.
4. Bonbright, J. C. (1961): *Principles of Public Utility Rates*. New York: Columbia University Press.
5. Buchanan, J. and Tullock, G. (1962): *The Calculus of Consent*. Ann Arbor: University of Michigan Press.
6. Cabinet Task Force on Oil Import Control (1970): *The Oil Import Question*. Washington, D.C.: U. S. Government Printing Office.
7. Coase, R. H. (1959): "The Federal Communications Commission," *Journal of Law and Economics*, 2 (2), October, 1–40.

8. Comanor, W. S. and Mitchell, B. (1972): "The Costs of Planning: The FCC and Cable Television," *Journal of Law and Economics*, 15 (1), April, 177–231.
9. Davis, K. C. (1958): *Administrative Law Treatise*. St. Paul: West. See also 1970 supplement.
10. Downs, A. (1957): *An Economic Theory of Democracy*. New York: Harper.
11. Eckert, R. D. (1972): "What do Regulatory Commissions Maximize?", unpublished manuscript, University of Southern California.
12. Ehrlich, I. and Posner, R. A. (1974): "An Economic Analysis of Legal Rule-making," *Journal of Legal Studies*. 3 (1), January, 257–86.
13. Friendly, H. J. (1962): *The Federal Administrative Agencies: The Need for Better Definition of Standards*. Cambridge: Harvard University Press.
14. Herring, E. P. (1936): *Public Administration and the Public Interest*. New York: McGraw-Hill.
15. Hilton, G. W. (1966): "The Consistency of the Interstate Commerce Act," *Journal of Law and Economics*, 9 (2), October, 87–113.
16. Hirshleifer, J., DeHaven, J. C., and Milliman, J. W. (1960): *Water Supply: Economics, Technology, and Policy*, Chicago: University of Chicago Press.
17. Huntington, S. P. (1966): "The Marasmus of the ICC: The Commission, the Railroads, and the Public Interest," in P. Woll (ed.), *Public Administration and Policy: Selected Essays*, New York: Harper & Row.
18. Jackson, R. (1969): "Regulation and Electric Utility Rate Levels," *Land Economics*, 45 (3), August, 372–6.
19. Jordan, W. A. (1970): *Airline Regulation in America: Effects and Imperfections*. Baltimore: Johns Hopkins Press.
20. ——(1972): "Producer Protection, Prior Market Structure and the Effects of Government Regulation," *Journal of Law and Economics*, 15 (1), April, 151–76.
21. Kitch, E. W., Isaacson, M., and Kasper, D. (1971): "The Regulation of Taxicabs in Chicago," *Journal of Law and Economics*, 14 (2), October, 285–350.
22. Kolko, G. (1965): *Railroads and Regulation, 1877–1916*. Princeton: Princeton University Press.
23. Leiserson, A. (1946): "Interest Groups in Administration," in F. M. Marx (ed.), *Elements of Public Administration*, New York: Prentice-Hall.
24. MacAvoy, P. W. (1965): *The Economic Effects of Regulation: The Trunk-Line Railroad Cartels and the Interstate Commerce Commission before 1900*. Cambridge: M.I.T. Press.
25. ——(1971): "The Regulation-Induced Shortage of Natural Gas," *Journal of Law and Economics*, 14 (1), April, 167–99.
26. MacPherson, C. B. (1972): "Tariff Structures and Political Exchange," unpublished Ph.D. dissertation, University of Chicago.
27. Moore, T. G. (1970): "The Effectiveness of Regulation of Electric Utility Prices," *Southern Economic Journal*, 36 (4), April, 365–75.
28. Olson, M. Jr. (1965): *The Logic of Collective Action*. Cambridge: Harvard University Press.
29. Pashigian, B. P. (1973): "Public vs. Private Ownership: Consequences and Determinants of Local Transit Systems," unpublished manuscript, University of Chicago Graduate School of Business, October.
30. Peltzman, S. (1966): "Entry in Commercial Banking," *Journal of Law and Economics*, 8 (2), October, 11–50.
31. ——(1973): "An Evaluation of Consumer Protection Legislation: The 1962 Drug Amendments," *Journal of Political Economy*, 81 (5), September–October, 1049–91.
32. Posner, R. A. (1972): "The Appropriate Scope of Regulation in the Cable Television Industry," *Bell Journal of Economics and Management Science*, 3 (1), Spring, 98–129.
33. ——(1972): "The Behavior of Administrative Agencies," *Journal of Legal Studies*, 1 (2), June, 305–23.
34. ——(1973): *Economic Analysis of Law*. New York: Little, Brown and Co.

35. ——(1969): "Natural Monopoly and Its Regulation," *Stanford Law Review*, 21, February, 548–643.

36. ——(1969): "Oligopoly and the Antitrust Laws: A Suggested Approach," *Stanford Law Review*, 21, June, 1562–75.

37. ——(1973): "Reflections on Consumerism," *University of Chicago Law School Records*, 20 (3), Spring, 19–25.

38. ——(1973): *Regulation of Advertising by the FTC*. American Enterprise Institute: Washington, D.C., November.

39. ——(1970): "A Statistical Study of Antitrust Enforcement," *Journal of Law and Economics*, 13 (2), October, 365–419.

40. ——(1971): "Taxation by Regulation," *Bell Journal of Economics and Management Science*, 2 (1), Spring, 22–50.

41. Stigler, G. J. (1968): "Price and Nonprice Competition," in G. J. Stigler (ed.), *Organization of Industry*, Homewood, Ill.: Richard D. Irwin.

42. ——(1971): "The Theory of Economic Regulation," *Bell Journal of Economics and Management Science*, 2 (1), Spring, 3–21.

43. —— and Friedland, C. (1962): "What Can Regulators Regulate? The Case of Electricity," *Journal of Law and Economics*, 5 (2), October, 1–16.

44. Truman, D. B. (1951): *The Government Process: Political Interests and Public Opinion*. New York: Knopf.

45. Wilson, J. (nd): *The Politics of Regulation*. Washington, D.C.: The Brookings Institution.

46. Ziegler, H. (1964): *Interest Groups in American Society*. Englewood Cliffs, N.J.: Prentice-Hall.

CHAPTER TWELVE

Surprises of Airline Deregulation

Alfred E. Kahn

Source: *American Economic Review*, Papers and Proceedings, 78 (1988), pp. 316–22. Reprinted with the permission of the author and the American Economic Association. © American Economic Association.

Surprises are a product of mistaken expectations and unforeseen outcomes. As for the former, I have no taste for the task of putting together a fair composite depiction of the expectations of the airline deregulation advocates; the fact that they ranged from Ralph Nader to the National Association of Manufacturers suggests how difficult that would be. I will therefore confine this account to my own expectations – and inevitably succumb to the temptation to deploy the evidence selectively, so as to demonstrate my prescience about both the good results and the unpleasant ones.

The subject is irresistible, however, partly because the aboriginal opponents of deregulation have been assembling collages of predictions by the proponents and depictions of the results that, even if authentic in their several parts, turn out to be caricatures in their composite.

The main more or less unpleasant surprises – be assured I will conclude with a brief but heartfelt summary of the pleasant ones – fall under four headings:

1 the turbulence and painfulness of the process;
2 the reconcentration of the industry;
3 the intensification of price discrimination and monopolistic exploitation; and
4 the deterioration in quality of airline service.

1. Turmoil

While the advocates of deregulation recognized that competitive markets are inherently more messy and unstable than tightly regulated ones (see my 1971 study, pp. 12–13, 325–26), and recognized also that radical changes were likely to follow removal of the pervasive restrictions that had been imposed on the industry over the preceding forty years, I doubt that most of us were fully prepared for the explosion of entry, massive restructurings of routes, price wars, labor-management conflict, bankruptices and consolidations and the generally dismal profit record of the last ten years.[1]

During the period of rapid deregulation, I scoffed at what

> seemed to be a general belief among defenders of the present regulatory regime that there is
> something about airlines that drives businessmen crazy – that once the CAB removes its body
> from the threshold, they will rush into markets pell-mell, en masse, without regard to the size
> of each, how many sellers it can sustain, and how many others may be entering at the same
> time.[2]

I was wrong – at least temporarily – but almost certainly will prove decreasingly so as time
goes on.

What inferences are we to draw, however, from these particular surprises?

The turbulent entry of new, much lower-cost carriers, and their ability to quote much
lower fares than the incumbents – typically across-the-board – were a clear reflection of
the extent to which the latter's costs had become inflated behind the protective wall of
regulation, and an illustration of competition doing exactly what we hoped and expected it
to do.

Considering the maniacally detailed restrictions on the operating authorities of airline
companies under regulation, it would have been shocking if their removal had *not* resulted
in a massive reordering of routes: what better proof could there be of the gross inefficiencies engendered by regulation?[3]

Of much greater significance than the changes in the operations of individual companies
has been the continuity and expansion of service in the aggregate. Thanks partly to the
Essential Air Services Program incorporated in the 1978 Act, not a single community that
enjoyed a minimum level of certificated service at the time of deregulation has lost it.
Many communities have lost uncertificated service since that date, just as many had under
regulation, but that had little or nothing to do with regulation or deregulation (U.S. GAO,
1985, p. 29). The smallest towns, the so-called nonhubs, have as a group experienced
practically no change in their average weekly departures between 1978 and 1987, while the
small hubs have enjoyed a 42 percent increase (Melvin Brenner, 1988, Figure 15; also
myself, 1988b).

The industry's severe financial losses in 1981–83 were the result primarily – perhaps
entirely[4] – of the severe recession, the fuel price explosion of 1979–81, and the air traffic
controllers strike. (On the other hand, the very poor financial showing in 1986, a year of
general economic prosperity, must be attributed preponderantly to the intense price
competition that deregulation unleashed.)

While the industry's return on equity has plummeted almost to zero, its average returns
on total invested capital have been no lower since 1978 than before (means shown with
standard deviations following in parentheses): 1965–77, 6.3(3.5); 1970–77, 5.3(3.1); 1978–
86, 7.2(3.1); 1979–86, 6.4(2.4). (Calcualted from Air Transport Association 1975–87; see
also myself, 1988) Perhaps equally striking, the volatility of these returns has not
increased.

The opponents of deregulation claim that what both they and investment analysts
generally see as the perverse tendency of the industry to continue to add to capacity in
the face of these poor financial results proves they were right in predicting that unregulated competition would tend chronically to be destructive. The ultimate public concern
about the possibility of destructive competition, however, is that it may result in an

impairment in the ability of an industry to finance needed expansions of capacity, and a consequent deterioration in service (myself, 1971, pp. 175–6). The triumphant assertions of the critics, therefore, are in effect a concession that this particular threat *to the consumer* has not in fact materialized – partly, no doubt, because several of the airline companies have been doing very well indeed.

Labor unrest and the insecurity and downward pressure on the wages of the preexisting labor force have been an undeniable cost of deregulation. From the standpoint of the public, however, grossly monopolistic wage levels are no more acceptable than monopoly profits. The fact that these costs have been usually severe may just as logically be blamed on the regulation that created vested interests in its perpetuation as on deregulation.

Total employment in the industry actually increased 39 percent between 1976 and 1986. The increase in revenue passenger enplanements by 87 percent during the same decade, and the increase in productivity reflected in these comparative changes are among the most important benefits of deregulation.

2. Reconcentration and the Attenuation of Competition

Just as one of the most pleasant surprises of the early deregulation experience was the large-scale entry of new, highly competitive carriers, so probably the most unpleasant one has been the reversal of that trend – the departures of almost all of them, the reconcentration of the industry both nationally (Brenner, Figure 3) and at the major hubs (Julius Maldutis, 1987, pp. 6–9), the diminishing disciplinary effectiveness of potential entry by totally new firms, and the increased likelihood, in consequence, of monopolistic exploitation. The reasons for these developments are generally familiar and in any event have been thoroughly expounded by Michael Levine (1987) – the advantages of controlled traffic feed, particularly by developing and dominating hubs; the difficulty of rivals mounting an effective challenge at those hubs; the advantages conveyed by ownership of computerized reservations systems (CRS) and frequent flyer programs; the discovery by the incumbents of the superior competitive attractiveness of deeply discounted fares – far lower than their smaller, lower-cost competitors were able to match on an across-the-board basis – targeted (with the help of increasingly sophisticated computerized scheduling) for seats that would otherwise be likely to go out empty; and the flood of mergers and operating agreements between competitors and potential competitors.

Were these developments surprises? Yes, to a large extent. We advocates of deregulation were misled by the apparent lack of evidence of economies of scale – the principal explanation of the differences in cost among the carriers appeared to be differences in their route structures, which we hoped to eliminate by permitting totally free entry and exit – and by the physical mobility of aircraft, which caused us to underestimate the other obstacles to entry. While recognizing the competitive advantages of controlled traffic feed, we were, as it turned out, overly impressed by the apparently equally great competitive opportunities for specialized turnaround service, and therefore did not anticipate the thoroughgoing movement to hub-and-spoke operations and the dominant role it would play in determining the balance of competitive advantage and disadvantage.

At the same time: as I specifically observed (1978a, pp. 18–22, and 1979, pp. 5–6), if it was impossible for government officials to predict what kind of route structures would prove ultimately to be the most effective, that was an argument not for perpetuating ignorant regulation but for leaving the decision to the competitive market.

Whatever misgivings one may have about this kind of competition-by-preemption of traffic (and I have more than most economists) one must recognize that the critical advantages of hub-and-spoke operations reflect genuine efficiencies: the superior quality of on-line service (in which passengers change planes from one flight to another of the same carrier) over interline, fuller utilization of larger planes and the possibility of offering a wider range of destinations from all originating points – the principal source, according to Morrison and Winston, 1986, (pp. 31–3), of the multibillion dollar annual benefit to the flying public attributable to deregulation.

The radical transformation of the operations of the incumbent carriers that enabled them so quickly to overcome the competitive threat of the new entrants was, in very large measure, the beneficent consequences of competition: the successful ones cut their costs, rationalized their route structures, developed extraordinarily efficient CRSs and learned to offer deep discounts to fill their planes.

The concentration process reflected also what many of the advocates of deregulation would characterize as a lamentable failure of the administration to enforce the policies of the antitrust laws – to disallow a single merger or to press for divestiture of the computerized reservation systems or attack a single case of predation. None of these cases would have been easy. All of the mergers, it could be argued, gave birth to more effective competitors; the harmful effects on competition of major carriers owning CRSs, on the one hand, and the feasibility and desirability of their divestiture, on the other, remain intensely contested; and the feasibility of identifying and moving against instances of predation are extremely uncertain. At the same time, I take perverse satisfaction in having predicted the demise of price-cutting competitors like World and Capitol Airways if we did nothing to limit the predictable geographically discriminatory response of the incumbent carriers to their entry, and in having rejected the conventional wisdom that predation would not pay because any attempt to raise fares after the departure of the price-cutting newcomers would elicit instantaneous competitive reentry.[5]

Despite the now markedly higher concentration of the industry at the national level, it is not at all clear that concentration has gone up in the economically pertinent markets – namely, individual routes. On the contrary, it *appears* that the average number of carriers per route is still higher today than it was under regulation (for a survey of the incomplete evidence, see my 1988 paper).

The relatively small number of airlines were under regulation prevented for the most part from competing with one another; since deregulation they have been free to invade one another's markets, offering whatever combinations of price and service they choose, and they have done so, vigorously.

While, therefore, travelers on flights originating and terminating at the concentrated hubs probably face fewer alternatives now than before deregulation, competition on longer, connecting flights over various hubs has clearly intensified: a Boston/Phoenix passenger, for example, has the choice of nine hubs at which to make connections (Maldutis, 1987, p. 9).

The industry remains to this very day far more intensely competitive than it was before 1978. The opponents of deregulation cannot have it both ways – asserting on the one hand that competition has proved to be a lost cause and, on the other, that it has been and remains catastrophically destructive. They will undoubtedly retort that the process of competition killing itself off is still incomplete. The response – now, as ten years ago – is that the possibility, which no one can deny with total certainty, that competition *may* one day prove not to be viable is hardly a reason to have suppressed it thoroughly in the first place.

3. Price Discrimination and Monopoly Exploitation

The benefits of price competition under deregulation have been very widespread. Between 1976 (the last year before the CAB began to permit widespread discounting) and 1986, average yields per mile dropped 28.5 percent in real terms. According to the Air Transport Association (1987, p. 5), 90 percent of all passengers in 1986 traveled on discount tickets, at an average 61 percent below coach fare. And while this means that the coach fares themselves have become increasingly fictional, the studies by the Meyer-Oster group show that they have not risen egregiously compared with the levels at which they would have been set under regulation (Meyer et al., 1987, pp. 112–13 and 121–2).

The very low fare levels of 1986 and early 1987, reflecting severe price wars, were not sustainable – the industry as a whole lost money – and yields have in the last months of 1987 almost regained 1985 levels.[6] But the decline from 1976 to those 1985 levels would still have represented savings of $11 billion to airline passengers in 1986 alone.

At the same time, the pressures and benefits of price competition have been unevenly distributed geographically. The troublesome disparities that have emerged are not, however, wholly discriminatory: it costs more to provide service on small airplanes, on thin routes, with the frequency required to meet the needs of business travelers, than it costs on the dense routes and to serve vacationers.

It is by no means obvious to what extent travelers in the less competitive markets have actually been exploited. What is extremely dubious is that, as is widely assumed, their fares have gone up *because* fares have declined, dramatically, in the more competitive markets – that is to say, that passengers in the thin markets are "subsidizing" the bargains in the dense ones. Such contentions assume that businesses would, irrationally, sell some services for substantial periods of time at prices below incremental costs and others at prices below profit-maximizing levels, raising the latter only after and because competition had forced them to reduce the former. On the contrary, if the introduction of intense price competition on the dense routes has had any effect on prices on the thin ones, it is more likely to have been to reduce than to increase them, because of the ability of many travelers to rearrange their routing to take advantage of the discounts.

The persistence – indeed, intensification – of price discrimination has been a surprise. While I pointed out (1978a, pp. 24–7; 1978c, pp. 39–40, 50–7) that the structure of airline costs – the inevitability and desirability (on quality grounds) of average load factors far below the 100 percent level, with the consequent availability of zero marginal cost seats – clearly suggested that widespread price discrimination would continue under competition, I was at other times so carried away by witnessing the introduction of across-the-board, nondiscriminatory low fares as to predict that, with competition increasingly pervasive, "much of the price discrimination will tend to disappear" (1979, pp. 11–12). I should have recognized that the naturally monopolistic or oligopolistic character of most airline markets (which I had myself observed, 1978a, p. 24) and the inevitable continuation of short-run marginal costs approximating zero promised that these discriminations would continue – indeed, expand – under deregulation.[7]

Competition in the real world is, inevitably, imperfect. The question before us in 1977–78 was whether the imperfections would be so severe as to justify continuation of the kind of regulation we had practiced in the airline industry in the preceding forty years, at costs to the economy of billions of dollars a year. At the worst, we might now decide that competition is so insufficiently protective of consumer interests on particular routes as to require us to reimpose price *ceilings* in those instances, although the practical difficulties would be enormous. In view of the CAB's advocacy of a continuation of such ceilings in markets dominated by a single carrier (myself, 1978b; 1978c, p. 46), I hope I do not shock anybody by observing that I probably would have been very reluctant to abandon price ceilings entirely had I had the choice. All the studies of airline pricing since deregulation confirm that reluctance: market concentration does matter; and their general trend over time has been toward the conclusion that it matters a great deal (compare Elizabeth Bailey et al. 1985, p. 199, with Gloria Hurdle et al., 1987, p. 16).

4. Congestion and Delay

Most of us probably did not foresee the deterioration in the average quality of the flying experience, and in particular the congestion and delays that have plagued air travelers in recent years. Fortunately, an audience of economists will readily understand how little this failure constitutes a legitimate criticism of deregulation:

To some considerable extent, these discomforts are a sign of the success of deregulation, not its failure, resulting as they have from the enormous response of travelers to the offer of very low fares for necessarily correspondingly lower-quality service – narrower seating, longer lines, fewer amenities.

The consequent similar deterioration in the quality of service enjoyed by full-coach-fare-paying-passengers as well has indeed reflected in part an imperfection of competition: they have lost an option they previously enjoyed. At the same time, their choices have been enriched in other ways – by the proliferation of business class and other such services and frequent flyer benefits.

In part, however, this spillover effect on them reflects the more general characteristic of a market economy that many of the allocative decisions it makes are in effect collective (see my article with William Shew, 1987, pp. 229–32): because of economies of scale, what gets produced is dictated by the preferences of the majority – in this case for a lower-cost and quality service than a minority would have preferred.

This deprivation has, however, resulted also from major derelictions by governments. Congestion at major airports at peak travel times (and the consequent inability of passengers to whom time is very valuable to get the delay-free travel they would willingly pay for) obviously means to an economist that the pertinent government authorities have on the one hand failed efficiently to expand airport and air traffic control capacity and, on the other, to price those scarce facilities at their marginal opportunity costs. No wonder there are shortages.

5. Completing the Balance

This assessment of the "surprises of deregulation" would be grossly distorted if it were not balanced with at least a mention of the respects in which the outcome has either not been surprising at all to its advocates, or the surprises have been happy ones. The last ten years have fully vindicated our expectations that deregulation would bring lower fares, a structure of fares on average in closer conformity with the structure of costs, an increased range of price-quality options, and great improvements in efficiency – made possible by the abandonment of regulatory restrictions and compelled by the greatly increased intensity of competition – all this along with a 35 percent or so decline in accident rates.

Notes

1   The industry's profit margin averaged only 1.30 percent in 1970–77, which was bad enough compared with industry generally, but fell to a puny 0.10 in the 1979–86 period. (Calcualtions from the Air Transport Association, 1975–87.)
2   "I cannot believe, in any event, that it requires governmentally-imposed cartelization to make this or any other industry creditworthy" (Kahn, 1978a, pp. 15–16, 28.)
3   It was precisely in recognition of the size of the resulting distortions and the unfitness for competitive survival of companies that had been nurtured in a regulatory hothouse for the preceding forty years that I attempted – unsuccessfully – to give the industry time to adjust, by deregulating only gradually. See my 1978b statement, pp. 5–13.
4   Steven Morrison and Clifford Winston (1986, p. 40) and John Meyer, Clinton Oster, and John Strong (1987, pp. 21–32) both conclude that during the 1980–82 period the financial showing of the industry might have been even worse had it not been deregulated.
5   Large portions of the memorandum to my fellow CAB members in which I expressed these opinions are reproduced in my 1987 paper.
6   Information from the Air Transport Association.
7   My colleague Robert Frank recalled this elementary principle to me and its pertinence in the airline context.

References

Air Transport Association of America (1975–87): *Air Transport – Annual Reports of the U.S. Scheduled Airline Industry*. Washington.
Bailey, E. E., Graham, D. R. and Kaplan, D. P. (1985): *Deregulating the Airlines*. Cambridge: MIT Press.
Brenner, M. A., (1988): "Airline Deregulation – A Case Study in Public Policy Failure," *Transportation Law Journal*, 16 (2), 179–228.
Hurdle, G. J. et al. (1987): *Concentration, Potential Entry, and Performance in the Airline Industry*, revised. Washington: Antitrust Division, U. S. Department of Justice, December.
Kahn, A. E. (1971): *The Economics of Regulation, II: Institutional Issues*. New York: Wiley & Sons.
——(1978a): "Talk to the New York Society of Security Analysts," Presented in New York City, February 2.
——(1978b): *Statement on H. R. 11145*, House Public Works and Transportation Committee, Aviation Subcommittee, March 6.

—— (1978c): "Deregulation of Air Transportation – Getting from Here to There," in C. Argyris et al. (eds), *Regulating Business: The Search for an Optimum*, San Francisco: Institute for Contemporary Studies, 37–59.

—— (1979): "Applying Economics To An Imperfect World," *American Economic Review Proceedings*, 69, May, 1–13.

—— (1987): "Deregulatory Schizophrenia," *California Law Review*, 75, 229–51.

—— (1988): "Airline Deregulation – a Mixed Bag, But a Clear Success Nevertheless," *Transportation Law Journal*, 16 (2), 229–35.

—— and Shew, W. B. (1987): "Current Issues in Telecommunications Regulation: Pricing," *Yale Journal on Regulation*, 4, Spring, 191–256.

Levine, M. E. (1987): "Airline Competition in Deregulated Markets: Theory, Firm Strategy, and Public Policy," *Yale Journal on Regulation*, 4, Spring, 393–494.

Maldutis, J. (1987): *Statement*, Senate Committee on Commerce, Science and Transportation, November 4.

Meyer, J. R., Oster, C. J., and Strong, J. S. (1987): "Airline Financial Performance since Deregulation" and "The Effect on Travelers: Fares and Service," in J. R. Meyer, C. J. Oster, Jr. and J. S. Strong (eds), *Deregulation and the Future of Intercity Passenger Travel*, Cambridge: MIT Press.

Morrison, S. and Winston, C. (1986): *The Economic Effects of Airline Deregulation*. Washington: The Brookings Institution.

U. S. General Accounting Office (1985): *Deregulation: Increased Competition Is Making Airlines More Efficient and Responsive to Consumers*. Washington: November 6.

CHAPTER THIRTEEN

The Economic Case Against Drug Prohibition

JEFFREY A. MIRON AND JEFFREY ZWIEBEL

Source: *Journal of Economic Perspectives*, 9, 4 (1995), pp. 175–92.
Reprinted with the permission of the authors and the American Economic
Association. © American Economic Association.

Drug use is widely blamed for a broad range of personal and social ills. According to
many observers, drug users suffer diminished health, decreased earnings and moral
degradation. Similarly, according to many accounts, the market in illegal drugs promotes
crime, destroys inner cities, spreads AIDS, corrupts law enforcement officials and politicians, produces and exacerbates poverty and erodes the moral fabric of society.

The most common response to these perceptions is a belief that governments
should prohibit the production, sale and use of the currently illegal drugs. This view
presumes that drug use causes the problems associated with illegal drugs and that
prohibition reduces these problems by discouraging use. A small but vocal minority,
however, suggests that prohibition itself causes many of the problems associated with
illegal drugs. This minority believes that policies other than prohibition might be preferable.[1]

The resolution of this debate matters. Almost a third of the population aged 12 and
older claims to have used marijuana at least once, and more than 10 percent claims to have
tried cocaine (U.S. Department of Justice, 1994, pp. 335–6). Revenues in the illegal drug
industry almost certainly exceed $10 billion and by some estimates surpass $50 billion
(WEFA, 1986, pp. 413–94). Federal, state and local governments currently spend more
than $20 billion per year on drug enforcement (U.S. Department of Justice, 1994,
pp. 22–3), and in 1992 law enforcement officials made more than one million arrests for
drug law violations (U.S. Department of Justice, 1994, p. 418). More than 20 percent of
the 700,000 state prisoners in 1991 and almost 60 percent of the 77,000 federal prisoners in
1993 were incarcerated for drug law violations (U.S. Department of Justice, 1994, pp. 612,
630). Rightly or wrongly, the enforcement of drug prohibition affects tens of millions of
Americans, involves substantial amounts of resources and has a profound influence on the
criminal justice system.

This paper discusses the costs and benefits of drug prohibition. It offers a detailed
outline of the economic consequences of drug prohibition and a systematic analysis of the
relevant empirical evidence. The bottom line is that a relatively free market in drugs is
likely to be vastly superior to the current policy of prohibition.

The Positive Analysis of Drug Prohibition

As a starting place for analyzing the economic consequences of drug prohibition, we compare a prohibited market with a free market in drugs. By prohibition, we mean a regime something like current U.S. policy. By a free market, we mean a regime something like that surrounding most legal goods. Many intermediate policy regimes are available, and we discuss these later in the paper.

The direct effects of prohibition on the drug market

Perhaps the most incontrovertible effect of prohibition is an upward shift in the supply curve for drugs. Enforcement and potential legal punishment effectively impose a "tax" on suppliers, thereby raising the costs of supplying drugs. This tax includes the jail sentences and fines that drug suppliers face if apprehended, along with any costs that suppliers incur in evading detection. In addition, supply costs increase because drug suppliers cannot rely on the legal and judicial system to enforce contracts or resolve disputes.

Prohibition is also likely to shift the demand curve for drugs downward. This shift results from legal penalties for possession of drugs, greater uncertainty about product quality, additional costs and danger associated with transactions in an illegal market and a "respect for the law" under which individuals abstain from illegal acts.

For several reasons, however, the downward shift in demand is likely to be small relative to the upward shift in supply. As a rule, both legal prescriptions and realized punishments are less extreme for consumers than suppliers (Bruno, 1984, p. 35). During alcohol Prohibition, for example, the purchase and use of alcohol were never explicitly prohibited (Clark, 1976), although some law enforcement officers and courts treated possession as evidence of intent to distribute. Similarly, increased transaction costs are likely to be greater for the supplier than for the consumer; for example, suppliers are more likely to be targets of violence than consumers.

The effect of "respect for the law" on the demand for drugs is also likely to be small. Many individuals regularly violate laws that are weakly enforced, including parking and speeding laws, certain tax laws, sodomy laws and blue laws. These examples differ in some respects from drug restrictions, but they support the view that individuals comply with laws selectively, based on the actual costs and benefits of the action in question. Furthermore, any reduction in demand due to "respect for the law" is mitigated to the extent prohibition glamorizes drug use.

Thus, prohibition is likely to cause a substantial upward shift in supply and a smaller downward shift in demand. Unless demand is far more elastic than supply, therefore, prices will increase under prohibition. In fact, widespread evidence indicates that prices of prohibited goods – be they drugs, alcohol or prostitution – are higher under prohibition. For example, Warburton (1932) estimates that alcohol prices were approximately three times higher during alcohol Prohibition than beforehand, and Morgan (1991) estimates that cocaine currently sells for at least 20 times its free market price.

The prohibition-induced shifts in supply and demand also imply that under prohibition, equilibrium consumption falls. The magnitude of the decline depends on a number of additional assumptions, and we argue below that the total decrease is likely to be small. Unless prohibition glamorizes drug use to a surprising extent, however, consumption will be lower under prohibition than in a free market.

These direct effects of prohibition on the drug market imply a number of additional effects. In the remainder of this section, we discuss the most important of these.

Violence

Prohibition is likely to lower marginal costs and raise marginal benefits to violence in an industry in several important manners. Because participants in the illegal drug trade cannot use the legal and judicial system, the marginal benefits to using violence to resolve disputes increases. Indeed, it is well known that in many situations, the first best can be asymptotically obtained only when arbitrarily large punishments can be imposed for bad outcomes; see, for example, Mirrlees (1975). While such punishments may be restricted due to other considerations, they will look more attractive if alternative legal remedies are not available.

Additionally, the marginal cost of violent acts is likely to be smaller in a prohibited market than in a free market, because evading apprehension for one set of illegal activities – drug dealing – is complementary with evading apprehension for another set – initiating violence. Likewise, the costs of legal punishment if apprehended may be concave in the number of offenses for which one is convicted; in other words, an extra few charges often leads to a less-than-proportional increase in the penalty. Furthermore, participants in an illegal enterprise, having no recourse to the law, have a greater need to protect themselves. Hiring a security force for protection, however, further lowers the marginal cost of initiating violent acts.

In addition to promoting violence in the drug trade itself, prohibition likely increases non-drug-related violence as well. As violence from the drug trade makes headlines, law-abiding citizens buy guns in self-defense, and these weapons are discharged accidentally or used in domestic and other non-drug-related disputes. The increased demand for guns, for both legal and illegal purposes, means that guns are widely available generally, for use in a broad range of violent activities.

Consequently, the marginal cost of violence is likely to decrease, and the marginal benefit is likely to increase under prohibition. This view proposed here, that drug *prohibition* promotes violence, contrasts sharply with the usual claim that drug *consumption* promotes violence. The evidence that drug consumption induces violence, however, is weak (Duke and Gross, 1993; U.S. Department of Justice, 1992). A host of historical examples supports the view that suppliers of various goods employ violence only when those goods are prohibited. We cite here only the most obvious examples.

Violence has occurred in the drug trade primarily since 1914, when drugs were first prohibited in the United States (Trebach, 1982). Similarly, violence was employed in the alcohol trade only during the years of Prohibition. The current lack of violence in this industry is notable given that alcohol consumption is widely linked with reduced inhibitions.

The behavior of the murder rate in the United States further supports the claim that prohibition increases violence (Friedman, 1991). The murder rate rose rapidly after 1910, when many states adopted drug and alcohol prohibition laws. The rate also rose through

World War I, when alcohol and drugs were first prohibited nationally, and it continued to rise during the 1920s as efforts to enforce alcohol prohibition increased. The rate then fell dramatically after Prohibition's repeal in 1934 and (except for wartime) remained at modest levels for several decades. In the late 1960s, the rate increased dramatically again and stayed at historically high levels through the 1970s and 1980s, coinciding with a drastic increase in drug law enforcement.

A more detailed examination of the violent acts associated with drugs also suggests that prohibition is responsible for considerable drug-related violence (Goldstein, Brownstein, Ryan and Bellucci, 1989). During the period from March to October 1988, 414 murders were recorded in New York City. Of these, 218 were classified by police as drug related. Of drug-related murders, only 31 resulted from a state of mind induced by drugs or alcohol, and only eight of these involved crack and/or cocaine (in three cases in combination with alcohol). By contrast, 21 deaths were attributed to the psycho-pharmacological effects of alcohol. The remaining drug-related murders were all "economic compulsive," which refers to killing while stealing to pay for a drug habit, or systemic, which refers to killing while stealing to pay for a drug habit, or systemic, which refers to battling over drug territory. Of these, the vast majority were systemic. No economic compulsive or systemic murders were reported relating to alcohol.

Cartelization, profits and violence

Together with increasing the incentives for violence, prohibition is likely to increase the ease with which a cartel can be established in an industry. Suppliers in a prohibited industry necessarily hide their activities from law enforcement officials, thereby lowering the marginal costs of evading the antitrust laws. Lower marginal costs to imposing severe punishments – violence – also serve to facilitate cooperation in repeated interactions (see, for example, Fudenberg and Maskin, 1986).

The willingness of a cartel to use violence also discourages small competitors from challenging the cartel. When a large incumbent in a legal industry fights a price war with a smaller competitor, the incumbent pays a higher cost (foregone sales) because it is larger. In a battle of guns, however, an equal loss (perhaps measured in the number of lives) is likely to hurt a small challenger more. Furthermore, even if challenges occur, violence is likely to settle disputes faster than legal remedies, restoring the dominance of a cartel more rapidly.

To the extent that prohibition does encourage cartelization, this will exacerbate the reduction in supply and increase in price discussed above. Cartelization also yields real profits (rather than just quasi-rents offsetting law-evasion costs), which may further increase the marginal benefits of violence. Similarly, the feasibility of real profits under cartelization increases the marginal benefits to the corruption of law enforcement officials and politicians, and it give suppliers a reason to support legal prohibitions.

The explanation of profits offered here, and the link suggested with increased violence, is to the best of our knowledge novel. Many observers suggest that prohibition raises profits, and many assert that profits explain the level of violence. Yet the foundation for these claims has been lacking. The mere fact that prohibition raises costs does not suffice, since a tax on suppliers merely lowers short-run profits until exit from the industry restores a situation where zero profits prevail. Likewise, high profits alone cannot account for elevated levels of violence; profits by themselves merely induce entry. Nevertheless, our analysis suggests that profits and violence are intimately related under prohibition. Although hard evidence is difficult to obtain, anecdotal evidence is consistent with our conjectures. Cartelization in the drug trade appears to exist at every stage of production, and battles over turf–market share – appear to be a primary source of violence in the industry.

Increased accidental poisonings and overdoses

Still another effect of prohibition is increased uncertainty about product quality. Government quality regulation does not exist for illegal commodities, and buyers cannot complain about quality without incriminating themselves. In response to such concerns, sellers of a prohibited product might endeavor to develop reputations for reliability through repeated transactions, but such reputation building is likely to be only a partial solution. Thus, accidental poisonings and overdoses will occur more frequently in a prohibited market.

A number of examples illustrate this point. During Prohibition, deaths due to alcoholism rose relative to other proxies for alcohol consumption (Miron and Zwiebel, 1991), presumably because consumption of adulterated alcohol increased. Indeed, federal regulation required manufacturers of industrial alcohol to adulterate their product with poisonous wood alcohol, knowing that much of this product was diverted to illegal consumption (Merz, 1932). In one case, an adulterant used by bootleggers to disguise alcohol as medicine turned out to cause permanent paralysis, victimizing thousands (Morgan, 1982). Similarly, the chemical paraquat, which the U.S. government encouraged Mexico to spray on marijuana fields, has caused sickness in many consumers (Duke and Gross, 1993, p. 195).

Increased property crime

Considerable evidence indicates a correlation between drug use and the perpetration of income-generating crimes such as theft or prostitution. A high fraction of those arrested for such crimes test positive for drug use, and several studies suggest that the rate of criminal activity is higher during periods of elevated drug use (Duke and Gross, 1993, pp. 65, 73, 108–10).

One interpretation of this correlation – the psycho–pharmacological explanation – is that drug consumption releases aggressions or reduces inhibitions, thereby making drug users more likely to commit crimes. Alternatively, drug users might commit crimes to finance their drug consumption. More specifically, if drug users have inelastic demands, face binding liquidity constraints and cannot supplement their income legally, increased prices are likely to both increase income-generating crime and induce substitution from consumption of "essentials." This effect may be magnified if individuals already inclined to commit crimes also happen to use drugs, a condition that appears consistent with the data (Greenberg and Adler, 1974).

Under the psycho–pharmacological explanation, prohibition should reduce crime by raising prices and decreasing consumption. Alternatively, if crimes are committed to finance drug consumption, prohibition should increase crime by raising prices. Reinforcing this effect, enforcement of prohibition may divert police resources from the deterrence of other crime.

Available evidence is generally consistent with the financing-consumption explanation and inconsistent with the psycho-pharmalogical explanation. For example, Silverman and Spruill (1977) document that increases in heroin prices are associated with increases in the rates of property crime, while Benson and Rasmussen (1991) and Benson, Kim, Rasmussen and Zuehlke (1992) find that increases in efforts to enforce prohibition are associated with increased rates of income-generating crime.

Other effects

Prohibition has a number of other likely effects. Attempts to enforce drug prohibition have promoted asset-forfeiture laws, which allow local police and the DEA to seize cars, boats, houses and financial assets from suspected drug users and suppliers without a trial or anything resembling due process. Likewise, attempts to enforce prohibition have weakened protections against unreasonable searches (Schlosser, 1994a, b).

The high prices caused by prohibition have increased the incentive to inject drugs (since this provides greater potency for a given expenditure) and, combined with restrictions on clean needles, thereby furthered the spread of HIV (Gostin, 1991). Restrictions on needle availability are not a necessary implication of drug prohibition, but these restrictions are widely imposed and usually supported by prohibitionists. This effect of prohibition-cum-needle-restrictions is potentially substantial; cross-sectional evidence suggests that HIV infection rates are lower in cities or countries with needle exchanges or greater legal access to clean needles (Gostin, 1991).

Drug prohibition has also had an important impact on foreign policy. In extreme cases like Peru, anecdotal evidence suggests that U.S. drug prohibition has helped create profits for drug cartels, who in turn have supported terrorism and fostered political instability (Barro, 1992).

Finally, as noted above, prohibition has substantial direct costs for law enforcement. The $20 billion figure cited in the introduction is undoubtedly an enormous underestimate, since it includes only direct expenditures on enforcement of the drug laws themselves. The expenditures necessitated by increased violent or income-generating crime might easily multiply this figure several times over.

The Normative Analysis of Drug Prohibition

The discussion above has reviewed the most important economic consequences of drug prohibition without addressing the welfare implications of each effect. For most of these effects, the welfare consequences are clearly negative. The most important possible exception is any reduction in drug consumption caused by prohibition. This section discusses whether policy-induced reductions in drug use are welfare enhancing and whether prohibition is an effective method of achieving whatever reductions are desirable.

Irrational behavior and drug consumption

In the standard economic paradigm, consumers make rational choices about consumption of goods. The fact that current drug consumption might lead to unpleasant future consequences in no way contradicts this presumption. Becker and Murphy (1988), for example, offer a model in which rational consumers anticipate any negative future utility from drug consumption, and they trade that off against present benefits. In this model, consumers only voluntarily initiate drug consumption when the effect on expected lifetime utility is positive. Thus, any reductions in drug consumption caused by prohibition constitute an additional cost of prohibition.

Despite this conclusion, however, many observers believe that policy should reduce consumption below the free market level. In particular, economists and others who espouse this view believe that some consumers systematically underestimate the degree to which current consumption of drugs influences the desire to consume drugs in the future – addictiveness – or underestimate the long-term costs of addiction. This kind of behavior is essentially equivalent to myopia and is usually referred to as such.

Even if some consumers underestimate the likelihood or costs of addiction, however, any benefits that drug users receive should still be included in cost–benefit calculations. Indeed, the utility obtained from social drinking is generally recognized as a benefit in discussions of alcohol policy, and as such it is remarkable how uniformly the utility from drug consumption is ignored in public discourse on drug policy – even by economists. The extent to which users (both casual and heavy) have pursued drugs, despite severe penalties and inflated prices under prohibition, suggests that the utility many users believe they derive is substantial.

In addition, the view that drug users systematically underestimate the costs of drug use or the likelihood of addiction is problematic. Information on the negative potential consequences of drugs is pervasive, and some drug "education" overstates the likely costs of drug use. In the case of cigarettes, for example, consumers appear to *overestimate* the relevant health risks (Viscusi, 1994). Thus, while we cannot deny that some consumers make a mistake in using drugs, we see little reason to label most or all such behavior as myopic.

Just as importantly, existing research suggests that many drugs are either not "addictive" or at least far less addictive than commonly portrayed. For example, across all categories of drugs at most a third of those who have ever used a drug say they have used that drug in the past year (U.S. Department of Justice, 1994, Tables 3.87–3.90, pp. 335–7). This does not mean drugs are never addictive, but it fails to suggest a high degree of addictiveness. The fact that continued use rates for marijuana, which is not regarded as addictive, are similar to those for crack, which is regarded as highly addictive, also challenges the more extreme claims about addictiveness of drugs. A sizable percentage of heroin users consume only occasionally, without becoming heavy users (Zinberg, 1979), and measurable withdrawal symptoms from opioids rarely occur until after several weeks of regular administration (Jaffee, 1991).

Existing evidence also suggests that the negative health consequences of drug use or addiction are often overstated. All drugs carry some health risk, but the degree to which illegal drugs are physically detrimental is far less than generally portrayed, provided they are consumed under safe circumstances. The *Merck Manual* (Berkow, 1992, pp. 1556–63) a standard reference book on diagnosis and treatment of diseases, states that "people who have developed tolerance [to heroin] may show few signs of drug use and function normally in their usual activities. . . . Many but not all complications of heroin addiction are related to unsanitary administration of the drug." It also writes that "there is still little evidence of biologic damage [from marijuana] even among relatively heavy users." Concerning cocaine, the manual does not mention effects of long-term use but emphasizes that all effects, including those that promote aggression, are short-lived. Many of the health risks discussed for all drugs result from overdoses or adulterated doses, not moderate or even heavy levels of use.[2]

Similarly, little evidence suggests that drug use lowers productivity. Laboratory studies have failed to document consistent effects – positive or negative – of drugs on performance, and individual earnings display, if anything, a positive relation with self-reported drug use, except for the very heaviest users (Normand, Lempert and O'Brien, 1994, pp. 107–23, 160–8). Winick (1991) documents that many regular drug users are productive, functioning members of society (as are many heavy alcohol users), with many claiming their greatest problem related to drug use is obtaining a steady supply.

Finally, the question for policy is not simply whether myopia has negative consequences but whether these consequences are greater under prohibition or an alternative policy. For example, prohibition raises the short-term rewards to working in the drug trade relative to the short-term benefits of getting an education. The "rational" choice – taking into account long-term considerations – might be education, but under prohibition, myopia could lead some teenagers to choose the drug trade. Similarly, prohibition might glamorize drugs, especially for those with myopic preferences.

Externalities of drug consumption

An alternative justification for policies to reduce drug consumption is that such consumption generates negative externalities. The existence of such externalities does not justify ignoring consumer benefits in an overall evaluation of drug policies, but their presence may imply that the socially optimal level of consumption is less than the individually optimal level. Again, the critical question is not whether drug consumption generates externalities, but how any such externalities compare to those generated by prohibition. In fact, it is possible that prohibition might increase certain externalities associated with consumption.

Note first that while prohibition (and other restrictive policies) might reduce the consumption of illegal drugs, these policies might increase the consumption of other products that also generate externalities, like alcohol and tobacco. Marijuana use increased and other drug use decreased in the 12 states that decriminalized marijuana during the 1970s (Model, 1993), and marijuana consumption of high school seniors rose while alcohol consumption fell after increases in minimum drinking ages during the 1980s (DiNardo and Lemieux, 1992). Similarly, data on actual marijuana prices along with indicators for decriminalization indicate that drinking frequency and heavy drinking episodes are positively related to the price of marijuana (Chaloupka and Laixuthai, 1994). Anecdotal evidence suggests that opiate consumption increased during the first few years of alcohol Prohibition (Feldman, 1927), and patients in drug-treatment programs appear to increase their marijuana and alcohol consumption as their opiate consumption declines (Apsler and Harding, 1991).

Existing evidence also suggests that externalities generated by consumption of substitutes for illegal drugs are at least as great as those for illegal drugs. For example, the deleterious effects of alcohol on driving ability are at least as great as those of marijuana (U.S. Department of Transportation, 1993; Crancer et al., 1969), and, consistent with this evidence, a decrease in the price of marijuana leads to a lower number of traffic fatalities, presumably because the lower price induces a substitution from alcohol to marijuana (Chaloupka and Laixuthai, 1994). The negative effects of cigarette smoking on pregnancy outcomes appear greater and are more consistently documented than those of marijuana or cocaine (Rosenzweig and Wolpin, 1995; Shiono et al., 1995).

It is also possible that prohibition increases rather than decreases the use of publicly funded health care resources. Prohibition raises the frequency of accidental poisonings and overdoses, contributes to the spread of HIV and increases emergency-room treatment of gunshot wounds. Additionally, prohibition has discouraged the use of illegal drugs for medical purposes. Marijuana cannot be used to treat a number of conditions for which it appears both safe and efficacious (Grinspoon and Bakalar, 1993); many doctors appear to undertreat pain because of hysteria over the use of narcotics (Trebach, 1982); and some patients refuse narcotics and other pain medication due to exaggerated fears of addiction (*New York Times*, 1994). Moreover, the net impact of drug policy on public funding is confounded by evidence that dying early, before receiving much Social Security or Medicare, may yield a net public inflow (Manning et al., 1989; Viscusi, 1994).

The externality-reducing effects of prohibition are further limited by the fact that externalities are likely to be disproportionately associated with heavy use, but enforcement probably discourages casual use more than heavy use. For example, the price elasticity of heavy drinkers is far less than that of moderate drinkers (Manning, Blumberg and Moulton, 1993). Thus, whereas proponents of the "war on drugs" cite survey evidence that use has fallen over the past 10–15 years, several factors suggest that heavy use has declined far less or even increased (Normand, Lempert and O'Brien, 1994, pp. 71–3). Meanwhile, many of the externalities that ostensibly justified the "war" remained constant or increased. For example, the reported rate of property crime is virtually unchanged compared to the late 1970s or early 1980s, and the rate of violent crime has increased substantially (U.S. Department of Justice, 1994, Table 3.107, p. 352).

Historical Evidence on Prohibition

The case for prohibition must rest on its ability to reduce drug use, especially that sort of use that produces externalities or is individually irrational. A critical empirical question is therefore whether drug prohibition produces a large or small effect in this direction. Historical evidence is informative here.

Although drug prohibition is almost universally practiced by the governments of the modern world, it is a recent phenomenon by historical standards. In the United States, federal prohibition of opium, heroin and cocaine dates only from 1914 and of marijuana only from 1937.[3] Before these dates, currently prohibited drugs were not only legal but widely available from drugs stores, street vendors and mail-order catalogs. They were also dispensed by pharmacists and physicians for a host of medical problems, particularly the alleviation of pain.

The lessons from this period are instructive. Although drugs were legal and widely available, the United States was not a country of addicts (Clark, 1976). Many individuals used opium, heroin, cocaine and other drugs without significant ill effects. For example, it was common to administer opium to infants and children, as in cough syrups, yet very few of these children became addicts.

Additionally, before 1914, opium use fluctuated substantially from year to year and declined significantly from about 1895 to 1914, in the absence of significant government prohibitions (Terry and Pellens, 1928). This implies that factors other than government drug policy, such as demographics, urbanization, the price of alcohol and unemployment rates, are important determinants of drug use. To the extent drug use was associated with negative outcomes, these were mainly confined to users, and society was not afflicted with the drug-related social ills that are commonly attributed to drug use today (Trebach, 1982). While a variety of factors make this evidence hard to apply to the present, it suggests the most dire predictions of prohibitionists – for example, that legalization would produce a boom in the number of "addicts" – were not borne out prior to prohibition restrictions.

Another source of historical evidence is provided by the U.S. experience with alcohol prohibition.[4] Prohibition began in 1917 as an emergency wartime measure, was made permanent by the 18th amendment in 1920 and continued until repeal at the end of 1933. Although no official data exist on alcohol consumption during Prohibition, data are available on a number of closely related series. These include the death rate from cirrhosis of the liver, the death rate from alcoholism, the drunkenness arrest rate and the number of first admittances to mental hospitals for alcoholic psychosis. In the periods before and after Prohibition, when official statistics on alcohol consumption are available, each of these measures seems to be an accurate proxy for the per capita consumption of alcohol.

The four different proxies tell a similar story about alcohol consumption during Prohibition. Taken together, they indicate that at the onset of Prohibition, consumption declined sharply, to approximately 30 percent of its pre-Prohibition level. Through the early 1920s, however, alcohol consumption increased significantly, rising to about 60–70 percent of the pre-Prohibition level.[5] Consumption grew slightly over the last few years of Prohibition and stayed approximately constant after repeal.

One natural interpretation of this pattern is that it took several years for illegal supply networks to organize, but by the early 1920s they were sufficiently well developed so that the return to a legal market for alcohol did not have a significant effect on availability. This pattern is particularly notable given the sharp increase in enforcement over this period.[6] Also notable is a shift from the consumption of beer and wine to hard liquors.

The data described above should not be taken as a direct estimate of alcohol Prohibition's effect on consumption, since other factors may have influenced consumption as well. For example, the political factors that led to passing Prohibition probably also reflected a social climate that frowned on alcohol consumption, while the political factors that led to repeal expressed a social climate that did not find alcohol consumption as threatening. Nevertheless, these data do not suggest that alcohol Prohibition had a significant deterrent effect on alcohol use. The absence of a substantial increase in alcohol consumption upon repeal is particularly relevant. Just as the illegal liquor supply was well developed by the late 1920s, the supply of illegal drugs is pervasive today.

What is the Optimal Drug Policy?

The possible policies toward drugs include many options between prohibition and a free market. This section offers a brief discussion of several main possibilities.

The degree of enforcement

One alternative to current prohibition is a regime with similar laws but substantially different amounts of resources devoted to enforcement. In the United States, the level of enforcement has changed substantially over time, and the level of enforcement varies widely across countries.

One key consideration in determining the optimal level of enforcement is that such expenditures likely exhibit decreasing marginal returns in reducing drug consumption. Cost-effective law enforcement is likely to address the easiest targets first, implying a diminishing marginal effect of enforcement in raising price. Moreover, any increases in price will yield diminishing returns in reducing consumption if market demand is convex, a condition that seems likely for drugs. Casual consumers have cheap substitutes like alcohol and tobacco available and thus have relatively elastic demands for drugs, while heavy users are likely to have inelastic demands. As price rises, the latter group will make up a higher proportion of the market, leading to a convex demand curve.

The U.S. experience with alcohol Prohibition is consistent with this conjecture. Early in alcohol Prohibition, enforcement was weak and alcohol consumption declined substantially; later enforcement was stronger, but consumption failed to decline further and actually increased. Part of the explanation is presumably that illegal supply networks became more efficient over time, but this evidence still suggests that increased enforcement yielded decreasing returns in reducing consumption.

Similarly, federal drug enforcement expenditures increased from less than $1 billion in 1981 to more than $7.5 billion in 1994.[7] Survey estimates indicate, however, that the fraction of the population using drugs declined by at most 50 percent (Normand, Lempert and O'Brien, 1994, p. 54), and this number almost certainly exaggerates the decline in drug consumption, both because heavy use appears to have remained relatively constant and because increased social stigmatization is likely to have biased survey responses.

Thus, while many prohibitionists believe present levels of enforcement are "inadequate," we see little evidence that increased enforcement would reduce drug use further. In contrast, decreases in enforcement would likely reduce violence – insofar as violence is likely to increase with higher prices – while leading to only modest increases in consumption, mainly by casual consumers. In the 1950s and 1960s, for example, the resources devoted to prohibition were proportionally smaller than during the last two decades, yet drug-related violence was less common and the consumption of drugs was, if anything, lower than during the 1970s and 1980s.

Which drugs to target

Any policy toward illegal drugs must decide whether all drugs should be treated alike. It is common for legalization advocates to focus on marijuana, for example.

If the only objective of drug policy were to reduce myopic or externality-producing *consumption*, without regard to externalities induced by prohibition, the case for a free market in marijuana might be clearer than that for cocaine or opiates. Marijuana is not believed to be physically addictive, nor does it appear to have significant negative health consequences, even in large doses. Although opiates and cocaine can be used safely over long periods, both can cause lethal overdoses, and both are potentially addictive.

Nevertheless, we have argued above that most of the negative consequences associated with illegal drugs derive from the prohibition rather than the consumption of the prohibited good. Although drugs differ from other commodities in important respects, their distinctive characteristics do not explain the effects of drug prohibition on the market for drugs. The markets for commodities that display similar distinctive characteristics but are not prohibited (like cigarettes and coffee) fail to exhibit the features of the market for drugs discussed here. Conversely, the markets for commodities that do not display these distinctive characteristics but that are often prohibited (like gambling and prostitution) exhibit many of the same negative features as the market for drugs.

The externalities generated by the prohibition of different drugs *are* likely to differ according to their respective supply and demand conditions. Perhaps most significantly, prohibitions of drugs with more inelastic demands are likely to cause a greater increase in violence and property crimes, through channels discussed above. Similarly, prohibitions of drugs that are more likely to be administered through injections will generally lead to greater externalities, through accidental poisonings and the spread of HIV. As such, the drugs that are primary targets of current enforcement policies – like cocaine and heroin – are likely to be among those whose restriction produces the most significant externalities.

Harm reduction and the Dutch model

One perspective often advanced by opponents of prohibition is that policy should continue to criminalize the supply of drugs while reducing or eliminating the penalties against possession and use. In addition, advocates of such an approach often suggest subsidizing treatment and encouraging needle exchanges to reduce the likely harm to users (Gostin, 1990). Such a system is often referred to as "harm reduction" or, slightly inaccurately, as the Dutch model. In Holland, possession and use are *de facto* decriminalized, although the legal penalties are similar in structure to those in the United States. The Dutch do devote considerable resources to harm reduction (Engelsman, 1991; Leuw, 1991; Oppenheimer, 1991).

If harm reduction means that supply restrictions are not seriously enforced, then harm-reduction regimes are likely to be significantly superior to current U.S. policy, consistent with our discussion above. On the other hand, if harm-reduction policies coexist with substantial enforcement of supply restrictions, the undesirable consequences of prohibition – violence, uncertainty over product quality and so on – will still occur, so harm reduction might differ insignificantly from current U.S. policy.

In addition, any policy that attempts to reduce the harm associated with drug consumption potentially encourages such consumption. For example, the availability of clean needless or subsidized drug abuse treatment might affect the likelihood that some consumers begin or renew their drug use. Moreover, such policies transfer resources from the population generally to those who willingly accept the risks of drug use and who, in some cases, are imposing externalities on others. This does not mean compassion for drug users is misplaced, nor that, say, clean needless should not be legally available. But it does suggest caution in adopting policies that in effect subsidize drug consumption. These policies require their own cost–benefit analyses, which in some cases do not appear favorable (for example, see Apsler and Harding, 1991, on treatment).

Medicalization and the British model

A different model for drug policy that receives widespread attention is the "British system." The system first evolved in the 1920s, shortly after Britain criminalized narcotics. In this system, doctors could legally prescribe narcotics not only for short-term pain relief but also to maintain a patient's habit over long periods if the doctor thought such a course the best option available. This policy continued until the 1960s, when the ability to maintain addicts was transferred from individual doctors to government clinics. With this exception, official British drug policy resembles U.S. drug prohibition (Oppenheimer, 1991; Turner, 1991; Howitt, 1990; Pearson, 1991).

Medicalization allows many drug users, especially those with the most inelastic demands and greatest consumption, to obtain drugs legally. Under such a policy, the size of the black market is likely to be smaller than under the pure prohibitionist model. In the extreme, the black market might never develop, because the unsatisfied demand is insufficient to overcome the fixed costs of setting up an illegal supply network. British experience is generally consistent with this view. Drug-related social ills such as violent crime were virtually nonexistent before the 1960s, when doctors prescribed narcotics freely. These ills have increased over the last three decades, but this increase is consistent with the view of many observers that government-operated maintenance clinics are far more restrictive in their supply of narcotics to users.

The alcohol/cigarette model

Although above we compared prohibition to a free market, most advocates of legalization endorse a number of government policies designed to reduce drug consumption, including taxation, drug education and/or subsidized treatment, age restrictions and similar policies. Loosely speaking, this means the legal regime associated with the production, sale and consumption of drugs would resemble that which is currently associated with alcohol and cigarettes.

We make two points about this type of regime. First, under this regime, the restrictions on supply are likely to be insufficient to generate a black market, so the most significant harms done by prohibition would be absent. For example, no well-developed black market in cigarettes or alcohol currently exists in the United States despite significant restrictions on their supply and use. Consumption of drugs might be higher than under prohibition, but our analysis suggests the difference would be smaller than commonly perceived and not necessarily undesirable. Moreover, some evidence suggests that policies like age restrictions can reduce consumption and related externalities (Safer, 1994; Grossman, Chaloupka, Safer and Laixuthai, 1993). Thus, such a regime is likely to be a vast improvement over prohibition.

Second, any particular policy toward drugs requires its own cost–benefit analysis. Certain restrictions may be beneficial in reducing externalities or uninformed consumption, but these restrictions are likely to have costs as well. Moderate "sin" taxes are plausibly a desirable policy, but they can easily be raised to levels that generate black markets. Age restrictions might make sense up to some age, but if extended too far, simply breed contempt for the law as widespread noncompliance occurs. Thus, while such policies are potentially useful, we believe they require more careful analysis and justification than has usually been given.[8]

Conclusion

The existing evidence relevant to drug policy is far from complete. Given the evidence, however, our conclusion is that a free market in drugs is likely to be a far superior policy to current policies of drug prohibition. A free market might lead to a substantial increase in the number of persons who use drugs and possibly to a significant increase in the total amount of drugs consumed. But that policy would also produce substantial reductions in the harmful effects of drug use on third parties through reduced violence, reduced property crime and a number of other channels. On net, the existing evidence suggests the social costs of drug prohibition are vastly greater than its benefits.

Notes

1   The literature on drug prohibition is too lengthy to cite in detail; see Evans and Berent (1992) and the references therein for a good sampling of the views on both sides.
2   For more detailed discussions of health effects, see Grinspoon and Bakalar (1979) on cocaine, Grinspoon and Bakalar (1993) on marijuana and Trebach (1982) and Zinberg (1979) on heroin.
3   Some states prohibited drugs before federal prohibition. These laws are not believed to have depressed consumption, however, because smuggling across state borders was easy and resources allocated for enforcement were modest.
4   The discussion here is based on Miron and Zwiebel (1991).
5   Similarly, data on convictions for drunkenness suggest that consumption of alcohol grew rapidly during Finnish prohibition in the 1920s after an initial sharp decline (Wuorinen, 1932).
6   Money appropriated by the federal government for enforcing Prohibition increased from $6.3 million in 1921 (the first year of large-scale enforcement) to $9.2 million in 1925 and to $13.4 million in 1930 (U.S. Department of Treasury, 1930, p. 2).
7   For data, see U.S. Department of Justice (1991, Table 1.12, pp. 16–17) and U.S. Department of Justice (1994, Table 1.14, pp. 19–21). The behavior of arrest rates suggests that state and local expenditures increased substantially as well, but precise estimates do not appear to be available.
8   By the same token, policies toward drug testing need their own cost–benefit analyses. Most legalizers not only oppose government-mandated drug testing but believe policy should prohibit private drug testing. Nothing in our argument for legalization requires this conclusion, however, Normand, Lempert and O'Brien (1994) provides a good introduction to these issues.

References

Apsler, R. and Harding, W. M. (1991): "Cost-Effectiveness Analysis of Drug Abuse Treatment: Current Status and Recommendations for Future Research," in *Drug Abuse Services Research: Background Papers on Drug Abuse Financing and Services Research*, Washington, D.C.: National Institute on Drug Abuse, 58–81.
Barro, R. J. (1992): "To Avoid Repeats of Peru, Legalize Drugs," *Wall Street Journal*, April 27, A14.
Becker, G. S. and Murphy, K. M. (1988): "A Theory of Rational Addiction," *Journal of Political Economy*, 96, August, 675–700.

Benson, B. L. and Rasmussen, D. W. (1991): "Relationship Between Illicit Drug Enforcement Policy and Property Crimes," *Contemporary Policy Issues*, 9, October, 106–15.

Benson, B. L., Kim, I., Rasmussen, D. W. and Zuehlke, T. W. (1992): "Is Property Crime Caused by Drug Use or by Drug Enforcement Policy?", *Applied Economics*, 24, July, 679–92.

Berkow, R. (ed.) (1992): *The Merck Manual*, 16th edn. Rahway, N.J.: Merck and Co., Inc.

Bruno, F. (1984): *Combatting Drug Abuse and Related Crime*. Rome: Frattelli Palombi Editori.

Chaloupka, F. J. and Laixuthai, A. (1994): "*Do Youths Substitute Alcohol and Marijuana? Some Econometric Evidence*," NBER working paper #4662.

Clark, N. H. (1976): *Deliver Us from Evil: An Interpretation of American Prohibition*. New York: W. W. Norton & Co.

Crancer, A. (et al.,) (1969): "Comparison of the Effects of Marihuana and Alcohol on Simulated Driving Performance," *Science*, (3882) 164, May, 851–4.

DiNardo, J. and Lemieux, T. (1992): "*Are Marijuana and Alcohol Substitutes? The Effect of State Drinking Age Laws on the Marijuana Consumption of High School Seniors*," NBER working paper #4212.

Duke, S. B. and Gross, A. C. (1993): *America's Longest War: Rethinking Our Tragic Crusade Against Drugs*. New York: G. P. Putnam's Sons.

Engelsman, E. L. (1991): "Drug Policy in the Netherlands from a Public Health Perspective," in M. B. Krauss and E. P. Lazear (eds), *Searching for Alternatives: Drug-Control Policy in the United States*, Standord, CA: Hoover Institution Press, 169–74.

Evans, R. L. and Berent, I. M. (eds) (1992): *Drug Legalization: For and Against*. La Salle, Ill.: Open Court Press.

Feldman, H. (1927): *Prohibition: Its Economic and Industrial Aspects*. New York: D. Appelton and Co.

Friedman, M. (1991): "The War We Are Losing," in M. B. Krauss and E. P. Lazear (eds), *Searching for Alternatives: Drug-Control Policy in the United States*, Stanford, CA: Hoover Institution Press, 53–67.

Fudenberg, D. and Maskin, E. (1986): "The Folk Theorem in Repeated Games with Discounting or with Incomplete Information," *Econometrica*, 54, May, 533–56.

Goldstein, P. J., Brownstein, H. H., Ryan, P. J. and Belluchi, P. A. (1989): "Crack and Homicide in New York City, 1988: A Conceptually Based Event Analysis," *Contemporary Drug Problems*, 16 (4), Winter, 651–87.

Gostin, L. (1990): "Waging a War on Drugs Users: An Alternative Public Health Vision," *Houston Law Review*, 18 (4), Winter, 385–94.

——(1991): "The Interconnected Epidemic of Drug Dependency and AIDS," *Harvard Civil Rights/ Civil Liberties Law Review*, 26 (1), Winter, 113–84.

Greenberg, S. W. and Adler, F. (1974): "Crime and Addiction: An Empirical Analysis of the Literature, 1920–1973," *Contemporary Drug Problems*, Summer, 3 (2), 221–69.

Grinspoon, L. and Bakalar, J. B. (1979): "Cocaine," in R. L. Dupont, A. Goldstein and J. O'Donnell (eds), *Handbook on Drug Abuse*, Washington, D.C.: National Institute on Drug Abuse, 241–8.

——(1993): *Marihuana: The Forbidden Medicine*. New Haven: Yale University Press.

Grossman, M., Chaloupka, F., Safer, H. and Laixuthai, A. (1993): "*Effects of Alcohol Price Policy on Youth*," NBER working paper #4385.

Howitt, D. (1990): "Britain's 'Substance Abuse Policy': Realities and Regulation in the United Kingdom," *International Journal of the Addictions*, 25 (3), 353–76.

Jaffee, J. H. (1991): "Opiates," in I. Glass (ed.), *The International Handbook of Addiction Behaviour*, New York: Routledge, 67.

Kleiman, M. A. (1992): *Against Excess: Drug Policy for Results*. New York: Basic Books.

Leuw, E. (1991): "Drugs and Drug Policy in the Netherlands," in *Crime and Justice: A Review of Research, Vol. 14*, Chicago: University of Chicago Press, 229–76.

Manning, W. G., Blumberg, L. and Moulton, L. H. (1993): "The Demand for Alcohol: The Differential Response to Price," manuscript, University of Minnesota, 1993.

Manning, W. G. et al. (1989): "The Taxes of Sin: Do Smokers and Drinkers Pay Their Way?", *Journal of the American Medical Association*, 261 (11), March, 1604–09.

Merz, C. (1932): *The Dry Decade*, Garden City, N.Y.: Doubleday, Doran & Co.

Miron, J. A. and Zwiebel, J. (1991): "Alcohol Consumption During Prohibition," *American Economic Review*, 81, May, 242–47.

Mirrlees, J. (1975): "*The Theory of Moral Hazard and Unobservable Behavior, Part I*," mimeo, Nuffield College, Oxford.

Model, K. E. (1993): "The Effect of Marijuana Decriminalization on Hospital Emergency Room Drug Episodes, 1975–1978," *Journal of the American Medical Association*, 88 (423), 737–47.

Morgan, J. P. (1982): "The Jamaica Ginger Paralysis," *Journal of the American Medical Association*, 245 (15), October, 1864–7.

——(1991): "Prohibition is Perverse Policy: What was True in 1933 is True Now," in M. B. Krauss, and E. P. Lazear (eds), *Searching for Alternatives: Drug-Control Policy in the United States*, Stanford, CA: Hoover Institution Press, 405–23.

New York Times (1994): "It Pains a Nation of Stoics to Say 'No' to Pain," April 3, E5.

Normand, J., Lempert, R. O. and O'Brien, C. P. (eds) (1994): *Under the Influence: Drugs and the American Work Force*. Washington, D.C.: National Academy Press.

Oppenheimer, G. M. (1991): "To Build a Bridge: The Use of Foreign Models by Domestic Critics of U.S. Drug Policy," *Millbank Quarterly*, 69 (3), 495–526.

Pearson, G. (1991): "Drug Control Policies in Britain," in *Crime and Justice, Vol. 14*, Chicago: University of Chicago Press, 167–227.

Rosenzweig, M. R. and Wolpin, K. I. (1995): "The Effect of the Timing and Frequency of Marijuana Use on Fetal Growth Based on Sibling Birth Data," manuscript, University of Pennsylvania.

Safer, H. (1994): "*Alcohol Advertising and Motor Vehicle Fatalities*," NBER working paper #4708.

Schlosser, E. (1994a): "Reefer Madness," *Atlantic Monthly*, 274 (2), August, 45–63.

——(1994b): "Marijuana and the Law," *Atlantic Monthly*, 274 (3), September, 84–94.

Shiono, P. H. et al. (1995): "The Impact of Cocaine and Marijuana Use on Low Birth Weight and Preterm Birth: A Multicenter Study," *American Journal of Obstetrics and Gynecology*, part 1, 171 (1), January, 19–27.

Silverman, L. P. and Spruill, N. L. (1977): "Urban Crime and the Price of Heroin," *Journal of Urban Economics*, 4, January, 80–103.

Terry, C. E. and Pellens, M. (1928): *The Opium Problem*. Montclair, N.J.: Pattern Smith Publishing Corporation.

Trebach, A. S. (1982): *The Heroin Solution*. New Haven: Yale University Press.

Turner, D. (1991): "Pragmatic Incoherence: The Changing Face of British Drug Policy," in M. B. Krauss, and E. P. Lazear (eds), *Searching for Alternatives: Drug-Control Policy in the United States*, Stanford, CA: Hoover Institution Press, 175–92.

U.S. Department of Justice (1991): *Sourcebook of Criminal Justice Statistics – 1990*. Washington, D.C.: U.S. Government Printing Office.

——(1992): *Drugs, Crime and the Justice System: A National Report for the Bureau of Justice Statistics*. Washington, D.C.: U.S. Government Printing Office.

——(1994): *Sourcebook of Criminal Justice Statistics – 1993*. Washington, D.C.: U.S. Government Printing Office.

U. S. Department of Transportation (1993): *Marijuana and Actual Driving Performance*. Washington, D.C.: U.S. Government Printing Office.

U.S. Department of Treasury (1930): *Statistics Concerning Intoxicating Liquors*. Washington, D.C.: U.S. Government Printing Office.

Viscusi, W. K. (1994): "*Cigarette Taxes and the Social Consequences of Smoking*," NBER working paper #4891.

Warburton, C. (1932): *The Economic Results of Prohibition*. New York: Columbia University Press.

WEFA (Wharton Econometric Forecasting Associates) (1986): *The Impact: Organized Crime Today*. Washington, D.C.: President's Commission on Organized Crime.

Winick, C. (1991): "Social Behavior, Public Policy, and Nonharmful Drug Use," *Millbank Quarterly*, 69 (3), 437–59.

Wuorinen, J. H. (1932): "Finland's Prohibition Experiment," in J. H. S. Bossard and S. Thorsten (eds), *Prohibition: A National Experiment*. Philadelphia: American Academy of Political and Social Science, 216–26.

Zinberg, N. E. (1979): "Non-Addictive Opiate Use," in R. I. Dupont, A. Goldstein and J. O'Donnell (eds), *Handbook on Drug Abuse*, Washington, D.C.: National Institute on Drug Abuse, 303–14.

CHAPTER FOURTEEN

Economic Foundations of the Current Regulatory Reform Efforts

W. KIP VISCUSI

Source: *Journal of Economic Perspectives*, 10, 3 (1996), pp. 119–34. Reprinted with the permission of the author and the American Economic Association. © American Economic Association.

Traditional economic regulation focused on issues such as antitrust and setting prices for public utilities. But in the last few decades, the emerging role of environmental and risk regulation has transformed the role of regulation in the American economy. Rough estimates of the economic costs of government regulations exceed $500 billion (Hopkins, 1992). This total can be divided up in various ways. More than half the cost is attributable to paperwork requirements arising out of regulation, but there is also more than $200 billion in direct costs of regulation, including costs to business. More than half of this amount is due to environmental regulation, and much of the remainder is attributable to various forms of risk regulation, and much of the remainder is attributable to various forms of risk regulation. About $100 billion involves government transfers, such as the effects of the minimum wage, while the rest involves costs paid by businesses. Regulatory benefits reduce the net burden of these efforts on society, but there are no good estimates of the total of regulatory benefits.

Regulatory interventions often have a sound economic foundation. Many economists would agree that markets have a difficult time spontaneously organizing to address all forms of environmental pollution and that consumers are unable to assess the risks associated with, say, prescription drugs. However, the existence of a rationale for some sort of government intervention in no way eliminates the need for obtaining the greatest benefit to society that can be derived from these regulatory expenditures.

During 1995 and 1996, the 104th Congress has considered a flurry of bills intended to foster more cost-effective regulatory policies by imposing greater structure on risk and environmental regulations.[1] These legislative efforts were quite broad in scope; it's fair to say that they attempted to revolutionize the criteria for approval of government regulations. For example, rather than cleaning up hazardous waste sites whenever hazardous chemicals are present, irrespective of the costs involved and whether any populations are actually exposed to the risk, the new legislative proposals were intended to require the

Environmental Protection Agency (EPA) to assess the risks and to show that the social benefits of these actions exceeded the associated costs.

The need for economic balancing is inevitable in a world of constrained resources. Suppose that we were to devote the entire U.S. gross domestic product to the prevention of fatal accidents. Even then, we would be only able to spend $55 million per fatality (Viscusi, 1992, p. 5). That expenditure would leave literally nothing for other goods, such as other risks or environmental pollution, let alone basics like food, housing and medical care. Unless mechanisms exist for placing bounds on our risk reduction efforts, we can end up pursuing policies of diminishing marginal impact and diverting resources from more productive uses.

A frequent approach of government regulations is to eliminate fatality risks that are one in a million annually or greater.[2] But risks of this magnitude are ubiquitous. Death risks of one in a million are incurred every time we have one chest x-ray, live two days in New York or Boston (air pollution), travel 10 miles by bicycle, eat 40 tablespoons of peanut butter (cancer from aflatoxin B) or drink Miami drinking water for one year.[3] If agencies devote their efforts to eliminating trivial risks of this magnitude, they are likely to be missing opportunities for policies that could be of much greater benefit.

It is interesting to consider why current governmental efforts do not already put the design of regulations on a sounder footing. Why is a reform even needed to influence the guidelines for promulgating regulation? Why are agencies not more balanced? What can the possible objections be to legislation that would foster greater balance in the design of governmental regulatory efforts? Put somewhat differently, is the recent impetus for establishing economic criteria to assess regulations simply a disciplinary concern of economists or does it, in fact, have substantive implications for the design of regulatory policy? Surely, the spirited nature of the policy debate, the fact that no consensus regulatory reform bill has yet been passed by both houses of Congress, and the threat of a presidential veto tend to imply that issues of importance are at stake here.

This article will review the process by which legislative mandates give regulatory agencies the power to promulgate regulations. I will argue that regulatory reforms that place the assessment of regulation on sounder footing and incorporate unbiased risk assessment practices can potentially enhance the performance of regulatory policies.

Legislative Mandates

Congress does not typically promulgate government regulations, with a few rare exceptions. Instead, Congress establishes broad legislative guidelines for regulatory policy that define the objectives that should be promoted by regulations that will be issued by the various regulatory agencies within the executive branch. These regulatory agencies in turn propose regulations that go through a rule-making process in which there is both a review by the Office of Management and Budget (OMB) as well as a public comment period, after which the agency can issue the regulation. In some instances, there is the threat that Congress will cut back funding if certain undesirable regulations are enacted.

The primary check on reckless regulatory policymaking is that if a regulation fails to be consistent with the legislative mandate defined by Congress, it can be challenged in court. However, judicial challenges or other reviews cannot overturn the legislative mandate itself (unless the mandate is unconstitutional) regardless of how restrictive it is. The Clean Air Act, for example, specifically excludes the consideration of costs in EPA's setting of national ambient air quality standards. Similarly, in its regulation of prescription drugs, the Food and Drug Administration (FDA) must ascertain the safety and efficacy of these products, but there is no overall benefit–cost test that must be met either by the drugs themselves or by the drug approval process. Since many useful drugs apparently become available more quickly to patients in western Europe, concern has been expressed that the U.S. drug approval process may be too cumbersome and cautious.

The principal judicial battleground over the breadth or narrowness of legislative mandates has involved the regulations of the Occupational Safety and Health Administration (OSHA). The legislative mandate of that agency has a safety-oriented character that is typical of other risk and environmental agencies. In particular, the Occupational Safety and Health Act of 1970 mandates the agency "to assure so far as possible every man and woman in the Nation safe and healthful working conditions."[4] Other language in the bill mandates that OSHA undertake actions to protect workers against health hazards as far as is "feasible." The agency has interpreted these mandates in a very aggressive fashion, claiming there is no obligation to show that there is any relation between the benefits derived from the policies and the cost. Put somewhat differently, any risk reduction is justified as long as it reduces risk, regardless of how costly or inefficient it may be.

Not surprisingly, this agency interpretation has been the subject of several major court cases, which in turn have influenced other agencies' interpretation of their own legislative mandates. In a 1980 decision involving the OSHA benzene standard, the U.S. Supreme Court sidestepped the benefit–cost tradeoff issue but did assess OSHA's risk mandate. In particular, before promulgating a regulation, the Court ruled that OSHA was required to demonstrate that the standard would generate significant reductions in risk and that the standard would be "reasonably necessary or appropriate to provide safe and healthful employment." The Court concluded that promoting safety was not the same as eliminating all risks, however small: "But 'safe' is not the equivalent of 'risk-free.' A workplace can hardly be considered 'unsafe' unless it threatens the worker with significant risk of harm."[5] The requirement to show that the risk reduction is "significant" is also intertwined with how the agency assesses the risk, which is one of the principal concerns of the regulatory reform bills.

In 1981, the U.S. Supreme Court considered the balancing issue with respect to the OSHA cotton dust regulation. One possible avenue for inserting economic tradeoff concerns would be to interpret the legislative requirements that OSHA regulations be "feasible" in terms of whether there is a sensible balance between the risks reduced and the money spent. However, the Court rejected this broader economic interpretation of feasibility and instead interpreted the agency's legislative mandate in terms of whether there is the technical possibility of compliance ("capable of being done") rather than meeting a benefit–cost test.[6]

However, a more recent decision of the U.S. Court of Appeals would open the door for potential use of a benefit–cost test. Although the act in no way requires a benefit–cost test, the court indicated that OSHA was not foreclosed from undertaking some kind of benefit–cost balancing in promulgating its regulations. Moreover, the Court went so far as to outline a new methodology of risk–risk analysis, which will be discussed below.[7]

These few cases aside, however, the courts have deferred to the agency's discretion in interpreting its legislative mandate. The pivotal court decision establishing this point was a 1984 case in which the Natural Resources Defense Council challenged EPA's introduction of the "bubble" policy, which would judge a firm's emissions from the standpoint of an artificial bubble around the plant rather than on a smokestack-by-smokestack basis. The bubble policy enables firms to select the most cost-effective emissions sources to control at a plant. The Supreme Court ruled that courts should permit agencies to interpret ambiguities in their legislative mandates reasonably.[8] Armed with these court rulings, regulatory agencies have had considerable discretion.

Regulatory Oversight

Since the Ford administration, there has been a formal regulatory oversight mechanism to provide a check on ill-chosen regulation. The Office of Management and Budget has been responsible for this activity since the Reagan administration. These oversight groups have been responsible for implementing executive orders with respect to regulatory criteria. In the Carter administration, these criteria required that regulations be cost-effective and that the agency quantify the benefits and costs of the regulation.[9] However, this effectiveness test did little to screen out inefficient regulations since truly dominant regulatory alternatives that were not selected could be identified in only a few cases. The more usual case is one in which the costs greatly exceeded the benefits by any usual economic measure, but there are no alternatives that provide exactly the same or more benefits at less cost.

Since the Reagan administration, regulations have also been required by executive order to show that the benefits of the regulation exceed the costs.[10] The Clinton administration has continued this policy, but emphasizes that this comparison should also recognize that not all benefits can be quantified in monetary terms.[11] However, this benefit–cost test provision is applicable only if it does not conflict with the agency's legislative mandate. The risk and environmental agencies invariably interpret their legislative mandate as excluding a formal benefit–cost balancing, using the Supreme Court decision in the cotton dust case and related cases to bolster their position. The result has been that the regulatory oversight effort has been restricted to generating marginal improvements in regulations and eliminating some of the very worst regulations. However, some agencies continue to issue many regulations that economists would judge to be inefficient, while other agencies may not be doing enough. A reallocation of regulatory priorities would be beneficial.

Tables 1 and 2 summarize the cost per life saved (with normal life expectancy) of a variety of regulations. These estimates do not, however, include all regulatory benefits, only the mortality effects that are typically the primary justification for the regulation. Suppose we take as our reference point an implicit value of life of $5 million as the cut off for an efficient regulation. This value is midway in the range of labor market estimates of value of a statistical life, which cluster from $3 million to $7 million, and should be a reasonable estimate of society's willingness to pay to avert a statistical death (Viscusi, 1993). By this standard, Table 1 shows regulations that have, in fact, met a benefit–cost test, while Table 2 lists some that have not.

Table 1   The cost of risk-reducing regulations that pass a benefit–cost test per life saved

Regulation	Agency year and status	Initial annual risk	Annual lives saved	Cost per life Saved (millions of 1984 $)
Unvented Space Heaters	CPSC 1980 F	2.7 in 10^5	63.000	$.10
Oil & Gas Well Service	OSHA 1983 P	1.1 in 10^3	50.000	.10
Cabin Fire Protection	FAA 1985 F	6.5 in 10^8	15.000	.20
Passive Restraints/Belts	NHTSA 1984 F	9.1 in 10^5	1,850.000	.30
Underground Construction	OSHA 1989 F	1.6 in 10^3	8.100	.30
Alcohol & Drug Control	FRA 1985 F	1.8 in 10^6	4.200	.50
Servicing Wheel Rims	OSHA 1984 F	1.4 in 10^5	2.300	.50
Seat Cushion Flammability	FAA 1984 F	1.6 in 10^7	37.000	.60
Floor Emergency Lighting	FAA 1984 F	2.2 in 10^8	5.000	.70
Crane Suspended Personnel Platform	OSHA 1988 F	1.8 in 10^3	5.000	1.20
Concrete & Masonry Construction	OSHA 1988 F	1.4 in 10^5	6.500	1.40
Hazard Communication	OSHA 1983 F	4.0 in 10^5	200.000	1.80
Benzene/Fugitive Emissions	EPA 1984 F	2.1 in 10^5	0.310	2.80

"Initial Annual Risk" indicates annual deaths per exposed population; an exposed population of 10^3 is 1,000, 10^4 is 10,000, etc. In "Agency Year and Status" column, *P, R* and *F* represent proposed, rejected and final rule, respectively.

Sources: Viscusi (1992) The table is also based on information presented in Morrall, (1986). These statistics were updated by Morrall via unpublished communication with the author, July 10, 1990.

Most noteworthy is that all regulations in Tables 1 and 2 that were issued by the U.S. Department of Transportation, whether as part of the Federal Aviation Administration (FAA) or the National Highway and Traffic Safety Administration (NHTSA), would pass a benefit–cost test. This strong policy performance is not an aberration. The U.S. Department of Transportation is one of the exceptional agencies that does, in fact, apply benefit–cost analysis in its regulatory efforts. The agency has recently employed an implicit value of life figure just under $3 million, which is at the low end of the value of life spectrum, and it refuses to issue any regulations that cost more than that amount for a statistical life saved. Another transportation-related regulation by the Federal Railroad

Table 2 The cost of risk-reducing regulations that fail a benefit–cost test

Regulation	Agency year and status	Initial annual risk	Annual lives saved	Cost per life saved (millions of 1984 $)
Grain Dust	OSHA 1987 F	2.1 in 10^4	4.000	5.30
Radionuclides/Uranium Mines	EPA 1984 F	1.4 in 10^4	1.100	6.90
Benzene	OSHA 1987 F	8.8 in 10^4	3.800	17.10
Arsenic/Glass Plant	EPA 1986 F	8.0 in 10^4	0.110	19.20
Ethylene Oxide	OSHA 1984 F	4.4 in 10^5	2.800	25.60
Arsenic/Copper Smelter	EPA 1986 F	9.0 in 10^4	0.060	26.50
Uranium Mill Tailings Inactive	EPA 1983 F	4.3 in 10^4	2.100	27.60
Uranium Mill Tailings Active	EPA 1983 F	4.3 in 10^4	2.100	53.00
Asbestos	OSHA 1986 F	6.7 in 10^5	74.700	89.30
Asbestos	EPA 1989 F	2.9 in 10^5	10.000	104.20
Arsenic/Glass Manufacturing	EPA 1986 R	3.8 in 10^5	0.250	142.00
Benzene/Storage	EPA 1984 R	6.0 in 10^7	0.043	202.00
Radionuclides/DOE Facilities	EPA 1984 R	4.3 in 10^6	0.001	210.00
Radionuclides/Elem. Phosphorous	EPA 1984 R	1.4 in 10^5	0.046	270.00
Benzene/Ethylbenzenol Styrene	EPA 1984 R	2.0 in 10^6	0.006	483.00
Arsenic/Low-Arsenic Copper	EPA 1986 R	2.6 in 10^4	0.090	764.00
Benzene/Maleic Anhydride	EPA 1984 R	1.1 in 10^6	0.029	820.00
Land Disposal	EPA 1988 F	2.3 in 10^8	2.520	3,500.00
EDB	OSHA 1989 R	2.5 in 10^4	0.002	15,600.00
Formaldehyde	OSHA 1987 F	6.8 in 10^7	0.010	72,000.00

"Initial Annual Risk" indicates annual deaths per exposed population; an exposed population of 10^3 is 1,000, 10^4 is 10,000, etc. In "Agency Year and Status" column, P, R and F represent proposed, rejected and final rule, respectively.

Sources: Viscusi (1992) The table is also based on information presented in Morrall, (1986). These statistics were updated by Morrall, via unpublished communication with the author, July 10, 1990.

Administration (FRA) also is quite effective in saving lives, with a cost per life saved of $500,000 for alcohol and drug control efforts.

In contrast, the regulations listed in Table 2 would fail a benefit–cost test. Clearly, some agencies like the EPA and OSHA are heavily represented among the regulations that fail such a test most severely. The difference across agencies highlights an opportunity to promote health and safety. If we could expand the safety-related efforts of the U.S. Department of Transportation and utilize the funds that would have otherwise been spent on very inefficient job safety and environmental regulations, we would save many more lives at less cost.

Perhaps the most striking aspect of Table 2 is the limited role that has been played by the OMB oversight effort. No regulation with a cost per life saved of under $142 million per life has ever been rejected by OMB as part of the oversight effort (indicated by R in the second column). Remember, agencies can override OMB objections by appealing to the absolute character of their legislative mandate. In addition, many regulatory efforts are not subject to OMB review. The OMB regulatory review process only pertains to new regulations issued by regulatory agencies; as a result, regulations on the books for many years are exempt from review. In other cases, such as the EPA Superfund program, the agency implements regulatory guidelines that are broadly specified in legislation without specifically issuing new regulatory policies. This Superfund program, which is devoted to the cleanup of hazardous waste, prevents expected cases of cancer at a median cost of $3.6 billion dollars per expected case (Viscusi and Hamilton, 1996), making it one of the least cost-effective government efforts. The OMB regulatory oversight unit has no leverage over governmental policies such as this in which no new regulatory policies are formally promulgated.

Regulatory Reform Legislation: An Overview

A variety of legislative changes have been proposed to remedy these deficiencies and to put risk regulations on sounder statistical footing, including both omnibus bills that would pertain to regulation generally and bills dealing with specific areas of regulation.[12] The political economy of these efforts to make regulations more efficient is often complex. Business interests presumably benefit from more regulatory restraint. However, corporate interests in less regulation are not always socially desirable. The beneficiaries of regulation also have mixed interests. Not all workers are made better off because of excessively stringent job safety regulations. Workers who lose their jobs because of inefficient regulations gain from reforms, as do average consumers. The most clear-cut political economy linkage was the prominent role of regulatory reform in Representative Gingrich's Contract with America.

These bills differ along a number of dimensions. Most focus exclusively on risk and environmental regulations; others also seek to reform more traditional rate regulation. The various regulatory reform bills have included a differing but wide range of provisions that would increase the requirements placed on the regulatory bodies. In some cases, regulatory agencies would be required to undertake retrospective analyses of existing regulations to determine their merits, whereas in others the emphasis is only on new regulations. Some bills would also require that agencies assess comparative risks for different regulatory policies, establish peer review panels to evaluate the scientific evidence underlying the regulatory proposal and create a formal recognition of the potential for judicial review of the regulatory proposal to assess whether the economic merits of the regulation do in fact meet the required test of benefits being in excess of the costs. These various institutional requirements do not introduce new economic tests that must be met by regulation, but nevertheless may have a strong impact on the structure of regulations and the speed with which regulations can be adopted. The transactions costs of issuing regulations are likely to soar under some of the proposals, particularly those that provide for judicial tests of economic analyses. This section will focus on the differences and issues that are of greatest interest to economists: benefit–cost analysis, performance vs. specification standards, the theories of risk–risk analysis, and the science and bias of risk assessment.

Benefit–cost analysis

From the standpoint of many economists, the centerpiece of the proposals for regulatory reform is the requirement that benefits of the regulation exceed the costs. In its most sweeping form, the requirement for passing a benefit–cost test would become a super-mandate, which overrides any possibly conflicting legislative guidelines.[13] Without such a super-mandate provision, the reform bills would be of little more than symbolic value, for the various reasons discussed earlier. But even if there were broad agreement on a super-mandate, exactly how this benefit–cost test is specified would be controversial. Under restrictive versions of the legislation, benefits are required to exceed costs before a regulation can be issued. These restrictive approaches may also exclude benefits that are judged to be speculative, thus limiting the potential range of commodities valued. More open-ended variants of the legislation would require that benefits bear a "reasonable relationship to costs" or some similarly structured language that falls short of a rigid benefit–cost test.

If all consequences of policies could be readily monetized, this distinction would not be consequential. However, many outcomes have nonmonetary consequences for which attaching dollar values remains quite controversial. For example, how might one measure the benefits of affirmative action requirements or improved access for the handicapped? Many of the most controversial issues of valuation involve the environment: what, for example, is the value to society of an endangered species? This value is almost entirely a passive use or non use value. Quantifying the passive use value of an endangered species might require contingent valuation survey techniques to elicit society's willingness to pay for preserving these species, but this approach is extremely controversial.[14] Since no market currently exists for society's value of endangered species, even conceptualizing how an individual might express such a valuation or think about this valuation process within the context of his or her current resource allocations raises considerable difficulties. Indeed, the debate over valuing passive use of environmental and natural resource out-comes is so fierce that there were even congressional proposals in 1995 to prevent agencies from considering such values on the grounds that they are too speculative.

The fact that many environmental outcomes cannot be readily monetized does not necessarily imply that they should be ignored. However, once the benefit–cost test becomes amended with language to encompass outcomes that cannot be readily monetized, the benefit–cost requirement may lose some of its appeal. But even an outcome that required a fuzzier benefit–cost test, without trying to monetize all benefits, would never-theless represent a substantial departure from the current approach in which agencies have little accountability with respect to balancing at all because of their narrow interpretation of their legislative mandates.

Another possibility is to have legislation that permits agencies to consider benefit–cost balancing, but not to require that they show that benefits are in excess of the costs. In this instance, the regulatory oversight group at OMB might be able to use this structure to monitor regulatory agency actions and promote more balanced policies without imposing a formal benefit–cost requirement.

Performance vs. specification standards

An economic corollary to the desirability of a benefit–cost test is that companies should have the flexibility to adopt the least cost means of meeting the risk reduction objective specified in the regulations, such as the bubble policy. A performance standard would give companies such leeway, whereas a specification standard would mandate specific compliance technologies, such as a particular type of guard for machinery.

A relatively large-scale experiment with the performance approach has taken place with respect to EPA emissions regulations. The most ambitious of these efforts, in effect, establishes a market for pollution using tradable pollution permits. Carlin (1992) has estimated that the more recent tradable permit system saves about $1 billion annually in pollution control costs by shifting the burden of pollution to sources where pollution can be reduced most cheaply.

Some of the regulatory reform bills included provisions to promote a performance-oriented rather than a technology-forcing approach.[15] These efforts have broad support among economists but are subject to two principal objections. First, agencies may be better able to monitor compliance with technology-forcing standards. In many instances, however, such as the OSHA grain dust standard, it has been possible to incorporate flexibility with a standard that can be monitored. Second, flexible standards may have political repercussions (Crandall, 1983). If companies could meet air pollution requirements by shifting to low sulphur coal from the American west rather than installing scrubbers, it would be more cost-effective but would adversely affect coal production in West Virginia. Not surprisingly, West Virginia legislators (notably Senator Byrd) opposed such discretion.

Risk–risk analysis

Perhaps in part because of the long-term failure of government agencies to adopt a balanced benefit–cost approach, economists have developed a series of other more limited tests that can be applied to policy. Three variants of this approach come under the heading of risk–risk analysis – that is, to compare the risks generated by the regulation with the risks reduced by the regulation to determine the net risk effects. The basic idea of this methodology is that government regulations have competing effects and that, even if one's sole concern is with risk levels, some regulations may not be desirable. Some thinking from this approach has been incorporated into proposed legislation.

The first type of risk–risk tradeoff is what economists might term moral hazard risks but which the regulatory reform legislation has termed "substitution risks."[16] In his analysis of the effect of seat belts on auto safety, for example, Peltzman (1975) hypothesized that drivers would drive faster and become less careful after wearing seat belts because the safety benefits from added care had been diminished. His empirical evidence suggested that offsetting behavior on the part of drivers may have accounted for the very weak effect that seat belts seem to have had on traffic safety. Other studies suggest that seat belts may have enhanced driver safety but may increase the risks to pedestrians and motorcyclists. However, there is considerable controversy with respect to the magnitude of the effect (Blomquist, 1988).

A variant of this moral hazard risk stems from what Viscusi (1984) termed the "lulling effect." Consumers may be lulled into a false sense of security by the existence of safety mechanisms. In the case of safety caps designed to prevent child poisonings, there is evidence that parents became excessively lax about access to the products once the caps were in place. The result is that there is no significant enhancement of the safety of products for which the caps were intended, and there was an apparent increase in risks for other risky products as the decrease in parental responsibility had apparent spillover effects with respect to safety protections more generally.

A second class of risk–risk analysis begins by noticing that regulatory efforts frequently generate new economic activity; for example, perhaps to manufacture pollution control devices or remove waste from hazardous waste sites. These risks, like most other economic activity, also generate new hazards. Viscusi and Zeckhauser (1994) show that the occupational risk cost of expenditures is approximately 3 to 4 percent of total costs, on average. Thus, every time the government incurs $100 million in regulatory costs, injuries and deaths created by these expenditures will have a total value of $3–4 million. This loss can become consequential in terms of assessing the overall attractiveness of the effort, particularly if the regulatory policy is extremely ineffective. If one assumes that 4 percent of all costs are fatality and injury costs, then there will be $5 million of fatality and injury losses for every $125 million in expenditures. Suppose the policy directly saves one statistical life for each $125 million in costs. If the implicit value of life is $5 million, then this policy will be exactly a break-even proposition in risk terms since it saves and loses one statistical life for each $125 million expenditure. For the regulations in Table 2 for which the cost per life saved exceeds $125 million, the value of the health losses directly generated by the regulation will be at least as great as the value of the health benefits provided by the regulation.

A third version of risk–risk analysis provides perhaps the strongest test of regulatory attractiveness. Regulatory expenditures, in effect, make society poorer by diverting resources that could be used for other purposes, such as food and housing. Because there is a link between higher income and longevity, the opportunity costs from regulations will impose mortality costs.

A vivid way to pose the empirical issue here is to determine what level of regulatory expenditure will lead to a statistical death. Using data relating international mortality rates to income levels, Lutter and Morrall (1994) calculate the expenditure level per statistical death to be between $9 million to $12 million. Of course, assessments such as these raise a variety of concerns, such as disentangling the simultaneous nature of the health–mortality linkage, as discussed by Smith, Epp and Schwabe (1994) and others. A more fundamental issue is the plausibility of this value range. Since evidence suggests that society is willing to spend $3–$7 million to save a statistical life, it seems unlikely that an only slightly higher expenditure would lead to the loss of a statistical life. It would barely be consistent to, on the one hand, be willing to spend, say, $7 million to save a statistical life, if every time we spent $9 million there was the loss of a statistical life. If that were the case, life saving expenditures would barely be a break-even proposition.

An alternative approach introduced in Viscusi (1994) gives another way to think about the expenditure level that leads to a statistical death. Instead of an econometric approach, this concept is specifically linked to estimates of the implicit value of saving a life. To be more specific, it relies on the insight that the expenditure level that leads to a statistical death equals the implicit value of life divided by the marginal propensity to spend on mortality-reducing commodities. Using this approach, Viscusi estimated that $50 million in expenditures would lead to the loss of a statistical life, which is a number that is more consistent with estimates of the amount society is willing to spend to save statistical lives.

The various approaches of risk–risk analysis are in early stages of development and remain controversial. However, as noted earlier, utilization of a risk–risk test has been suggested by a federal court judge as well as by a head of the OMB regulatory oversight group.[17] These risk–risk tests are only very partial tests of policy efficacy. But if benefit–cost analysis is not permitted, then some much weaker test can at least help in weeding out the most inefficient regulations. Naturally, the ideal outcome is to develop a meaningful overall test of the attractiveness of regulatory policies so that it will not be necessary to resort to these more partial policy evaluation criteria.

The science and bias of risk assessment

Along with benefit–cost analysis, guidelines for risk assessment comprise the core of all the regulatory reform proposals. These issues may seem largely scientific, but they also pertain to the appropriate economic policy criteria for policy assessment as well. The issue is whether government agencies should use "conservative" risk assessments that pertain to upper bounds, even if these involve unlikely scenarios that might create particularly adverse consequences, or whether they should rely instead on unbiased risk assessments pertaining to the mean risk.

From a statistical decision theory standpoint, if we are concerned with maximizing the expected benefits of government efforts, we should rely upon the mean risk values in making these assessments rather than some other value along the risk distribution. However, the prevailing practice in the federal government is to utilize some kind of upper bound for the risk in the interest of "conservatism." This bias toward conservatism can intrude upon the risk assessment to a considerable extent (Nichols and Zeckhauser, 1986) because it is typically manifested on a parameter by parameter basis, not simply by selecting the 95th percentile of the overall risk distribution. Thus, in the case analysis of Superfund risks from groundwater contamination, the agency uses the maximum concentration of the chemical found at the site and an upper bound value of four other parameters to calculate the risk. The result is that the sequence of conservative assumptions is compounded, so that the overall degree of conservatism is much greater. Indeed, in the case of Superfund, the estimated risk values are well beyond the 99th percentile of the overall risk distribution (Viscusi and Hamilton, 1996).

It is probably impossible for policymakers to ascertain the degree of conservative bias. The extent of the bias varies according to agency and even according to the particular policy action within each agency. Since government analysts do not typically report the lower bound or the mean risk assessment, policymakers have no sense of the true risk, only what might prevail under a worst case scenario. Virtually all the regulatory reform bills would require that the agency report some type of mean or central tendency of the risk. If agencies choose to report an upper bound, the bills would also require them to report a lower bound so that policy analysts can assess the range of risk and scientific opinion.

This controversy relates more generally to the economic problems arising with respect to risk ambiguity. The well-known Ellsberg paradox (1961), for example, demonstrated that individuals have a preference for precise opportunities of winning a prize. In particular, how do people react to "hard" probabilities, such as those based on detailed objective evidence as opposed to "soft" probabilities that are subjectively determined relying primarily on individual judgment? A rational decision maker should be indifferent to a lottery that offers a "hard" 0.5 probability of a prize to a lottery that offers a "soft" 0.5 probability that is known with less precision; for example, people prefer choosing a black or white ball from an urn where the proportion of balls is known to be half and half, rather than choosing from an urn where they do not know the proportion of balls and thus must make a rational default assumption that the chance of drawing a black or white ball is 50:50. People generally prefer the lottery for which the probability is known with precision. In the loss dimension, the counterpart result is that people are averse to ambiguous chances of harms, including those from environmental damage (Viscusi, 1992). This anomaly does not arise because of risk aversion. Rather, there is aversion to imprecisely defined probabilities, which is one of the classic contradictions of economic rationality. One possible explanation for the conservatism bias is that government agencies have institutionalized the ambiguity aversion bias in decision making through their risk assessment practices.

From a policy standpoint, providing a fuller statistical characterization could eliminate potential distortions in regulatory priorities. Suppose that for Policy A the risk of cancer is 59 per million and that this probability is known with precision, whereas with Policy B the scientists are evenly divided as to whether the risk is zero or 60 per million. Their mean risk assessment is 30 per million. Current risk assessment practices would summarize the risk levels based solely on the upper bound values, giving Policy B a higher risk ranking even though its mean value is about half that of Policy A, and its upper bound value is almost the same as the risk for Policy A that is known with precision. The result is that agencies tilt policy priorities toward risks that are least precisely understood rather than those risks for which the expected benefits to society from regulation are the greatest. Legislation to change this treatment of uncertainty could save a greater expected number of lives.

Conclusion

The controversy over the regulatory reform legislation is really over the practical applicability of economic principles. In the abstract, it is difficult (at least for an economist) to disagree with benefit–cost analysis. But in practice, what provision should be made for benefits that cannot be quantified? Must all benefits and costs be monetized? Should estimation of risks be delegated to scientists? Is there a legitimate role for the public to play in deciding whether these risk estimates should be taken from the conservative edge of existing estimates or from the mainstream? The policy debate over applying benefit–cost analysis has been further clouded because the bills include a myriad of institutional reforms that would affect the process of issuing regulation and could often lead to additional delays, such as the establishment of peer review panels and judicial review.

Almost since the inception of the risk and environmental agencies in the early 1970s, there has been a continuing concern with ensuring that regulations yield societal benefits commensurate with their costs. This recognition of the need for balance, in turn, has led policymakers to seek a greater role for economists, and the principles of economic analysis undoubtedly will continue to play a central role in the debate over the future of regulatory policy.

Notes

1   All subsequent discussion of House and Senate bills will refer to those introduced in the 104th Congress. In March 1995, the House of Representatives inserted the regulatory reform bill H.R. 1022 into another piece of legislation, H.R. 9, which was passed.

2   The Food and Drug Administration (FDA) and EPA, for example, target lifetime risks of 1 in 100,000 which, over a 70-year assumed lifetime, are actually much smaller than 1 in a million. In the case of the EPA Superfund program, cleanup is mandatory for lifetime cancer risks in excess of 10^{-4} and discretionary for risks between 10^{-4} and 10^{-6}.

3   See Wilson (1979) for a more comprehensive tally of one in a million risks.

4   Section 26 of the Occupational Safety and Health Act of 1970, 29 U.S.C. §651 (1976).

5   See the decision of the U.S. Supreme Court in *Industrial Union Department, AFL-CIO v American Petroleum Institute*, 448 U.S. 607 (1980).

6   See the decision of the U.S. Supreme Court in *American Textile Manufacturer's Institute v Donovan*, 452 U.S. 490 (1981).

7   See *UAW v Occupational Safety & Health Administration*, 938 F.2d 1310 (D.C. Circuit 1991).

8   See *Chevron USA Inc. v NRDC*, 467 U.S. 837 (1984).

9   The Carter effort was defined by Executive Order 12044, March 23, 1978 (Carter, 1979). The principal precursor was the Ford Executive Order 11821, November 27, 1974 (Ford, 1974).

10   Executive Order 12291, February 17, 1981, was the pivotal action that led to the adoption of the benefit–cost approach (Reagan, 1982).

11   The Clinton Executive Order No. 12866, issued September 30, 1993, broadened the definition of benefits to emphasize the nonmonetary character of many effects (Clinton, 1993).

12   For examples of omnibus bills, see H.R. 1022 (passed as part of H.R.9), H.R. 690, H.R. 1923, and S. 343. For examples of particular bills, see H.R. 1028, which pertains to Superfund, and S. 333, which deals with energy risk management.

13   One example of a bill in which there is an exemption for conflicting legislative provisions is S. 343. H.R. 1022 would override current legislative mandates.

14   See, for example, the symposium on contingent valuation in the Fall 1994 issue of this journal, with papers by Portney, Hanemann, and Diamond and Hausman. See also Carson et al. (1994).

15   See, for example, S.291 and S. 343.

16   H.R.1022, for example, includes extensive provisions requiring that agencies recognize substitution risks and incorporate them into theiranalysis. Graham and Wiener (1995) consider a variety of these examples, as does Lave (1981).

17   See in particular *UAW v OSHA*, United States Court of Appeals for the District of Columbia Circuit 89–1559 and the letter from James MacRae, Acting Administrator, Office of Information and Regulatory Affairs to Nancy Risque-Rohrbach, Assistant Secretary for Policy, U.S. Department of Labor, Washington, D.C., September 16, 1992.

References

Blomquist, G. (1988): *The Regulation of Motor Vehicle and Traffic Safety*. Boston: Kluwer Academic Publishers.

Carlin, A. (1992): "The United States Experience with Economic Incentives to Control Environmental Pollution," draft, EPA Office of Policy, Planning and Evaluation, No. 230-R-92-001, February.

Carson, R. T., Mitchell, R. C., Hanemann, W. M., Kopp, R. J., Presser, S. and Rudd, P. A. (1994): *Contingent Valuation and Lost Passive Use: Damages from the Exxon Valdez*. Discussion paper, 94 (18), March, Washington, D.C.: Resources for the Future.

Carter, J. (1979): "Improving Government Regulations, Executive Order 12044," March 23, 1978, in *Public Papers of the President of the United States, Jimmy Carter, 1978, Book I: January 1 to June 30, 1978*. Washington, D.C.: U.S. Government Printing Office, 558–61.

Clinton, B. (1993): "Regulatory Planning and Review, Executive Order 12866," September 30, 1993, in *Weekly Compilation of Presidential Documents, 1993: October–December Index*. Vol 29, Nos. 39–52, Washington, D.C.: U.S. Government Printing Office, 1925–33.

Crandall, R. (1983): *Controlling Industrial Pollution: The Economics and Politics of Clean Air*. Washington, D.C.: Brookings Institution.

Diamond, P. and Hausman, J. (1994): "Contingent Valuation: Is Some Number Better Than No Number?", *Journal of Economic Perspectives*, 8 (4), 45–64.

Ellsberg, D. (1961): "Risk, Ambiguity, and the Savage Axioms," *Quarterly Journal of Economics*, 75, November 643–69.

Ford, G. (1974): "*Inflation Impact Statements, Executive Order 11821*." 3 Code of Federal Regulations, November 27, 926.

Graham, J. D. and Wiener, J. B. (eds) (1995): *Risk vs. Risk: Tradeoffs in Protecting Health and the Environment*. Cambridge: Harvard University Press.

Hanemann, W. M. (1994): "Valuing the Environment Through Contingent Valuation," *Journal of Economic Perspectives*, 8 (4), 19–43.

Hopkins, T. D. (1992): *Costs of Regulation: Filling the Gaps*. Report prepared for Regulatory Information Service Center, Washington, D.C., August.

Lave, L. B. (1981): *The Strategy of Social Regulation: Decision Frameworks for Policy*. Washington, D.C.: Brookings Institution.

Lutter, R. and Morrall, J. F. III, "Health-Health Analysis: A New Way to Evaluate Health and Safety Regulation," *Journal of Risk and Uncertainty*, 8 (1), 43–66.

Morrall, J. F. III (1986): "A Review of the Record," *Regulation*, 10 (2), 25–34.

Nichols, A. and Zeckhauser, R. J. (1986): "The Perils of Prudence: How Conservative Risk Assessments Distort Regulation," *Regulation*, 10 (2), 13–24.

Peltzman, S. (1975): "The Effects of Automobile Safety Regulation," *Journal of Political Economy*, 83 (4), 677–725.

Portney, P. (1994): "The Contingent Valuation Debate: Why Economists Should Care," *Journal of Economic Perspectives*, 8 (4), 3–17.

Reagan, R. (1982): "Federal Regulation, Executive Order 12291," February 17, 1981. In *Public Papers of the President of the United States, Ronald Reagan, 1981: January 20 to December 31, 1981*. Washington, D.C.: U.S. Government Printing Office, 104–08.

Smith, V. K., Epp, D. and Schwabe, K. (1994): "Cross-Country Analyses Don't Estimate Health-Health Responses," *Journal of Risk and Uncertainty*, 8 (1), 67–84.

Viscusi, W. K. (1984): "The Lulling Effect: The Impact of Child-Resistant Packaging on Aspirin and Analgesic Ingestions," *American Economic Review*, 74, May, 324–7.

——(1992): *Fatal Tradeoffs: Public and Private Responsibilities for Risk*. New York: Oxford University Press.

——(1993): "The Value of Risks to Life and Health," *Journal of Economic Literature*, 31 (4), 1912–46.

——(1994): "Mortality Effects of Regulatory Costs and Policy Evaluation Criteria," *Rand Journal of Economics*, 25 (1), Spring, 94–109.

——and Hamilton, J. T. (1996): "Cleaning Up Superfund," *The Public Interest*.

——and Zeckhauser, R. (1994): "The Fatality and Injury Costs of Expenditures," *Journal of Risk and Uncertainty*, 8 (1), 271–93.

Wilson, R. (1979): "Analyzing the Daily Risks of Life," *Technology Review*, 81 (4), 40–6.

PART V

Public Goods and Investment

Introduction

Chapter 15 is a seminal article by Samuelson in which he formalizes the introduction of public goods into the computation of a social welfare maximum (given the existence of a social welfare function, for a discussion of which see chapter 7). In the first-order necessary conditions for such an optimum, the marginal rates of substitution for each public good whose consumption is nonrivalrous must be summed over all consumers and equated to the marginal rate of technical substitution in their production. In addition, along with private goods which can be consumed by only one consumer, the marginal social worth of each consumer's marginal consumption of each product must be equal to every other consumer's marginal social worth of their marginal consumption of that good.

The most important contribution of the article is the demonstration of the need to add consumers' marginal rates of substitution for public goods vertically to compute their optimal production. However, Samuelson also discusses the inability of the market to yield the individuals' preferences for such goods as raw material for the Wise People who formalize the social welfare function. Because, unlike the private goods whose marginal rates of substitution are equated to prices in purely competitive markets by the rational actions of consumers, the consumers of public goods do not reveal their preferences in this way, and have an incentive to present, in nonmarket ways, indications of the utility they derive from such which are smaller than the true values. This is true because the Wise People must devise an optimal set of flat taxes and subsidies to bring about the optimal income distribution necessary for the social welfare optimum, and the revelation of smaller-than-true marginal rates of substitutions for public goods will reduce such taxes or increase subsidies. Moreover, fewer public goods will be produced than would be if the social welfare optimum reflected their true psychic values.

Individuals discount private investments' expected returns for time and for risk, at a risk discount that is dependent on their attitudes to risk. In decisions concerning uncertain public investments, how should the government treat their riskiness? Should the discount rate ruling in private markets, reflecting in part private attitudes to risk, be adopted straightforwardly for public decision making? Or should governments, because of their ability to spread risks over a large number of projects and to ignore such potentials as moral hazard or fraudulent behavior, adopt risk neutrality and discount for time alone? Or should governments ignore the atomistic decision making of the private market and search for a public rate of risk discount that reflects the pecularities of the public investment gestalt?

In chapter 16, Arrow and Lind opt for an approach of the first type, in which private attitudes toward risk should be taken into account in public investment, but modify the usual argument for such procedure (based largely on Hirshleifer's work). The necessity of the modification is based on Arrow's well-known argument that first-best Pareto optima can be achieved only if perfectly competitive markets for insurance exist on risky payoffs in all potential states of nature over the life of the investment.

For uncertain government investments, therefore, given different individual attitudes to risk bearing that cannot be neutralized by hedging in markets, net benefits, after taking into account the costs of risk-bearing, depend on which individuals benefit and which bear the costs. The social cost of risk bearing is the expected value of the investment over its life, less the costs of risk bearing of beneficiaries and cost-bearers. The authors' basic argument is that the social cost of risk bearing is spread over n beneficiaries and cost-bearers, and, where n is large, the individual share approaches zero. Hence, the individual cost of risk bearing is negligible and, although taken into account, government investment under uncertainty can essentially ignore it. Because it is taken into account, the procedure is consistent with the need to treat such risk-bearing costs on the same basis as private investment. The second-best optimum approaches the first-best (if it exists) very closely.

Arrow and Lind also take into account the case where the beneficiaries of a public investment do not receive negligible benefits, in which case their cost of risk bearing should be taken into account. Interestingly, they extend their arguments to the case of large corporations with large numbers of stockholders, in which case their conclusion is the same as the general case discussed above. However, they indicate that the managers of the corporation may be quite risk-averse and capable of injecting their risk-bearing costs into the computation of net benefits.

Chapter 17 and 18 deal with the social welfare aspects of governmental divestiture of assets rather than their acquisition, and do so in an enlightening manner. In chapter 17, McMillan, who acted as a Federal Communications Commission (FCC) economist, discusses the questions raised by economists in structuring the auctions that took place in 1994 to divest the radio spectrum relinquished by the military for personal communications services (PCS). Congress mandated that award of spectrum licenses by auction was to replace their haphazard award by lottery. The distinctive characteristic of the spectra awards was their complementarity by region and spectrum location. Efficiency demanded that contiguous "networks" be constructed by successful bidders.

Auction theory, originating largely as a tool of game theorists in analyzing competitive behavior, took on a life of its own in designing efficient policy and analyzing deficiencies of auction procedures, and the FCC took advantage of economic expertise in designing auction specifics to achieve its ends. These were the implementation of fair and feasible auction procedures to achieve efficient geographic and spectrum aggregates, avoiding monopolistic control of regional PCS, awarding favorable treatment to certain minorities, women and small businesses, while at the same time, within these primary constraints, maximizing government revenue. Licenses granted the use of spectrum for ten years, with effective *de facto* renewal at the end of the period.

Faulty auctions in New Zealand and Australia, discussed in the chapter, provided cautionary guidance to economists, but the task remained a formidable one. No markets existed for such PCS services (as opposed to cellular phone service). The basic questions debated by economists, and resolved by the FCC, concerned the type of auction that best suited social purposes, simultaneously or sequentially run, aggregated by area or spectrum bloc, with or without government royalties, and method of granting favored-party preferences. McMillan discusses the issues involved in such choices and the FCC decisions resolving them.

The chapter, therefore, is an *ex ante facto* study of economic policy design by economic theoriests in the face of uncertainty and within a dominantly game theoretic context. The effort was to foresee potential pitfalls that might interfere with the social objectives specified broadly by Congress and in detail by the FCC, and to design auction procedures to forestall them. What makes the discussion doubly interesting is that in chapter 18, written by McAfee and McMillan, the former also an economist who participated actively in the design phase, we are presented with an early postmortem of the auction that permits a tentative evaluation of the economists' and FCC auction design.

Chapter 18, then, offers an early judgment of the success of the spectrum auction experiment, in that it was written after the first three of the five auctions. Two of the three were for narrowband sales and one for broadband portions of the spectrum. The authors judge the outstanding success of the auctions to be the form selected: simultaneous ascending auctions of spectra with strong substitution or complementary characteristics, conducted by sequences of rounds during which successful bidders in prior rounds could cancel earlier winning bids in light of their successes in later rounds in fulfilling hopes of creating efficient aggregations. At the end of each round, the government released information concerning the bids and bidders, and the rounds continued until bidding ceased. The authors do not discuss how much signaling, if any, occurred among the bidders, implying collusion. They analyze the bidding strategies in the auctions, the apparent efficiency in creating efficient aggregations, the success in awarding spectra to "designated" minority and other favored bidders, and the potential for application to auctions in other areas where complementarities exist.

CHAPTER FIFTEEN

The Pure Theory of Public Expenditure

Paul A. Samuelson

Source: *Review of Economics and Statistics*, 36 (1954), pp. 387–9. Reprinted with the permission of The MIT Press. © The MIT Press.

1. Assumptions

Except for Sax, Wicksell, Lindahl, Musgrave, and Bowen, economists have rather neglected the theory of optimal public expenditure, spending most of their energy on the theory of taxation. Therefore, I explicitly assume two categories of goods: ordinary *private consumption goods* $(X_1 \ldots, X_n)$ which can be parcelled out among different individuals $(1, 2, \ldots, i, \ldots, s)$ according to the relations

$$X_j = \sum_1^s X_j^i$$

and *collective consumption goods* $(X_{n+1}, \ldots, X_{n+m})$ which all enjoy in common in the sense that each individual's consumption of such a good leads to no subtraction from any other individual's consumption of that good, so that $X_{n+j} = X_{n+j}^i$ simultaneously for each and every ith individual and each collective consumptive good. I assume no mystical collective mind that enjoys collective consumption goods; instead I assume each individual has a consistent set of *ordinal preferences* with respect to his consumption of all goods (collective as well as private) which can be summarized by a regularly smooth and convex utility index

$$u^i = u^i \left(X_1^i, \ldots, X_{n+m}^i \right)$$

(any monotonic stretching of the utility index is of course also an admissible cardinal index of preference). I shall throughout follow the convention of writing the partial derivative of any function with respect to its jth argument by a j subscript, so that $u_j^i = \partial u^i / \partial X_j^i$, etc. Provided economic quantities can be divided into two groups, (1) *outputs* or goods which everyone always wants to maximize and (2) inputs or factors which everyone always wants to minimize, we are free to change the algebraic signs of the latter category and from then on to work only with "goods," knowing that the case of factor inputs is covered as well. Hence by this convention we are sure that $u_j^i > 0$ always.

To keep production assumptions at the minimum level of simplicity, I assume a regularly convex and smooth production-possibility schedule relating totals of all outputs, private and collective; or $F(X_1, \ldots, X_{n+m}) = 0$, with $F_j > 0$ and ratios F_j/F_n determinate and subject to the generalized laws of diminishing returns.

Feasibility considerations disregarded, there is a *maximal* (ordinal) *utility frontier* representing the Pareto-optimal points – of which there are an $(s-1)$ fold infinity – with the property that from such a frontier point you can make one person better off only by making some other person worse off. If we wish to make normative judgments concerning the relative ethical desirability of different configurations involving some individuals being on a higher level of indifference and some on a lower, we must be presented with a set of ordinal interpersonal norms or with a *social welfare function* representing a consistent set of ethical preferences among all the possible states of the system. It is not a "scientific" task of the economist to "deduce" the form of this function; this can have as many forms as there are possible ethical views; for the present purpose, the only restriction placed on the social welfare function is that it shall always increase or decrease when any one person's ordinal preference increases or decreases, all others staying on their same indifference levels: mathematically, we narrow it to the class that any one of its indexes can be written $U = U(u^1, \ldots, u^s)$ with $U_j > 0$.

2. Optimal Conditions

In terms of these norms, there is a "best state of the world" which is defined mathematically in simple regular cases by the marginal conditions

$$\frac{u^i_j}{u^i_r} = \frac{F_j}{F_r} \qquad (i = 1, 2, \ldots, s; r, j = 1, \ldots, n) \text{ or} \tag{1}$$

$$(i = 1, 2, \ldots, s; r = 1; j = 2, \ldots, n)$$

$$\sum_{i=1}^{s} \frac{u^i_{n+j}}{u^i_r} = \frac{F_{n+j}}{F_r} \qquad (j = 1 \ldots, m; r = 1, \ldots, n) \text{ or} \tag{2}$$

$$(j = 1, \ldots, m; r = 1)$$

$$\frac{U_i u^i_k}{U_q u^q_k} = 1 \qquad (i, q = 1, \ldots, s; k = 1, \ldots, n) \text{ or } (q = 1; i = 2, \ldots, s; k = 1) \tag{3}$$

Equations (1) and (3) are essentially those given in the chapter on welfare economics in my *Foundations of Economic Analysis*. They constitute my version of the "new welfare economics." Alone (1) represents that subset of relations which defines the Pareto-optimal utility frontier and which by itself represents what I regard as the unnecessarily narrow version of what once was called the "new welfare economics."

The new element added here is the set (2), which constitutes a pure theory of government expenditure on collective consumption goods. By themselves (1) and (2) define the $(s-1)$ fold infinity of utility frontier points; only when a set of interpersonal normative conditions equivalent to (3) is supplied are we able to define an unambiguously "best" state.

Since formulating the conditions (2) some years ago, I have learned from the published and unpublished writings of Richard Musgrave that their essential logic is contained in the "voluntary-exchange" theories of public finance of the Sax–Wicksell–Lindahl–Musgrave type, and I have also noted Howard Bowen's independent discovery of them in Bowen's writings of a decade ago. A graphical interpretation of these conditions in terms of *vertical* rather than *horizontal* addition of different individuals' marginal-rate-of-substitution schedules can be given; but what I must emphasize is that there is a different such schedule for each individual at each of the $(s-1)$ fold infinity of different distributions of relative welfare along the utility frontier.

3. Impossibility of Decentralized Spontaneous Solution

So much for the involved optimizing equations that an omniscient calculating machine could theoretically solve if fed the postulated functions. No such machine now exists. But it is well known that an "analogue calculating machine" can be provided by competitive market pricing, (a) so long as the production functions satisfy the neoclassical assumptions of constant returns to scale and generalized diminishing returns and (b) so long as the individual's indifference contours have regular convexity and, we may add, (c) so long as all goods are private. We can then insert between the right-and left-hand sides of (1) the equality with uniform market prices p_j/p_r and adjoin the budget equations for each individual

$$p_1 X_1^i + p_2 X_2^i + \ldots + p_n X_n^i = L^i \ (i = 1, 2, \ldots, s) \tag{1}$$

where L^i is a lump-sum tax for each individual so selected in algebraic value as to lead to the "best" state of the world. Now note, if there were no collective consumption goods, then (1) and (1)' can have their solution enormously simplified. Why? Because on the one hand perfect competition among productive enterprises would ensure that goods are produced at minimum costs and are sold at proper marginal costs, with all factors receiving their proper marginal productivities; and on the other hand, each individual, in seeking as a competitive buyer to get to the highest level of indifference subject to given prices and tax, would be led as if by an Invisible Hand to the grand solution of the social maximum position. Of course the institutional framework of competition would have to be maintained, and political decision making would still be necessary, but of a computation-ally minimum type: namely, algebraic taxes and transfers $(L^1, \ldots L^s)$ would have to be varied until society is swung to the ethical observer's optimum. The servant of the ethical observer would not have to make explicit decisions about each person's detailed consump-tion and work; he need only decide about generalized purchasing power, knowing that each person can be counted on to allocate it optimally. In terms of communication theory and game terminology, each person is motivated to do the signaling of his tastes needed to define and reach the attainable-bliss point.

Now all of the above remains valid even if collective consumption is not zero but is instead *explicitly set* at its optimum values as determined by (1), (2), and (3). *However no decentralized pricing system can serve to determine optimally these levels of collective consumption.* Other kinds of "voting" or "signaling" would have to be tried. But, and this is the point sensed by Wicksell but perhaps not fully appreciated by Lindahl, now it is in the selfish interest of each person to give *false* signals, to pretend to have less interest in a given collective consumption activity than he really has, etc. I must emphasize this: taxing according to a benefit theory of taxation can not at all solve the computational problem in the decentralized manner possible for the first category of "private" goods to which the ordinary market pricing applies and which do not have the "external effects" basic to the very notion of collective consumption goods. Of course, utopian voting and signaling schemes can be imagined. ("Scandinavian consensus," Kant's "categorical imperative," and other devices meaningful only under conditions of "symmetry," etc.) The failure of market catallactics in no way denies the following truth: given sufficient knowledge the optimal decisions can always be found by scanning over all the attainable states of the world and selecting the one which according to the postulated ethical welfare function is best. The solution "exists"; the problem is how to "find" it.

One could imagine every person in the community being indoctrinated to behave like a "parametric decentralized bureaucrat" who *reveals* his preferences by signaling in response to price parameters or Lagrangean multipliers, to questionnaires, or to other devices. But there is still this fundamental technical difference going to the heart of the whole problem of *social* economy: by departing from his indoctrinated rules, any one person can hope to snatch some selfish benefit in a way not possible under the self-policing competitive pricing of private goods; and the "external economies" or "jointness of demand" intrinsic to the very concept of collective goods and governmental activities makes it impossible for the grand ensemble of optimizing equations to have that special pattern of zeros which makes *laissez-faire* competition even *theoretically* possible as an analogue computer.

4. Conclusion

To explore further the problem raised by public expenditure would take us into the mathematical domain of "sociology" or "welfare politics," which Arrow, Duncan Black, and others have just begun to investigate. Political economy can be regarded as one special sector of this general domain, and it may turn out to be pure luck that within the general domain there happened to be a subsector with the "simple" properties of traditional economics.

CHAPTER SIXTEEN

Uncertainty and the Evaluation of Public Investment Decisions

KENNETH J. ARROW AND ROBERT C. LIND

Source: *American Economic Review*, 60 (1970), pp. 364–78. Reprinted with the permission of the authors and the American Economic Association. © American Economic Association.

The implications of uncertainty for public investment decisions remain controversial. The essence of the controversy is as follows. It is widely accepted that individuals are not indifferent to uncertainty and will not, in general, value assets with uncertain returns at their expected values. Depending upon an individual's initial asset holdings and utility function, he will value an asset at more or less than its expected value. Therefore, in private capital markets, investors do not choose investments to maximize the present value of expected returns, but to maximize the present value of returns properly adjusted for risk. The issue is whether it is appropriate to discount public investments in the same way as private investments.

There are several positions on this issue. The first is that risk should be discounted in the same way for public investments as it is for private investments. It is argued that to treat risk differently in the public sector will result in overinvestment in this sector at the expense of private investments yielding higher returns. The leading proponent of this point of view is Jack Hirshleifer (Hirshleifer, 1965, 1966; Hirshleifer et al., 1960, pp. 139–50). He argues that in perfect capital markets, investments are discounted with respect to both time and risk and that the discount rates obtaining in these markets should be used to evaluate public investment opportunities.

A second position is that the government can better cope with uncertainty than private investors and, therefore, government investments should not be evaluated by the same criterion used in private markets. More specifically, it is argued that the government should ignore uncertainty and behave as if indifferent to risk. The government should then evaluate investment opportunities according to their present value computed by discounting the expected value of net returns, using a rate of discount equal to the private rate appropriate for investments with certain returns. In support of this position it is argued that the government invests in a greater number of diverse projects and is able to pool risks to a much greater extent than private investors.[1] Another supporting line of argument is that many of the uncertainties which arise in private capital markets are related to what may be termed moral hazards. Individuals involved in a given transaction may hedge against the possibility of fraudulent behavior on the part of their associates. Many such risks are not present in the case of public investments and, therefore, it can be argued that it is not appropriate for the government to take these risks into account when choosing among public investments.

There is, in addition, a third position on the government's response to uncertainty. This position rejects the notion that individual preferences as revealed by market behavior are of normative significance for government investment decisions, and asserts that time and risk preferences relevant for government action should be established as a matter of national policy. In this case the correct rules for action would be those established by the appropriate authorities in accordance with their concept of national policy. The rate of discount and attitude toward risk would be specified by the appropriate authorities and the procedures for evaluation would incorporate these time and risk preferences. Two alternative lines of argument lead to this position. First, if one accepts the proposition that the state is more than a collection of individuals and has an existence and interests apart from those of its individual members, then it follows that government policy need not reflect individual preferences. A second position is that markets are so imperfect that the behavior observed in these markets yields no relevant information about the time and risk preferences of individuals. It follows that some policy as to time and risk preference must be established in accordance with other evidence of social objectives. One such procedure would be to set national objectives concerning the desired rate of growth and to infer from this the appropriate rate of discount.[2] If this rate were applied to the expected returns from all alternative investments, the government would in effect be behaving as if indifferent to risk.

The approach taken in this paper closely parallels the approach taken by Hirshlefer, although the results differ from his. By using the state-preference approach to market behavior under uncertainty, Hirshleifer demonstrates that investments will not, in general, be valued at the sum of the expected returns discounted at a rate appropriate for investments with certain returns. (Hirshleifer, 1965, pp. 523–34; 1966, pp. 268–75). He then demonstrates that using this discount rate for public investments may lead to non-optimal results, for two reasons. First, pooling itself may not be desirable (Hirshleifer, 1966, pp. 270–5). If the government has the opportunity to undertake only investments which pay off in states where the payoff is highly valued, to combine such investments with ones that pay off in other states may reduce the value of the total investment package. Hirshleifer argues that where investments can be undertaken separately they should be evaluated separately, and that returns should be discounted at rates determined in the market. Second, even if pooling were possible and desirable, Hirshleifer argues correctly that the use of a rate of discount for the public sector which is lower than rates in the private sector can lead to the displacement of private investments by public investments yielding lower expected returns (Hirshleifer, 1966, pp. 270–5).

For the case where government pooling is effective and desirable, he argues that rather than evaluate public investments differently from private ones, the government should subsidize the more productive private investments. From this it follows that to treat risk differently for public as opposed to private investments would only be justified if it were impossible to transfer the advantages of government pooling to private investors. Therefore, at most, the argument for treating public risks differently than private ones in evaluating investments is an argument for the "second best" (Hirshleifer, 1966, p. 270).

The first section of this paper addresses the problem of uncertainty, using the state-preference approach to market behavior. It demonstrates that if the returns from any particular investment are independent of other components of national income, then the present value of this investment equals the sum of expected returns discounted by a rate appropriate for investments yielding certain returns. This result holds for both private and public investments. Therefore, by adding one plausible assumption to Hirshleifer's formulation, the conclusion can be drawn that the government should behave as an expected-value decision maker and use a discount rate appropriate for investments with certain returns. This conclusion needs to be appropriately modified when one considers the case where there is a corporate income tax.

While this result is of theoretical interest, as a policy recommendation it suffers from a defect common to the conclusions drawn by Hirshleifer. The model of the economy upon which these recommendations are based presupposes the existence of perfect markets for claims contingent on states of the world. Put differently, it is assumed that there are perfect insurance markets through which individuals may individually pool risks. Given such markets, the distribution of risks among individuals will be Pareto optimal. The difficulty is that many of these markets for insurance do not exist, so even if the markets which do exist are perfect, the resulting equilibrium will be sub-optimal. In addition, given the strong evidence that the existing capital markets are not perfect, it is unlikely that the pattern of investment will be Pareto optimal. At the margin, different individuals will have different rates of time and risk preference, depending on their opportunities to borrow or to invest, including their opportunities to insure.

There are two reasons why markets for many types of insurance do not exist. The first is the existence of certain moral hazards.[3] In particular, the fact that someone has insurance may alter his behavior so that the observed outcome is adverse to the insurer. The second is that such markets would require complicated and specialized contracts which are costly. It may be that the cost of insuring in some cases is so high that individuals choose to bear risks rather than pay the transaction costs associated with insurance.

Given the absence of some markets for insurance and the resulting sub-optimal allocation of risks, the question remains: How should the government treat uncertainty in evaluating public investment decisions? The approach taken in this paper is that individual preferences are relevant for public investment decisions, and government decisions should reflect individual valuations of costs and benefits. It is demonstrated in the second section of this paper that when the risks associated with a public investment are publicly borne, the total cost of risk- bearing is insignificant and, therefore, the government should ignore uncertainty in evaluating public investments. Similarly, the choice of the rate of discount should in this case be independent of considerations of risk. This result is obtained not because the government is able to pool investments but because the government distributes the risk associated with any investment among a large number of people. It is the risk- spreading aspect of government investment that is essential to this result.

There remains the problem that private investments may be displaced by public ones yielding a lower return if this rule is followed, although given the absence of insurance markets this will represent a Hicks–Kaldor improvement over the initial situation. Again the question must be asked whether the superior position of the government with respect to risk can be made to serve private investors. This leads to a discussion of the government's role as a supplier of insurance, and of Hirshleifer's recommendation that private investment be subsidized in some cases.

Finally, the results obtained above apply to risks actually borne by the government. Many of the risks associated with public investments are borne by private individuals, and in such cases it is appropriate to discount for risk as would these individuals. This problem is discussed in the final section of the paper. In addition, a method of evaluating public investment decisions is developed that calls for different rates of discount applied to different classes of benefits and costs.

1. Markets for Contingent Claims and Time-Risk Preference[4]

For simplicity, consider an economy where there is one commodity and there are I individuals, S possible states of the world, and time is divided into Q periods of equal length. Further suppose that each individual acts on the basis of his subjective probability as to the states of nature; let π_{is} denote the subjective probability assigned to state s by individual i. Now suppose that each individual in the absence of trading owns claims for varying amounts of the one commodity at different points in time, given different states of the world. Let $\bar{x}_{isq}$ denote the initial claim to the commodity in period $q + 1$ if state s occurs which is owned by individual i. Suppose further that all trading in these claims takes place at the beginning of the first period, and claims are brought and sold on dated commodity units contingent on a state of the world. All claims can be constructed from basic claims which pay one commodity unit in period $q + 1$, given state s, and nothing in other states or at other times; there will be a corresponding price for this claim, p_{sq} ($s = 1, \ldots, S; q = 0, \ldots, Q - 1$). After the trading, the individual will own claims x_{isq}, which he will exercise when the time comes to provide for his consumption. Let

$$V_i\left(x_{i1,0}, \ldots, x_{i1,Q-1}, x_{i2,0}, \ldots, x_{iS,Q-1}\right)$$

be the utility of individual i if he receives claims x_{isq} ($s = 1, \ldots, S; q = 0, \ldots, Q - 1$). The standard assumptions are made that V_i is strictly quasi-concave ($i = 1, \ldots, I$)

Therefore each individual will attempt to maximize,

$$V_i\left(x_{i1,0}, \ldots, x_{i1,Q-1}, x_{i2,0}, \ldots, x_{iS,Q-1}\right) \tag{1}$$

subject to the constraint

$$\sum_{q=0}^{Q-1}\sum_{s=1}^{S} p_{sq} x_{isq} = \sum_{q=0}^{Q-1}\sum_{s=1}^{S} p_{sq}\bar{x}_{isq}$$

Using the von Neumann–Morgenstern theorem and an extension by Hirshleifer (von Neumann and Morgenstern, 1964; Hirshleifer, 1965, pp. 534–6), functions $U_{is}(s = 1, \ldots, S)$ can be found such that

$$V_i(x_{i1,0}, \ldots, x_{iS,Q-1}) = \sum_{s=1}^{S} \pi_{is} U_{is}(x_{is0}, x_{is1}, \ldots, x_{iS,Q-1}) \tag{2}$$

In equation (2) an individual's utility, given any state of the world, is a function of his consumption at each point in time. The subscript s attached to the function U_{is} is in recognition of the fact that the value of a given stream of consumption may depend on the state of the world.

The conditions for equilibrium require that

$$\pi_{is}\frac{\partial U_{is}}{\partial x_{isq}} = \lambda_i p_{sq} \quad (i = 1, \ldots I; s = 1, \ldots, S; q = 0, \ldots, Q-1) \tag{3}$$

where λ_i is a Lagrangian multiplier.

From (3) it follows that

$$\frac{p_{sq}}{p_{rm}} = \frac{\pi_{is}\frac{\partial U_{is}}{\partial x_{isq}}}{\pi_{rm}\frac{\partial U_{ir}}{\partial \lambda_{irm}}} \quad (i = 1, \ldots, I; r, s = 1, \ldots, S; m, q = 0, \ldots, Q-1) \tag{4}$$

Insight can be gained by analyzing the meaning of the prices in such an economy. Since trading takes place at time zero, p_{sq} represents the present value of a claim to one commodity unit at time q, given state s. Clearly,

$$\sum_{s=1}^{S} p_{s0} = 1$$

since someone holding one commodity unit at time zero has a claim on one commodity unit, given any state of the world. It follows that p_{sq} is the present value of one commodity at time q, given state s, in terms of a certain claim on one commodity unit at time zero. Therefore, the implicit rate of discount to time zero on returns at time q, given state s, is defined by $p_{sq} = 1/1 + r_{sq}$.

Now suppose one considers a certain claim to one commodity unit at time q; clearly, its value is

$$p_q = \sum_{s=1}^{S} p_{sq}$$

and the rate of discount appropriate for a certain return at time q is defined by

$$\frac{1}{1+r_q} = \sum_{s=1}^{S} \frac{1}{1+r_{sq}} = \sum_{s=1}^{S} p_{sq} \tag{5}$$

Given these observations, we can now analyze the appropriate procedure for evaluating government investments where there are perfect markets for claims contingent on states of the world.[5] Consider an investment where the overall effect on market prices can be assumed to be negligible, and suppose the net return from this investment for a given time and state is h_{sq} ($s = 1, \ldots, S; q = 0, \ldots, Q - 1$). Then the investment should be undertaken if

$$\sum_{q=0}^{Q-1} \sum_{s=1}^{S} h_{sq} p_{sq} > 0 \tag{6}$$

and the sum on the left is an exact expression for the present value of the investment. Expressed differently, the investment should be adopted if

$$\sum_{q=0}^{Q-1} \sum_{s=1}^{S} \frac{h_{sq}}{1+r_{sq}} > 0 \tag{7}$$

The payoff in each time-state is discounted by the associated rate of discount. This is the essential result upon which Hirshleifer (1965, pp. 523–34) bases his policy conclusions.

Now suppose that the net returns of the investment were

(a) independent of the returns from previous investment,
(b) independent of the individual utility functions, and
(c) had an objective probability distribution, i.e., one agreed upon by everyone.

More specifically, we assume that the set of all possible states of the world can be partitioned into a class of mutually exclusive and collectively exhaustive sets, E_t, indexed by the subscript t such that, for all s in any given E_t, all utility functions U_{is} are the same for any individual i ($i = 1, \ldots, I$), and such that all production conditions are the same. Put differently, for all s in E_t, U_{is} is the same for a given individual, but not necessarily for all individuals. At the same time there is another partition of the states of the world into sets, F_u, such that the return, h_{sq}, is the same for all s in F_u. Finally, we assume that the probability distribution of F_u is independent of E_t and is the same for all individuals.

Let E_{tu} be the set of all states of the world which lie in both E_t and F_u. For any given t and u, all states of the world in E_{tu} are indistinguishable for all purposes, so we may regard it as containing a single state. Equations (3) and (5) and the intervening discussion still hold if we then replace s everywhere by tu. However, $U_{is} = U_{itu}$

actually depends only on the subscript, t, and can be written U_{it}. From the assumptions it is obvious and can be proved rigorously that the allocation x_{isq} also depends only on t, i.e., is the same for all states in E_t for any given t, so it may be written x_{itq}. Finally, let π_{it} be the probability of E_t according to individual i, and let π_u be the probability of F_u, assumed the same for all individuals. Then the assumption of statistical independence is written:

$$\pi_{itu} = \pi_{it}\pi_u \tag{8}$$

Then (3) can be written

$$\pi_{it}\pi_u \frac{\partial U_{it}}{\partial x_{itq}} = \lambda_i p_{tuq} \tag{9}$$

Since p_{tuq} and π_u are independent of i, so must be

$$\left(\pi_{it}\frac{\partial U_{it}}{\partial x_{itq}}\right)/\lambda_i$$

on the other hand, this expression is also independent of u and so can be written μ_{tq}. Therefore,

$$p_{tuq} = \mu_{tq}\pi_u \tag{10}$$

Since the new investment has the same return for all states s in F_u, the returns can be written h_{uq}. Then the left-hand side of (6) can, with the aid of (10), be written

$$\sum_{Q=0}^{Q-1}\sum_{s=1}^{S} h_{sq}p_{sq} = \sum_{q=0}^{Q-1}\sum_{t}\sum_{u} h_{uq}p_{tuq}$$
$$= \sum_{q=0}^{Q-1}\left(\sum_{t}\mu_{tq}\right)\sum_{u}\pi_u h_{uq} \tag{11}$$

But from (10)

$$p_q = \sum_{s=1}^{S} p_{sq} = \sum_{t}\sum_{u} p_{tuq} = \left(\sum_{t}\mu_{tq}\right)\left(\sum_{u}\pi_u\right) = \sum_{t}\mu_{tq} \tag{12}$$

since of course the sum of the probabilities of the F_u's must be 1. From (11),

$$\sum_{q=0}^{Q-1}\sum_{s=1}^{S} h_{sq}p_{sq} = \sum_{Q=0}^{Q-1}\frac{1}{1+r_q}\sum_{u} \pi_u h_{uq} \qquad (13)$$

Equation (13) gives the rather startling result that the present value of any investment which meets the independence and objectivity conditions, equals the expected value of returns in each time period, discounted by the factor appropriate for a certain return at that time. This is true even though individuals may have had different probabilities for the events that governed the returns on earlier investments. It is also interesting to note that each individual will behave in this manner so that there will be no discrepancy between public and private procedures for choosing among investments.

The independence assumption applied to utility functions was required because the functions U_{is} are conditional on the states of the world. This assumption appears reasonable, and in the case where U_{is} is the same for all values of s, it is automatically satisfied. Then the independence condition is simply that the net returns from an investment be independent of the returns from previous investments.

The difficulty that arises if one bases policy conclusions on these results is that some markets do not exist, and individuals do not value assets at the expected value of returns discounted by a factor appropriate for certain returns. It is tempting to argue that while individuals do not behave as expected-value decision makers because of the nonexistence of certain markets for insurance, there is no reason why the government's behavior should not be consistent with the results derived above where the allocation of resources was Pareto optimal. There are two difficulties with this line of argument. First, if we are to measure benefits and costs in terms of individuals' willingness to pay, then we must treat risk in accordance with these individual valuations. Since individuals do not have the opportunities for insuring assumed in the state- preference model, they will not value uncertainty as they would if these markets did exist. Second, the theory of the second best demonstrates that if resources are not allocated in a Pareto optimal manner, the appropriate public policies may not be those consistent with Pareto efficiency in perfect markets. Therefore, some other approach must be found for ascertaining the appropriate government policy toward risk. In particular, such an approach must be valid, given the nonexistence of certain markets for insurance and imperfections in existing markets.

2. The Public Cost of Risk-Bearing

The critical question is: What is the cost of uncertainty in terms of costs to individuals? If one adopts the position that costs and benefits should be computed on the basis of individual willingness to pay, consistency demands that the public costs of risk-bearing be computed in this way too. This is the approach taken here.

In the discussion that follows it is assumed that an individual's utility is dependent only upon his consumption and not upon the state of nature in which that consumption takes place. This assumption simplifies the presentation of the major theorem, but it is not essential. Again the expected utility theorem is assumed to hold. The presentation to follow analyzes the cost of risk-bearing by comparing the expected value of returns with the certainty equivalent of these returns. In this way the analysis of time and risk preference can be separated, so we need only consider one time period.

Suppose that the government were to undertake an investment with a certain outcome; then the benefits and costs are measured in terms of willingness to pay for this outcome. If, however, the outcome is uncertain, then the benefits and costs actually realized depend on which outcome in fact occurs. If an individual is risk-averse, he will value the investment with the uncertain outcome at less than the expected value of its net return (benefit minus cost) to him. Therefore, in general the expected value of net benefits overstates willingness to pay by an amount equal to the cost of risk-bearing. It is clear that the social cost of risk-bearing will depend both upon which individuals receive the benefits and pay the costs and upon how large is each individual's share of these benefits and costs.

As a first step, suppose that the government were to undertake an investment and capture all benefits and pay all costs, i.e., the beneficiaries pay to the government an amount equal to the benefits received and the government pays all costs. Individuals who incur costs and those who receive benefits are therefore left indifferent to their pre-investment state. This assumption simply transfers all benefits and costs to the government, and the outcome of the investment will affect government disbursements and receipts. Given that the general taxpayer finances government expenditures, a public investment can be considered an investment in which each individual taxpayer has a very small share.

For precision, suppose that the government undertook an investment and that returns accrue to the government as previously described. In addition, suppose that in a given year the government were to have a balanced budget (or a planned deficit or surplus) and that taxes would be reduced by the amount of the net benefits if the returns are positive, and raised if returns are negative. Therefore, when the government undertakes an investment, each taxpayer has a small share of that investment with the returns being paid through changes in the level of taxes. By undertaking an investment the government adds to each individual's disposable income a random variable which is some fraction of the random variable representing the total net returns. The expected return to all taxpayers as a group equals expected net benefits.

Each taxpayer holds a small share of an asset with a random payoff, and the value of this asset to the individual is less than its expected return, assuming risk aversion. Stated differently, there is a cost of risk-bearing that must be subtracted from the expected return in order to compute the value of the investment to the individual taxpayer. Since each taxpayer will bear some of the cost of the risk associated with the investment, these costs must be summed over all taxpayers in order to arrive at the total cost of risk-bearing associated with a particular investment. These costs must be subtracted from the value of expected net benefits in order to obtain the correct measure for net benefits. The task is to assess these costs.

Suppose, as in the previous section, that there is one commodity, and that each individual's utility in a given year is a function of his income defined in terms of this commodity and is given by $U(Y)$. Further, suppose that U is bounded, continuous, strictly increasing, and differentiable. The assumptions that U is continuous and strictly increasing imply that U has a right and left derivative at every point and this is sufficient to prove the desired results; differentiability is assumed only to simplify presentation. Further suppose that U satisfies the conditions of the expected utility theorem.

Consider, for the moment, the case where all individuals are identical in that they have the same preferences, and their disposable incomes are identically distributed random variables represented by A. Suppose that the government were to undertake an investment with returns represented by B, which are statistically independent of A. Now divide the effect of this investment into two parts: a certain part equal to expected returns and a random part, with mean zero, which incorporates risk. Let $\bar{B} = E[B]$, and define the random variable X by $X = B - \bar{B}$. Clearly, X is independent of A and $E[X] = 0$. The effect of this investment is to add an amount $\bar{B}$ to government receipts along with a random component represented by X. The income of each taxpayer will be affected through taxes and it is the level of these taxes that determines the fraction of the investment he effectively holds.

Consider a specific taxpayer and denote his fraction of this investment by s, $0 \leq s \leq 1$. This individual's disposable income, given the public investment, is equal to

$$A + sB = A + s\bar{B} + sX$$

The addition of sB to his disposable income is valued by the individual at its expected value less the cost of bearing the risk associated with the random component sX. If we suppose that each taxpayer has the same tax rate and that there are n taxpayers, then $s = 1/n$, and the value of the investment taken over all individuals is simply $\bar{B}$ minus n times the cost of risk-bearing associated with the random variable $(1/n)X$. The central result of this section of the paper is that this total of the costs of risk-bearing goes to zero as n becomes large. Therefore, for large values of n the value of a public investment almost equals the expected value of that investment.

To demonstrate this, we introduce the function

$$W(s) = E[U(A + s\bar{B} + sX)] \qquad 0 \leq s \leq 1 \tag{14}$$

In other words, given the random variables A and B representing his individual income before the investment and the income from the investment, respectively, his expected utility is a function of s which represents his share of B. From (14) and the assumption that U' exists, it follows that

$$W'(s) = E[U'(A + s\bar{B} + sX)(\bar{B} + X)] \tag{15}$$

Since X is independent of A, it follows that $U'(A)$ and X are independent; therefore,

$$E[U'(A)X] = E[U'(A)]E[X] = 0$$

so that

$$W'(0) = E[U'(A)(\bar{B} + X)] \\ = \bar{B}E[U'(A)] \tag{16}$$

Equation (16) is equivalent to the statement

$$\lim_{s \to 0} \frac{E[U(A + s\bar{B} + sX) - U(A)]}{s} = \bar{B}E[U'(A)] \tag{17}$$

Now let $s = 1/n$, so that equation (17) becomes

$$\lim_{n \to 0} nE\left[U\left(A + \frac{\bar{B} + X}{n}\right) - U(A)\right] = \bar{B}E[U'(A)] \tag{18}$$

If we assume that an individual whose preferences are represented by U is a risk-averter, then it is easily shown that there exists a unique number, $k(n) > 0$, for each value of n such that

$$E\left[U\left(A + \frac{\bar{B} + X}{n}\right)\right] = E\left[U\left(A + \frac{\bar{B}}{n} - k(n)\right)\right] \tag{19}$$

or, in other words, an individual would be indifferent between paying an amount equal to $k(n)$ and accepting the risk represented by $(1/n)X$. Therefore, $k(n)$ can be said to be the cost of risk-bearing associated with the asset B. It can easily be demonstrated that $\lim_{n \to \infty} k(n) = 0$, i.e., the cost of holding the risky asset goes to zero as the amount of this asset held by the individual goes to zero. It should be noted that the assumption of risk aversion is not essential to the argument but simply one of convenience. If U represented the utility function of a risk preferrer, then all the above statements would hold except $k(n) < 0$, i.e., an individual would be indifferent between being paid $-k(n)$ and accepting the risk $(1/n)X$ (net of the benefit $(1/n)\bar{B}$).

We wish to prove not merely that the risk-premium of the representative individual, $k(n)$, vanishes, but more strongly that the total of the risk-premiums for all individuals, $nk(n)$, approaches zero as n becomes large.

From (18) and (19) it follows that

$$\lim_{n \to 0} nE\left[U\left(A + \frac{\bar{B}}{n} - k(n)\right) - U(A)\right] = \bar{B}E[U'(A)] \tag{20}$$

In addition, $\bar{B}/n - k(n) \to 0$, when $n \to \infty$.
It follows from the definition of a derivative that

$$\lim_{n \to 0} \frac{E[U(A + \frac{\bar{B}}{n} - k(n)) - U(A)]}{\frac{\bar{B}}{n} - k(n)} = E[U'(A)] > 0 \tag{21}$$

Dividing (20) by (21) yields

$$\lim_{n \to 0}[\bar{B} - nk(n)] = \bar{B} \tag{22}$$

or

$$\lim_{n \to 0} nk(n) = 0 \qquad (23)$$

The argument in (21) implies that $\bar{B}/n - k(n) \neq 0$. Suppose instead the equality held for infinitely many n. Substitution into the left-hand side of (20) shows that $\bar{B}$ must equal zero, so that $k(n) = 0$ for all such n, and hence $nk(n) = 0$ on that sequence, confirming (23).

Equation (23) states that the total of the costs of risk-bearing goes to zero as the population of taxpayers becomes large. At the same time the monetary value of the investment to each taxpayer, neglecting the cost of risk, is $(1/n)\bar{B}$, and the total, summed over all individuals, is $\bar{B}$, the expected value of net benefits. Therefore, if n is large, the expected value of net benefits closely approximates the correct measure of net benefits defined in terms of willingness to pay for an asset with an uncertain return.

In the preceding analysis, it was assumed that all taxpayers were identical in that they had the same utility function, their incomes were represented by identically distributed variables, and they were subject to the same tax rates. These assumptions greatly simplify the presentation; however, they are not essential to the argument. Different individuals may have different preferences, incomes, and tax rates; and the basic theorem still holds, provided that as n becomes larger the share of the public investment borne by any individual becomes arbitrarily smaller.

The question necessarily arises as to how large n must be to justify proceeding as if the cost of publicly borne risk is negligible. This question can be given no precise answer; however, there are circumstances under which it appears likely that the cost of risk-bearing will be small. If the size of the share borne by each taxpayer is a negligible component of his income, the cost of risk-bearing associated with holding it will be small. It appears reasonable to assume, under these conditions, that the total cost of risk-bearing is also small. This situation will exist where the investment is small with respect to the total wealth of the taxpayers. In the case of a federally sponsored investment, n is not only large but the investment is generally a very small fraction of national income even though the investment itself may be large in some absolute sense.

The results derived here and in the previous section depend on returns from a given public investment being independent of other components of national income. The government undertakes a wide range of public investments and it appears reasonable to assume that their returns are independent. Clearly, there are some government investments which are interdependent; however, where investments are interrelated they should be evaluated as a package. Even after such groupings are established, there will be a large number of essentially independent projects. It is sometimes argued that the returns from public investments are highly correlated with other components of national income through the business cycle. However, if we assume that stabilization policies are successful, then this difficulty does not arise. It should be noted that in most benefit–cost studies it is assumed that full employment will be maintained so that market prices can be used to measure benefits and costs. Consistency requires that this assumption be retained when considering risk as well. Further, if there is some positive correlation between the returns of an investment and other components of national income, the question remains as to whether this correlation is so high as to invalidate the previous result.

The main result is more general than the specific application to public investments. It has been demonstrated that if an individual or group holds an asset which is statistically independent of other assets, and if there is one or more individuals who do not share ownership, then the existing situation is not Pareto-efficient. By selling some share of the asset to one of the individuals not originally possessing a share, the cost of risk-bearing can be reduced while the expected returns remain unchanged. The reduction in the cost of risk- bearing can then be redistributed to bring about a Pareto improvement. This result is similar to a result derived by Karl Borch (1960). He proved that a condition for Pareto optimality in reinsurance markets requires that every individual hold a share of every independent risk.

When the government undertakes an investment it, in effect, spreads the risk among all taxpayers. Even if one were to accept that the initial distribution of risk was Pareto-efficient, the new distribution of risk will not be efficient as the government does not discriminate among the taxpayers according to their risk preferences. What has been shown is that in the limit the situation where the risk of the investment is spread over all taxpayers is such that there is only a small deviation from optimality with regard to the distribution of that particular risk. The overall distribution of risk may be sub-optimal because of market imperfections and the absence of certain insurance markets. The great advantage of the results of this section is that they are not dependent on the existence of perfect markets for contingent claims.

This leads to an example which runs counter to the policy conclusions generally offered by economists. Suppose that an individual in the private sector of the economy were to undertake a given investment and, calculated on the basis of expected returns, the investment had a rate of return of 10 percent. Because of the absence of perfect insurance markets, the investor subtracted from the expected return in each period a risk premium and, on the basis of returns adjusted for risk, his rate of return is 5 percent. Now suppose that the government could invest the same amount of money in an investment which, on the basis of expected returns, would yield 6 percent. Since the risk would be spread over all taxpayers, the cost of risk-bearing would be negligible, and the true rate of return would be 6 percent. Further, suppose that if the public investment were adopted it would displace the private investment. The question is: Should the public investment be undertaken? On the basis of the previous analysis, the answer is yes. The private investor is indifferent between the investment with the expected return of 10 percent, and certain rate of return of 5 percent. When the public investment is undertaken, it is equivalent to an investment with a certain rate of return of 6 percent. Therefore, by undertaking the public investment, the government could more than pay the opportunity cost to the private investor of 5 percent associated with the diversion of funds from private investment.

The previous example illustrates Hirshleifer's point that the case for evaluating public investments differently from private ones is an argument for the second best. Clearly, if the advantages of the more efficient distribution of risk could be achieved in connection with the private investment alternative, this would be superior to the public investment. The question then arises as to how the government can provide insurance for private investors and thereby transfer the risks from the private sector to the public at large. The same difficulties arise as before, moral hazards and transaction costs. It may not be possible for the government to provide such insurance, and in such cases second-best solutions are in order. Note that if the government could undertake any investment, then this difficulty would not arise. Perhaps one of the strongest criticisms of a system of freely competitive markets is that the inherent difficulty in establishing certain markets for insurance brings about a sub-optimal allocation of resources. If we consider an investment, as does Hirshleifer, as an exchange of certain present income for uncertain future income, then the misallocation will take the form of under-investment.

Now consider Hirshleifer's recommendation that, in cases such as the one above, a direct subsidy be used to induce more private investment rather than increase public investment. Suppose that a particular private investment were such that the benefits would be a marginal increase in the future supply of an existing commodity, i.e., this investment would neither introduce a new commodity nor affect future prices. Therefore, benefits can be measured at each point in time by the market value of this output, and can be fully captured through the sale of the commodity. Let $\bar{V}$ be the present value of expected net returns, and let V be the present value of net returns adjusted for risk where the certainty rate is used to discount both streams. Further, suppose there were a public investment, where the risks were publicly borne, for which the present value of expected net benefits was P. Since the risk is publicly borne, from the previous discussion it follows that P is the present value of net benefits adjusted for risk. Now suppose that $\bar{V} > P > V$. According to Hirshleifer, we should undertake the private investment rather than the public one, and pay a subsidy if necessary to induce private entrepreneurs to undertake this investment. Clearly, if there is a choice between one investment or the other, given the existing distribution of risk, the public investment is superior. The implication is that if a risky investment in the private sector is displaced by a public investment with a lower expected return but with a higher return when appropriate adjustments are made for risks, this represents a Hicks–Kaldor improvement. This is simply a restatement of the previous point that the government could more than pay the opportunity cost to the private entrepreneur.

Now consider the case for a direct subsidy to increase the level of private investment. One can only argue for direct subsidy of the private investment if $V < 0 < \bar{V}$. The minimum subsidy required is $|V|$. Suppose the taxpayers were to pay this subsidy, which is a transfer of income from the public at large to the private investor, in order to cover the loss from the investment. The net benefits, including the cost of risk-bearing, remain negative because while the subsidy has partially offset the cost of risk-bearing to the individual investor, it has not reduced this cost. Therefore, a direct public subsidy in this case results in a less efficient allocation of resources.

We can summarize as follows: It is implied by Hirshleifer that it is better to undertake an investment with a higher expected return than one with a lower expected return. (See 1965, p. 270.) This proposition is not in general valid, as the distribution of risk-bearing is critical. This statement is true, however, when the costs of risk-bearing associated with both investments are the same. What has been shown is that when risks are publicly borne, the costs of risk-bearing are negligible; therefore, a public investment with an expected return which is less than that of a given private investment may nevertheless be superior to the private alternative. Therefore, the fact that public investments with lower expected return may replace private investment is not necessarily cause for concern. Furthermore, a program of providing direct subsidies to encourage more private investment does not alter the costs of risk-bearing and, therefore, will encourage investments which are inefficient when the costs of risk are considered. The program which produces the desired result is one to insure private investments.

One might raise the question as to whether risk-spreading is not associated with large corporations so that the same result would apply, and it is easily seen that the same reasoning does apply. This can be made more precise by assuming there were n stockholders who were identical in the sense that their utility functions were identical, their incomes were represented by identically distributed random variables, and they had the same share in the company. When the corporation undertakes an investment with a return in a given year represented by B, each stockholder's income is represented by $A + (1/n)B$. This assumes, of course, that a change in earnings was reflected in dividends, and that there were no business taxes. Clearly, this is identical to the situation previously described, and if n is large, the total cost of risk-bearing to the stockholders will be negligible. If the income or wealth of the stockholders were large with respect to the size of the investment, this result would be likely to hold. Note that whether or not the investment is a large one, with respect to the assets of the firm, is not relevant. While an investment may constitute a major part of a firm's assets if each stockholder's share in the firm is a small component of his income, the cost of risk-bearing to him will be very small. It then follows that if managers were acting in the interest of the firm's shareholders, they would essentially ignore risks and choose investments with the highest expected returns.

There are two important reasons why large corporations may behave as risk averters. First, in order to control the firm, some shareholder may hold a large block of stock which is a significant component of his wealth. If this were true, then, from his point of view, the costs of risk-bearing would not be negligible, and the firm should behave as a risk averter. Note in this case that the previous result does not hold because the cost of risk-bearing to each stockholders is not small, even though the number of stockholders is very large. Investment behavior in this case is essentially the same as the case of a single investor.

The second case is when, even though from the stockholder's point of view, risk should be ignored, it may not be in the interest of the corporate managers to neglect risk. Their careers and income are intimately related to the firm's performance. From their point of view, variations in the outcome of some corporate action impose very real costs. In this case, given a degree of autonomy, the corporate managers, in considering prospective investments, may discount for risk when it is not in the interest of the stockholders to do so.

Suppose that this were the case and also suppose that the marginal rate of time preference for each individual in the economy was 5 percent. From the point of view of the stockholders, risk can be ignored and any investment with an expected return which is greater than 5 percent should be undertaken. However, suppose that corporate managers discount for risk so that only investments with expected rates of return that exceed 10 percent are undertaken. From the point of view of the stockholders, the rate of return on these investments, taking risk into account, is over 10 percent. Given a marginal rate of time preference of 5 percent, it follows that from the point of view of the individual stockholder there is too little investment. Now suppose further that the government were considering an investment with an expected rate of return of 6 percent. Since the cost of risk-bearing is negligible, this investment should be undertaken since the marginal rate of time preference is less than 6 percent. However, in this case, if the financing were such that a private investment with a 10 percent expected rate of return is displaced by the public investment, there is a loss because in both cases the risk is distributed so as to make the total cost of risk-bearing negligible. The public investment should be undertaken, but only at the expense of consumption.

3. The Actual Allocation of Risk

In the idealized public investment considered in the last section, all benefits and costs accrued to the government and were distributed among the taxpayers. In this sense, all uncertainty was borne collectively. Suppose instead that some benefits and costs of sizeable magnitudes accrued directly to individuals so that these individuals incurred the attendant costs of risk-bearing. In this case it is appropriate to discount for the risk, as would these individuals. Such a situation would arise in the case of a government irrigation project where the benefits accrued to farmers as increased income. The changes in farm income would be uncertain and, therefore, should be valued at more or less than their expected value, depending on the states in which they occur. If these increases were independent of other components of farm income, and if we assume that the farmer's utility were only a function of his income and not the state in which he receives that income, then he would value the investment project at less than the expected increase in his income, provided he is risk averse. If, however, the irrigation project paid out in periods of drought so that total farm income was not only increased but also stabilized, then the farmers would value the project at more than the expected increase in their incomes.

In general, some benefits and costs will accrue to the government and the uncertainties involved will be publicly borne; other benefits and costs will accrue to individuals and the attendant uncertainties will be borne privately. In the first case the cost of risk-bearing will be negligible; in the second case these costs may be significant. Therefore, in calculating the present value of returns from a public investment a distinction must be made between private and public benefits and costs. The present value of public benefits and costs should be evaluated by estimating the expected net benefits in each period and discounting them, using a discount factor appropriate for investments with certain returns. On the other hand, private benefits and costs must be discounted with respect to both time and risk in accordance with the preferences of the individuals to whom they accrue.

From the foregoing discussion it follows that different streams of benefits and costs should be treated in different ways with respect to uncertainty. One way to do this is to discount these streams of returns at different rates of discount ranging from the certainty rate for benefits and costs accruing to the government and using higher rates that reflect discounting for risk for returns accruing directly to individuals. Such a procedure raises some difficulties of identification, but this problem does not appear to be insurmountable. In general, costs are paid by the government, which receives some revenue, and the net stream should be discounted at a rate appropriate for certain returns. Benefits accruing directly to individuals should be discounted according to individual time and risk preferences. As a practical matter, Hirshleifer's suggestion of finding the marginal rate of return on assets with similar payoffs in the private sector, and using this as the rate of discount, appears reasonable for discounting those benefits and costs which accrue privately.

One problem arises with this latter procedure which has received little attention. In considering public investments, benefits and costs are aggregated and the discussion of uncertainty is carried out in terms of these aggregates. This obscures many of the uncertainties because benefits and costs do not in general accrue to the same individuals, and the attendant uncertainties should not be netted out when considering the totals. To make this clear, consider an investment where the benefits and costs varied greatly, depending on the state of nature, but where the difference between total benefits and total costs was constant for every state. Further, suppose that the benefits and costs accrued to different groups. While the investment is certain from a social point of view, there is considerable risk from a private point of view. In the case of perfect markets for contingent claims, each individual will discount the stream of costs and benefits accruing to him at the appropriate rate for each time and state. However, suppose that such markets do not exist. Then risk-averse individuals will value the net benefits accruing to them at less than their expected value. Therefore, if net benefits accruing to this individual are positive, this requires discounting expected returns at a higher rate than that appropriate for certain returns. On the other hand, if net benefits to an individual are negative, this requires discounting expected returns at a rate lower than the certainty rate. Raising the rate of discount only reduces the present value of net benefits when they are positive. Therefore, the distinction must be made not only between benefits and costs which accrue to the public and those which accrue directly to individuals, but also between individuals whose net benefits are negative and those whose benefits are positive. If all benefits and costs accrued privately, and different individuals received the benefits and paid the costs, the appropriate procedure would be to discount the stream of expected benefits at a rate higher than the certainty rate, and costs at a rate lower than the certainty rate. This would hold even if the social totals were certain.

Fortunately, as a practical matter this may not be of great importance as most costs are borne publicly and, therefore, should be discounted using the certainty rate. Benefits often accrue to individuals, and where there are attendant uncertainties it is appropriate to discount the expected value of these benefits at higher rates, depending on the nature of the uncertainty and time-risk preferences of the individuals who receive these benefits. It is somewhat ironic that the practical implication of this analysis is that for the typical case where costs are borne publicly and benefits accrue privately, this procedure will qualify fewer projects than the procedure of using a higher rate to discount both benefits and costs.

Notes

1 For this point of view, see P. A. Samuelson and W. Vickrey (1964).
2 For this point of view, see O. Eckstein (1961) and S. Marglin (1963).
3 For a discussion of this problem see M. V. Pauly (1968) and Arrow (1968).
4 For a basic statement of the state-preference approach, see Arrow (1964) and G. Debreu (1959).
5 The following argument was sketched in Arrow (1966, pp. 28–30).

References

Arrow, K. J. (1964): "The Role of Securities in the Optimal Allocation of Risk-Bearing," *Review of Economic Studies*, 31, April, 91–6.

——(1966): "Discounting and Public Investment Criteria," in A. V. Kneese and S. C. Smith (eds), *Water Research*, Baltimore: Johns Hopkins Press (for Resources for the Future).

——(1968): "The Economics of Moral Hazard: Further Comment," *American Economic Review*, 58, June, 537–8.

Borch, K. (1960): "The Safety Loading of Reinsurance," *Skandinavisk Aktuarietid-skrift*, 163–84.

Debreu, G. (1959): *Theory of Value*. New York: John Wiley.

Eckstein, O. (1961): "A Survey of the Theory of Public Expenditure," and "Reply," *Public Finances: Needs, Sources, and Utilization*, Princeton: National Bureau of Economic Research, 493–504.

Hirshleifer, J. (1965): "Investment Decision under Uncertainty: Choice-Theoretic Approaches," *Quarterly Journal of Economics*, 79, November, 509–36.

——(1966): "Investment Decision under Uncertainty: Applications of the State-Preference Approach," *Quarterly Journal of Economics*, 80, May, 252–77.

——De Haven, J. C. and Milliman, J. W. (1960): *Water Supply: Economics, Technology, and Policy*. Chicago: University of Chicago Press.

Marglin, S. (1963): "The Social Rate of Discount and the Optimal Rate of Investment," *Quarterly Journal of Economics*, 77, February, 95–111.

Pauly, M. V. (1968): "The Economics of Moral Hazard: Comment," *American Economic Review*, 58, June, 531–7.

Samuelson, P. A. and Vickrey, W. (1964): "Discussion," *American Economic Review Proceedings*, 59, May, 88–96.

von Neumann, J. and Morgenstern, O. (1964): *Theory of Games and Economic Behavior*, 3rd edn. New York: John Wiley.

CHAPTER SEVENTEEN

Selling Spectrum Rights

JOHN McMILLAN

Source: *Journal of Economic Perspectives*, 8, 3 (1994), pp. 145–62. Reprinted with the permission of the author and the American Economic Association. © American Economic Association.

"It has shades of the '49 California gold rush," remarked one industry observer. "It's the 21st century equivalent of the Oklahoma land rush," said another.[1] The sought-after item is the radio spectrum, which the U.S. government has put on the auction block. The wavelengths on offer, formerly reserved for the military, are to be used for newly invented personal communications services (PCS): pocket telephones, portable fax machines, and wireless computer networks.

The auction is one of the biggest and most complicated in history. The spectrum on offer is estimated by the Office of Management and Budget (1993, p. 21) to be worth $10.6 billion. Thousands of spectrum licenses are for sale.

The bidders include most U.S. telecommunications firms: long-distance, local, and cellular telephone companies and cable-television companies. After spending billions for the spectrum licenses, the firms will invest still bigger sums installing transmitters and developing a customer base. The return is highly uncertain. The new PCS operators will compete not only with each other but also with entrenched cellular-telephone companies. The PCS technology is still being developed. The potential size of the market is unknown. (Will cordless telephones eventually replace many of the telephones now tethered by wires? Will the new wireless multimedia systems – carrying video and data as well as the spoken word – be in wide demand?) Successful bidders face daunting risks, but could make huge profits.

The story of how the spectrum auction was designed is a case study in the policy application of economic theory. The major telephone companies and the government relied on the advice of theorists. Paul Milgrom, Robert Wilson, and Charles Plott were hired by Pacific Bell, Jeremy Bulow and Barry Nalebuff by Bell Atlantic, Preston McAfee by Airtouch Communications, Robert Weber by Telephone and Data Systems, Mark Isaac by the Cellular Telecommunications Industry Association, Robert Harris and Michael Katz by Nynex, Daniel Vincent by American Personal Communications, Peter Cramton by MCI, John Ledyard and David Porter by the National Telecommunications and Information Administration, and the author of this article by the Federal Communications Commission (FCC). This was perhaps the biggest use of economic theorists as consultants since that other telephone-industry revolution, the break-up of AT&T ten years earlier.

The analysis of how auctions work is one of the successes of modern mathematical economics. Developed to try out new ideas in game theory, auction theory has turned out to have considerable practical content. The theory looks at the strategy of competition: how bidders choose their bids, not knowing the value of the item for sale and not knowing what their rivals know; and what the seller can do to stimulate the bidding competition, not knowing how much any of the bidders is willing to pay.[2] When the theorists met the policy-makers, concepts like Bayes–Nash equilibrium, incentive-compatibility constraints, and order-statistic theorems came to be discussed in the corridors of power.

The Decision to Auction

Spectrum licenses used to be assigned by administrative decision. Prospective license-holders filed applications and the Federal Communications Commission held comparative hearings to decide which applicant was the most worthy. This method broke down under its cumbersomeness: there was a big backlog of unassigned licenses. Congress replaced it with lotteries, assigning each license randomly among the applicants. The lotteries succeeded in assigning licenses quickly, but the prospect of a windfall gain attracted large numbers of applicants: there were nearly 400,000 applications for cellular licenses. In one not atypical case, an obscure group called the RACDG partnership was chosen by lottery in 1989 to run cellular telephones on Cape Cod; the partners then sold their license to Southwestern Bell for $41 million. The total value of cellular licenses the government gave away during the 1980s, according to a Commerce Department estimate, was $46 billion.[3] Congress could not shrug off such figures.

Auctioning spectrum rights is not a new idea. The U.S. Congress held hearings on it as early as 1958, and R. H. Coase advocated it in a 1959 article. A 1985 FCC discussion paper showed that auctions would be workable (Kwerel and Felker, 1985). New Zealand legislated spectrum auctions in 1989, as did the United Kingdom in 1990. It was not until August 1993, however, that Congress passed legislation giving the FCC the authority to auction licenses. The FCC was to "design and test multiple alternative methodologies" for competitive bidding, and auctioning was to begin in May 1994. Auctioning did not change property rights: the restrictions on what the spectrum can be used for remain as before. A license lasts for a fixed term of up to ten years, but renewal is almost automatic provided it is being used appropriately. The Act specifies a range of aims for the auction: achieving an "efficient and intensive use of the electromagnetic spectrum;" promoting rapid deployment of new technologies; preventing excessive concentration of licenses; and ensuring some licenses go to minority-owned and women-owned companies, small businesses, and rural telephone companies (U.S. Congress, 1993, pp. 80–3).

The Act downplays revenue as an objective, and by its actions also the government showed that revenue was not its overriding objective (as, indeed, it should not be). If revenue had been paramount, the government could have offered a single monopoly license in each region – at the cost, obviously, of creating future inefficiencies. The government allocated a large swath of spectrum for PCS (120 megahertz, as compared with 50 megahertz for cellular telephones), even though maximizing revenue would have meant allocating less spectrum. Nevertheless, the wide publicity given to the forecasts of over $10 billion to be raised in the auction put pressure on the FCC to generate revenue.

The FCC canvassed a variety of auction-design possibilities and made some preliminary recommendations in its October 1993 Notice of Proposed Rule Making, and then called for comments from the industry. Over 220 firms and lobby groups filed submissions (some written by academics). The auction structure chosen by the Commissioners in March 1994 followed the recommendations of the FCC officials. Although pork-barrel politics had shaped the debate on whether to use auctions, the auction-design process was driven not by politics, but by economics.

Theory helped to answer key questions of auction design. Which of the basic auction forms should the government use? An open auction, in which bidders raise their bids until only one remains, who wins and pays the final bid? A first-price sealed-bid auction, in which each bidder submits a single sealed bid and the high bidder wins, paying that bid? Or a second-price sealed-bid auction, in which each bidder submits a single sealed bid and the high bidder wins, but the price is the second-highest bid? Should the licenses be auctioned in sequence, or should they all be bid for at once in a large simultaneous auction? Should the government help the bidders to aggregate licenses by accepting bids for combinations of licenses, or should it allow only bids for individual licenses? How should the auction be structured to promote the interests of minority-owned and other designated firms? Should the government demand royalty payments? Should reserve (or minimum) prices be imposed? How much should the bidders be informed about their competition? Faulty choices over issues such as these could mean the auction produces a mismatch of licenses to firms, or the government misses out on revenue it could have earned, or the auction in some way breaks down.

Cautionary Tales from the Antipodes

That auction design matters is illustrated by the experience of the innovator in the field of spectrum auctions, New Zealand, which began auctioning the spectrum for radio, television, and cellular-telephone use in 1990. Following the advice of a U.S.–U.K. consulting firm, National Economic Research Associates (NERA), the government adopted second-price auctions (NERA, 1988). Politically embarrassing newspaper headlines resulted, as winners paid prices far below their bids (Mueller, 1991). In one extreme case, a firm that bid NZ$100,000 paid the second-highest bid of NZ$6. In another the high bid was NZ$7 million and the second bid NZ$5,000. (NZ$1 equaled US$0.55.) An Otago University student bid NZ$1 for a television license for a small city; no one else bid so he won and paid nothing. The revenue fell far short of the advance estimate: the cellular licenses fetched NZ$36 million, one-seventh the NZ$240 million that NERA had predicted.

The auction form had a political defect. By revealing the high bidder's willingness to pay, the second-price auction exposed the government to criticism, because after the auction everyone knew that the firm valued the license at more than it paid for it. This scope for criticism would exist even if it was unjustified, in that the auction had generated the best possible price. But theory says the auction form had another defect. No reserve (or minimum) prices were imposed. More revenue would have been earned if there had been reserve prices because, when there are few bidders (as in New Zealand), a reserve price substitutes for the missing bidding competition. The government abandoned the second-price auctions following the complaints in the media, and now uses first-price sealed-bid auctions instead. The auctions worked better than the alternative, bureaucratic decisions. They assigned the spectrum to its highest-value users, and did so quickly and with low administrative costs. But less revenue was raised than could have been.

An Australian government auction illustrates that it pays to think through the details of auction design. Two licenses for satellite-television services were offered in April 1993 by first-price sealed-bid auction. What followed was high comedy – though it did not seem funny to the communications minister, Senator Bob Collins, who almost lost his job. An opposition politician called it "one of the world's great media license fiascoes." The licenses were won by dark-horse bidders called Hi Vision Ltd. and Ucom Pty. Ltd., who beat the favorites – including a consortium of the big players, Rupert Murdoch, Kerry Packer, and Telecom Australia – by offering startlingly high bids of A$212 million and A$177 million. (A$1 equaled US$0.68.) The government hailed the auction results as opening up "a whole new era," bringing new firms into the closed shop of the Australian television industry. The press quoted one of Hi Vision's directors expressing confidence in his firm's ability to raise the bid amount, despite having issued capital of just A$100.

It soon became apparent that the two parvenu bidders had, in the Australian argot, pulled the wool over the eyes of the government. They had no intention of paying their bids; they had bid high merely to guarantee they won. They had also put in a series of lower bids – reportedly up to 20 such bids at A$5 million intervals. The two proceeded to default on their highest bids, which meant that the licenses had to be re-awarded at the next-highest bids, also theirs. The government had neglected to require a deposit, so default cost the bidders nothing. The prices cascaded down as Ucom and Hi Vision failed to produce the cash for their bids. Four months later, after several defaults by the same two bidders, Ucom paid A$117 million for its license, A$95 million less than its initial bid. Shortly afterwards Ucom sold it to a firm called Australis Media Ltd., earning an agreeable A$21 million profit. The cascading continued on the other license for another five months, with Hi Vision dropping out but then other firms successively defaulting on their bids. The final price was A$77 million, A$100 million less than the original bid. The successful bidder for the second license was none other than Ucom – which then sold it to a joint venture called Continental Century.[4]

This botched auction delayed by almost a year the introduction of pay television into Australia, already one of the few countries in the world still without it. The flaw in the auction rules, the source of the cascading bids, was the absence of a penalty for default, which meant bids were not meaningful. The lesson is that the fine print matters. Any oversight in auction design can have harmful repercussions, as bidders can be counted on to seek ways to outfox the mechanism.

What is the Role of Theory in Auction Design?

Any kind of auction will result in better matches of licenses to firms than allocating the licenses at random, as was done before. But some kinds of auctions work better than others: this was why so much effort went into designing the spectrum auction.

What makes the spectrum auction distinctive are the potential efficiencies from license aggregation. The FCC divided the United States geographically and the spectrum by wavelength, making over 2,500 licenses. There are 51 major trading areas (MTAs), each of which has two large blocks of spectrum (of 30 megahertz). There are also 492 basic trading areas (BTAs), subdivisions of the MTAs, each of which has four spectrum blocks (one of 30 megahertz and four of 10 megahertz). Efficiencies will be realized if bidders succeed in aggregating some of the licenses.

The aggregation efficiencies rest on both engineering and economics. First, firms that have several licenses can spread their fixed costs of technology, acquisition and customer-base development. Second, problems of interference at the boundaries of license areas mean there are production-cost economies from operating adjacent licenses. Third, several different, incompatible technologies are vying to become the industry standard. Consumers will value roaming capability – the ability to use the same telephone when they travel around the country – and this is more likely to be achieved if some firms own enough licenses to cover reasonably large areas. As well as these complementarities, there is also the opposite kind of interdependency: substitution among licenses. Each region contains several slices of the spectrum, so a firm that fails to win one license may bid for another in its place, and the auction design must be flexible enough to allow bidders to switch. It is impossible to foresee what will comprise efficient aggregations of licenses. Different firms want different license combinations. The ideal auction procedure should therefore be flexible enough to enable the bidders to construct their own aggregations.[5]

The government's multiple aims complicated the task of auction design: achieving an efficient outcome, promoting minority-owned and other designed firms, preventing monopolization. An extra goal, not written in the legislation but critical, was that the auction not misfire and cause political damage. Revenue was low on the list. These objectives are not necessarily in conflict with each other. Pursuing efficiency, for example, is usually consistent with pursuing revenue (because efficiency usually means awarding the license to the bidder willing to pay the most). The auction designers took the view that, after the other aims had been met, the auction form should be chosen to maximize revenue.

Theory has limits. Any nontheorist will readily assent to this proposition; but it is useful to be specific about where those limits lie. First, while theory can identify the relevant variables, it cannot tell us much about their size. Theory sometimes shows that there are effects that work in opposite directions from each other, and data are needed to establish which effect is likely to be dominant. Second, transactions costs arise in carrying out some of the policies that the theory recommends, and these costs may swamp the theoretical benefits of the policies. Third, implementing a recommendation of the theory may require knowledge that is unavailable. In particular, some of what auction theory identifies as optimal seller strategies depend on the distributions of bidders' valuations, which were not known. Fourth, the theory does not specify an unambiguously best form for the spectrum auction, which is so complex that no existing theorem covers it.[6]

Each of these limits of theory was met during the spectrum-auction design process. Judgment and guesswork were needed to merge the various partial theories, to weigh the government's various objectives, to estimate the relative sizes of the different effects, and to evaluate whether a proposed scheme was workable. Laboratory experiments also were used to test whether people bid as the theory predicts, and to look for hidden gaps in the rules that might leave the auction open to manipulation by the bidders.

Open Auction or Sealed Bids?

The FCC, following the theorists' recommendation, chose an open auction ahead of a sealed-bid auction. The advantage of an open auction is that it reduces the force of the "winner's curse."[7] The high bidder is the one who most overestimates the value of the item for sale, and thus may find, too late, that it has paid more than the license is worth. However, with billions of dollars at stake (and, for that matter, having been advised by economists) the bidders might anticipate the winner's curse when they decide their bids. A bidding firm that understands the winner's curse avoids falling victim to it by bidding cautiously, discounting its own estimate of the license's value. This discount is large – and rational bidders bid low – if the estimates can range widely around the true value. If bidders bid to avoid the winner's curse, then anything that improves the bidders' information is to the government's advantage, in that it induces the bidders to be less cautious.

Theory says, then, that the government can increase its revenue by publicizing any available information that affects the licenses' assessed value: providing assurances about future regulatory developments, or announcing how much new spectrum will be allocated to telecommunications in the future.

By the same logic of winner's curse avoidance, an open auction yields more revenue than a sealed-bid auction (Milgrom and Weber, 1982a). In a first-price sealed-bid auction, the price is based solely on the winner's own initial value estimate. In an open auction, by contrast, each bidder gets some indirect information about the other bidders' estimates from their bids, so the bidders are more confident and, on average, bid higher.

Two caveats apply to the choice of an open auction. First, the spectrum-auction bidders are likely to be risk averse, given the huge sums being bid. Bidder risk aversion tends to make bids higher in a sealed-bid auction than in an open auction (Riley and Samuelson, 1981). Whether the winner's curse effect exceeds the risk-aversion effect is an empirical issue. Second, if bidder collusion is anticipated, the government might prefer a sealed-bid auction, because it deters collusion more effectively than an open auction (Milgrom, 1987). The FCC and the economist-consultants judged these two effects to be outweighed by the bidders' ability to learn from others' bids in the open auction.

Instead of using a conventional open auction, in which the bidders call out their bids, the FCC chose to run multiple rounds of sealed bids, announcing the bids after each round, and with a minimum bid increment between rounds. This has the informational advantages of a literally open auction, but offers the government extra control. With oral bidding, the bidders automatically know against whom they are competing. With multiple-round sealed bidding, the government can choose what to tell the bidders about the competition. Although the winner's curse idea suggests full information release – all bid amounts and bidder identities – fears of anticompetitive behavior suggest concealing the bidders' identities during the bidding: revealing identities may help bidders to collude. The compromise was to announce the bids during the bidding, but not the bidders' identities.

Simultaneous or Sequential Auction?

The most contentious question during the auction-design process was whether the licenses should be sold in sequence or simultaneously. The debate pitted theoretical virtues against practical feasibility. A simultaneous mechanism promises efficient aggregation of licenses; but the skeptics questioned whether it can realistically deliver on this promise.

Sequential auctions are the usual practice when multiple related items (parcels of real estate, coins, stamps) are sold. The advantage of the sequential method, as some of the economists pointed out, is its administrative simplicity; also, bidders know which licenses they already own and which have gone to others.[8] A drawback of the sequential mechanism in the case of spectrum licenses is that it impedes aggregation by eliminating backup strategies. A bidding firm may rethink its evaluation of one of the early licenses in the light of the bidding activity it observes on the later licenses; but in a sequential setting the bidder cannot go back. Also, predatory bidding can occur (Pitchik and Schotter, 1988). A bidder may try to drive prices for the early licenses up to excessive levels so the winners will be unable to afford to compete for the later licenses.

A simultaneous auction with multiple rounds of bidding allows bidders to take advantage of any information revealed during the bidding. It gives bidders, bidding license by license, full flexibility in constructing license aggregations, and in being able to switch to their backup aggregations should their first-choice aggregations turn out to be too expensive. Its symmetry prevents predatory bidding. Thus a simultaneous mechanism, if it works, creates better license aggregations than a sequential mechanism. The crucial question about any simultaneous mechanism is whether it is workable. It will fail unless an effective stopping rule can be devised.

The two simplest stopping rules are inadequate. One would be to close licenses one by one, as the bidding ceases on each. But this is not really a simultaneous auction: it is effectively sequential, with a random ordering of the licenses. Another simple stopping rule leaves all licenses open until bidding ceases on all. This gives bidders complete flexibility in constructing aggregations, but gives them little incentive to bid actively: they could hold back, waiting for others to show their hands. A bidder wanting to game the mechanism could repeatedly bid on one small license, causing it to take interminably long to close. An effective stopping rule, then, must

1 end the auction in a reasonable time;
2 close the licenses almost simultaneously, to aid license aggregation; and
3 be simple enough to be understandable by the bidders.

Three stopping rules were discussed. One, offered by Paul Milgrom and Robert Wilson, keeps all licenses open until all close, but reduces gaming by means of an activity rule. Bidders must specify in advance, and pay deposits on, the total number of licenses they intend to own. In each round, a bidder must be active on a minimal number of licenses (a specified fraction of the bidder's pre-announced total), which means either being the current high bidder or putting in a bid that exceeds the current high bid by at least the specified increment. The mechanism has three phases, each with an increasingly stringent activity rule. A second stopping rule, offered by Preston McAfee, closes each license separately as the bidding stops on it, but tries to ensure that all licenses close at roughly the same time by slowing down the bidding as final prices are approached. It does this by reducing the minimum bid increment for a given license as the number of active bidders falls, so that when only two bidders remain the price rises slowly. The third stopping rule, offered by the FCC staff and the author of this paper, uses the skewedness of the population distribution among licenses. A relatively small number of licenses (one-fifth) account for 50 percent of the U.S. population: define these licenses to be the core. The all-open-until-all-close rule applies to the licenses in the core. After the core licenses close, all at the same time, the bidding continues in the remaining, smaller licenses, with license-by-license stopping on them. This mechanism therefore permits full efficiency in the core licenses, and sacrifices efficiency to speed of closing in the smaller licenses.

For bids to be meaningful, there must be some penalty on bidders who withdraw their bids (an important consideration, as the Australian example shows). If bids can be freely withdrawn, then the bidders cannot infer any reliable information from each other's bids. How to ensure sincerity of bidding without unduly restricting the bidders' flexibility to shift to backup plans needed a judgment call. One proposal was that, when a bidder withdraws while having the highest bid, the government require the bidder to pay the difference between its bid and the price at which the license ultimately sells (thus having the bidder compensate the government for the loss it causes by reneging on its bid).

The rules of a simultaneous auction, then, are necessarily quite complicated. Critics pointed to a risk of system breakdown: either from an inadvertent gap in the rules that allows bidders to game the mechanism, or from a clerical flaw in the bid-transmission process. The bidders also must be capable of processing a lot of information. The proponents of the simultaneous mechanism (including the author of this article) replied that the potential gains from achieving good license aggregations justified a little complexity.[9]

The FCC, in announcing the auction rules in March 1994, left itself the option of choosing from a range of auction forms, depending on the degree of license inter-dependency and whether the license values are high or low. "Because the Commission expects most licenses to be of high value and interdependent, it found that simultaneous multiple round auctions...should be the Commission's preferred auction design....Be-cause of the superior information and flexibility provided by simultaneous multiple round auctions, this method will facilitate efficient aggregations across spectrum bands" (FCC, 1994, p. 2). The FCC left itself the possibility of using sequential auctions in those cases where the licenses have little interdependence, or single-round sealed bidding where there are large numbers of low-value licenses. For the simultaneous auction, the FCC chose the stopping rule that keeps the bidding open on all licenses until bidding stops on all. An activity rule would be used to ensure the auction closes within a reasonable time. Bidders would be required to pay a substantial deposit, so as to limit the bidding to serious bidders. Bid-withdrawal penalties were imposed to ensure sincere bidding. A high bidder withdrawing its bid during the course of the auction would have to pay the difference between its bid and the price for which the license ultimately sold. For withdrawing a bid after close of the auction there would be an extra 3 percent penalty.

Should Combinational Bids be Permitted?

Should bidders be permitted to bid on combinations of licenses – that is, bids for bundles of licenses together – or should bids be accepted only license-by-license? Private-sector auctions sometimes use combinational bidding when the items are worth more together than separately. When a factory is being sold, for example, the buildings and machines are offered as a set as well as piece by piece (Cassady, 1967, pp. 156–61). In the spectrum auctions it is possible that the license complementarities are large enough that, for efficiency, one or more firms should cover the entire country. This means winning every one of a large number of licenses (51 in the case of MTAs, 492 in the case of BTAs). With so many licenses to be won, it is possible that idiosyncratic events in a few auctions might prevent the efficient aggregation from being achieved. Because of a worry that the FCC had doomed the industry to fragmentation by dividing the nation into so many pieces, some suggested aggregation be aided by allowing nationwide bids, with the nationwide bid winning if it exceeds the sum of the highest bids on the individual licenses.

Theory says, however, that with nationwide bidding, licenses may not end up with the firms that are willing to pay the most (Palfrey, 1983). Nationwide bids can reduce the bidding competition, as the nationwide bidders refrain from driving up the separate-license prices. There is a free-rider problem. Separate-license bidders may not raise their bids by enough to beat a nationwide bidder because only part of the gain from raising their bid accrues to them. As a result, a nationwide bidder may win even though the total value of licenses if awarded separately would exceed the nationwide bidder's value. The auction is biased toward the nationwide bidders.[10] A variant of the nationwide proposal sought to mitigate this implicit favoritism by handicapping nationwide bidders: putting a premium on any nationwide bid, so it wins only if it is at least, say, 5 percent more than the sum of the individual bids (as is sometimes done in the private sector; see Cassady, 1967, p. 160). Most of the economists recommended against permitting nationwide bids, even with a premium.

The ideal level of aggregation may not be nationwide. Some subnational aggregations are likely to be efficient. A more ambitious mechanism allows bidders to express their preferences over aggregations (Banks, Ledyard, and Porter, 1989). Bidders may bid for groups of licenses, in any combinations they choose. A group bid wins if it exceeds the sum of the individual bids. Experiments have found that this mechanism works better than separate-license bidding when the bidders' preferences are idiosyncratic, in that bidders rank the various aggregations differently. (One source of aggregation idiosyncrasies is government regulation: firms that already own cellular licenses are limited in the amount of PCS spectrum they can own in the same region.) If the different bidders have reasonably similar rankings across alternative aggregations, on the other hand, they can construct their own aggregations from individual auctions, and there is no need for combinational bidding. The disadvantage of the full-combinational mechanism is its complexity: both for bidders in understanding how it works and for the government in running it. A huge number of possible combinations exists (for the 492 BTA licenses, more than 10^{148}). Computer or other administrative breakdowns may occur. In the judgment of most of the economists involved in the auction design, the complexity costs outweighed the potential efficiency gains: the full-combinational mechanism was ahead of its time.

The FCC decided that bids for combinations of licenses should not be permitted in a simultaneous auction (at least not before significant proven advances have been made in combinational bidding procedures). If a sequential auction is used, and if it is clear that some particular level of license aggregation is efficient (such as nationwide), then the FCC might adopt combinational bidding, possibly with a bid premium.

How to Aid Designated Bidders?

Congress required the FCC to "ensure that small businesses, rural telephone companies, and businesses owned by members of minority groups and women are given the opportunity to participate in the provision of spectrum based services" (U.S. Congress, 1993, p. 81). Theory says that auctions usually produce efficient outcomes: in most cases the winner is the bidder with the highest use-value for the license. This argues for laissez-faire: letting level-playing-field auctions determine who gets the license. Favoring certain bidders is justified, on the other hand, if bidders' willingness to pay does not reflect social value, because of externalities or capital-market imperfections, or for distributional reasons.

The FCC initially proposed that one-fourth of the spectrum for sale be set aside for bidding by the designated firms only. A skeptic might question this policy for its arbitrariness. Why does one-fourth give the right amount of correction: why not one-third or one-fifth? Also, setting aside some of the licenses lowers revenue by reducing the bidding competition. Theory offers an alternative way of aiding the designated bidders (Myerson, 1981; McAfee and McMillan, 1987, pp. 714–16). The government could allow any firm to bid on any license, but give the designated firms a price preference. With a preference of, say, 10 percent, a designated firm would win if its bid was no more than 10 percent less than the highest nondesignated-firm bid. This is a free-lunch policy. It would not only address the public-policy goal of increasing the number of licenses won by the designated firms, but it would also actually increase the government's revenue. Most of the designated bidders, presumably, have a lower willingness to pay for the licenses than the nondesignated firms (otherwise there would be little need for preferences). With level-playing-field bidding, they would therefore impose little competitive pressure on the nondesignated firms, who could get away with bidding relatively low. A price preference for the designated firms stimulates the bidding competition, forcing the nondesignated firms to bid higher. If the government sets the price preference at the right level, its revenue-raising effect (from the higher bids from the nondesignated firms) outweighs its revenue-lowering effect (from the chance that a designated firm wins and pays a low price). The net effect of the price preference, therefore, is to increase the government's revenue.

A difficulty in applying price preferences is in knowing the appropriate level at which to set them: the only practical approach would be to experiment with different levels (between, say, 5 and 15 percent). As with other choices between price and quantity tools (for example, in the environmental arena), quantity controls can seem more predictable, while price-based instruments seem more uncertain. But, as a rule of thumb, a 10 percent preference would result in about 10 percent more of the licenses being won by designated firms than would have happened without the preference.

In the end, the FCC retained the ability to favor designated bidders in a variety of ways, by using set-asides, price preferences, or installment payments. The FCC also said it would monitor any resale of licenses by these firms. To prevent what it called "unjust enrichment" by auction winners, the rules on resale require any designated firm selling its license to return to the government that part of the profit earned from the sale that is attributable to the artificially low purchase price.

Another kind of special treatment is the award of pioneer preferences. In December 1993 the FCC gave licenses to Omnipoint Communications, Personal Communications, and Cox Enterprises, as a reward for their having developed new PCS technologies. This removed from the auction three of the most valuable licenses, covering New York, Los Angeles, and Washington D.C. Had they been auctioned, they might have fetched up to $1 billion – an implausibly generous reward to the inventors.

Should Royalties or Reserve Prices be Used?

Should winning bidders make a single up-front payment, or should the government extract royalties based on value in use? Theory says royalties increase the revenue from the sale. A three-way tradeoff exists (McAfee and McMillan, 1986; Laffont and Tirole, 1987). Royalties have two revenue-raising effects. First, royalties shift to the government part of the risk otherwise borne by the firm and, if the firm is risk-averse, raise the firm's willingness to pay. Second, and more subtly, royalties stimulate the bidding competition, for they reduce the effect of differences in valuations among the bidders. The cost of using royalties, on the other hand, is that they act as a disincentive to post-auction investment, since the license-holder keeps only a fraction of any revenue generated. The theory shows that, on balance, royalties benefit the government. Royalties on spectrum licenses are probably unworkable, however, since the government would have to compute the profits attributable to the licenses. In a telecommunications firm with multiple lines of business, it would be difficult to isolate the profit from the license alone, and easy for the firm to use creative accounting to understate it. The FCC decided against royalties.

Should the government impose reserve (or minimum) prices? Theory says it should. A reserve price, if set at the right level, can raise the government's revenue by driving up the price in the event that all bidders except one place little value on the license (Myerson, 1981; Riley and Samuelson, 1981). But the reserve price has its effect only when bidding competition is weak. The U.S. spectrum auctions (unlike in New Zealand, with its small population) will probably attract enough bidders to make reserve prices unnecessary. The FCC decided reserve prices, if used at all, would only be on licenses for which only two or three firms had applied to bid.

Spectrum Auctions and Auction Theory

Auctioning spectrum licenses is an idea whose time has come. Nations with inadequate telephone systems – less-developed countries and the formerly Communist countries – are leapfrogging technologies and going straight to wireless rather than laying wires. Once telecommunications ceases to be a state monopoly, a method for allocating the spectrum must be chosen: administrative process, lottery, or auction. An auction offers two advantages over the alternatives: it not only raises revenue, but also identifies the firms with the highest use-values for the spectrum. Egypt, India, and Colombia have auctioned cellular licenses. Argentina's 1993 cellular-license auction illustrates the variety of public-policy purposes to which auctions can be put. The competition was not over price, but over which bidder could offer to set up cellular-telephone service in the fastest time. A consortium including GTE and AT & T won by promising to provide cellular service across a vast area of Argentina's countryside in only one month.[11]

The FCC's spectrum auction is unprecedented in its use of economic theory in the design of the auction. The theorists' contribution showed in the choice of an auction with multiple rounds of bids; in the preference for a simultaneous auction when licenses are interdependent and have high value; in the form of the stopping rule and the use of an activity rule for the simultaneous auction; and in the nature of the bid-withdrawal penalties. The FCC's adoption of a simultaneous multiple-round auction ahead of a sequential or a single-round-sealed-bid auction – which are more conventional but arguably less effective for selling spectrum licenses – was a triumph for game theory. The auction runs through the summer and fall of 1994. The intriguing next step will be to appraise its performance.

Notes

1 *Business Week*, November 29, 1993, p. 128; and Tom Wheeler, president of the Cellular Telecommunications Industry Association, in the *Financial Times*, October 18, 1993, p. VIII.

2 Wilson (1969, 1977) started the theory of auctions. Milgrom and Weber (1982a) developed many of the ideas used in designing the spectrum auction. For surveys of the theory, see McAfee and McMillan (1987), Milgrom (1987, 1989), and Wilson (1992); and on its practical content, see McMillan (1992; chs. 11–13).

3 For more on the methods the U.S. government has used for allocating the spectrum, see Kwerel and Felker (1985), Kwerel and Williams (1993), U.S. Department of Commerce (1991), and Congressional Budget Office (1992). The estimate of cellular-license values, based on the stock market value of cellular firms, is from U.S. Department of Commerce (1991, p. D6). The Cape Cod story is from the *New York Times*, May 30, 1991, p. A1.

4 The saga did not end with the award of the licenses. Outsmarted by the upstarts, the Murdoch–Packer–Telecom consortium belatedly tried some gaming of its own, seeking to undermine the auction. It investigated using alternative technologies for delivering pay television, to squeeze the two new entrants out of the market. It tried to make a side-deal to gain control of another satellite license that the government had reserved for the state-run Australian Broadcasting Corporation. When that failed it sued to overturn the auction outcome, alleging the government had not complied with the bid guidelines; it withdrew its suit five minutes into the court hearing. (This story has been pieced together from reports in the *Age*, the *Australian*, the *Australian Financial Review*, the *Financial Times*, and the *Sydney Morning Herald* between April 1993 and March 1994.)

5 The secondary market in licenses will help to correct any mismatches of licenses to firms that result from defects in auction design (as it did when the licenses went by lottery). This does not, however, render auction design unimportant. The secondary market is likely to be thin; transactions costs will limit its ability to fix inefficiencies.

6 The main shortcoming of the existing theory is the lack of a model of aggregation of the items for sale. Engelbrecht-Wiggans and Weber (1979), Milgrom and Weber (1982b), Palfrey (1983),

Hausch (1986), McAfee and McMillan (1988), Maskin and Riley (1990), and McAfee and Vincent (1993) model auctions of multiple items, but without interdependencies. Gale (1990) models an auction with aggregation efficiencies and shows that the seller optimally bundles all the licenses; but the assumption that full aggregation is ideal makes this inapplicable to the PCS auction. Lang and Rosenthal (1991) model the auctioning of items that are substitutes for each other. Bernheim and Whinston (1986) characterize equilibria in the bidding for combinations of items, assuming the bidders know each others' valuations. Much of what is known about multi-unit auctions with interdependencies comes from experiments: Grether, Isaac and Plott (1981, 1989), Rassenti, Smith, and Bulfin (1982), Banks, Ledyard, and Porter (1989), Brewer and Plott (1993).

7   The winner's curse was first identified by Wilson (1969). Auction theory has two basic models: the common-value model and the independent-private-values model. The spectrum auction has aspects of both of these polar cases (so the bidders' valuations are affiliated: Milgrom and Weber, 1982a). Values are private insofar as different bidders have different stocks of capital, labor, and knowledge, and so different prospects for earning profits from the licenses. Values are common, on the other hand, insofar as there is uncertainty about technological possibilities and about consumer demand for the new mobile communication services: the bidders have their own estimates of technology and demand, but are trying to estimate the same number, the common value. The secondary market also induces a common-value aspect, as the bids reflect guesses of the prices that will rule there. Winner's curse effects reflect common values.

8   If a sequential mechanism is used, should the licenses covering the largest populations go first or last? For efficiency, the best ordering is large to small, as the large regions are the key parts of any aggregations. This ordering may mean sacrificing some revenue. The bidders learn from the early bidding, so the winner's curse discounts are smaller – and bids higher – the more regions have already been sold. If the smaller regions go first, then by the time the big regions are sold the winner's curse effect is reduced. An opposite revenue effect also exists, however: as the large-to-small ordering generates more efficiency, it raises the potential revenue and may raise realized revenue. Since Congress said efficiency had precedence over revenue, large-to-small was the recommended ordering.

9   A precedent – a large-scale simultaneous auction that worked – is the 1992 sale by Czechoslovakia (as it was then) of shares in nearly 1,500 state-owned firms (Svejnar and Singer, 1992). The auction was Walrasian. In the first round, the privatization ministry set a price per share. A bid, by vouchers, consisted of a request for a stated number of shares at the set price. In subsequent rounds, the ministry set the price as a function of earlier-round excess demands or supplies. Only five rounds were held, so price adjustments between rounds had to be large and misjudgments occurred, with some big swings from excess demand to excess supply and back. The Czechoslovakian auction was successful, however, in that it established equilibrium relative prices for the firms' shares, and disposed of all but 7 percent of the 22 million shares.

10 Imagine there are three bidders, E, W, and N, and two licenses, East and West (this example is due to Preston McAfee). Firm E values owning East alone at $2 billion, West alone at $1 billion, and the nation at $3 billion. Firm W values East at $1 billion, West at $2 billion, and the nation at $3 billion. Firm N values East at $1.6 billion, West at $1.6 billion, and the nation at $3.3 billion. Suppose first that nationwide bidding is not allowed. In the two open auctions, W wins West at a price slightly above $1.6 billion (which is the price at which the second-last bidder, who happens to be N, drops out), and E wins East at slightly above $1.6 billion. This is the ideal outcome, in that the licenses go to their highest-value users. The total value of the licenses to their new owners is $4 billion, of which the government gets a little over $3.2 billion. Now suppose there is a national auction in addition to the separate auctions. Anticipating winning the nationwide auction, N has no incentive to bid for the separate licenses. Only E and W bid for them, so the price in each stops at slightly more than $1 billion. All three bidders compete in

the national auction. Firm N wins the nationwide bidding at slightly above $3 billion, which is where both E and W drop out. The nationwide bid of $3 billion exceeds the sum of the two separate bids, so the nationwide bidder N wins. This is not the efficient outcome: the total use-value is $3.3 billion and government revenue slightly above $3 billion. The free-rider point is that E and W would have to raise their nationwide bids by a total of $1 billion to beat N; but neither alone will raise its bid this much, as that would mean bidding more than value. Now make one change to the example: increase N's value of the nation to $4 billion, so ideally N would win the nation. But N wins even without nationwide bidding, by bidding slightly more than $2 billion in each separate auction.

11 *Financial Times*, January 25, 1994, p. 6; *Wall Street Journal*, January 28, 1994, p. A8; *New York Times*, November 9, 1993, p. C16.

References

Banks, J. S., Ledyard, J. O. and Porter, D. P. (1989): "Allocating Uncertain and Unresponsive Resources: An Experimental Approach," *Rand Journal of Economics*, 20, Spring, 1–22.

Bernheim, B. D. and Whinston, M. D. (1986): "Menu Auctions, Resource Allocation, and Economic Influence," *Quarterly Journal of Economics*, 101, February, 1–32.

Brewer, P. and Plott, C. R. (1993): "Decentralized Allocation of the Use of a Transportation Network," mimeo, California: Institute of Technology, Pasadena, November.

Cassady, R. (1967): *Auctions and Auctioneering*. Berkeley: University of California Press.

Coase, R. H. (1959): "The Federal Communications Commission," *Journal of Law and Economics*, 2, October, 1–40.

Congressional Budget Office (1992): "Auctioning Radio Spectrum Licenses," Washington, D.C., March.

Engelbrecht-Wiggans, R. and Weber, R. J. (1979): "An Example of a Multi-Object Auction Game," *Management Science*, 25, December, 1272–7.

Federal Communications Commission (FCC) (1993): "Notice of Proposed Rule Making," Washington, D.C., October.

——(1994): "FCC Adopts Rules to Implement Competitive Bidding to Award Spectrum Licenses," press release, Washington D.C., March 8.

Gale, I. (1990): "A Multiple-Object Auction with Superadditive Values," *Economics Letters*, 34, December, 323–8.

Grether, D. M, Isaac, R. M. and Plott, C. R. (1981): "The Allocation of Landing Rights by Unanimity Among Competitors," *American Economic Review Papers and Proceedings*, 71, May, 166–71.

——(1989): *The Allocation of Scarce Resources: Experimental Economics and the Problem of Allocating Airport Slots*. Boulder: Westview Press.

Hausch, D. B. (1986): "Multi-Object Auctions: Sequential vs. Simultaneous Sales," *Management Science*, 32, December, 1599–610.

Kwerel, E. R. and Felker, A. (1985): "Using Auctions to Select FCC Licenses," OPP working paper 16, Office of Plans and Policy, ECC, May.

Kwerel, E. R. and Williams, J. R. (1993): "Moving Toward a Market for Spectrum," *Regulation*, 16 (2), 53–62.

Laffont, J-J. and Tirole, J. (1987): "Auctioning Incentive Contracts," *Journal of Political Economy*, 95, October, 921–37.

Lang, K. and Rosenthal, R. W. (1991) "The Contractors' Game," *Rand Journal of Economics*, 22, Autumn, 329–38.

Maskin, E. and Riley, J. (1990): "Optimal Multi-Unit Auctions," in F. Hahn (ed.), *The Economics of Missing Markets and Information*, Oxford: Oxford University Press, 312–33.

McAfee, R. P. and McMillan, J. (1986): "Bidding for Contracts: A Principal-Agent Analysis," *Rand Journal of Economics*, 17, Autumn, 326–38.

——(1987): "Auctions and Bidding," *Journal of Economic Literature*, 25, June, 699–738.

——(1988): "Multidimensional Incentive Compatibility and Mechanism Design," *Journal of Economic Theory*, 46, December, 335–54.

McAfee, R. P. and Vincent, D. (1993): "The Declining Price Anomaly," *Journal of Economic Theory*, 60, June, 191–212.

McMillan, J. (1992): *Games, Strategies, and Managers.* New York: Oxford University Press.

Milgrom, P. (1987): "Auction Theory," in T. Bewley (ed.), *Advances in Economic Theory*, Cambridge: Cambridge University Press, 1–32.

——(1989): "Auctions and Bidding: A Primer," *Journal of Economic Perspectives*, 3, Summer, 3–22.

—— and Weber, R. J. (1982a): "A Theory of Auctions and Competitive Bidding," *Econometrica*, 50, September, 1089–122.

—— and Weber, R. J. (1982b): "A Theory of Auctions and Competitive Bidding II," mimeo, Northwestern University.

Mueller, M. (1991): "Reform of Spectrum Management: Lessons from New Zealand," Policy Insight 135, Reason Foundation, Los Angeles, November.

Myerson, R. (1981): "Optimal Auction Design," *Mathematics of Operations Research*, 6, February, 58–73.

National Economic Research Associates (NERA), (1988): *Management of the Radio Frequency Spectrum in New Zealand. A report for the New Zealand Government.* London: NERA, November.

Office of Management and Budget (OMB), (1993): *Mid-Session Review of the 1994 Budget.* Washington, D.C., September.

Palfrey, T. R. (1983): "Bundling Decisions by a Multiproduct Monopolist with Incomplete Information," *Econometrica*, 51, March, 463–85.

Pitchik, C. and Schotter, A. (1988): "Perfect Equilibria in Budget-Constrained Sequential Auctions: An Experimental Study," *Rand Journal of Economics*, 19, Autumn, 363–88.

Rassenti, S. J., Smith, V. L. and Bulfin, R. L. (1982): "A Combinational Auction Mechanism for Airport Time Slot Allocation," *Bell Journal of Economics*, 13, Autumn, 402–17.

Riley, J. and Samuelson, W. (1981): "Optimal Auctions," *American Economic Review*, 71, June, 381–92.

Svejnar, J. and Singer, M. (1992): "The Czechoslovak Voucher Privatization: An Assessment of Results," mimeo, University of Pittsburgh, December.

U.S. Congress, (1993): Omnibus Budget Reconciliation Act of 1993, Conference Report [HR 2264], Title VI, "Communications Licensing and Spectrum Allocation Improvement," report 103–213, August 4.

U.S. Department of Commerce, (1991): *U.S. Spectrum Management Policy: Agenda for the Future.* Washington, D.C., NTIA Special Publication February, 91–23.

Wilson, R. B. (1969): "Competitive Bidding with Disparate Information," *Management Science*, 15, March, 446–8.

——(1977): "A Bidding Model of Perfect Competition," *Review of Economic Studies*, 44, October, 511–18.

——(1992): "Strategic Analysis of Auctions," in R. J. Aumann and S. Hart (eds), *Handbook of Game Theory with Economic Applications*, vol. 1, Amsterdam: North-Holland, 227–80.

CHAPTER EIGHTEEN

Analyzing the Airwaves Auction

R. PRESTON MCAFEE AND JOHN MCMILLAN

Source: *Journal of Economic Perspectives*, 10, 1 (1996), pp. 159–75. Reprinted with the permission of the authors and the American Economic Association. © American Economic Association.

Just as the Nobel committee was recognizing game theory's role in economics by awarding the 1994 prize to John Nash, John Harsanyi and Reinhard Selten, game theory was being put to its biggest use ever. Billions of dollars worth of spectrum licenses were being sold by the U.S. government, using a novel auction form designed by economic theorists. Suddenly, game theory became news. William Safire in the *New York Times* called it "the greatest auction in history." *The Economist* remarked, "When government auctioneers need worldly advice, where can they turn? To mathematical economists, of course.... As for the firms that want to get their hands on a sliver of the airwaves, their best bet is to go out first and hire themselves a good game theorist." *Fortune* said it was the "most dramatic example of game theory's new power.... It was a triumph, not only for the FCC and the taxpayers, but also for game theory (and game theorists)." *Forbes* said, "Game theory, long an intellectual pastime, came into its own as a business tool." The *Wall Street Journal* said, "Game theory is hot."[1]

The government auctioned licenses to use the electromagnetic spectrum for personal communications services (PCS): mobile telephones, two-way paging, portable fax machines and wireless computer networks. Thousands of licenses were offered, varying in both geographic coverage and the amount of spectrum covered. The bidders were the local, long-distance and cellular telephone companies, as well as paging and cable television companies and a host of smaller firms. The Federal Communications Commission (FCC) chose an innovative form of auction over the time-tested alternatives (like a sealed-bid auction), because theorists predicted it would induce more competitive bidding and a better match of licenses to firms.

The designing of the spectrum auction has been described in this journal by McMillan (1994).[2] In what follows, we examine how the auction actually worked. We describe the strategies used by the bidders, and analyze the success of the auction in realizing the government's goals. While theory was used in designing the auction, in turn the auction has stimulated further theorizing, as we discuss. We also propose some other potential uses of the auction form that the FCC pioneered.

The Simultaneous Ascending Auction

In the 1993 legislation authorizing the FCC to hold auctions, Congress charged the FCC with encouraging an "efficient and intensive use of the electromagnetic spectrum." Congress also said the auction should advance various public-policy goals and in particular ensure some licenses went to minority-owned and women-owned firms. Congress said revenue raising was an aim of the auction, but gave it a low priority.

The auction the FCC adopted is a *simultaneous ascending auction*, first proposed by Paul Milgrom and Robert Wilson (consultants for Pacific Telesis) and Preston McAfee (a consultant for Air Touch Communications). Multiple licenses are open for bidding at the same time, and remain open as long as there is some bidding on any of the licenses. Bidding occurs over rounds, with the results of each round announced to the bidders before the start of the next. The auction is run by computer, with on-line bidding.

Many detailed rules are needed to support the broad principles of the simultaneous ascending auction. Months of work by FCC officials (Evan Kwerel's contribution to the design process was crucial) and the theorist-consultants (including John McMillan, who worked for the FCC) went into writing the auction rules to close any gaps that could be exploited by clever bidders: the rules, in FCC (1994), cover more than 130 pages. The most important of these details are the activity rules (devised by Milgrom and Wilson). A bidding firm might play cautiously, waiting to see how the others bid while not revealing its own intentions. If all bid in this way the auction would take inordinately long to close. The activity rules are designed to prevent the bidders from holding back, so the auction proceeds at a reasonable pace. Before the auction, each bidder must specify how many licenses it hopes to win and must post a proportionate bond. A bidder is defined to be active on a particular license if either it has the standing high bid from the previous round or it submits an acceptable bid in this round. The auction has three stages, each containing an unspecified number of bidding rounds. In the first stage a bidder must be active on licenses that add up to one-third of its desired total; in the second stage, two- thirds; and in the final stage, 100 percent. If a bidder ever falls short of the required activity level, the number of licenses it is eligible to own shrinks proportionately. There is no prespecified final round; instead, the auction closes when no one wants to continue bidding. Other rules define the size of bid increments, the penalties for bid withdrawal,[3] provisions for waivers from the activity rules, the length of time for a bidding round, and so on.

Why use a simultaneous ascending auction? Why not use the time-tested method, a sequential auction, in which the licenses are simply offered one after the other? Or why not use the quickest method, offering all the licenses simultaneously in a single round of sealed bids? The main reason is that the licenses are interdependent. For most of the licenses there is a close substitute: a twin license that covers the same region and the same amount of spectrum. Licenses are also complementary: a license may be more valuable if the holder also has the license for a contiguous region.

Efficiency in a spectrum auction – which means assigning the licenses to the firms best able to use them – requires that some bidders win multiple licenses, because of the license complementarities. The FCC did not know before the sale how the licenses should be aggregated: partly because the technology was new, but also because different bidders had different, mutually inconsistent preferred aggregations (for various reasons, such as their cellular-telephone holdings and local expertise). The simultaneous ascending auction was designed to let market processes establish the shape of the license aggregations.

Both features of the auction form – the *simultaneous* bids and the *ascending* bids – aid efficiency. The ascending bids let bidders see how highly their rivals value each license and which aggregations they are seeking. By the time equilibrium is approached, each bidding firm knows whether it is likely to be able to construct its preferred aggregation and roughly how much it is going to cost. With all licenses open for bidding simultaneously, a bidder has flexibility to seek whatever license aggregation it wishes, as well as to switch to a back-up aggregation if its first-choice aggregation becomes too expensive.

As well as aiding license aggregation, the ascending bidding, by allowing bidders to respond to each others' bids, diminishes the winner's curse: that is, the tendency for naive bidders to bid up the price beyond the license's actual value, or for shrewd bidders to bid cautiously to avoid overpaying. Also, ascending simultaneous bidding means it is likely that substitute licenses fetch similar prices, because bidders can switch across the substitutes if their bid prices differ, bidding up any lower-priced licenses.

The alternative auction forms do not assure either efficient aggregation or that similar items will fetch the same price.[4] A single-round, sealed-bid auction, for example, would almost certainly cause a poor match of licenses to firms. Bidders must bid blind, unable to know how high they must bid to win a particular license. Only by good luck would a bidding firm win all the licenses it needs for an efficient aggregation; bad luck could mean the firm wins more licenses than it needs. Also, the bidders' fear of the winner's curse induces more cautious bidding and lower prices than ascending bids would yield. The risk of winning too many licenses further induces low bidding from budget-constrained bidders. Simultaneous single-round, sealed-bid auctions were used in New Zealand for spectrum licenses and in Australia for satellite-television licenses, with disappointing results: low revenues and inefficient license allocations (McMillan, 1994).

Sequential auctions also have problems. First, identical items can sell for quite different prices: items sold later in the sequence typically fetch less than items sold earlier (Ashenfelter, 1989; McAfee and Vincent, 1993). Second, a firm might bid in a predatory manner, driving early prices unreasonably high to eliminate its budget-constrained rivals from the later bidding (Pitchik and Schotter, 1988). Third, and most important, the sequential form hinders license aggregation. In the early auctions, a firm must bid without knowing whether it will win complementary licenses offered later. Later, a firm may wish to rebid on a license already sold if it discovers it needs that license to complete its set; but in a sequential auction it cannot go back. One of the pitfalls of the sequential auction is shown by the 1981 sale of seven identical licenses to use RCA's communications satellite for cable television broadcasts. Sotheby Parke Bernet ran a sequential auction. The winning bids varied widely. The highest (on the first license sold) was $14.4 million, and the lowest (the sixth license) was $10.7 million.[5] The FCC nullified the auction, saying the procedure was "unjustly discriminatory" in levying different prices for the same service, and ordered RCA to charge the same price to all. The inflexibility of the sequential auction caused the $3.7 million (or 26 percent) price difference. It would not have arisen had a simultaneous ascending auction been used, as price disparities would be bid away.[6]

After-market trading of licenses is permitted, subject to FCC approval, and such trading will assist in ultimately producing an efficient allocation of spectrum rights. But it is unrealistic to believe that the after-market can completely solve the allocation problem no matter what the initial allocation – which would mean the auction form would not matter – because it will be far from fully competitive. There will be few buyers and few sellers. Also, the firms possess private information about license values through their knowledge of customers, local conditions and technology. Modern theory shows that private information can hinder efficient trade (Akerlof, 1970; Myerson and Satterthwaite, 1983).

Persuaded of the superiority of the simultaneous ascending auction by the theorists, and of its workability by some experiments, the FCC decided to adopt it. The FCC's courage in using an untried mechanism devised by a set of mathematical economists was rewarded: the simultaneous ascending auction came to be widely regarded as a success.

Auction Performance

Because of the logistical complexities of running a huge simultaneous auction, not all of the roughly 2,000 licenses were offered for sale at once. The FCC planned five auctions, each in the simultaneous ascending format. Three have been held at the time of this writing. The first two sold narrowband licenses, thin slivers of the spectrum to be used for paging services: nationwide licenses were sold in July 1994 and regional licenses in October 1994, covering 1.2 mHz of spectrum between them. The other auctions offer broadband licenses, which cover a wide enough slice of spectrum to be usable for voice and data mobile communications services. The third and largest auction, which ran from December 1994 to March 1995, sold 60 mHz of spectrum: two 30 mHz broadband licenses covering relatively large geographic areas (the "major trading areas," or MTAs, which divide the United States into 51 regions). The fourth and fifth auctions will each offer broadband licenses covering 30 mHz of spectrum over smaller areas (the "basic trading areas," or BTAs, which divide the United States into 492 regions).

The Office of Management and Budget estimated in 1993 that $10 billion would be paid for the broadband spectrum – enough to make a dent in the budget deficit. The industry's immediate response to this estimate was (possibly strategic) skepticism. BellSouth chairman John Clendenin said, "There is no rational methodology on which that $10 billion was calculated." The government estimate, he asserted, "was sort of pulled out of thin air" (and perhaps he was right). MCI chairman Bert Roberts said, "The government is smoking something to think they are going to get $10 billion for these licenses." As it turned out, however, the government's estimate was low.

"For once, the government is doing a great job of dragging money out of people," said Wayne Perry of McCaw Cellular Communications during the first auction. The two narrowband auctions raised over $1 billion, far more than most predictions. Then the broadband MTA auction attracted the big spenders: Wirelessco L.P. (a consortium of the Sprint Corp. with the cable television companies TCI, Comcast and Cox), which bid a total of $2.1 billion; the AT&T Corp., $1.7 billion; PCS Primeco L.P. (a consortium of Bell Atlantic, U.S. West, AirTouch and Nynex), $1.1 billion; and the Pacific Telesis Group (or PacTel), $0.7 billion. Selling half the 120 mHz of broadband spectrum, this auction raised $7.7 billion.[7]

The simultaneous ascending auction should yield similar prices for similar items. Did it? The nationwide narrowband auction priced similar licenses very closely (see Table 1:

Table 1   Auction results for nationwide narrowband licenses

Licence	Winning bid ($ millions)	Winning bidder
50/50 kHz	80.0	Paging Network of Virginia
50/50 kHz	80.0	Paging Network of Virginia
50/50 kHz	80.0	KDM Messaging Co.
50/50 kHz	80.0	KDM Messaging Co.
50/50 kHz	80.0	Nationwide Wireless Network Corp.
50/12.5 kHz	47.0	AirTouch Paging
50/12.5 kHz	47.5	BellSouth Wireless
50/12.5 kHz	47.5	Nationwide Wireless Network Corp.
50 kHz	37.0	Paging Network of Virginia
50 kHz	38.0	Pagemart II, Inc.
Total	617.0	

The 50/50 and 50/12.5 licenses each have two separated slices of spectrum, to allow two-way pager communication.
Source: FCC (1994).

Table 2   Auction results for regional narrowband licenses (*discounted final prices in millions and winning bidder by region and spectrum block*)

Region/ Block	1	2	3	4	5	6
(kHz)	(50/50)	(50/50)	(50/12.5)	(50/12.5)	(50/12.5)	(50/12.5)
Northeast	17.5	14.9	9.5	9.0	8.7	10.3
	Pagemart	PCSD	Mobile	Am.W.	AirTouch	L.G.S.
South	18.4	18.8	11.8	11.5	8.0	11.3
	Pagemart	PCSD	Mobile	Am.W.	Instacheck	L.G.S.
Midwest	16.8	17.4	9.3	10.1	9.5	10.3
	Pagemart	PCSD	Mobile	Am.W.	Ameritech	L.G.S.
Central	17.3	17.1	8.3	8.8	8.3	10.5
	Pagemart	PCSD	Mobile	Am.W.	AirTouch	Benbow
West	22.6	22.8	14.9	14.3	14.3	10.9
	Pagemart	PCSD	Mobile	Am.W.	AirTouch	Benbow
Total	92.6	90.9	53.7	53.6	48.7	53.2

Spectrum blocks 1 and 2 consisted of two 50 kHz channels; blocks 3, 4, 5 and 6 consisted of one 50 kHz and one 12.5 kHz channel. Spectrum blocks 2 and 6 had the 40 percent minority/woman credit; the prices shown for these two licenses are net of this discount. "PCSD" is the PCS Development Corp. "Mobile" is Mobilemedia, Inc. "Am.W." is American Wireless Messaging. "L.G.S." is Lisa-Gaye Shearing.
Source: FCC (1994).

the five 100 kHz licenses are close substitutes, as are the three 65.5 kHz licenses and the two 50 kHz licenses). In the regional narrowband auction, prices for substitute licenses were similar, though not as close as in the nationwide auction (see Table 2: licenses 1 and 2 are substitutes, as are licenses 3, 4, 5 and 6). A price disparity existed across the two auctions, however: prices in the regional auction were higher than in the earlier nationwide auction (compare the last row of Table 2 with Table 1).

Prices were lower in the broadband MTA auction than in the narrowband auctions. The average broadband price per pop (that is, price per person covered by the license) was $15.51, which meant the price per mHz-pop was just 16 percent of the narrowband price. The lower prices had several sources. First, the broadband spectrum has intrinsically lower value, as some of it has incumbent users who will have to be moved. Second, the firms had budget constraints, the sums bid being large even for a firm as big as AT&T. Third, the competition was less intense, as the ratio of initially expressed demand to licenses for sale was just two-to-one.

The broadband prices varied greatly from license to license. The winners of the ten largest-population licenses are shown in Table 3. Highest in price per pop were Chicago ($31.90 and $30.88), Atlanta ($28.58 and $26.60) and Seattle ($27.79 and $27.48). Lowest in price per pop were Guam ($0.61 for both licenses) and Alaska ($1.82 and $3.00). Variations in price in part reflect regional variations in predicted demand for PCS services. The profitability of a license varies with income level, population density, predicted population growth and so on. There are also bidder-specific effects, such as home-base advantages for the local Bell companies or the ownership of a cellular license in a neighboring area. Some of the price differences, however, do not seem to be explained by value differences: for example, the Chicago price per pop is nearly twice New York and 20 percent higher than Los Angeles. Few bidders were eligible to bid on some licenses. Chicago was the only license among the top ten for which all three of the big bidders competed: AT&T, Primeco and Wirelessco. Some of the price variations reflect differences in the strength of competition.

Revenue is not the only criterion for evaluating the FCC auctions; it is not even the main goal. Another criterion is whether the auctions generated an economically efficient

Table 3   Auction results for broadband MTA licenses *(top 10 licenses, winner and price bid in $ millions)*

Region/Block	A		B	
New York	[a]		Wirelessco	443
Los Angeles	[a]		PacTel	494
Chicago	AT&T	373	Primeco	385
San Francisco	Wirelessco	207	PacTel	202
Detroit	AT&T	81	Wirelessco	86
Charlotte	AT&T	67	BellSouth	71
Dallas	Primeco	88	Wirelessco	88
Boston	AT&T	122	Wirelessco	127
Philadelphia	AT&T	81	Phillieco	85
Washington	[a]		AT&T	212
Total revenue:	$7.7 billion (including pioneer preference awards)			

Wirelessco includes Sprint, TCI, Comcast and Cox. Primeco includes Bell Atlantic, US West, AirTouch and Nynex.
[a]Pioneer preference award.
Source: FCC (1994).

allocation; that is, assigned the licenses to the firms best able to use them, given the complementarities among licenses and the gains from aggregations.

Only time will tell whether the auctions put the licenses into the hands of the right firms. The secondary market will give some evidence. A large number of licenses being resold would suggest that the auction had produced an inefficient allocation. Little secondary-market activity would not provide decisive evidence of efficiency, however, because the secondary market will be thin, with few players and large informational asymmetries, and cannot be expected to work smoothly. Conclusive evidence on the efficiency of the auction outcome will come only after the firms have their mobile-communications services operating, which will take several years. The bid data do, however, allow us to speculate on whether the simultaneous ascending auction allowed the bidders to construct efficient license aggregations.

For the regional narrowband auction, the FCC divided the country into five regions, with six licenses in each. Four bidders – Pagemart, PCS Development Corp., Mobileme-dia, Inc., and American Wireless Messaging – assembled nationwide licenses, winning all five licenses in a particular wavelength. Also, two bidders built consistent subnational aggregations: AirTouch won three of the licenses on one waveband, and Lisa-Gaye Shearing won three on another (see Table 2). This suggests that the auction did enable the bidders to build their desired aggregations.

Did the bidders in the broadband MTA auction achieve efficient aggregations? PacTel won the aggregation that it had made no secret it was seeking: northern plus southern California. The other three big bidders appeared to bid for the licenses that filled gaps in their cellular holdings.[8] They did not fill all of their gaps, but they came close. Of the 46 contiguous-U.S. licenses, when previous cellular holdings are added to the new PCS winnings, AT&T owns 40, Wirelessco owns 39 and Primeco owns 38. Each of these firms holds cellular or PCS licenses in each of the top ten markets (with the exception of Wirelessco's missing Chicago, since all three competed for the two Chicago licenses).

The bid data suggest, then, that the auctions facilitated license aggregation. The bidders agreed. After the broadband auction, Primeco president George F. Schmitt said his group expected to have a complete nationwide network operating within two years. Steven Hooper, chairman of AT&T's mobile-telephone subsidiary, said, "This enables us to build a nationwide network."[9]

A failure some feared for the auction appears not to have occurred. A bidder seeking a particular aggregation might unexpectedly fail to win a crucial license. Then the licenses that bidder wins might be worth less than their total price, bid in anticipation of winning the lost license. Some economists argued that, for this reason, bidders should be allowed to bid for combinations of licenses, rather than bidding license by license.[10] It does not appear, however, that bidders became exposed in this way. If they had, we would expect to see them withdrawing bids. In fact there were few withdrawals, and those that occurred did not seem to result from license aggregation failures. In the broadband MTA auction, for example, Wirelessco seemed not to change its bidding behavior after it lost the Chicago licenses. Failure to complete an aggregation might not be serious. The complementarities may not be so sizable as to generate large discontinuities in the values of aggregations. Also, substitution is possible: Wirelessco could complete its set by winning licenses in a later auction, or by forming alliances with other firms.

Congress stated a further criterion for the auction, beyond efficiency and revenue. Some licenses should go to minority-and woman-owned firms, small businesses and rural telephone companies. The initial auction design had ambitious provisions to aid these so-called "designated entities." FCC chairman Reed E. Hundt said this would be "the single most important economic opportunity made available to women and minorities in our country's history." The first two auctions ran under these rules. Then a June 1995 Supreme Court judgment that an affirmative-action program must be "narrowly tailored" to support "a compelling governmental interest" induced the FCC to scrap the race-and gender-based preferences. Some preferences remain, however. The fourth auction, offering 30 mHz (not held at the time of writing), is to be limited to entrepreneurs (defined as firms with less than $125 million in annual revenue and $500 million in assets) and small businesses (revenue under $40 million), with the latter receiving bid discounts.

The designated entities were eligible for a discount in the nationwide narrowband auction: if they won they would pay 25 percent less than their bid. The size of this discount was set by guesswork as, this being the first auction, there were no data from which to estimate its effects. As it turned out, 25 percent was too small for any of them to win licenses. For the second auction, the regional narrowband auction, the FCC used higher preferences. On two of the six wavebands the designated firms were offered a 40 percent discount. Minority bidders won all 10 licenses on which they were offered discounts (see Table 2). PCS Development Corp., a start-up minority company, won a nationwide aggregation. The prices on the designated licenses were bid so much higher than the other licenses that in net terms, after subtracting the discount, the designated firms paid approximately as much as the nonfavored firms. (The designated entities still received some special treatment, however, as they were permitted to pay in installments.)

Bid discounts not only address the policy goal of getting licenses into the hands of the designated firms, but also can actually boost the government's revenue (Myerson, 1981; McAfee and McMillan, 1988, 1989). The designated bidders, presumably, have a lower willingness to pay for the licenses than the nondesignated firms – otherwise preferences would not be needed. With level-playing-field bidding, they would therefore not be competitive with the nondesignated firms, who could bid low. A discount for the designated firms stimulates the bidding competition, forcing the nondesignated firms to bid higher. This may have happened in the narrowband auctions. Prices rose 12 percent higher in the regional auction than in the nationwide auction (the average price per mHz-pop was $3.10 in the nationwide auction and $3.47 net of discounts in the regional auction). Perhaps, as the theory says, the discounts did increase the bidding competition.

Bidder Strategies

"Bidding for the PCS licenses is like playing a dozen hands of billion-dollar poker at once," said the *Wall Street Journal* (23.12.1995, p. B1) Bidder strategies can be aggressive or passive. The theorists, when designing the auction, expected that the bidders would be cagey, revealing to their rivals as little of their intentions as the auction rules permitted. As it happened, in the first two auctions many of the bidders behaved much more aggressively than this. But in the third, the broadband MTA auction, the huge amounts of money at stake induced the bidders to be circumspect, as the theorists had predicted.

Aggressive bidding took the form of "jump bidding:" entering bids that were far above the required minimum. In the nationwide narrowband auction, one spectacular jump bid was 138 percent above the previous high bid. In nine instances, bids were between 40 and 70 percent above the previous high, and in 20 cases they were 20 to 40 percent higher (minimum increments were typically 5 to 10 percent). The jump bidding occurred in the early rounds, including the opening bids. The 30 bids that beat the standing bid by 20 percent or more all came in the first 27 rounds of the auction (which took 46 rounds to close). An extreme form of jump bidding, which happened on several occasions, involved submitting a higher bid for a license on which the bidder already had the standing high bid. Jump bidding was common also in the regional narrowband auction.

Jump bidding is intended to signal the jump bidder's toughness, to try to persuade the others it is pointless to compete (Avery, 1993). Did jump bidding achieve the bidders' aims, or did it just aid the FCC by speeding up the auction? Despite jump bidding's prevalence in the two narrowband auctions, most of the jump bids were eventually overtaken. Few of the final prices were reached by a jump bid; instead, the final prices were reached gradually, by a series of minimum-increment bids. This suggests that the jump bids had little effect, for they did not deter competitors.

By the time of the third and biggest of the auctions, the broadband MTA auction, the bidders, having observed the two narrowband auctions, had apparently decided that jump bids did not work, for they mostly eschewed them. A few jump bids were used. Some-times a bid beat the standing bid by twice the minimum increment; in round 30 ALAACR Communications, Inc., raised Pacific Telesis's $183 million bid on Los Angeles to $300 million; in round 81 Wirelessco submitted bids on four small markets that exceeded the standing bids by 10 times the minimum increment; and on a handful of occasions bidders such as SouthWest Bell and ALAACR raised their own standing bid. But most bids beat the standing bid by just the minimum increment or slightly more.

The broadband bidders bid cautiously in another way, by not bidding for more licenses than the activity rule required. The auction's pace was driven by the auction rules more than by the bidders' decisions. Total revenue rose at the rate set by the mechanism. The effect of the three stages of the activity rule is seen in Figure 1.[11] In each stage, bid activity steadily dropped off, until the imposition of the next stage (in rounds 12 and 65), with its stricter activity requirements, caused a jump in bid activity. The revenue curve is scallop shaped, steepening when a new stage starts and roughly concave within each stage.

The broadband MTA auction had few bidders relative to the number of licenses on offer. The low excess demand, just two-to- one, gave rise to fears that the bidders might collude. A drawback of the simultaneous ascending auction is that collusion is easier than under a single round of sealed bids. Through their bidding patterns in the early rounds, the bidders might in effect say to each other: "This is 'my' territory. Stay away from it, and I will stay away from 'yours.' If you ever bid on it, I will drive up the price of 'yours' in retaliation." The FCC could have hindered collusion by revealing only the bid amounts between rounds, and not the bidders' identities. It chose not to do this in the broadband auction and instead gave out full details of each round's bidding, because it judged that the risk of collusion was outweighed by benefits of the information. (Bidder identities are useful to the bidders for evaluating the meaning of others' bids, reducing the winner's

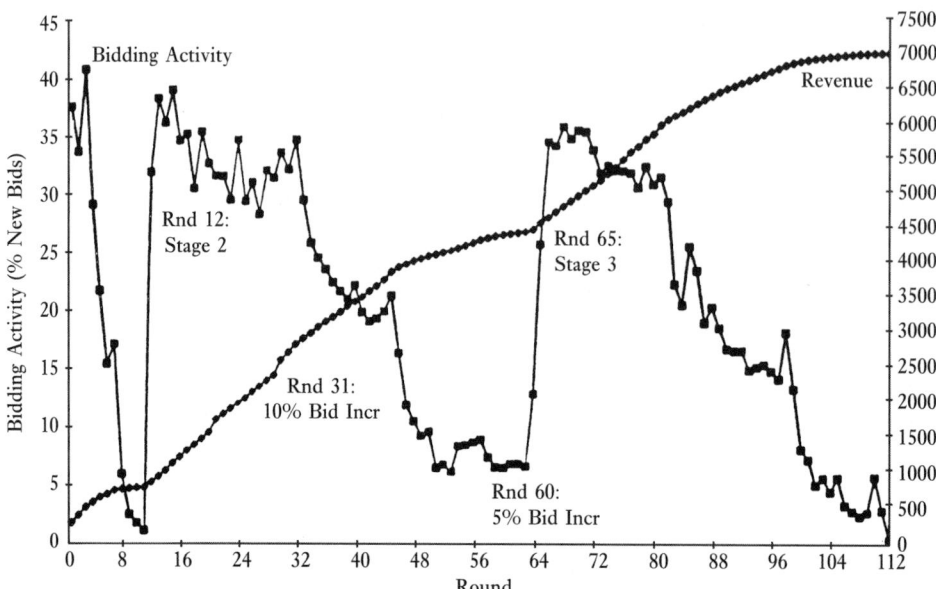

Figure 1   Revenue and Bidding Activity, MTA Broadband PCS Auction

curse and generally assisting sensible bidding.) Some of the firms may have tried to coordinate their bids. Primeco president George F. Schmitt was reported as saying during the broadband MTA auction: "You mess with me in Chicago, you pay."[12] Primeco won its Chicago license, however, only after a bruising three-way battle for the two licenses, involving Primeco, Wirelessco and AT&T, which drove the bids to the highest level in the nation. Schmitt's threat, if such it was, had little effect. It takes only one maverick bidder to upset an attempt at collusion. ALAACR, in particular, seems to have used a strategy of bidding on any major license that was relatively underpriced (and American Portable Telecommunications seems to have bid similarly); and this helped to keep the bidding competitive.[13]

One of the reasons for adopting the simultaneous ascending auction was to aid efficient license aggregation by allowing a bidder to switch to a back-up aggregation if the bid prices in its first-choice aggregation rose too high. The bid data contain many examples of back-up strategies. In the nationwide narrowband auction, Nationwide Wireless Network began by bidding for two of the 62.5 kHz licenses. In round 26, about the halfway point, it apparently decided that the prices were too high, and it switched to bidding for a single 100 kHz license, which is what it won. In the regional narrowband auction, Air Touch began by apparently seeking a nationwide aggregation of five licenses. Then it scaled back, and sought and won three licenses, supplementing the nationwide license it had won in the first auction. During the broadband MTA auction, firms such as GTE and Wirelessco often shifted their bidding across different license sets.

A consistent pattern of closing (especially in the narrowband auctions, but less clearly in the broadband MTA auction) was that, as equilibrium came near, the winning bidders tended to be established first on the highest-valued licenses. Then the activity shifted progressively to lower-valued licenses, with the lowest-valued settling last.

New Theory of Multiunit Auctions

The spectrum sale is more complicated than anything in auction theory. No theorem exists – or can be expected to develop – that specifies the optimal auction form. The auction designers based their thinking on a range of models, each of which captures a part of the issue. The basic ideas used in designing the auction and in advising the firms on bidding strategy include the way the different bidders' valuations are related – they are partly idiosyncratic and partly common, or *affiliated* – and the effects of this on bidder behavior (Milgrom and Weber, 1982); how auctions reveal and aggregate dispersed information (Wilson, 1977); and the logic of bidding in the face of the winner's curse (Wilson, 1969; Milgrom and Weber, 1982). Other ideas used include the revenue-increasing effect of bid discounts (Myerson, 1981; McAfee and McMillan, 1988, 1989) and reserve prices as substitutes for bidding competition (Myerson, 1981; Riley and Samuelson, 1981).[14]

A lesson from this experience of theorists in policymaking is that the real value of the theory is in developing intuition. The role of theory, in any policy application, is to show how people behave in various circumstances, and to identify the tradeoffs involved in altering those circumstances. What the theorists found to be the most useful in designing the auction and advising the bidders was not complicated models that try to capture a lot of reality at the cost of relying on special functional forms. Such theorizing fails to develop intuition, as it confounds the effects of the functional forms with the essential elements of the model. Instead, a focused model that isolates a particular effect and assumes few or no special functional forms is more helpful in building understanding.

The spectrum auction, itself based on theory, has in turn sparked a new wave of theorizing. Although sequential auctions and single-round simultaneous auctions had been modeled, there had been little formal work on simultaneous ascending auctions of the sort the FCC used. Most of the existing theory omitted the crucial feature of the spectrum auction: the fact that the licenses complement and substitute for each other. Prompted by the FCC auctions, theorists are beginning to address this issue, though because of the intrinsic difficulty of the question, the existing attempts are preliminary.

One promising approach is to assume away asymmetries of information and the strategic behavior they induce, in order to focus on how bidding proceeds when the goods complement and substitute for each other. Complementarities mean market-clearing prices may not exist. Equilibrium is likely to exist if the buyers have similar views about how the goods should be aggregated, whereas it may not if they disagree about what constitutes good aggregations.[15] Some recent research has identified conditions for the existence of equilibrium in this sort of auction. Gul and Stacchetti (1995a,b), for example, show that a certain kind of substitutability among goods ensures existence. Their model also yields a decentralized price-setting process in which prices rise when demand exceeds supply.

Strategic behavior in a simultaneous ascending auction is analyzed by Menezes (1995), again assuming complete information. Prices are quoted and rise until excess demand becomes zero. The bidders' game playing means there are many equilibria. On applying a natural way of selecting one of the equilibria – the iterated elimination of weakly dominated strategies – Menezes shows, remarkably, that the sale takes place at the opening prices. Bidders forecast how much they will eventually purchase and shrink the amounts they demand in the first round to this level; the consequence of iterating this logic is immediate sale. This result rests on the unrealistic assumption of complete information; but it provides a warning about the peculiar possibilities in simultaneous ascending auctions.[16]

More new theory is needed. Features of the FCC's auction should be modeled. How should the activity rule parameters be set? How do the bid withdrawal rules affect the bidding? If bidders fear being stuck holding an incomplete bundle by losing a crucial license, do they bid unduly cautiously? Is this caution lessened by the availability of substitute licenses? How does the FCC-style auction, with its single-license bidding, compare in efficiency and revenue with combinational bidding under certain prespecified permissible combinations? Together with experiments (Plott, 1994), theory will map the scope and the limits of the simultaneous ascending auction.

Other Uses of the Simultaneous Ascending Auction

Auctions are used when the seller does not know the bidders' willingness to pay for idiosyncratic items for which there is no well-functioning market. The fundamental purpose of any auction is to reveal the bidders' valuations, thereby extracting a good price for the seller. The simultaneous ascending auction extends this notion of value-discovery to multiple items and how they fit together. The seller need not know how the items for sale complement or substitute for each other, as the auction induces the bidders to express their ideas about serviceable aggregations, and so the market process determines the outcome.

The evidence from the FCC auctions is that the simultaneous ascending auction is an effective mechanism for selling interdependent items. The simultaneous ascending auction has many other potential uses for selling multiple items that are complements or sub-stitutes. Further possible public-sector uses include the sale of oil and mineral rights, timber and grazing rights, houses held by the Resolution Trust Corp. or the Federal Deposit Insurance Corp., and airport landing rights. The FCC might also begin selling spectrum rights to broadcasters, who currently receive a huge hidden subsidy through receiving spectrum for free. In the private sector, the simultaneous ascending auction could be used for art and real estate.

More innovative uses might also emerge. One possible use is by a firm buying inputs from other firms. Conventional procurement specifies the level of assembly at which components are to be purchased. If instead a simultaneous mechanism were used, the procuring firm could define the components finely and have the potential suppliers bid component by component, with the possibility of winning several contracts and so supplying a bundle of components. By the set of components it bid for, each supplier would reveal its economies of scope. Another possible application is in the sale of a multidivisional corporation. The simultaneous auction could allow buyers to bid division by division. The bidders could thereby express their ideas on which parts of the firm fit together and which should be spun off. The uses of this new auction have just begun.

Notes

1 The citations for the quotations in this paragraph are *New York Times*, March, 16, 1995, p. A17; *The Economist*, July 23, 1994, p. 70; *Fortune*, February 6, 1995, p. 36; *Forbes*, July 3, 1995, p. 62; *Wall Street Journal*, February 13, 1995, p. A19.

2 For more on game theory's role in the design of the FCC auction, see Milgrom (1995). For more on auction performance and bidder strategies, see Cramton (1995a, b) and Salant (1995). On the case for using auctions to assign the spectrum, see McMillan (1995), and on the history and politics of spectrum allocation, see Hazlett (1995).

3 The withdrawal penalty involved guaranteeing the price bid. If after the license was reoffered, the final price was less than the withdrawn bid, the bidder who withdrew owed a penalty equal to the difference.

4 There was, however, considerable disagreement among the theorists involved in the design process, based on differing judgments about the sizes of various effects and the workability of the simultaneous ascending auction. Some advocated a sequential auction; others, an auction in which bidders could bid for license combinations, not just single licenses. On this debate, see McMillan's (1994) article in this journal.

5 The story is told in several places: *PR Newswire*, November 9, 1981; *Christian Science Monitor*, June 29, 1982, p. 11; *Time*, December 13, 1982, p. 148.

6 Prices sometimes rise rather than fall during a sequential auction. In Israel's 1987–1990 sequential auctions of cable television licenses, Gandal (1994) finds that the prices tended to be higher for licenses auctioned later. The competition seems to have intensified later, because by then some bidders held complementary licenses and so were willing to pay more. If a simultaneous ascending auction had been used instead, the earlier licenses may have been bid higher, and different bidders may have won the later licenses. Whether prices rise or fall, the uncertainty in a sequential auction creates difficulties for bidders, exacerbating the winner's curse and hindering efficient aggregation.

7 The complete auction data, including round-by-round bids, can be found on the Internet at the FCC web server, www.fcc.gov. The $7.7 billion sum includes the revenue from the licenses awarded as "pioneer preferences." Before the auction the FCC awarded three MTA licenses – New York, Los Angeles and Washington D.C. – to three firms as a reward for developing new technologies. These firms paid concessionary prices based on the winning bids. (The quotations in the paragraph are from *Reuters Financial Report*, October 20, 1993, and *Wall Street Journal*, August 1, 1994, p. A1.)

8 Marketing and brand-name gains come from offering nationwide mobile services. Cellular and PCS are not perfect substitutes, however, as telephones that transmit on both spectrum bands are expected to be more expensive than those specialized to a single band. The FCC's antimonopoly rules prevented a bidder from acquiring a broadband license in a region where it already held a cellular license.

9 Reactions from a story in the *Wall Street Journal*, March 14, 1995, p. A12.

10 Combinational bidding has some problems. Because of the huge number of license aggregations, combinational bids create impossibly complex computations. The FCC could pre-specify a limited number of aggregations. But the existing theory of combinational bidding (Bernheim and Whinston, 1986; Banks, Ledyard and Porter, 1989; Branco, 1995; Rothkopf, Pekec and Harstad, 1995) offers little guidance on the effects of combinational bidding with restricted permissible aggregations. Experiments often find gains from combinational bidding; but the theory currently does not say when restricted combinational bidding would work better, for either revenue or efficiency, than the much simpler single-license bidding.

11   This figure was devised by Peter Cramton for the FCC.
12   The Schmitt quotation is from the *New York Times*, March 27, 1995, p. C9.
13   ALAACR is owned by Craig McCaw, who became a billonaire by building America's leading
     cellular company and then, after selling it to AT&T, bid on his own account for the PCS
     licenses. Despite its aggressive bidding, ALAACR ended up without a single license. However,
     according to *Forbes* (July 3, 1995, p. 64), "McCaw had a grand time giving ulcers to the
     functionaries at the big bidders and adding hundreds of millions to the U.S. Treasury. 'Craig
     McCaw thought he was playing Nintendo. He was having the time of his life,' says Sam Ginn,
     chief executive of AirTouch." Incidentally, McCaw envisages novel uses of the spectrum:
     according to *Fortune* (December 12, 1994, p. 102), he "once suggested in all apparent serious-
     ness – as color drained from the face of a PR man in attendance – that the FCC should reserve
     spectrum for telepathic communications to be made possible by brain implants he thinks will
     exist some day."
14   There is a direct link between game theory's Nobel laureates and the spectrum auction. The
     ideas with which Nash, Harsanyi and Selten are associated – Nash, Bayesian and perfect
     equilibrium – are the basic tools of the theory used in designing the auction.
15   An example with no equilibrium has two items and two buyers. Buyer 1 sees the two goods as
     perfect substitutes, but buyer 2 sees them as perfect complements. Buyer 1 puts a value of 2 on
     getting either good 1 or good 2 or both. Buyer 2 puts zero value on having either good alone,
     but puts a value of 3 on having both. The allocation that is efficient, and therefore the only
     candidate for a Walrasian equilibrium, gives buyer 2 both goods, for a value of 3. Since buyer 1
     gets nothing, the price of each good must be 2, for otherwise buyer 1 would buy one of them.
     But buyer 2 will not buy the goods at those prices. (If buyer 2 were allowed to bid all-or-
     nothing for the aggregation, however, the efficient outcome would result.) For more on
     existence, see Bikhchandani and Mamer (1994).
16   Krishna and Rosenthal (1995) model a simultaneous auction with bidders who are either local
     bidders, who want only one of the items, or global bidders, who get extra value if they acquire
     both, and show the global bidders' strategies may be discontinuous. Rosenthal and Wang (1995)
     extend this to a common-value case. In Jehiel, Moldovanu and Stacchetti (1995), one bidder's
     ownership has externalities for the others (for example, MCI may prefer GTE to obtain a
     license rather than AT&T). The negative externalities mean a bidder may pay even when the
     item is not sold, and the item may fail to sell even though a bidder is willing to pay more than
     the seller's value. Jehiel and Moldovanu (1995) add an after-market to the auction, finding that
     after-market trading does not ensure efficiency.

References and Further Reading

Akerlof, G. A. (1970): "The Market for 'Lemons': Quality Uncertainty and the Market Mecha-
     nism," *Quarterly Journal of Economics*, 84, August, 488–500. [Reprinted as Ch. 9 in this volume.]
Ashenfelter, O. (1989): "How Auctions Work for Wine and Art," *Journal of Economic Perspectives*, 3,
     Summer, 23–36.
Avery, C. (1993): "Strategic Jump Bidding and English Auctions," discussion paper, Kennedy
     School of Government, Harvard University.
Banks, J. S., Ledyard, J. O. and Porter, D. (1989): "Allocating Uncertain and Unresponsive
     Resources: An Experimental Approach." *Rand Journal of Economics*, 20, Spring, 1–22.
Bernheim, B. D. and Whinston, M. D. (1986): "Menu Auctions, Resource Allocation, and Eco-
     nomic Influence," *Quarterly Journal of Economics*, 101, February, 1–32.
Bikhchandani, S. and Mamer, J. W. (1994): "Competitive Equilibrium in an Economy with
     Indivisibilities," unpublished paper, University of California, Los Angeles, October.

Branco, F. (1995): "Multi-Object Auctions: On the Use of Combinatorial Bids," unpublished paper, Universidade Catolica Portuguesa, April.

Cramton, P. C. (1995a): "Money Out of Thin Air: The Nationwide Narrowband PCS Auction," *Journal of Economics and Management Strategy*, 4, Summer, 267–343.

—— (1995b): "The PCS Spectrum Auctions: An Early Assessment," unpublished paper, University of Maryland, July.

Federal Communications Commission (FCC), (1994): "Fifth Report and Order," FCC 94–178, Washington DC, July 15.

Gandal, N. (1994): "Sequential Auctions of Cable Television Licenses: The Israeli Experience," working paper 31–94, Tel-Aviv University, December.

Gul, F. and Stacchetti, E. (1995a): "English Auctions with Multiple Goods," unpublished paper Northwestern University, June.

—— and (1995b): "Walrasian Equilibrium without Consumption Complementarities," unpublished paper, Northwestern University, June.

Hazlett, T. W. (1995): "Assigning Property Rights to Radio Spectrum Users: Why Did FCC License Auctions Take 67 Years?", unpublished paper, University of California, Davis, July.

Jehiel, P. and Moldovanu, B. (1995): "Resale Markets and the Assignment of Property Rights," discussion paper 1196, Centre for Economic Policy Research, London, June.

——and Stacchetti, E. (1995): "Multidimensional Mechanism Design for Auctions with Externalities," unpublished paper. Bonn University, February.

Krishna, V. and Rosenthal, R. W. (1995): "Simultaneous Auctions with Synergies," unpublished paper, Boston University, March.

McAfee, R. P. and McMillan, J. (1987): "Auctions and Bidding," *Journal of Economic Literature*, 25, June, 699–738.

——(1988): *Incentives in Government Contracting*. Toronto: University of Toronto Press.

——(1989): "Government Procurement and International Trade," *Journal of International Economics*, 26, May, 291–308.

McAfee, R. P. and Vincent, D. (1993): "The Declining Price Anomaly," *Journal of Economic Theory*, 60, June, 191–212.

McMillan, J. (1994): "Selling Spectrum Rights," *Journal of Economic Perspectives*, 8, Summer, 145–62. [Reprinted as Ch. 17 in this volume.]

——(1995): "Why Auction the Spectrum?", *Telecommunications Policy*, 19, April, 191–99.

Menezes, F. (1995): "Multiple-Unit English Auctions," unpublished paper, Australian National University, May.

Milgrom, P. (1995): "Auction Theory for Privatization," draft, Stanford University.

—— and Weber, R. J. (1982): "A Theory of Auctions and Competitive Bidding," *Econometrica*, 50, September, 1089–122.

Myerson, R. (1981): "Optimal Auction Design," *Mathematics of Operations Research*, 6, February, 58–73.

—— and Satterthwaite M. A. (1983): "Efficient Mechanisms for Bilateral Trading," *Journal of Economic Theory*, 29, April, 265–81.

Pitchik, C. and Schotter, A. (1988): "Perfect Equilibria in Budget-Constrained Sequential Auctions: An Experimental Study," *Rand Journal of Economics*, 19, Autumn, 363–88.

Plott, C. R. (1994): "Market Architectures, Institutional Landscapes and Testbed Experiments," *Economic Theory*, 4 (1), 3–10.

Riley, J. and Samuelson, W. (1988): "Optimal Auctions," *American Economic Review*, 71, June, 381–92.

Rosenthal, R. W. and Wang, R. (1995): "Simultaneous Auctions with Synergies and Common Values," unpublished paper, Boston University, August.

Rothkopf, M. H., Pekec, A. and Harstad, R. M. (1995): "Computationally Manageable Combinatorial Auctions," unpublished paper, Rutgers University, April.
Salant, D. J. (1995): "Up in the Air: GTE's Experience in the MTA Auctions for PCS Licenses,"
unpublished paper, Charles River Associates, July.
Wilson, R. B. (1969): "Competitive Bidding with Disparate Information," *Management Science*, 15,
March, 446–48.
——(1977): "A Bidding Model of Perfect Competition," *Review of Economic Studies*, 44, October,
511–18.

Index